LAW AND NARRATIVE IN THE BIBLE

CALUM M. CARMICHAEL

LAW AND NARRATIVE IN THE BIBLE

The Evidence of the Deuteronomic Laws and the Decalogue

CORNELL UNIVERSITY PRESS
ITHACA AND LONDON

This book has been published with the aid of a grant
from the Hull Memorial Publication Fund of Cornell University.

First published 1985 by Cornell University Press.

International Standard Book Number 0-8014-1792-9
Library of Congress Catalog Card Number 85-4214
Printed in the United States of America
*Librarians: Library of Congress cataloging information
appears on the last page of the book.*

*The paper in this book is acid-free and meets
the guidelines for permanence and durability
of the Committee on Production Guidelines for
Book Longevity of the Council on Library Resources.*

CONTENTS

PREFACE

In quoting biblical texts I have relied on the King James Authorized Version of 1611, but made changes where these were called for. I have used the AV because it is almost always a more literal rendering of the Hebrew original than any other translation. The texts that I quote, though sometimes paraphrased, constitute but a convenient selection of the more pertinent ones.

I am indebted to the John Simon Guggenheim Foundation for its support of my research during 1982, when I was a visiting scholar at the Oxford Centre for Postgraduate Hebrew Studies and a guest of the Institute for Advanced Studies at the Hebrew University, Jerusalem. In the preparation of the manuscript I have also received support from the Cornell Humanities Fund. Patricia Williams of the Department of Comparative Literature ably typed different versions of the manuscript, and Emily Wheeler provided valuable editorial assistance for Cornell University Press. At various stages in its preparation I received helpful comments from Norman W. Porteous and John F. A. Sawyer. I owe a special debt of gratitude to David Daube. Since I first studied under him some twenty years ago he has honored me with a deep friendship and a keen interest in everything that I have done. His erudition and originality have made him a legend in his own time, and my association with him over the years has been a source of pride and inspiration.

CALUM M. CARMICHAEL

Ithaca, New York

ABBREVIATIONS

AB	Anchor Bible
ATD	Das Alte Testament Deutsch
AV	Authorized Version
BZ	*Biblische Zeitschrift*
CBC	Cambridge Bible Commentary
CBQ	*Catholic Biblical Quarterly*
E	The Elohistic literary strand in the Pentateuch
ETL	*Ephemerides theologicae lovanienses*
HTR	*Harvard Theological Review*
HUCA	*Hebrew Union College Annual*
IB	Interpreter's Bible
ICC	International Critical Commentary
J	The Y(J)ahwistic literary strand in the Pentateuch
JAOS	*Journal of American Oriental Society*
JBL	*Journal of Biblical Literature*
JE	The Y(J)ahwistic and Elohistic literary strand in the Pentateuch
JJS	*Journal of Jewish Studies*
JSOT	*Journal for the Study of the Old Testament*

NCBC	New Century Bible Commentary
NICOT	New International Commentary on the Old Testament
NTS	*New Testament Studies*
P	The Priestly literary strand in the Pentateuch
RB	*Revue Biblique*
RSV	Revised Standard Version
SVT	*Supplement to Vetus Testamentum*
VT	*Vetus Testamentum*
ZAW	*Zeitschrift für die alttestamentliche Wissenschaft*

LAW AND NARRATIVE IN THE BIBLE

INTRODUCTION

It is no easy task to overturn longstanding views on material that has always been in center stage in the study of the Bible. Novel solutions to old problems might be welcomed inasmuch as they stimulate renewed awareness and provide insights, but a new theory, with its inevitable excesses, is destined to meet much resistance. The one put forward in this book, although radical in its results, in fact stays close to conventional theory. There is but one fundamental difference, which leads to the novel way of understanding the material in question.

The regnant theory relates the decalogue and the Deuteronomic laws directly to a historical background that is largely inferred from other biblical material. A link is thus forged between the laws and the literary traditions, but the overriding aim is to uncover the circumstances in the life of ancient Israel that may explain the substance of the laws. The assumption is always that the laws issue from real-life situations with their complex web of social, religious, political and economic elements. It seems a sensible approach, reflecting confidence in the application of the historical mode of inquiry. But it is precisely this method that I claim not to be applicable to an understanding of this large body of legal material (around a hundred rules).

"A fork is a marvellous instrument, but not for supping soup" (as my friend, N. S. Doniach, editor of the *Oxford English-Arabic Dictionary of Current Usage,* once commented to me in reference to certain linguistic methods). Historical and literary criticism is undeniably useful when working with ancient sources, but not only has it limitations, it sometimes leads nowhere. One manifest restriction in its application to most biblical material is that the historical results hypothesized cannot be corroborated. The speculative character of most such results is easily overlooked because the historical method is so deeply entrenched in scholarly approaches. With a little distance, we can see just how shaky the historical method is. No professional historian working on recent history could proceed with any confidence if the material available to him or her were in any way comparable to the biblical documents. Not only is their range of material exceedingly small, but also they cover hundreds of years and they often purport to relate history when, in effect, they report others' inventions.

In regard to the Deuteronomic laws and the (miscalled) Ten Commandments, the attempt at historical illumination has in fact, despite the spate of recent research, produced little that is agreed to. The problem is reckoned to be the complexity of the final form of the documents, which is believed to be an amalgam of materials belonging to various periods of time. Inevitably the quest for background becomes correspondingly more difficult in proportion to the layers of texts that can supposedly be uncovered by historical and literary analysis. The procedure is a dispiriting one, dull to read, difficult to follow, and largely illusory given the paucity of the results and the conjectured historical realities dotted here and there over a vast span of time. Its most depressing aspect is the no doubt unintentional demeaning of the intelligence of the lawgiver who was responsible for the presentation of the material available tc us. E. M. Forster, struck by the cavalier way in which we treat the past, attributed the attitude to the fact that those who lived then are all dead and cannot rise up and protest. Biblical scholars who observe discrepancies and contradictions in the texts before them never consider whether, if they really do exist, they did not bother the ancient author or redactor. There is no denying that similar such discrepancies can be cited, but the process of separating new material from old is largely dependent upon a one-dimensional type of literary criticism.[1] Texts are read and apparent difficulties in sense, style, and language are singled out as evidence of editorial activity, and hence an indication of disparate sources. While this procedure has its place, it does not follow that the evidence means what conventional views make of it. Consider two examples of the typical process.

In Deut 16:21 the rule refers to planting an Asherah, any tree, "beside the altar of Yahweh thy God which thou shalt make thee." Critics assume that an old rule has been taken over because the Deuteronomic law lacks the distinctive Deuteronomic reference to the chosen, central sanctuary. I shall argue, however, that the rule is indeed a Deuteronomic invention that is based upon an old rule for a quite specific reason. The matter is more complex and sophisticated than critics imagine it to be. In Deut 24:19–22 the oddity of the direction (it stands out from the related ones about olives and grapes) to let lie a sheaf of grain that has been forgotten by the harvester, so that the needy may have it, is again viewed as a sign that the law must come from an early period when propitiatory offerings were left in the field for the deity. Apart from the dubious understanding of the term "forgotten," not a shred of biblical evidence exists to support such a practice in Israelite antiquity. The assumption seems to be that either the old rule was taken over thoughtlessly or that its very age conferred upon it some measure of sanctity. But the latter view clashes seriously with the Deuteronomic view of how offerings should be presented to Yahweh, and thus suggests that the lawgiver failed to see the problem. One cannot really argue against many such attempts to postulate old rules for the simple reason that there is no historical evidence open to evaluation. Evidence of another kind can be produced, however, for a quite different interpretation of the rule, one that at least restores the human dimension of intelligence and imagination to its formulator. Only by recovering this dimension can we claim that the laws collected in Deuteronomy are not to a considerable extent the result of accidental deposit but are, rather, im-

[1]For a cogent attack on the process, see C. Rabin, "Discourse Analysis and the Dating of Deuteronomy," *Interpreting the Hebrew Bible: Essays in Honour of E. I. J. Rosenthal,* ed. J. A. Emerton and S. C. Reif (Cambridge: Cambridge University Press, 1982), 171–77.

pressively wrought individual compositions. Each such composition, I shall argue, had a status that made it deserving of incorporation in a larger work whose outstanding literary value has never been in question.

The thesis presented in this book takes it for granted that, with certain notable exceptions, old rules contribute to those before us now. This point should always be borne in mind when I claim that incidents in the early narratives prompted the later Deuteronomic or decalogue versions of them. There is, however, again with certain exceptions (rules in the Book of Exodus), no way to discover what form they took in their earlier existence.[2] What can be demonstrated is how the present rules achieved their form, and why they contain what they do, with illuminating results for a whole range of problems.

The key to an understanding of what is going on lies in taking up two longstanding, universally agreed to, insights of critical scholarship whose implications, however, have never been worked out. First is the fictional attribution of the laws in Deuteronomy to Moses. He it is who gives them in a farewell address to Israel. This well-recognized literary convention in biblical and ancient Near Eastern antiquity has him cast in the role of a seer, a combination of sage and prophet. As such he looks back on events in his own lifetime, some of which are openly cited, and also to the formative period of his nation, the history of the patriarchs.[3] He similarly looks forward to events

[2]For example, there may have been influence from ancient Near Eastern sources at this prior stage. Attempts to demonstrate such links have not met with much acceptance. Indeed, the striking difference between Deuteronomic laws and comparable rules in the Near Eastern source is often the subject of comment, for example, the rule about the runaway slave (M. Weinfeld, *Deuteronomy and the Deuteronomic School* [Oxford: Clarendon, 1972], 272). It can be difficult to decide that similar rules are not just the product of similar human and social factors. W. W. Hallo links an eighteenth-century B.C. case from Nippur, which appears to deal with a bride slandered by the groom before the consummation of the marriage, with the Deuteronomic rule about the bride slandered after her marriage. He chooses to minimize this (surely rather significant) difference in order to forge the link ("The Slandered Bride," *Studies Presented to A. Leo Oppenheim,* ed. W. W. Hallo [Chicago: Oriental Institute, 1964], 95–105). On the often insurmountable difficulty of determining customary rules in any society, see W. A. J. Watson, *The Evolution of Law* (Baltimore: Johns Hopkins University Press, 1985), chap. called *Custom.*

[3]For examples of his judgments upon matters in the patriarchal period, see my *Women, Law, and the Genesis Traditions* (Edinburgh: Edinburgh University Press, 1979), and "Forbidden Mixtures," *VT* 32 (1982):394–415.

that are to occur after his time, because he is endowed with supernatural insight. Because this convention was used, a convention also appearing in the decalogue only with Yahweh in the role of seer, the laws must represent judgments upon events in literary history, not in real history. As a result we can locate the source of the problems handled in the laws: the literary traditions to be found in the Books of Genesis, Exodus, Numbers (events before and during Moses' life); Joshua, Judges, Samuel, and Kings (events after it).

The second insight is the recognition that a Deuteronomic writer (or a number of them) has worked with the traditions recounted in most of these books. Not only are the traditions recorded and put together in a way that reveals this redactor's views, but now and again his explicit judgments upon developments are actually cited—for example, those in regard to the history of Israelite kingship. I shall argue that the laws in Deuteronomy and the decalogue are likewise judgments upon matters in this same material.

With these two insights in mind the thesis presented in this book can be spelled out more precisely. The laws in both Deuteronomy and the decalogue arise not as a direct, practical response to the conditions of life and worship in Israel's past, as is almost universally held, but from a scrutiny of historical records about these conditions. The link is between law and literary account, not between law and actual life. One way of viewing the Deuteronomic laws is to see them as embodying both the retrospective and prospective judgments of Moses. He looks back on events in his life and before, but he also looks forward to events long after his time, for example, to the Israelite request for a king, because as a prophet he has foreknowledge.[4] From our rational, critical point of view we can infer that the laws are the product of someone other than Moses who is surveying the sweep of history from the patriarchal period through to the end of the period of the kings of Israel and Judah. This lawgiver sees himself in the prophetic line of Moses, Samuel, Nathan, Ahijah, Jehu, Micaiah, Elijah, and Elisha. He is "a prophet like unto me," namely, Moses (Deut 18:15). He sincerely believes he has authority to make judgments on issues that arose in his nation's past because he possesses the

[4]Note how the seer Balaam predicts the existence of Israel's king (Num 24:7). The reference seems to be to Saul.

mind of Israel's first lawgiver.[5] This identification is crucial for understanding how the Deuteronomist has proceeded in constructing his laws. The procedure should be compared with the manifest fiction of the prophetic judgment to be followed by its fulfillment in the writing up of the history of the kings (for example, Joshua's judgment against rebuilding Jericho in Josh 6:26, 27, comes to pass in Ahab's reign [1 Kings 16:34], and the anonymous prophet's judgment about the altar at Bethel in 1 Kings 13:1–3 in Josiah's reign [2 Kings 23:15–20]). The events had already taken place, but a hindsight based upon a certain ideological perspective sees their inevitability and casts it in the form of prophetic foresight.[6]

A thesis that argues for a close link between the laws and the narratives in the Bible need not occasion much surprise, even if the results are unexpected. The Pentateuch has been put together in such a way that both are mixed together, for example, the decalogue is embedded in a narrative structure, and the rules about killing animals and humankind in the story of the flood (Gen 9:5, 6). An even more integrated relationship is manifest in some narratives when, for example, laws are attributed to the occasions in question. Moses makes a judgment on what is to be done to a man who gathers sticks on the

[5]For illuminating comments on comparable beliefs and procedures, from St. John to Marx, Freud, and Wittgenstein, see D. Daube, "The Influence of Interpretation on Writing," *Buffalo Law Review* 20 (1970):41–59.

[6]See G. von Rad, *Studies in Deuteronomy* (London: SCM, 1953), 78–91. In my view the same writer(s) is responsible for both the laws and the redaction of the historical material from Joshua to 2 Kings up until the time of Josiah at least. M. Noth (*Überlieferungsgeschichtliche Studien*, 2d ed. [Tübingen: Niemeyer, 1957], 16) felt no need to inquire into the literary history of the laws, and his one argument for placing them before the redaction of the historical material appears to be based on his acceptance of the account of the lawbook's discovery in Josiah's time. In that Noth's Deuteronomic redactor took into account the end of the history of the kings of Israel and Judah, he must have been writing around 562 B.C., and hence at least sixty years after the Book of Deuteronomy. There may have been, however, a process of redaction up until Josiah's time, followed by another that took the record up to the close of the kingship; see F. M. Cross, *Canaanite Myth and Hebrew Epic* (Cambridge, Mass: Harvard University Press, 1973), 274–89; R. Nelson, "Josiah in the Book of Joshua," *JBL* 100 (1981):531–40. I have purposely refrained from discussing the question about different Deuteronomic authors for two reasons: the issue does not affect the substance of my thesis, and it is too difficult a task to make such judgments with any degree of assurance. Even in regard to the record about Josiah it is virtually impossible to separate fact from fiction. In some ways, I incline to the simple proposition that a single Deuteronomic writer—whom I refer to as the Deuteronomist or the lawgiver—is responsible for the composition of Deuteronomy and the redaction of the historical books.

sabbath (Num 15:32–36) and pronounces a rule that distinguishes between married and unmarried female captives (Num 31:17, 18). More oblique links between a law and a narrative are observable in, for example, the story about Jacob's wrestling the divine warrior, which ends with an explanation of why Israelites do not eat the flesh of a certain part of an animal (Gen 32:32). This kind of oblique relationship turns out to be characteristic of a great many rules that are not incorporated in narratives but that are brought together in the separate collections, Deuteronomy and the decalogue.

It might well be asked why the links between the laws and the narratives have not hitherto been seen in the history of exegesis. Only those incidents in Moses' own time are referred to in the laws, and exegetes have viewed these references as additions not closely related to them.[7] Three factors should be noted. First is our inability to appreciate just how intimately acquainted a certain kind of ancient audience was with a body of tradition. Some idea of this intimacy may be seen in circles that, up until three hundred years ago, enjoyed the cento literature. The listener took pleasure in recognizing that part of Homer or Virgil from which a line or half line was taken, as well as its new meaning in the cento. The familiarity with the classical texts was deep and detailed. Both the compiler of the biblical laws we are interested in as well as some original, literate audience might be assumed to have had a similarly intimate acquaintance with the written body of texts underlying the laws. Accordingly, we can expect that the merest allusion to a story or legend was easily picked up.

A second, more significant factor is that the fictional, Mosaic character of the material had to be preserved. References to events in Moses' own time contributed to the notion that the laws originated from him. But if those rule-engendering events before and after his time had been revealed to an outside audience, then the fiction would have been suspect. The result has been one of the most successful cover-ups of all time. Even those modern scholars who acknowledge

[7]They are: frequent references to the time in Egypt (Deut 13:5, 10, 15:15, 16:1, 3, 6, 12, 20:1, 23:7, 24:18, 22, 26:5–8). Others are: the experience at Horeb (Deut 18:16); Ammon's and Moab's bad treatment of the Israelites after they left Egypt (Deut 23:3); Miriam's leprosy (Deut 24:9); Amalek's attack (Deut 25:17, 18). The speech made at the presentation of the first fruits contains an allusion to Jacob as the "Aramean ready to perish was my father" (Deut 26:5). This speech, however, is one of historical recall and is therefore irrelevant to the observation in question.

the fiction have paid lip service to it only, for they have been convinced of the antiquity of the material. For them a traditional code of laws has been embedded in a paranetic framework, and only the latter has been the distinctive Deuteronomic feature.

A third factor is that, apart from the notable exceptions that should have prompted further inquiry, the links between a law and a narrative are not easily detected. The main reason for this difficulty lies not in the demands imposed by the creation of a fiction, but in the nature of the relationship itself. There is no one-to-one correspondence between the two, because there was little point in expressing in a rule what was clearly communicated in a narrative, especially when many of the narratives had already undergone a didactic orientation. On the contrary, just as the story about Jacob's wrestling with the angel unexpectedly ends with a notice about a food law, so in many laws a similarly unexpected use of the narratives shows up. Their use, moreover, is systematic in the sense that the lawmaker moves from one to another (or to another part of the same incident), because he is interested in a certain topic. As a result, the logic that underlies the sequence of the laws becomes clear. For both the Deuteronomic laws and the decalogue this problem of their sequential arrangement has been a major one.

Although we might find the links between the laws and the narratives unexpected, from the lawgiver's perspective his use of the latter is straightforward: he is primarily exploring their legal and ethical implications. This inevitably means that the extraordinary features that constitute the essence of narrative literature, and largely account for both its creation and preservation, have to be translated into more ordinary terms for the purpose of his constructions. Sometimes this translation takes the form of stating a well-recognized rule that is general in scope. More often it leads to a rule whose range is narrow precisely because of the special feature in the narrative. A major problem, though barely acknowledged, is why so many rules exhibit this narrowness of focus. Why, for example, in the midst of rules that are general in nature does the prohibition in the decalogue confine itself to false witness against someone, rather than condemning lying as such? Or why in Deuteronomy does the only rule about inheritance rights concern itself with the exceptional case where there are two wives, one loved, the other hated, and the firstborn son is by the latter? In every instance we can explain the bias of a law, whether it is general or particular, because we can see how a narrative has determined its formulation.

We shall find that the lawgiver brings out a problem (for example, individual responsibility) that is obscured by other elements in a narrative (an innocent father, Hamor, is slain along with his guilty son, Shechem, but Jacob is solely taken up with the jeopardy his group is put in because Simeon and Levi had slain a group of Canaanites); or he formulates a hypothetical problem (for example, straying animals) that is suggested by narrative details (the Reubenites and Gadites have to leave their many cattle unprotected when they go off on war duty to help their brother Israelites attain their land); or he focuses on a problem (for example, false witness within a town) that is explicit but not the central concern of a narrative (a town's officials collude with Queen Jezebel in the injustice done to Naboth); or (and this is common) he transfers a problem (for example, renovating a marriage) to circumstances more conventional than the extreme or idiosyncratic ones found in the narrative (Sarah is passed off as Abraham's sister and goes from her husband to another man and then back to her first husband). Frequently, especially in the decalogue, Yahweh's judgments or actions in a tradition (for example, putting a mark on Cain) are seen to imply certain rules, and these are then given explicit expression (a rule against murder). Sometimes the deity's action (for example, causing the Egyptians to give valuables to the departing Hebrew slaves) cannot be encapsulated in a rule and the lawgiver's task is to come up with an equivalent for the rule (a release of debts every seven years). In doing so he often has to recognize that at the mundane level the imitation of divine action (for example, God's aiding Jacob at Laban's expense) is not satisfactory and adjust his rule (the treatment of hired servants who are poor) accordingly.

There are detectable patterns in the Deuteronomist's handling of traditions. His interest in a topic—for example, kingship and the cult, sexual offenses, war and peace—determines which traditions he turns to and consequently the order of the laws. Why he chooses the topics he does cannot be answered, although both the prophetic and wisdom traditions are relevant. In general, a starting point for dealing with a topic is the first-time-ever occurrence of a problem pertinent to it. He typically proceeds by looking at comparable problems in succeeding generations. For example, in regard to kingship and the cult, he turns to the period of the judges when the issue of kingship first arose, then, in order, to Saul's reign, David's, Solomon's, Jeroboam's, and Ahab's. A change in topic, for instance, from apostasy in its link with famine to food matters, causes him to switch his reference point from a tradition belonging to a later period of history to one belonging to an early period, because that is when the problem of famine and the provision of food first arose for the Israelites. A succession of laws usually follows the switch, but sometimes a single law comprehends the history of the problem in question. In looking for schematic elements in the handling of traditions, it is important always to bear in mind that the topic under consideration will determine which tradition is looked at, and that the latter can modify the topic such that a tradition from a quite different period of time then comes under scrutiny. There is no artificial adherence to chronological sequences of traditions.

An objection to the thesis concerns the question of what the hearers of the laws were meant to understand by them. Were they to pick up all the historical allusions concealed in them? That appears unlikely. Neither traditional exegetes nor modern scholars have been alert to the allusions.[8] One response to this objection is to emphasize again the fictional character of the book of Deuteronomy (and the decalogue), and to appreciate what happens when material is so composed that hearers understand it as ancient. Those Israelites who knew their national traditions would acknowledge with awe the ancient capacity of Moses to anticipate later problems and to provide solutions for them. That is a different perspective, and no doubt what is intended, from one in which the hearers were expected to identify the incidents that originally prompted the formulation of the laws. A distinction should be drawn between a first group of recipients, and a later more general audience for whom the legislation (in Deuteronomy) came from Moses in a historical sense because the fiction was

[8]Although not entirely; consider, for example, S. R. Driver's statement (in small print): "Unless, indeed, the other alternative be adopted, and the author of Deut 17:14–20 about the king be supposed to have been influenced, as he wrote, by his recollections of the narrative of Sam. As the nucleus of 1 S 8; 10:17–27a, 12 appears to be pre-Deuteronomic the latter alternative is not the least probable one." For the names of other scholars whom he cites in support of this view, see *Deuteronomy* ICC (Edinburgh: T. and T. Clark, 1902), 213.

successful. In some original setting, a scribal school or some analogue, the task was undertaken of evaluating existing records about the nation's past from the perspective of some ideal understood to be Mosaic. In this setting the process of lawmaking that has been described above occurred, and the first recipients of the laws were indeed taken through the various traditions that have been used in their construction. At this stage, because it was fundamental to the exercise, the laws were cast as if they had come from Moses. The distinction between the two types of audience corresponds to the alleged historical one in the biblical record (2 Kings 22, 23): a law book had its origin somewhere before turning up in the temple, after which it took on a new life.

CHAPTER 1

KINGSHIP AND THE CENTRALIZATION OF THE CULT

The prevailing views about the Deuteronomic laws share a common approach. Wherever they can, for they acknowledge the difficulty of the task, critics correlate clues in the laws with clues in the narrative records and postulate the same historical background.[1] These critics infer that the cultic laws in Deuteronomy 12, for example, have a history before reaching the Deuteronomist. He in turn is not really interested in this history but finds that the old laws can be usefully refashioned to serve his aims. He refashions a number of surviving laws even though their presentation proves repetitious, verbose, and redactionally clumsy.

I too choose to make correlations between the laws and the narrative records, but on a different basis and on a scale far more exten-

[1]A. Welch, for example, locates Deut 12:13–19 in a time when Israel was settled in Canaan but the Canaanites were still strong enough to have their own altars; Deut 12:8–12 in an unsettled period within Israel; and verses 2–7 in a time when the Canaanites had been overrun and Israel was master of the land. See his *Code of Deuteronomy* (London: Oxford University Press, 1924), 47–51; cp., A. Rofé, "The Strata of the Law about the Centralization of Worship in Deuteronomy and the History of the Deuteronomic Movement," *SVT* 22 (1972), 221–26. M. Weinfeld is more cautious in his assessment. He is not sure to what extent the variation between the second-person singular and the second-person plural is an indication of the composite nature of the material. He also finds that clues about their proper historical and religious context are lacking. See *Encyclopedia Judaica* 5 (Jerusalem: Keter, 1971), s.v. "Deuteronomy."

sive than that attempted by other critics. The laws are intimately related to the narratives, their formulation being a response to issues in them. This is not to deny that the Deuteronomist was acquainted with existing law and custom in regard to, for example, cultic life. He certainly would have been,[2] but what he did not have before him was a collection of cultic laws whose original form we can deduce by historical and literary analysis, and that he worked over and presented in his own distinctive way. What critics believe to be different sources in the material do not indicate such layers of legal traditions but are the background narratives that were used in formulating the laws. These narratives tell of different times in Israel's existence, and the laws, because they are a response to the narratives, appear to reflect such a varied past. But this diversity of historical backgrounds is by appearance only and is the source of the understandable but

[2]Alas, only in regard to his familiarity with the laws in the Book of the Covenant (Exod 21:2–23:19) can we indicate with some degree of assurance the nature and extent of this acquaintance. Scholars commonly fail to distinguish clearly between custom and *jus scriptum*. It is difficult to know whether G. von Rad (*Deuteronomy* [Philadelphia: Westminster, 1966], 16, 17, 90, 91) and E. W. Nicholson (*Deuteronomy and Tradition* [Oxford: Blackwell, 1967], 54, 57) view the cultic laws as developments of existing written laws, so probably von Rad, or of customary usage, so possibly Nicholson. This failure additionally means that there is no awareness of how custom functions in contrast to the role of *jus scriptum*.

J. Milgrom's attempt in "Profane Slaughter and a Formulaic Key to the Composition of Deuteronomy," *HUCA* 47 (1976):1–17, to understand certain formulas as indicating Deuteronomy's sources, namely, E and P, is unconvincing. Consider two examples he claims are easy to demonstrate. In the decalogue in Deuteronomy the formula "As Yahweh thy God hath commanded thee" (Deut 5:12, 16) is claimed to indicate that E's version is being referred to (Exod 20:3–12). This may be correct, but he pays no attention to the fact that the decalogue in Deuteronomy is set in the midst of a historical retrospect and that the reminder is attached to positive duties that ordinarily are more in need of reinforcement than are prohibitions. The claim will not be correct if the decalogue itself is in fact a Deuteronomic creation, for which view see chapter 12. In regard to the formula in Deut 24:8, he claims that the reference is "unquestionably" to Leviticus 13 and 14 (P). Yet the Deuteronomic law explicitly refers to the Miriam story (Numbers 12, JE) and not to the material in Leviticus. No mention is made of this reference, but he should at least attempt to link the formula with this tradition. Such an attempt reveals that Miriam was afflicted with leprosy because she refused to acknowledge Moses' superior authority. When she and Aaron eventually learnt their lesson she was healed. The inference that the Deuteronomist could have made was that for any future cure Moses was to be understood as possessing the authoritative directions and that Aaron as head of the Levitical priests derived them from him. A question Milgrom does not raise is why the Deuteronomist uses his formula in certain instances only. The fact that an explicit reminder has to be given that Moses had commanded something suggests doubt in the matter.

mistaken view that the laws contain old material, in the sense that they incorporate previous legal formulations.[3] In reality they are new constructions by one author, or scribal school, living at one particular time, possibly Josiah's, possibly later.

The four laws in Deuteronomy 12 illustrate well the Deuteronomist's distinctive process of lawmaking. In regard to the first we can observe that, in reviewing the national history from Moses through the period of the kings, he has been alert to the recurring problem of idolatry. The reason this topic receives attention in the opening law is because foreign gods, on the one hand, and human kingship, on the other, constitute a threat to the sovereignty of the Israelite god. Where, as later happened, kingship became more closely identified with foreign cults, the threat was all the greater and the need to preserve the idea of God as the sovereign power the more pressing. The law in Deut 12:2–7 has in mind all the idolatrous kings of Israel (and Judah). The second law (Deut 12:8–12) looks at that period of time when the judges, or sometimes prophets, were the rulers, and the need for a king first surfaced (Judg 17:6, 18:1, 19:1). The third (Deut 12:13–28) considers an act of disobedience to the prophet Samuel that led to the failure of Israel's first king, Saul, to achieve hereditary rule.[4] The fourth (Deut 12:29–31) focuses initially on a potential act of idolatry into which Saul tried to force David, but generalizes to include the influence of alien cults upon David's successors.

In these cultic laws the Deuteronomist concentrates on certain developments in regard to worship, from Moses—making his farewell speech on the plains of Moab—through the time of the judges, through Saul's rejection as king, to the establishment of Jerusalem by David, and then decisively by Solomon, as the location for the central sanctuary. The pivotal feature of his overview for our analysis is the switch from direct rule by God, through his legitimate prophet, to the institution of kingship, with its ambivalent capacity to introduce order and discipline throughout all the tribes of Israel and yet compete with the deity's continuing claim to sovereignty.

[3]It is why one claim has Deuteronomy as originally the lawbook laid up by Samuel in Mizpah (1 Sam 10:25), and another as the foundation document of Solomon's temple. See G. Henton Davies, *Peake's Commentary* (London: Nelson, 1962), 269.

[4]For the sake of clarity I am treating the material in Deut 12:13–28 as one law. When I discuss it in detail separate issues will arise, but they can all be related to Saul's career.

Law: Foreign cultic influence

[2] Ye shall utterly destroy all the places, wherein the nations which ye shall possess served their gods, upon the high mountains, and upon the hills, and under every green tree: [3] and ye shall overthrow their altars, and break their pillars, and burn their Asherim with fire; and ye shall hew down the graven images of their gods, and destroy the names of them out of that place. [4] Ye shall not do so unto Yahweh your God. [5] But unto the place which Yahweh your God shall choose out of all your tribes to put his name there, even unto his habitation shall ye seek, and thither thou shalt come: [6] and thither ye shall bring your burnt offerings, and your sacrifices, and your tithes, and heave offerings of your hand, and your vows, and your freewill offerings, and the firstlings of your herds and of your flocks: [7] and there ye shall eat before Yahweh your God, and ye shall rejoice in all that ye put your hand unto, ye and your households, wherein Yahweh thy God hath blessed thee. (Deut 12:2–7)

Background: From the aftermath of the golden calf to Solomon's temple

[12] Take heed to thyself, lest thou make a covenant with the inhabitants of the land whither thou goest, lest it be for a snare in the midst of thee: [13] but ye shall destroy their altars, break their pillars, and cut down their Asherim. (Exod 34:12, 13)

[15] And he [Solomon] said, Blessed be Yahweh God of Israel, which spake with his mouth unto David my father, and hath with his hand fulfilled it, saying, [16] Since the day that I brought forth my people Israel out of Egypt, I chose no city out of all the tribes of Israel to build an house, that my name might be therein; but I chose David to be over my people Israel. [17] And it was in the heart of David my father to build an house for the name of Yahweh God of Israel. [18] And Yahweh said unto David my father, Whereas it was in thine heart to build an house unto my name, thou didst well that it was in thine heart. [19] Nevertheless thou shalt not build the house; but thy son that shall come forth out of thy loins, he shall build the house unto my name. [20] And Yahweh hath performed his word that he spake, and I am risen up in the room of David my father, and sit on the throne of Israel, as Yahweh promised, and have built an house for the name of Yahweh God of Israel. (1 Kings 8:15–20)

> [21] And Rehoboam the son of Solomon reigned in Judah. . . . in Jerusalem, the city which Yahweh did choose out of all the tribes of Israel, to put his name there. And his mother's name was Naamah an Ammonitess. [22] And Judah did evil in the sight of Yahweh, and they provoked him to jealousy with their sins which they had committed, above all that their fathers had done. [23] For they also built them high places, and pillars, and Asherim, on every high hill, and under every green tree. (1 Kings 14:21–23)

> [6] In the ninth year of Hoshea the king of Assyria took Samaria, and carried Israel away into Assyria, and placed them in Halah and in Habor by the river of Gozan, and in the cities of the Medes. [7] For so it was, that the children of Israel had sinned against Yahweh their God, which had brought them up out of the land of Egypt, and had feared other gods, [8] and walked in the statutes of the heathen, whom Yahweh cast out from before the children of Israel, and of the kings of Israel, which they had made. [9] And the children of Israel did secretly those things that were not right against Yahweh their God, and they built them high places in all their cities, from the tower of the watchmen to the fenced city. [10] And they set them up pillars and Asherim in every high hill, and under every green tree. (2 Kings 17:6–10)

We are meant to hear Moses speak in the laws but it soon becomes clear that he is thinking of events and religious practices of a much later time. After all, the setting for the laws is Moses looking ahead to the future life of the Israelites in their new land. The places where the Canaanite nations worshipped their gods, "upon the high mountains, and upon the hills, and under every green tree," are, as S. R. Driver noted,[5] especially associated with the period of the kings. The objects of their worship, the Asherahs and the pillars, are likewise well attested to in this period. The emphasis upon the places in nature where they worshipped is to be understood in light of the distinctive Deuteronomic concern with the sacrosanct, life-giving nature of the land. There would be a strange mixture of life and nonlife should these places continue to be associated with alien gods who, from the Israelite perspective, are not gods at all. To acknowledge them is to attribute life in some special sense where none exists. Immediately preceding the reference to these natural places is the call to observe

[5]Driver, *Deuteronomy* ICC (Edinburgh: T. and T. Clark, 1902), 139.

the laws about to be given "all the days that you live *upon the earth* [my emphasis]."

Understandably, because his speech is set at the time of the imminent entry into the new land, the lawgiver has Moses first reject the religious practices of the indigenous inhabitants. The almost identical prohibition in Exod 34:13 is also Deuteronomic and is issued in the context of Moses' experience with the first example of the Israelite's propensity to apostasy, their creation of the golden calf. The appearance of the prohibition in this setting reveals the typical Deuteronomic concern with linking subsequent periods of apostasy, especially in the time of the kings, which began in Moses' own lifetime.[6]

Another factor that will account for the initial concentration upon foreign religious practices is the Deuteronomist's view that Israelite kingship was an imitation of the institution as it existed in surrounding cultures. His law regarding the establishment of kingship begins with an acknowledgment of this fact (Deut 17:14; cp., 1 Sam 8:5, 20). The need to proscribe the religious practices of the kings of these nations would have been all the more pressing in light of the permission received by Israel to establish kingship.

In Deut 12:2–7 the lawgiver goes on to oppose Israelite worship at Canaanite places with the command to serve God at the chosen place in one of the tribes. Presumably his judgment is that the Solomonic temple is to be regarded, from his later standpoint (or alternatively from Moses' prophetic one), as a culminating event in Israelite history because it is highlighted both by the sheer impressiveness of the development and by the united nature of all the tribes at that time. Solomon, moreover, fully acknowledged the derivative character of his royal rule: his capacity was a gift from the deity (1 Kings 3:3–12). The Jerusalem sanctuary should therefore be regarded as the norm for Israelite religious orientation. The exclusiveness he urges upon it, moreover, is believed by the Deuteronomist to constitute the best strategy for stamping out the influence of foreign cults upon the Israelites.

The feasting and rejoicing that characterize the blessing bestowed upon Solomon's new order of worship (1 Kings 8:65, 66) can also be

[6]M. Noth assigns Exod 34:13 to his Deuteronomic redactor: *Exodus* (Philadelphia: Westminster, 1962), 262. B. S. Childs speaks of the influence of Deuteronomy; see *The Book of Exodus* (Philadelphia: Westminster, 1974), 613.

viewed as the inspiration for the command, really the blessing, that the Israelite worshipper should rejoice in all that he does in his cultic life (Deut 12:7, 12, 18). The link between the law and the tradition about Solomon is further indicated by the fact that it has undergone Deuteronomic editing and comment.

This expression of the law of the central sanctuary, perhaps because it is the first, ranges over the history of Israel's and Judah's apostasy from the first exposure to Canaanite worship through its imitation by many of their kings. Each of the following laws will reveal a more specific focus upon a historical episode. The lawgiver's awareness, however, of comparable problems at times other than the one under consideration is not excluded because he is abreast of the entire range of traditions.

Law: Cultic competitiveness

> [8] Ye shall not do after all the things that we do here this day, every man whatsoever is right in his own eyes. [9] For ye are not as yet come to the rest and to the inheritance, which Yahweh your God giveth you. [10] But when ye go over Jordan, and dwell in the land which Yahweh your God giveth you to inherit, and when he giveth you rest from all your enemies round about, so that ye dwell in safety; [11] then there shall be a place where Yahweh your God shall choose to cause his name to dwell there; thither shall ye bring all that I command you; your burnt offerings and your sacrifices, your tithes, and the heave offering of your hand, and all your choice vows which ye vow unto Yahweh: [12] and ye shall rejoice before Yahweh your God, ye, and your sons, and your daughters, and your menservants, and your maidservants, and the Levite that is within your gates; forasmuch as he hath no part nor inheritance with you. (Deut 12:8–12)

Background: Household and tribal shrines

Micah restored to his mother the money he had stolen. She had already promised it to Yahweh on behalf of her son, and now had an image made and placed in Micah's home. He first appointed one of his sons as a priest, but was pleased to appoint a sojourning Levite to the position. The tribe of Dan, in seeking their inheritance in the land, came upon him and requested his services. Micah was helpless to resist their request, which was backed by force. The Levite became a priest to them in the city of Dan, which they built after destroying the inhabitants of the region, and where they set up the image they had taken from Micah (Judges 17, 18).

In the review of history that determines the sequence of his laws, the lawgiver moves from Moses' awareness of the problem of Canaanite religious influence to unsatisfactory Israelite religious practice. One specific time in mind, because it concerns the beginnings of kingship in Israel, is the period of the judges, in particular, the accounts in Judges 17 and 18 about Micah's setting up his own household shrine and the Danites their tribal one. The fear, already expressed in these traditions, is that anarchy is spreading among Israelites because of their cultic competitiveness. The preceding stories in the Book of Judges often reveal a concern with alien religion—though sometimes only indirectly, as in Samson's taking a daughter of the Philistines to be his wife (cp., Deut 7:3–5)—so that even the material in Judges can be seen to switch from the external menace to internal Israelite problems. Even more to the point, Samson's last act, in fact the climax to the story about him, was his destruction of the place where the Philistines worshipped their god Dagon (Judg 16:23–31).[7] The similar juxtaposition of concerns in the laws and in the material in Judges suggests the common hand of the Deuteronomist.[8]

The negative reflection that is incorporated into the accounts about Micah and the Danites, "There was no king in Israel, every man did that which was right in his own eyes" (Judg 17:6; cp., 18:1), is the basis for the statement in Deut 12:8: "Ye shall not do after all the things that we do here this day, every man whatsoever is right in his own eyes."[9] Although these words apply to Moses' own situation on the plains of Moab, for example, the people's bowing down to Moabite gods (Num 25:2), and although the recipients of the laws,

[7]It is the climax both in the sense that it was the final event in Samson's life as well as the result of the Israelite God "seeking an occasion" against the Philistines (Judg 14:4).

[8]On the Deuteronomic redaction of the Samson material in Judges 16 and the stories about the cult in Judges 17 and 18, see R. G. Boling, *Judges* AB (New York: Doubleday, 1975), 252–55, 258–59.

[9]The change from the second person to the third is unnecessary and indicates some such external influence as the statement in Judg 17:6.

presumably in Josiah's time, would recognize a situation similar to the one at which Moses hints, their primary focus has been the episode in Judges. The lawgiver has Moses speak this way because he has to have him committed to the view that kingship is a necessary institution. Not only will order and discipline be fully established when kingship comes into existence (Deut 17:14–20), but the fact of kingship provides for the correct order of cultic life.[10] The model in mind is, as emerged in the preceding law, the arrangement between the deity and Solomon to have a temple built in Jerusalem such that the house of David will always be subordinate to the deity's house, an earthly kingship affirming that religious sovereignty is primary. The command to worship at the chosen place therefore follows in verses 11 and 12. Intervening remarks explain why even Moses in his own life is in the midst of undisciplined cultic activity: Israel has not yet attained its rest and inheritance (note, for example, the position in Numbers 32).

Again Solomon's achievement is to be seen as determining this view of all preceding Israelite history. Rest from enemies and complete tenure of the land was the hallmark of his reign (1 Kings 5:1, 18). The establishment of God's house was dependent upon Solomon's achievement. It therefore follows that all preceding cultic practices are to be regarded as less than ideal. Given the conditions of Israelite life, these practices were often acceptable.[11] The particular conditions, however, described in Judges 17 and 18 are especially illuminating, revealing as they do an undisciplined freedom of action in the cultic sphere that produced friction among the Israelites themselves. The Danites stole from Micah his priest, the Levite, in order to enhance their own shrine. The complaint made to them by Micah and his fellow clansmen met with a life-threatening response. This tradi-

[10]The chosen cultic place is Jerusalem, and the warning against the king's multiplying horses, wives, silver, and gold (Deut 17:16, 17) is made with Solomon in mind. Neither is mentioned by name because such specificity is not appropriate for the fictional view of Moses as a prophet. Indeed from Moses' point of view an openness of possibilities is to be understood, for example, the tribe of Benjamin could well have been chosen for the sacred site if Saul had not been disobedient. Failure to appreciate the nature of this fiction has led to pointless attempts to identify the chosen place with different shrines at different historical periods.

[11]This explains why, contra Y. Kaufmann, *Tôledôt hā'emûnâ hayyiśre'ēlît* 2 (Tel Aviv: Dvir, 1957), 358, the Deuteronomist does not condemn local altars when he edits the material in the Book of Judges, for example.

tion of the Book of Judges is particularly in mind when the lawgiver speaks of every Israelite doing what he thinks right. Moreover, when he refers to Israel's not yet attaining its inheritance, it is worth noting that the Danites had not yet attained theirs at this point in time. To do so, they had to destroy a people who themselves had been dwelling in a state of security (Judg 18:7–10, 27).

When the lawgiver goes on to mention that every Israelite household should celebrate at the chosen place,[12] he includes the Levite for special consideration because he has no inheritance in Israel. The Levite of Judges 17 and 18 would have prompted this concern. His livelihood was manifestly dependent upon the cultic life of different people and groups in Israel. His employment first with Micah and then in the local cult of the Danites at the time they first attained their inheritance gave him a living. Once a judgment was made that this kind of arrangement should only be viewed as a temporary interlude in Israelite history, because a proper cultic order that excluded a diversity of places was yet to be established, his position required comment. The lawgiver's explicit interest in it arises from a consideration of this story in light of his overall scrutiny of Israelite history.

Law: Presenting burnt offerings at every place that is seen

> [13] Take heed to thyself that thou offer not thy burnt offerings in every place that thou seest: [14] but in the place which Yahweh shall choose in one of thy tribes, there thou shalt offer thy burnt offerings, and there thou shalt do all that I command thee. (Deut 12:13, 14)

Background: Saul's burnt offerings

> [8]And he [Saul] tarried seven days according to the set time that Samuel had appointed: but Samuel came not to Gilgal; and the people were scattered from him. [9] And Saul said, Bring hither a burnt offering to me, and peace offerings. And he offered the burnt offering. [10] And it came to pass, that as soon as he had made an

[12]The list of items to be brought to the central sanctuary ends, unlike the preceding list in Deut 12:6, with "all your choice vows which ye vow unto Yahweh" (v. 11). The vow of Micah's mother constituted a major element in the cultic developments described in Judges 17.

> end of offering the burnt offering, behold Samuel came; and Saul went out to meet him, that he might salute him. [11] And Samuel said, What hast thou done? And Saul said, Because I saw that the people were scattered from me, and that thou camest not within the days appointed, and that the Philistines gathered themselves together at Michmash; [12] therefore said I, The Philistines will come down now upon me to Gilgal, and I have not made supplication unto Yahweh; I forced myself therefore, and offered a burnt offering. [13] And Samuel said to Saul, Thou hast done foolishly: thou hast not kept the commandment of Yahweh thy God, which he commanded thee: for now would Yahweh have established thy kingdom upon Israel for ever. [14] But now thy kingdom shall not continue: Yahweh hath sought him a man after his own heart, and Yahweh hath commanded him to be captain over his people, because thou hast not kept that which Yahweh commanded thee. (1 Sam 13:8–14)

The prohibition against doing whatever anyone thinks is right in his own eyes does not in fact mention the problem that prompted the law in the first place. The lawgiver wants to keep the matter as open as possible even though he has in mind a specific problem in the past. From a reading of the law itself, without regard to any set of historical circumstances, we can infer that it refers not to general lawlessness but to cultic arrangements that are not satisfactory. The next law makes this point explicit: "Take heed to thyself that thou offer not thy burnt offerings in every place that thou seest" (v. 13).[13] From a consideration of the time when there was no king in Israel and different places of worship, the lawgiver switches to the time when the first king, Saul, lived and to a particular incident, namely, when he worshipped at a place that he should not have. His offense, in fact, can be accurately characterized as "doing what he thought was right in his own eyes."[14]

Deut 12:13 is formulated so as to presuppose the availability of

[13]This rule can therefore be regarded as closely tied to the preceding instruction. One can see why many Hebrew and translated texts introduce no division after verse 12.

[14]The problem of the continued existence of the tribe of Benjamin constitutes the tradition (Judges 19–21) that follows the tradition about Micah and the Danites. Saul is a Benjaminite, and his failure to establish hereditary rule dominates the Deuteronomist's attention in the law following the one that deals with the cultic activity of Micah and the Danites. If there is a structural parallel here it could be accounted for by the fact that the material in Judges has been shaped by the Deuteronomist.

various places ("in every place that thou seest") where one might think that it is acceptable to present offerings; in other words, the situation current in Samuel's time.[15] The prophet condemned the king for disobeying a divine command. This breach was regarded as so serious that Saul's kingship was to be terminated because of it. Little wonder that the Deuteronomist focuses on this incident and its interpretation. The primacy he gives in his legislation to the worship of God, that is, to acknowledging divine kingship, would incline him to concentrate on a king's, especially the first Israelite king's, cultic activity.[16] After all, the norm for correct worship, making offerings at one chosen place only, he derives from contemplating what transpired in King Solomon's time. Saul's offense would have been interpreted as denying Saul the eventual establishment of the one exclusive place of worship in his time, just as David's record of bloodshed prevented the development in his reign (1 Kings 5:3; 1 Chron 22:8, 28:3).

Commentators draw attention to the single reference to burnt offerings in the statement in Deut 12:13, with its omission of the other sacrifices, in order to contrast it to the comprehensive statements in verses 6 and 11. Saul, in offering at a place he should not have, presented burnt offerings. His intention was to present peace offerings as well, but the narrator twice indicates that only the burnt ones were sacrificed (1 Sam 13:9, 12). The Deuteronomist, in giving his prohibition against offering at any place that one sees, has been contemplating this incident, involving as it does the single person of Saul. It is noteworthy that the prophetic voice of Moses declares itself in this law ("And there thou shalt do all that I command thee" [v. 14]). Saul disobeyed such prophetic authority.[17] Another point of note is the form of the prohibition, "Take heed not to do," as against, for

[15]While this particular episode constitutes the basis for the law it has to be borne in mind that the lawgiver is also generalizing. This would mean that theoretically any place that had received divine approval could have been the chosen one, not just Jerusalem. If, for example, Jeroboam had not proceeded presumptuously to set up high places in Bethel and Dan, it is conceivable that some form of worship might have been approved at either or both of these places.

[16]On the relationship between kingship and obedience to Yahweh as the central theme in the stories about Saul, see P. Kyle McCarter, Jr., *I Samuel* AB (New York: Doubleday, 1980), 229–30.

[17]Note the repeated emphasis upon this failure: "Thou hast not kept the commandment of Yahweh thy God, which he commanded thee" (1 Sam 13:13); "Because thou hast not kept that which Yahweh commanded thee" (v. 14).

example, "Thou shalt not do." As David Daube has shown, the characteristic of this form is cautionary emphasis with a view to stressing the importance of the rule in question.[18] The form is especially suitable in light of Saul's offense, which by itself was hardly an infraction at all. He waited the seven days for Samuel to come and only then when the prophet failed to show did he think that it was proper for him to sacrifice. His offense was not inherently cultic in nature, for example, usurping a priestly function or being ritually unfit in some other way, but that as God's chosen king or anointed one he had opposed his way of thinking to the deity's.[19] A cautionary emphasis in support of a prohibition against presenting burnt sacrifices at a place one might think is suitable is most appropriate if Saul's situation has been the primary focus of attention.

We may ask why the incident at Gilgal prompted the lawgiver to set down yet another statement about the chosen place of worship; the answer is that it illustrates why even royal authority must yield to religious in regard to cultic requirements. If this requirement were true for Saul's situation at Gilgal, it would also be true for any problem involving Jerusalem. Thus King Jeroboam's decision to sacrifice at places other than Jerusalem (1 Kings 12:25–33) constituted similar disobedience—he had been warned by the prophet Ahijah (1 Kings 11:29–39)—and met with the harshest condemnation.

Not surprisingly, because he is the first king and David is his successor, other incidents from the traditions about Saul's sacrificial activity (sometimes involving David, too), have come under scrutiny. The result is the construction of the rules in Deut 12:15–27. In this context the incident concerning Saul's failure to exterminate all the animals of the Amalekites deserves comment. Acting together he and the people spared the best animals in order to sacrifice them at Gilgal. Saul's fault was again his failure to obey Samuel's religious authority. As the prophet put it: "Hath Yahweh as great delight in burnt offerings and sacrifices, as in obeying the voice of Yahweh? Behold, to obey is better than sacrifice" (1 Sam 15:22). Samuel's indictment of Saul in this matter reinforces the judgment underlying the prohibition

[18]Daube, *Ancient Jewish Law* (Leiden: Brill, 1981), 93.

[19]We have to remind ourselves that in his time Saul could have legitimately sacrificed at Gilgal. Solomon sacrificed burnt offerings at the place Gibeon (1 Kings 3:4) and was not condemned for it. There was no accompanying divine injunction.

against sacrificing at every place: the sacrificial activity itself is not the primary concern but, rather, obedience to recognized divine authority about matters more important than sacrifice—for example, if, or where, or when it should be done.

Law: Profane slaughter

> [15] However, with all the desire of thy soul thou mayest slaughter and eat flesh, according to the blessing of Yahweh thy God which he hath given thee, in all thy towns: the unclean and the clean may eat thereof, as of the roebuck, and as of the hart. [16] Only ye shall not eat the blood; ye shall pour it upon the earth as water. (Deut 12:15, 16)

Background: Saul adheres to a rule separating blood from flesh; and a feast of his

The Israelites, faint with hunger because Saul had imposed an oath upon them not to eat until the Philistine enemy was defeated, could not control their appetite after their victory. Slaughtering their acquired animals, they proceeded to eat the flesh with the blood. Saul reacted by ordering that they bring their remaining animals to him so that they "sin not against Yahweh in eating with the blood" (1 Sam 14:31–35).

David, fearful of Saul's intent, did not come to the king's feast at the time of the new moon. As an excuse, he spoke of attending his family's yearly sacrifice in Bethlehem. After the first day Saul had not commented on his absence because he thought David must be unclean for some reason. On the second, however, he made inquiry, and on being told of David's family feast, went into a rage and sought his death (1 Sam 20:1–30).

Driver thought that the reference to burnt offerings by themselves in verse 13 was included because the temptation to offer this type of sacrifice at other places might be peculiarly strong.[20] We have seen, however, that it is Saul's presumptuous offer of them at Gilgal that is behind this particular statement. What follows (and it has to be understood in the context of Saul's offense at Gilgal) is the topic of

[20]Driver, *Deuteronomy,* ICC, 145.

sacrifices that are secular in character. It is quite acceptable to slaughter (the same term *zābaḥ* is used as for sacred slaughter) within the towns of Israel for the purpose of feasting.

Interpreters, attempting a historical approach, assume that prior to the Deuteronomic rule limiting all offerings to a single sanctuary, domestic animals were only slaughtered in a cultic context at the various shrines that existed throughout Israel. This view is inherently improbable.[21] While the actual slaughter of the animal undoubtedly evoked religious ideas about the nature of life and death, this evocation need not entail a cultic act. If it were true that domestic animals were always taken to a shrine for sacrifice and that the Deuteronomic law altered this requirement, the change would have been momentous enough to warrant much more explicit comment. Instead the supposed change, with its emphasis actually upon the needs of an Israelite's appetite—"However, with all the desire of thy soul, thou mayest slaughter and eat flesh . . . in all thy towns, the unclean and clean may eat thereof"—is found in a subordinate position attached to the main contrasting command about the proper place to celebrate cultically (v. 14). This suggests that the issue of noncultic slaughter is in fact not of such great moment but reflects a practice that requires attention only in regard to the proper separation of the blood from the carcass—hence the rule in verse 16.

We can explain why the issue is brought up at this point in the code. In the survey of Saul's sacrificial activity we have, after the Gilgal incident, the story of his supervision of the slaughter of the animals captured from the Philistines (1 Sam 14:33–35). Saul imposed his authority because the people had initially eaten the flesh of the animals and drunk the blood. The one remaining story concerns David's failure to turn up for Saul's feast at the time of the new moon (1 Sam 20:5, 18, 24). Both these stories are highlighted in the formulation of the law about profane slaughter, with the interesting result that the two acceptable actions of Saul in regard to sacrificial matters converge. Saul's adherence to a rule about separating out blood from flesh is recognized and approved of. But so too is the

[21]It ignores such practices as hospitality to guests (e.g., Gen 18:7), feasting among the wealthy (e.g., Job 1:13, 18), and demands for food as payment for protection of a man's flocks (e.g., 1 Sam 25:8). The story of Nabal in 1 Samuel 25 is instructive; see, for example, verse 11, "Shall I then take my bread, and my water, and my flesh that I have killed for my shearers, and give it unto men, whom I know not whence they be?"

legitimacy of the customary feasts mentioned for both Saul and David. It is their existence that is the primary focus of the law. A subsequent law in Deut 12:20–28 considers more fully the implications of the incident involving the spoil of the Philistines.

The excuse that was given to Saul for David's failure to appear at the feast was that he had to be in his own town for his family's yearly sacrifice (1 Sam 20:6, 29). The real reason was that he feared for his life. The lawgiver has concentrated on Saul's feast because it brings up an issue that can be generalized. David's nonappearance has been used as the basis for raising the more fundamental question about the legitimacy of such feasts. In response the Deuteronomist sees no reason not to approve of this kind of noncultic feasting so long as blood is not consumed. The incorporation of the latter concern in the rule can be attributed to the inference that because Saul had acted properly in separating the blood from the flesh when dealing with the spoil of the Philistines, he would similarly have ensured its separation on the occasion of his feasts.

It was perhaps all the more important to set the seal of approval on this type of slaughter because of the seemingly harsh condemnation of the sacrifices at Gilgal. As already indicated, it was not the sacrificing as such that brought condemnation, and hence the move to underline ("However, with all the desire of thy soul") that this secular type of animal sacrifice was perfectly in order. In that the Deuteronomist is making a judgment that has national relevance (the particular circumstances of Saul's reign merely constitute the inspiration for it),[22] the rule about profane sacrifice appears as a concession to the wider prohibition against sacrificing at any place, that is, at any shrine. The rule only appears to be a concession, however, because the distinction between towns and shrines does not in fact involve a proper comparison (not all towns would have had shrines).[23] This lack of rigor in

[22]It is crucial to keep in mind this move from the idiosyncratic to the typical in understanding how the Deuteronomist has consistently formulated his laws. It is perhaps worth recalling the main characteristic of law: "In general the function of the statute is to regulate the typical so that guide lines are provided for future conduct"; statement of W. A. J. Watson, *The Nature of Law* (Edinburgh: Edinburgh University Press, 1977), 66.

[23]Commentators seem to assume that the feast at the time of the new moon in 1 Samuel 20 was cultic in character. H. P. Smith (*Samuel* ICC [Edinburgh: T. and T. Clark, 1904], 192), makes of Saul's feast a religious one and likens David's yearly family sacrifice in his home town of Bethlehem to Elkanah's at the Shiloh sanctuary (185), a sanctuary not in his home town. McCarter (*I Samuel*, 341, 343), assumes,

laying out the rules is one indication that the awkwardness, admittedly minor, is a product of the lawgiver's scrutiny of the particularities of past events. Indeed the concessive language used ("However") is intelligible once it is seen that the contrast between the apparently harmless but in the event wrongful sacrifices at Gilgal and the acceptable sacrifices on other occasions, typically at local family feasts, has been in the background. A further indication that the Gilgal sacrifices and Saul's family feast have been under joint consideration is that Samuel's nonappearance at the former and David's at the latter brought up the issues in question in the first instance.

Three other observations also direct us to Saul's time. The law states that the unclean and the clean alike may eat at one of these family feasts, just as ordinarily, without any ritual questions being raised, individuals in both these categories eat game animals. Instead of interpreting this rule as arising from the supposed change to a new, secular type of sacrifice, in which previous religious associations are shed, we can observe its origin in the fact that the Deuteronomist takes up Saul's speculation about why David does not come to the feast ("Something hath befallen him, he is not clean; surely he is not clean" [1 Sam 20:25]). The question has been taken further: suppose David was unclean (this in fact turned out not to be the issue), should he have felt barred from a feast such as Saul's? The lawgiver sees no reason for such an exclusion. Rather, David, who was at that point in the field (1 Sam 20:5) and probably obtaining his sustenance from the killing of game animals, should, if not prevented by other circumstances, eat at these feasts in the same way as he would eat the game animals.[24]

Second, the feasting in Saul's home went on for three days. The

---

without evidence, that the priestly requirements in Num 28:11–15 were always in effect and that in the monarchical period the king had particular responsibility for them. For useful observations on family festal observances (which he believes were often cultic in character), see M. Haran, "*Zebaḥ hayyāmîm*," *VT* 19 (1969):11–22. His arguments for the existence of a sanctuary at Bethlehem are strained. There is nothing in 1 Samuel 20 about cultic sacrifice. The issue of David's uncleanness need not imply a cultic problem. A special feast can acquire an aura of sanctity without being linked to a shrine. The uncleanness could have regard to mourning or to military custom (Abner, Saul's commander, is beside Saul at the feast). The term *zebaḥ* is used in reference to David's seasonal feast. We noted that the verb *zābaḥ* is used in Deut 12:15 for killing within the towns.

[24]Note Solomon's attachment to hunting and the mention of the two animals in the rule, the roebuck and the hart (1 Kings 4:23).

permission in the law to eat as much as desired points to feasting on this scale.

Third, when David himself was being hunted (as if he were game [1 Sam 26:20]), a group called the Ziphites informed Saul of David's hiding place and invited him to come to them, whereupon they would deliver David over (1 Sam 23:20). The language of invitation to Saul is identical to that in the rule about doing something "with all the desire of thy soul," and only occurs in these two places in addition to Deut 12:20, 21, 18:6.

In summary, each disparate element in the unified section, verses 13–16—not to present burnt offerings at any place that one sees, approval of local feasts, avoidance of eating blood—is related to issues that arose with Saul.

Law: Sacred dues not to be eaten within the cities

> [17] Thou mayest not eat within thy gates the tithe of thy corn, or of thy wine, or of thy oil, or the firstlings of thy herds or of thy flock, nor any of thy vows which thou vowest, nor thy freewill offerings, or heave offering of thine hand: [18] but thou must eat them before Yahweh thy God in the place which Yahweh thy God shall choose, thou, and thy son, and thy daughter, and thy manservant, and thy maidservant, and the Levite that is within thy gates: and thou shalt rejoice before Yahweh thy God in all that thou puttest thine hands unto. [19] Take heed to thyself that thou forsake not the Levite as long as thou livest upon the earth. (Deut 12:17–19)

Background: David at Nob

David, fleeing from Saul, came to the priestly city of Nob and requested food to eat. Only hallowed bread was available, but after some discussion with the priest Ahimelech about the fitness of nonpriests to eat it, David was given some. For assisting David, Saul had the priests and the other inhabitants of the city destroyed. Only Abiathar escaped to inform David of the massacre (1 Samuel 21, 22).

In Deut 12:6 and again in 12:11 we have the listing altogether of the various offerings: burnt offerings, sacrifices, tithes, heave offering, vows (free will offerings and firstlings in v. 6 but not in v. 11). A similar sequence begins in verse 13, but it is interrupted twice to incorporate rules deemed to be important at these points. We have explained why a statement about the chosen place of worship is given after the prohibition not to present burnt offerings at any place. We have also explained the rule about profane sacrifices (vv. 15 and 16). Yet another statement follows, demanding that the tithes, firstlings, vows, free will offerings, and heave offering be presented at the chosen place. Why is this so? A straightforward answer appears to be that in contrast to the preceding permission to sacrifice within the cities of Israel, there has to be a reminder that no such permission applies to these other offerings. But the recipients of these laws already have the rule in question. Poor drafting on the part of a redactor is the usual reason given. But again an explanation in terms of the Deuteronomist's response to a matter that arises in a tradition can be provided.

The question, answered in the affirmative, of whether one might participate in a local feast, along with the question of whether one might be unclean and still participate, likewise answered affirmatively, was taken up from the story about David in 1 Samuel 20. The following story in 1 Samuel 21 raises a related, if contrasting question, which this time is resolved with a negative answer. David, fleeing from Saul, and in a hungry state, arrived in Nob, the city of the priests, and requested sacred bread, cakes that have been made from pure grain (Lev 24:5–9). By its very nature, because David is deceiving the priest Ahimelech and inventing facts, the story is confusing. Claiming to be in a state of cleanness (he and his nonexistent companions have kept themselves from women, supposedly because they are involved in military activities), David asked for and was permitted to eat the sacred bread. In the correct cultic order that is to prevail, so Moses (the Deuteronomist) judges, no comparable action to David's can be upheld. That is, even if there should no longer be a local sanctuary such as Nob, pressing circumstances comparable to those he supposedly experienced cannot justify the consumption of sacred food within an Israelite town. In that David is such a major figure in Israelite lore, hearers of the story might think that his eating of sacred food in one of the towns in Israel could constitute a precedent for later Israelites.[25]

[25]That this story, with its controversial issue of the appropriateness of David's action, continued to be debated in later circles is evidenced by Jesus' use of it in defense of his disciples' action (Mark 2:23–28; Matt 12:1–8; Luke 6:1–5). Alas, only Jesus' side of the argument is given.

In light of this link with the tradition about David in the priestly city of Nob, four aspects of the law are illuminated. First, its negative formulation of the rule about centralization is determined by the negative reaction to David's act, or, more precisely, to some anticipated comparable act at the time when centralization comes about. Second, this formulation begins with, "Thou mayest not eat within thy gates the tithe of thy corn."[26] David, we saw, ate of the shewbread that would have been made from cereal probably received as a sacred revenue by the sanctuary. This focus would have inclined the lawgiver to give precedence to the tithe of the corn, the main cereal offering, in his listing of the sacred revenues. Third, the fact that the law begins with a statement about appetite recalls not only the similar concern in the preceding law but also David's presumed needs as a fugitive from Saul. Fourth, the law singles out the Levite for special consideration: "Take heed to thyself that thou forsake not the Levite as long as thou livest upon the earth." The fate of the Nob priests would explain why the Deuteronomist singles out again at this point the priestly estate in general for special regard. Recall that Saul had these priests killed because of the assistance David received at their sanctuary (1 Sam 22:9–19). Only one of them, Abiathar, escaped death, and David promised him future protection (1 Sam: 22:20–23). From the Mosaic point of view, only after David's time would there arise the one, centralized sanctuary. No other should then exist. The priests of the previously established sanctuaries would therefore require attentiveness to their well-being, especially in regard to their share in the sacred revenues that had been theirs in the local shrines. For example, no longer would the shewbread be available to them. The fact that the particular priestly line of Abiathar was to meet with its demise in Solomon's time (1 Kings 2:26, 27) (because of the previous conduct of Eli's sons in such matters as their greedy appropriation of the sacred dues [1 Sam 2:12–17]), serves to underline all the more the existence and needs of the surviving lines.[27]

[26]On the form *lō' tûkal,* really "Thou cannot," see D. Daube, "The Culture of Deuteronomy," *Orita* 3 (1969):41–43.

[27]For the Levitical descent of the house of Eli, see McCarter, *I Samuel,* 59, 239, 349, and F. M. Cross, *Canaanite Myth and Hebrew Epic* (Cambridge: Harvard University Press, 1973), 196. The use of the form "Guard thyself" in reference to the Levite's welfare is understandable against the background of traditions recording the extinction of many of them.

Law: Enlargement of territory and the availability of meat

[20] When Yahweh thy God shall enlarge thy border, as he hath promised thee, and thou shalt say, I will eat flesh, because thy soul longeth to eat flesh; thou mayest eat flesh, whatsoever thy soul lusteth after. [21] If the place which Yahweh thy God hath chosen to put his name there be too far from thee, then thou shalt kill of thy herd and of thy flock, which Yahweh hath given thee, as I have commanded thee, and thou shalt eat in thy gates whatsoever thy soul lusteth after. [22] Even as the roebuck and the hart is eaten, so thou shalt eat them: the unclean and the clean shall eat of them alike. [23] Only be sure that thou eat not the blood: for the blood is the life; and thou mayest not eat the life with the flesh. [24] Thou shalt not eat it; thou shalt pour it upon the earth as water. [25] Thou shalt not eat it; that it may go well with thee and with thy children after thee, when thou shalt do that which is right in the sight of Yahweh. [26] Only thy holy things which thou hast, and thy vows, thou shalt take, and go unto the place which Yahweh shall choose: [27] and thou shalt offer thy burnt offerings, the flesh and the blood, upon the altar of Yahweh thy God: and the blood of thy sacrifices shall be poured out upon the altar of Yahweh thy God, and thou shalt eat the flesh. [28] Observe and hear all these words which I command thee, that it may go well with thee, and with thy children after thee for ever, when thou doest that which is good and right in the sight of Yahweh thy God. (Deut 12:20–28)

Background: The spoil of the Philistines

Saul's son, Jonathan, received the deity's approval and aid in overcoming the Philistine enemy. His efforts were increased when Saul and the rest of Israel joined in the successful attack on the Philistines. The extent of the victory, and its potential gain to Israel—the displacement of the Philistines from their territory—was lessened, however. Saul had imposed an oath upon the people not to eat food that day until the foe was overcome. The result, as Jonathan pointed out, was that by foregoing the consumption of the enemies' spoil the people were too weak to achieve a greater victory. But worse was to happen. In the end the Israelites' desire for food was so intense that they could not control themselves, and they "flew upon the spoil and took sheep, and oxen, and calves, and slew them on the ground: and the people did eat them with the blood" (1 Samuel 14).

Events in Saul's time continue to determine the rules about the Israelite's desire to consume meat. Again the lawgiver addresses himself to the matter in terms of what constitutes the appropriate place to consume nonsacred and sacred items. In the law beginning in Deut 12:20 the connection that is made between God's enlargement of Israel's border, which will happen when Israel's enemies are routed (cp., Exod 34:24), and the Israelite's desire for meat is strange.[28] But in 1 Samuel 14 we find just such a linking of the two concerns. By scrutinizing this incident the Deuteronomist sets out what he takes the position of Moses to be in regard to what one might expect (without the complication introduced by Saul's oath) when Israel overcomes an enemy, enlarges its border, and finds livestock available to it. There is support for Jonathan's position against Saul. The animals should be freely eaten (they are like game animals in that they have been captured), the clean and unclean alike may eat them, only they must be slaughtered in the proper way. The blood must be separated out from the flesh and never consumed. The repeated emphasis upon not consuming the blood is readily explained as a reaction to the incident described in 1 Sam 14:31–33.[29]

More of the law's content is illuminated by linking it to the issues that are raised by the story. The lawgiver prefers that the consumption of what is probably a large number of animals take place at the chosen sanctuary. Only if distance from this sanctuary causes a problem should the animals be eaten within the various towns. The view expressed is not in conflict with the bald permission in verse 15 to eat flesh in the towns (without any mention of what is deemed preferable practice). The statement in verse 15 primarily concerns the kind of feast that Saul had in his home town at the time of the new moon, when the desire to consume the flesh with the blood would be less likely to arise. In verse 21 the communal activity of the Israelites at

[28]B. Halpern overlooks this primary link and concentrates on the secondary one, which seems to make more immediate sense, between a larger territory and increased distance from the central sanctuary. A little reflection, however, indicates that this problem would exist without territorial expansion. See "The Centralization Formula in Deuteronomy," *VT* 31 (1981):25.

[29]In his use of material the Deuteronomist proceeds from 1 Samuel 21 (David at Nob) to 1 Samuel 14. The factor that determines priority of use is his primary concern with manifest cultic matters; then he considers matters either marginally cultic or those that fall outside the cultic domain.

the time of a military success, when there might well be a problem of uncontrolled appetite, is central, and the lawgiver is thinking of what took place after the defeat of the Philistines in 1 Sam 14:31. Then Saul himself, in attempting to right the wrong that had been committed with the spoil, ordered the people to bring their animals to a central spot where they slew them in a proper manner. Saul even built an altar, his first ever, at that place (v. 35). In rebuking them for eating the flesh with the blood, and in order to instruct in the matter, he had commanded them to roll a great stone before him. The animals were slain upon it so that, presumably, the blood visible to all poured down and into the ground.

The lawgiver's following direction that the holy things and the vows must be exclusively associated with the central place mentions what has not hitherto been made explicit, that the flesh and the blood are to be offered upon the altar, with the blood being poured out upon it (v. 27). Proper supervision of the division between life and death—the life of the animal, its blood, and its carcass—is considered absolutely essential for sacred slaughter. But even in regard to profane slaughter the lawgiver, remembering Saul's problem with his fellow Israelites, prefers this centralized supervision. That the votive offerings are the only ones singled out in the law may also be noteworthy. Saul's vow not to have anyone eat food until victory was attained caused the people's offense. The lawgiver may have judged that by limiting vows to the central sanctuary, the kind of problem that Saul's ill-thought-out vow gave rise to might be avoided.

We can again understand why this incident from Saul's time required the Deuteronomist to state once more the law of the centralization of the cult. The slaughter of the animals taken in war appeared to be brought into a cultic context by Saul's building of an altar. But their slaughter, for the purpose of satisfying human appetite, is of an order different from those sacrifices required for the purpose of honoring the deity. Saul's activity, justifiable in the circumstances, calls for a clarification of the distinction between slaughter that must always be cultic in character and slaughter that need not be, but is nonetheless best carried out in that context.

Immediately after these cultic laws comes a general admonition to obey all of Moses' commandments. To do so will confer well-being upon each generation ("That it may go well with thee, and with thy children after thee"). The inspiration for this statement may well have come from the Deuteronomist's overall reflection upon Saul's life, and upon the lives of succeeding kings and their lines. Because Saul disobeys the prophet Samuel's commands, and hence those of Moses because Samuel is a prophet "like unto him," he is rejected as king and his children face grim problems. The same negative development is true for most of his successors as king. They offended against the cult, just as this admonition is appended to the laws about the cult.

Before proceeding (in the following chapter) to show that it is another incident from Saul's life that prompts the lawgiver to make the transition to the subject of idolatry, we can support from another angle the thesis that the institution of kingship—the need for it, and its beginnings in Saul's time— prompts the rules in Deuteronomy 12 with their intention to guarantee the supremacy of the deity's place in Israelite life.[30] We have the following sequence of historical episodes underlying these rules: Moses' anticipation in the aftermath of the golden calf of the Israelite's exposure to Canaanite religious influences; that period of time when the judges lived and the view arose that without a king discipline in cultic practice would be wanting; Saul's offense in sacrificing at Gilgal and subsequent events during his reign. When we turn to the actual accounts of the institution of kingship in 1 Samuel we find features similar to those we have observed for the origin of the rules in Deuteronomy 12.

The failure of Samuel's sons to rule justly prompted the Israelite elders to request a king (1 Sam 8:1–9).[31] The request was interpreted as a rejection of God as king and another example of their propensity to worship other gods (v. 8), an inclination, well illustrated in the incident of the calf, that is observed to go back to Moses' time when God led them out of Egypt. This link between giving allegiance to an

[30]M. Noth fails to appreciate the true significance of the rules in Deuteronomy 12 and as a result is wrong in his assessment that King Josiah revealed too narrow a concentration upon them (*Überlieferungsgeschichtliche Studien*, 2d ed. [Tübingen: Niemeyer, 1957], 93, 94). M. Weinfeld's view that the cultic laws in Deuteronomy have been secularized in contrast to those in P cannot be upheld; see *Deuteronomy and the Deuteronomic School* (Oxford: Clarendon, 1972), 188, 210–14. We are not in a position to judge that the Deuteronomist had no interest in the technical aspects of sacrifice. All we can say is that he focuses upon the fundamental issue of preserving the notion of the deity's sovereignty.

[31]It follows that the king must himself have laws to rule by if he in turn is to do justice. The Deuteronomic laws serve this purpose (cp., Deut 17:18–20).

earthly king and paying regard to other gods is relevant to Samuel's understanding of the undesirability of the competing demands of the Israelite God and the Israelite king. It is perhaps even implied that the king will be competing with God for the tithes of the land's produce (1 Sam 8:15). However that may be, both Samuel and the Deuteronomist permit the institution of kingship but make sure, by stressing the supremacy of God, that the king acknowledges the higher authority.

Samuel's views are more fully expressed in a speech (1 Samuel 12) that is decidedly Deuteronomic in character and whose historical retrospect leading up to the occasion of the people's request for a king is comparable to the Deuteronomist's review of past events in setting out his cultic laws. Samuel's historical survey is part of his farewell address. In this regard what he is doing is analogous to what Moses is portrayed as doing in the Book of Deuteronomy. Each is a prophet, and the looking back on the past is a prelude to their concern for and anticipation of what will occur in the future. In his address Samuel recounts the history of the nation Israel from the time that Jacob went down to Egypt; God's deliverance of them through Moses and Aaron; their taking up residence in their present location, the land of Canaan; their forgetting their God, their deliverance into the hands of foreign rulers and groups, their recognition of their defection and idolatry, and their consequent rescue from these enemies by the judges, up to and including Samuel himself. In language almost identical to Deut 12:10 (behind which, we saw, was a focus upon the latter period of the judges, that is, close to Samuel's time) he refers to their being delivered out of the hand of "your enemies on every side; and ye dwelled safe" (1 Sam 12:11). This promising stage of development was fundamentally upset again by the people's request for a king, a request that in effect meant the rejection of God as their king. Even this crisis, however, was ordered in such a way that God accommodated himself to the rejection and, through the prophet Samuel, appointed the king himself. In the remaining part of his address, Samuel, again in language that is Deuteronomic, calls for the people to obey and serve God. By means of a sign (the miracle of thunder and rain at wheat harvest), that is characteristic of the true Deuteronomic prophet who is known by his sign coming to pass (Deut 18:22), Samuel instills fear in the people. He then assures them that all will go well for them and their king should they serve God with all their heart. As in Deuteronomy 12, the service of God is affirmed as primary, with kingship being legitimized only in so far as kingship recognizes its derivative character.

In conclusion, two interrelated results deserve further comment. First, a precise, detailed, and coherent account of those much discussed laws in Deuteronomy 12, including an explanation of why the command to worship at one place is repeated so often, follows from recognizing that these laws are the product of reflection upon historical records. This thesis, which should occasion no surprise because of the well-recognized Deuteronomic redaction of these records, does justice to the manifest sophistication and intelligence of the author of Deuteronomy in a way that conventional critical theory does not. In opting for a link between law and actual historical circumstances it postulates different layers of legal material lacking in coherence, order, and conciseness. While such a procedure is understandable, it undervalues the work of the supposed final redactor of the material in a way that leaves him bereft of much sense in matters legal or literary.

Second, on the evidence of the laws and how they have come to be formulated there is no warrant for the commonly accepted view that the Book of Deuteronomy lay before some later Deuteronomic redactor of Joshua through 2 Kings. Indeed the evidence is that the Deuteronomist, in handling that material and sometimes inserting his judgments, at the same time focused on issues that arose in it and compiled judgments which he set down in the Book of Deuteronomy. The scribal activity that shaped Joshua through 2 Kings is the same as that which produced the Deuteronomic laws.

What this thesis does not attempt is an assessment of the actual history underlying the Deuteronomist's demand for the centralization of the cult and any parallels to it before and after his time. In regard to this history it is most probable that centralization was an issue in the early tribal period; that in Solomon's time the exclusiveness of the new temple was urged; that in the ninth and eighth centuries there was a bias in favor of the sanctuary in Jerusalem and a polemic against those at Bethel and Dan; that after the fall of the northern kingdom Jerusalem's exclusiveness became important; that its worship was the total focus after the exile. Only in regard to Josiah's reform does the matter come into the open. I am arguing that the

Deuteronomic legal material cannot be used, as it has been, for sketching some presumed history of centralization. It may not exclude the possibility, but I know of no way in which the historical questions can be put with any degree of confidence. Literary redaction (the latter description not doing justice to what is going on) is the hallmark of the legal material as well as other sections of Deuteronomy, and Joshua through 2 Kings.

SUMMARY The history of the apostasy of successive kings in Israel, which represented a declension from the model of worship established in the Solomonic temple, informs the rule about the source of this apostasy and the call to adhere to the Solomonic model. The need for a king in Israel and a centralized place of worship emerged in the time of the judges, because, lacking a king, the Israelites competed among themselves in cultic matters. The rule about not doing in such matters what people think is right takes up the problem of cultic competitiveness. Saul, the first approved king, offered burnt offerings at a place he thought was acceptable. He offended in doing so and thereby lost his authority as king. The development underlies the rule that warns against presenting burnt offerings at a place that may appear suitable.

In his other sacrificial activity Saul knew to separate the blood of the animal from its flesh, and his family feast, at which David's uncleanness was an issue, involved eating on a grand scale. Positive evaluation of such customary occasions, with a reminder to separate the blood from the flesh, is behind the permission to hold local feasts and to let those who are unclean participate. At the priestly town of Nob the hungry David was permitted to eat the shewbread normally reserved for the priests. Similar permission to eat sacred food in the towns, when the central sanctuary comes into existence, is denied. The rule also takes up the needs of the priests when this sanctuary is established as the exclusive one. The hungry Israelites, in consuming the spoil of their enemies, ate the flesh with the blood still in it. Saul intervened and imposed a centralized supervision of the slaughtering. The rule, addressing itself to a comparable situation in which Israel expands its territory and finds livestock available to it, warns about eating the flesh with the blood, and requires the slaughter to be supervised at the central sanctuary if possible.

CHAPTER 2

APOSTATE RULERS

The Deuteronomist concentrates in the initial laws upon serving the Israelite god in the proper way, acknowledging his supreme authority. This concern began with a rule (Deut 12:2–7) in which fear about the attraction of other gods was present. The appeal of other gods was linked to supreme secular authority in the form of successive kings of Israel (and Judah). It is no surprise to find that the subject of apostasy among Israel's leaders comes into full focus in subsequent laws. We find that the Deuteronomist scrutinizes activities in which this tendency shows up or is acted upon. His scrutiny proves to be systematic: kings are looked at in chronological order (as in the preceding cultic laws). At the same time, however, because Moses is purportedly issuing the rules, the Deuteronomist's judgment is based on Moses' reaction to apostasy in his lifetime. The first law in the code (Deut 12:2–7) reveals the same link between Moses' own time and the history of the monarchy.

Law: Exposure to foreign gods

[29] When Yahweh thy God shall cut off the nations from before thee, whither thou goest to possess them, and thou succeedest them, and dwellest in their land; [30] take heed to thyself that thou be not

> snared by following them, after that they be destroyed from before thee; and that thou enquire not after their gods, saying, How did these nations serve their gods? even so will I do likewise. [31] Thou shalt not do so unto Yahweh thy God: for every abomination to Yahweh, which he hateth, have they done unto their gods; for even their sons and their daughters they have burnt in the fire to their gods. (Deut 12:29–31)

Background: Saul's threat to David's religious loyalty

Saul, informed by the Ziphites of David's hideout in the wilderness, pursued him but was outwitted by David, who came upon the king while he was sleeping and removed his spear. In the ensuing conversation, conducted at a distance, David accused Saul of driving him from his inheritance and forcing him into a position where he might have to give allegiance to foreign gods. Each left in his own fashion. David, knowing that he was not safe from Saul, took up residence with a Philistine group. During his stay in their midst he was able to go out and destroy many of Israel's traditional enemies (1 Samuel 26, 27). There is no indication that he participated in Philistine cults, but many of his royal successors, as recorded in the Book of Kings, came under such foreign religious influence.

Deut 12:29–31 concerns an Israelite's entrapment by foreign gods when he enters the new land and asks, "How did these nations serve their gods?"; this subject is taken up and continued in the following laws in Deuteronomy 13. In 1 Samuel 26, David, forced from his people because of Saul's hostility to him, had occasion to protest his situation to Saul in person. The lawgiver, with his interest in beginnings, notes that this incident is the first in the history of the kings in which the subject of idolatry arises. David did not in fact become involved in idolatry, but such involvement is readily suggested: Saul was forcing David to "go and serve other gods."[1] The lawgiver takes up the subject at this point and goes on to consider how future kings

[1]In the judgments made upon idolatrous kings, David's avoidance of idolatry is cited (e.g., 2 Kings 16:2, 18:3). The rare verb *nāqaš* is found three times in the Psalms; in Deut 12:30, in which, we have argued, David's complaint to Saul about the threat to his life informs the law; and in 1 Sam 28:9, where the woman of Endor complains that Saul is threatening her life. Also noteworthy is the use of the form "guard thyself" in Deut 12:30. David proved to be on guard for his own religious well-being (1 Sam 26:19).

were open to the abominable practices of foreign cults. He cites the example of passing a son or daughter through fire (to the god Molech). David's successors as king, for example, Ahaz (2 Kings 16:3) and Manasseh (2 Kings 21:6), imitated this Canaanite ritual. Of Ahaz the Deuteronomic redactor states that he "did not that which was right in the sight of Yahweh his God, like David his father" (2 Kings 16:2), and then cites how he made his son pass through fire. The lawgiver prefaces his condemnation of this practice with "Thou shalt not do so unto Yahweh thy God" (Deut 12:31). These words are identical to those in Deut 12:4, in which the copying of Canaanite practices by the later kings of Israel (and Judah) is a subtext.

In the law Moses refers to the time when God will cut off the nations that occupy the territory Israel is to receive as its inheritance. This prophecy can be seen to include David's time. Under divine guidance David achieved victory against the Philistines at this period in his life when Saul was harassing him (1 Sam 23:1–5; cp., 1 Sam 27:8). As a result of his triumph, he found himself being threatened with the loss of his own inheritance in the land (1 Sam 26:19). His position is an odd one. Moses is understandably legislating for the more typical situation in which Israel's enemies are being destroyed and the Israelites are possessing their land.

The topic of David's threatened loss of his inheritance can be linked to similar interests in the traditions underlying the preceding laws. The first law prescribed the loss of the religious emblems of the Canaanite inheritance of the land, but, more important, it concerned the engagement of the kings of Israel and Judah in Canaanite ways that led to Israel's eventual loss of its land. The second law focused on the period when the tribe of Dan was establishing its inheritance and the tribe of Benjamin was threatened with loss of its. The third concerned the Benjaminite Saul's loss of hereditary rule.

A law in which someone causes someone else to serve other gods logically follows laws about serving the native God in the proper way. It is nonetheless interesting to note that these two topics come together in David's complaint to Saul: if God had incited Saul against him, then David could have God accept an offering (1 Sam 26:19);[2] if, however, human agency motivated the antagonism, those responsi-

[2]The term *minḥāh* has here an inclusive meaning, an offering of any kind, grain or animal.

ble should be cursed before God, because they were forcing him to serve other gods.

Law: Not to add or subtract from what has been commanded by Moses

> [32] What thing soever I command you, observe to do it: thou shalt not add thereto, nor diminish from it. (Deut 12:32)

Background: Aaron's and Jeroboam's initiative with the golden calves

When Moses delayed to return from Mount Sinai, the people requested Aaron to make them gods to go before them in their journeyings. He fashioned the golden calf of which they declared, "These be thy gods, O Israel, which brought thee up out of the land of Egypt." Aaron built an altar before the calf and proclaimed the following day to be a feast to Yahweh. The people duly celebrated. Yahweh informed Moses of the situation and threatened to destroy the people, but Moses pleaded with him to spare them. Moses came down the mountain with the two tablets and, on seeing the calf and the dancing, broke them. He burnt the calf and made the people drink water with its powdered contents. He asked Aaron, "What did this people unto thee, that thou hast brought so great a sin upon them?" Aaron recounted the people's request and claimed, "And I said unto them, Whosoever hath any gold, let them break it off. So they gave it me: then I cast it into the fire, and there came out this calf." The sons of Levi came forward in response to Moses's call for those who were loyal to Yahweh and proceeded to slay "every man his brother, and every man his companion, and every man his neighbour." Some three thousand men died (Exodus 32).

> [25] Then Jeroboam built Shechem in mount Ephraim, and dwelt therein; and went out from thence, and built Penuel. [26] And Jeroboam said in his heart, Now shall the kingdom return to the house of David: [27] if this people go up to do sacrifice in the house of Yahweh at Jerusalem, then shall the heart of this people turn again unto their lord, even unto Rehoboam king of Judah, and they shall kill me, and go again to Rehoboam king of Judah. [28] Whereupon the king took counsel, and made two calves of gold, and said unto them, It is too much for you to go up to Jerusalem: behold thy

gods, O Israel, which brought thee up out of the land of Egypt. [29] And he set the one in Beth-el, and the other put he in Dan. [30] And this thing became a sin: for the people went to worship before the one, even unto Dan. [31] And he made an house of high places, and made priests of the lowest of the people, which were not of the sons of Levi. [32] And Jeroboam ordained a feast in the eighth month, on the fifteenth day of the month, like unto the feast that is in Judah, and he offered upon the altar. (1 Kings 12:25–32)

In the preceding law Moses condemns in advance the idolatrous practices of the kings, for example, their imitation of the Canaanite activity of passing sons and daughters through fire to the gods. This history of apostasy is very much the concern of the following laws in Deuteronomy 13, beginning with the statement in Deut 12:32: "What thing soever I command you, observe to do it: thou shalt not add thereto, nor diminish from it." There are two interrelated traditions that account for the presentation of this commandment.

In the preceding laws Kings Saul, David, and Solomon have been a focus of attention for the lawgiver. The building of the temple in Jerusalem by Solomon was behind the rule centralizing the cult. Solomon, however, was the first king to be enticed into apostasy (1 Kings 11:1–8). The result, according to the Deuteronomist, was the division of the previously united kingdom. Jerusalem remained in the control of Solomon's oppressive son, Rehoboam, while the tribes that broke away were united under Jeroboam who was not a member of David's family. The conflict between Jeroboam and Rehoboam resembles the one between Saul and David in that it prompted Jeroboam's actual, as against David's potential, involvement in unacceptable worship.[3] He set up the golden calves in the cities Bethel and Dan so that his subjects would not be tempted to renew their allegiance to the Davidic dynasty in Jerusalem. The Deuteronomist judges Jeroboam's action harshly and interprets it as recurring evidence of Israel's apostasy. Worship of the calves in these cities is seen as a rejection of the central place of worship—and, presumably, all that centralization stood for—and as signaling the downfall of the northern kingdom of Israel. In 2 Kings 17:16, 17, worship of them is

[3]There is the further parallel, namely, that the tribes of Israel declared that their inheritance is imperiled under the reigning house (1 Kings 12:16), just as David, faced with Saul's antagonism, complained about the threat to his inheritance.

coupled with the practice of passing sons and daughters through the fire to indicate why Israel fell to the Assyrians in the time of King Hoshea. Little wonder that the Deuteronomist, after his repeated emphasis on the need for a central place to worship and just after citing the abhorrent use of fire by the Canaanites should turn to this development. Incidentally the creation of the idols, like Aaron's creation of a calf in his time, would have involved the use of fire.

In judging Jeroboam's idolatry, the Deuteronomist typically goes back to some comparable example as close to Moses' own time as possible; in this instance, to the worship of the golden calf under Aaron's supervision. Commentators have surely been correct in claiming a connection between the tradition about Jeroboam and the one about Aaron in Exodus 32.[4] Especially revealing of a link is Jeroboam's assertion, "Behold thy gods, O Israel, which brought thee up out of the land of Egypt" (1 Kings 12:28). Aaron's provision of a calf to the people in his time was accompanied by the words, "These be thy gods, O Israel, which brought thee up out of the land of Egypt" (Exod 32:4), a statement more obviously appropriate to his situation than to Jeroboam's.

The lawgiver evaluates these two traditions in his law about not adding to or subtracting from the commandments issued by Moses and in the subsequent laws about instigation to idolatry by a prophet or dreamer of dreams, by a close family intimate, and by certain persons within a city. Moses is represented as asserting his personal and supreme authority: "What thing soever I command you, observe to do it." No one else, not Aaron, not Jeroboam,[5] no other king, can issue rules pertaining to the worship of the Israelite god. Ahijah, who is a prophet "like unto Moses," speaks with the latter's authority in warning Jeroboam not to depart from the deity's statutes and commandments (1 Kings 11:31–39). The need to make Moses' authority explicit in this context of new leadership is readily apparent in the incident involving Aaron.[6] He was Moses' brother and the people

[4]J. Coert Rylaarsdam points out how the people's rejection of the charismatic leadership of the prophet, Moses, in favor of "a more stable representation of deity" has much in common with the people's request for a king in 1 Sam 8:5. See his *Exodus* IB 1 (New York: Abingdon, 1952), 1064.

[5]Like Moses in Deut 12:32, Jeroboam uses both "you" and "thou" in his order to the people in 1 Kings 12:28: "It is too much for you to go up to Jerusalem: behold thy gods."

[6]At the beginning of the reign of Jehoiakim, the son of Josiah, there is a similar exhortation to obey, "all the words that I [Yahweh] command thee [Jeremiah] to

wanted him to become their leader because Moses appeared to be lost on Mount Sinai. As a result, Aaron asserted his assumed authority and created the golden calf, which they identified as their god who had been responsible for leading them out of Egypt.

The lawgiver focuses on the problem of the deviant exercise of authority that this narrative poses. Aaron (along with Hur) was left in charge of affairs while Moses was on Mount Sinai (Exod 24:14). The issue therefore arises as to how far he should go in discharging his duty. The lawgiver, in the spirit of Moses as depicted in the narrative, is in no doubt that Aaron far exceeded his authority. The people were to bring any unresolved cases to him, and, it is implied, he was to decide them according to the rules and directions already laid down by Moses. No additions to, no subtractions from them were warranted. The representation of the deity by an image would constitute such an addition. This is so because the contents of the decalogue, in particular the prohibition of an image of Yahweh (Exod 20:4), had not yet been imparted to Aaron or the people.[7] Instruction in the decalogue's contents awaited the second delivery of them in writing (Exod 34:32). It is, in fact, difficult to believe that Aaron would have made the golden calf if he had known of a prohibition against the creation of such an image. If in his historical record the Deuteronomist did not include such an original prohibition of Moses, then we can better understand the narrative itself and the lawgiver's response to it. Aaron's action is not from our perspective such a reprehensible one at all but, rather, an attempt to make Israel's deity more tangible. What is at stake is the potential crisis of authority between Moses and his brother as to whose rule is to be given precedence. Both the narrative in its present form and the Deuteronomist

speak unto them, diminish not a word" (Jer 26:1, 2). In Deut 4:2 we find the almost identical prohibition about not adding to or subtracting from the commandments in a context recalling the apostasy to Baal at Peor (Num 25:1–5). Similar considerations apply to its use in this context. The foreign prophet Balaam appears to be held responsible by Moses for Israel's apostasy then (Num 31:8, 16). He was a prophet who earlier lived up to the claim that he could not go beyond the command of Yahweh to do less or more (Num 22:18). Later, however, he presumably no longer spoke only the words put in his mouth by Yahweh (Num 22:35, 38), but spoke in the name of Baal and was heeded by the Israelites.

[7]The prohibition in Exod 20:23 against making "with me [Yahweh]" gods of silver or gold is a different matter. Aaron regarded his calf as a representation of Yahweh (Exod 32:5) and not, although it could be (and was) so interpreted, as a god alongside Yahweh.

come down on the side of Moses, and each, unfairly in terms of the actual historical situation, condemns Aaron's action by imputing apostasy and idolatry.

Laws: Three instigators to idolatry

[1] If there arise in thy midst a prophet, or a dreamer of dreams, and giveth thee a sign or a wonder, [2] and the sign or the wonder come to pass, whereof he spake unto thee, saying, Let us go after other gods which thou hast not known, and let us serve them; [3] thou shalt not hearken unto the words of that prophet, or that dreamer of dreams: for Yahweh your God proveth you, to know whether ye love your God with all your heart and with all your soul. [4] Ye shall walk after Yahweh your God, and fear him, and keep his commandments, and obey his voice, and ye shall serve him, and cleave unto him. [5] And that prophet, or that dreamer of dreams, shall be put to death; because he hath spoken defection against Yahweh your God, which brought you out of the land of Egypt, and redeemed you out of the house of bondage, to thrust thee out of the way which Yahweh thy God commanded thee to walk in. So shalt thou put the evil away from the midst of thee.

[6] If thy brother, the son of thy mother, or thy son, or thy daughter, or the wife of thy bosom, or thy friend, which is as thine own soul, entice thee secretly, saying, Let us go and serve other gods, which thou hast not known, thou, nor thy fathers; [7] namely, of the gods of the people which are round about you, nigh unto thee, or far off from thee, from the one end of the earth even unto the other end of the earth; [8] thou shalt not consent unto him, nor hearken unto him; neither shall thine eye pity him, neither shalt thou spare, neither shalt thou conceal him: [9] but thou shalt surely kill him; thine hand shall be first upon him to put him to death, and afterwards the hand of all the people. [10] And thou shalt stone him with stones, that he die; because he hath sought to thrust thee away from Yahweh thy God, which brought thee out of the land of Egypt, from the house of bondage. [11] And all Israel shall hear, and fear, and shall do no more any such wickedness as this in thy midst.

[12] If thou shalt hear in one of thy cities, which Yahweh thy God hath given thee to dwell there, saying, [13] Certain men, the children of Belial, are gone out from thy midst, and have drawn

away the inhabitants of their city, saying, Let us go and serve other gods, which ye have not known; [14] then shalt thou enquire, and make search, and ask diligently; and, behold, if it be truth, and the thing certain, that such abomination is wrought in thy midst; [15] thou shalt surely smite the inhabitants of that city with the edge of the sword, destroying it utterly, and all that is therein, and the cattle thereof, with the edge of the sword. [16] And thou shalt gather all the spoil of it into the midst of the street thereof, and shalt burn with fire the city, and all the spoil thereof every whit, for Yahweh thy God: and it shall be an heap for ever; it shall not be built again. [17] And there shall cleave nought of the devoted thing to thine hand: that Yahweh may turn from the fierceness of his anger, and shew thee mercy, and have compassion upon thee, and multiply thee, as he hath sworn unto thy fathers; [18] when thou shalt hearken to the voice of Yahweh thy God, to keep all his commandments which I command thee this day, to do that which is right in the eyes of Yahweh thy God. (Deut 13:1–18)

Background: Aaron's role in the incident of the golden calf (Exodus 32); idolatry within royal families (1, 2 Kings); Jeroboam's counselors (1 Kings 12:25–33); the destruction of Jericho

After Israel entered the promised land the first Canaanite city to be given over by Yahweh for destruction was Jericho. No Israelite was to touch anything of it, and the silver and gold, and the vessels of brass and iron, were to be devoted to Yahweh. With the exception of the harlot Rahab, who had protected the Israelite spies, the city and all its human and animal inhabitants were destroyed. It was then burnt. "And Joshua adjured them at that time, saying, Cursed be the man before Yahweh, that riseth up and buildeth this city Jericho: he shall lay the foundation thereof in his firstborn, and in his youngest son, shall he set up the gates of it" (Josh 6:26).

Achan of the tribe of Judah offended by acquiring some of Jericho's valuables. The result was a curse upon Israel and a search to ascertain who was responsible. "And Joshua and all Israel with him, took Achan the son of Zerah, and the silver, and the garment, and the wedge of gold, and his sons, and his daughters, and his oxen, and his asses, and they brought them unto the valley of Achor. And Joshua said, Why hast thou troubled us? Yahweh shall trouble thee this day. And all Israel stoned him with stones, and burned them with fire, after they had stoned them with stones. And they raised over him a great heap of stones unto this day. So Yahweh turned from the fierceness of his anger" (Josh 7:24–26).

The false prophet or dreamer of dreams

The law concerns a prophet or dreamer of dreams who is able to give a sign or wonder and make it come to pass, namely, Aaron.[8] We can accurately characterize him as a prophet or dreamer of dreams. Even more to the point, because of the context out of which the Deuteronomist produces his laws, this characterization defines Aaron precisely in relation to Moses. Aaron is made a prophet to Moses (Exod 7:1), the latter's spokesman to the people (Exod 4:16). As Moses' prophet he is able to perform miracles in the sight of the people, the purpose of which is to cause them to believe in a divine being, namely, the Israelite god (Exod 4:1–9, 30, 31). The distinction between Moses and Aaron as prophets is that Moses receives direct communication from the deity, whereas Aaron (and their sister Miriam) by vision and dream only (Num 12:6). In the relationship between Aaron and Moses, Moses has the greater authority. We have just noted how Moses' statement, "What thing soever I command you, observe to do it," represents an assertion of his authority over such as Aaron.

In the incident of the golden calf Aaron informed Moses that the calf constituted a miracle (Exod 32:24). From Moses' point of view Aaron's idolatry had thus begun with a miracle (and not with an act of engraving). Moses is giving the laws and he focuses on this aspect of Aaron's wrongful use of his power to perform signs and wonders, and fashions a law accordingly.[9] In that he is constructing a law, he has to make the nature of the issue explicit. A reading of the narrative

[8]In that the Deuteronomist is familiar with Balaam (Deut 4:3, 23:4) the tradition about him should not be excluded. He was a diviner, presumably able to perform signs and wonders, and he received word from Yahweh at night, presumably by dreams (Num 22:7, 8, 13, 19, 20).

[9]Because of the way in which the Deuteronomist uses traditions in his legal constructions, it is irrelevant that Aaron's claim to have performed a wonder might not be true. The topic presents itself regardless of the historical veracity. Commentators often point to a conflict with the instruction in Deut 18:22, in which the distinguishing feature of a true prophet is said to be that his predictions come to pass. Apart from the problem whether they should be comparing a prophet who predicts the future with a prophet who performs a wonder, the important comparison is between each law and its relevant tradition, not between the two laws.

leaves the nature of Aaron's role unclear. The lawgiver has therefore to spell out in detail some comparable matter. The prophet, unlike Aaron, has to declare openly that he wants the people to follow other gods. In Exodus 32 after Aaron produced the calf, the people themselves declared, "These be thy gods, O Israel, which brought thee up out of the land of Israel" (v. 4). The lawgiver, noting Aaron's supporting and hence influential role in the incident, but especially noting also his assertion about the wonder in Exod 32:24, constructs a law that will give expression to a situation where a prophet's role is unambiguous. It is precisely the lack of clarity or detail in a narrative that prompts the lawgiver to offer a clear statement on a subject.[10]

The gods referred to do not appear to be foreign ones in the sense that they are worshipped in the surrounding cultures. It is simply said of them that they are ones the people of Israel have not known. The gods mentioned in Exodus 32 were not those of foreign groups but ones that the people of Israel had not known from their previous experience with Moses and Aaron, especially the God, Yahweh, revealed by the signs (Exod 4:1–9, 28–31, and so on).[11] The false prophet is one who tempts the people to turn away from "Yahweh your God, which brought you out of the land of Egypt, and redeemed you out of the house of bondage" (Deut 13:5). This is how the matter is perceived in Exod 32:7, 8. The language of the law is similar to that used in the Deuteronomist's own description of the incident of the golden calf (Deut 9:12, 16, 26).[12]

The intimate relative or friend

The lawgiver examines both the incident of the golden calf and the history of the apostasy of the kings when he considers the topic of

[10]M. Aberbach and L. Smolar note that when Moses descended from Mount Sinai he angrily accused Aaron of having instigated, not just submitted to, the apostasy of the people: "What did this people unto thee, that thou hast brought so great a sin upon them?" (Exod 32:31). See their "Aaron, Jeroboam, and the Golden Calves," *JBL* 86 (1967):137.

[11]*nātan,* "to give" a sign, is used in the law and in Exod 7:9.

[12]The "You" form in Deut 13:5 is paralleled in Deut 7:8 and 9:16. Note too the use of the verb *nādaḥ,* in the sense of thrusting aside Yahweh for idolatry, in 13:5, 13, and 4:19. The last citation refers to the incident of the golden calf (4:16). The verb *bʿr* (*piʿel*), "to exterminate," is used in a number of laws beginning with this one. In the history of the kings it is first used similarly in regard to the removal of the house of Jeroboam because of his apostasy with the calves (1 Kings 14:10).

instigation to idolatry within an intimate circle such as the family. As in the preceding law, he would again have noted that Aaron's role in relation to his brother was to be his spokesman and to perform signs before the people. In defending himself against Moses' accusation that he caused the people to sin, Aaron blamed them for forcing him to act on their behalf. He claimed that he threw their gold into the fire and out came the calf. His assertion could be taken as an implication that this miracle was a sign in keeping with his previous function as his brother's surrogate. It would follow that one brother was trying to convince another that the sign was a true one, when in fact the sign incited the people to idolatry, to claim that they now knew the gods which had brought them out of Egypt. We could then explain why the law begins with a comparable example of a man's attempt to persuade his blood brother to recognize a god (or gods) not previously known to him. In accounting for the reference to a friend's influence, as well as a brother's, we might note that those killed by the Levites in the incident of the calf were the Levites' brothers and friends (*rēaʿ* as in Deut 13:6). Why some were killed and not others, even though all were apparently culpable, suggested to C. F. Keil that a distinction between tempters, who were killed, and those tempted must be borne in mind.[13] The Deuteronomist may have made this distinction.

As well as observing the role of close acquaintances in the narrative of Exodus 32, the Deuteronomist ranges over the succession of royal families in which one member incited another to idolatry. The loyalty of the kings to Yahweh was, we recall, the overriding interest in the preceding cultic laws. Solomon's wives turned away his heart toward other gods (1 Kings 11:4). Jezebel's influence upon Ahab was profound (1 Kings 16:31). She enticed him (*sût*), the same verb as in the law (1 Kings 21:25). Jehoram was given to idolatry because of his wife, who was the daughter of Ahab and Jezebel (2 Kings 8:18). The law refers to an instigator who is "thy daughter or the wife of thy bosom." Plainly in Ahab's house both were to be found. Events in his apostate reign come under scrutiny in the presentation of some of the following laws.

In the incident of the golden calf the Levites were assigned to the role of executioners (Exod 32:26–29). A similar role is given in the

[13]C. F. Keil and F. Delitzsch, *Commentar über das Alte Testament* vol. 2, part 1 2d ed. (Leipzig: Dorffling und Franke, 1870), 228.

law to a man who is aware of an instigator to idolatry in his midst. For example, like the Levites in regard to their own brothers and companions (Exod 32:27), the family member is to be the first in putting his relative or close friend to death. Afterwards the people are to be involved just as Moses would no doubt have hoped that all the people might have imitated the example of the Levites in Exodus 32.[14] The Deuteronomist understands that Aaron too deserved death for his role but that the deity intervened—thus the statement in Deut 9:20 about how God was going to destroy him. Because Aaron avoided punishment the lawgiver would have had all the more reason to formulate a law to cover some future example where one brother sought to influence another.

It is said of the gods which the idolater calls to serve that unlike those in the preceding law, they are those of peoples nearby and far off. The lawgiver is thinking of such idolatrous foreign influence as that of Jezebel and the wives of Solomon. He took wives from near and far, and they successfully incited him to idolatry (1 Kings 11:1–8).

Instigators within a city

To account for the lawgiver's switch from the laws concerning the false prophet and the member of the family or close friend to the law concerning certain men within a city who incite to idolatry, we must recall Jeroboam's situation. In order to establish his kingship he built two cities, Shechem and Penuel, and set up a golden calf in Bethel and one in Dan. By having the people recognize these calves as the gods that brought them out of Egypt, he sought to break their allegiance to the temple in Jerusalem (1 Kings 12:28). If in the preceding law the idolatrous influence upon (among others) King Solomon has been a concern, so now the source of his successor's apostasy comes under scrutiny.

Like King Rehoboam in Jerusalem when he sought to consolidate his rule, Jeroboam solicited advice before he set up the golden calves

[14]Those interpreters, for example, M. Weinfeld (*Deuteronomy and the Deuteronomic School* [Oxford: Clarendon, 1972], 94, 95), who observe the influence of lynch law in the details about the punishment are correct up to a point, but they are wrong to think of the instruction as reflecting some historical reality. The "history" behind the law is the nonjudicial action of the Levites in the narrative.

(1 Kings 12:6–11, 28). The lawgiver, concerned with the topic of influencing counsel, is alert to this element in the tradition and on the basis of it constructs a law of more general application. It is not said who these counselors were, or from which city they arose, whether Shechem, Penuel, Bethel, or Dan. The Deuteronomist accordingly formulates a statement about this source of idolatry: "If thou shalt hear in one of thy cities . . . ." Equally revealing of a link with the tradition is that the lawgiver does not concentrate upon the instigators, as he had done in the preceding two laws, but upon those who have responded positively to their incitement, namely, a city's inhabitants. In 1 Kings 12:30 the residents of Bethel and Dan who fell in with the new cultic arrangement are the focus. The nameless counselors, whose role was decisive, are not mentioned again, just as the rule switches from a description of the evil counsel to its effect upon sympathetic listeners.

Elsewhere in the history of the kings (1 Sam 30:22; 1 Kings 21:10, 13) men of the kind the Deuteronomist describes are called base fellows, "sons of Belial," the expression used in the law.[15] Like the false prophet they counsel that other gods, whom the people of Israel have not known, be worshipped. There is no reference to gods of other cultures, and hence the explanation again appears to be that the lawgiver refers to the example of the golden calves, which represents an internal development. In considering the role of these counselors from one of the cities of Israel, the lawgiver has to spell out in greater detail than is found in the narrative in 1 Kings 12:28 what exactly constitutes instigation to idolatry. Their actual counsel must unambiguously call to serve alien gods. Although we cannot know for certain, it is likely that in light of their success the instigators mentioned in the law already enjoyed some standing in their city. Counselors of the kind cited in 1 Kings 12:28 come to mind.

That no punishment is mentioned for the inhabitants of Bethel and Dan is significant. In the law the punishment for the city and its inhabitants is comparable to what was done to the city of Jericho

[15]Cp. the expression *yōʿēṣ bᵉliyyāʿal* in Nah 1:11. *yāʿaṣ* is used in reference to Jeroboam's seeking counsel. Aberbach and Smolar ("Aaron, Jeroboam, and the Golden Calves," 129) point out that the term primarily implies taking counsel with the leading elements of the kingdom (1 Kings 12:6, 8; 2 Kings 6:8; 1 Chron 13:1; 2 Chron 10:6, 8, 30:2, 32:3).

(Josh 6:21). There is a reason for this. Jericho represented the threat of Canaanite religious influence upon the newly arriving Israelites. The destruction of Jericho is the first example of the attempt to extirpate such influence in the new land. The law explicitly deals with the prospect of the first instance of idolatry breaking out in an newly acquired Israelite city. Given the Deuteronomist's interest in first occurrences it is likely that there is a link between his law and this tradition; what was done in Joshua's time may have served as a useful guide to his decision regarding an appropriate punishment for an idolatrous city within Israel. The tradition itself has undergone Deuteronomic redaction.

The link between the law and the tradition is made even closer when it is noted that the Israelite Achan was indeed infected by Jericho's accursed state and that his punishment shows up as the precise model for what has to happen to the Israelite city infected by idolatry. Achan took objects that had been devoted to the sacred ban (*ḥerem*) and as a consequence was put to death with all his household and livestock (Josh 7:24–26). Stoning was the mode of execution and this was followed by burning. A heap of stones was raised over the spot, after which it is stated that God turned from the fierceness of his anger. In the law a city within Israel that has succumbed to the call to serve other gods is to be devoted to the ban. This means that both the inhabitants and the cattle are slain and that fire is used to burn the city and its spoil. The remains then form a heap, preventing anyone from ever building upon the site. The same language is used in the law about God's turning from the fierceness of his wrath once the idolatrous city has been disposed of (cp., too, Exod 32:12, 13). The unique description of its destruction as "a whole-offering to Yahweh thy God" becomes more intelligible in light of Jericho's and Achan's fate.

Law: An Israelite is not to cut himself for the dead

[1] Ye are the children of Yahweh your God: ye shall not cut yourselves, nor make any baldness between your eyes for the dead. [2] For thou art an holy people unto Yahweh thy God, and Yahweh hath chosen thee to be a peculiar people unto himself, above all the nations that are upon the earth. (Deut 14:1, 2)

Background: Ahab's reign and the destruction of the prophets of Baal

Elijah announced to Ahab that Yahweh was bringing famine to the land by withholding moisture. By the performance of certain miracles Elijah demonstrated that he had a special relationship to Yahweh and that the latter acted for him. Ahab accused Elijah of troubling Israel, but he responded by telling Ahab that it was his breach of Yahweh's commandments and his following the Baalim that had brought famine. Together they arranged for the whole of Israel to assemble on Mount Carmel along with the hundreds of prophets of the Baal and the Asherim. Elijah requested of the people that they either follow Yahweh or Baal, but there was no response. He then suggested that the prophets of Baal sacrifice a bullock to their gods and that he sacrifice one to Yahweh. Whichever god answered by fire would be God. The prophets tried first, but despite strenuous efforts there was no response from Baal. They even "cried aloud, and cut themselves after their manner with knives and lancets, till the blood gushed out upon them" (1 Kings 18:28). But still there was no response. Elijah then built an altar in the name of Yahweh and sacrificed his bullock. Fire came forth and consumed it. The people acknowledged Yahweh as God and obeyed Elijah's instruction to slaughter the prophets of Baal. Rain fell (1 Kings 18).

His interest continuing to be taken up with the apostasy of the Israelite kings, the lawgiver next turns to Ahab's reign and an incident occurring then. He looks at the worst record of idolatry after Jeroboam's—Ahab's. His was "above all that were before him," "doing more to provoke Yahweh God of Israel to anger than all the kings of Israel that were before him" (1 Kings 16:30–33). Immediately following these judgments is a notice about how in his days Hiel the Bethelite built Jericho at the cost of the lives of his two sons (v. 34). This, it is said, was in fulfillment of Joshua's word on the subject (Josh 6:26). We have just noted the role of the Jericho narrative, from which the lawgiver constructs a sanction appropriate to a city within Israel that has proved idolatrous, and that, when destroyed, must never, like Jericho at Joshua's command, be built again. It is equally noteworthy that Hiel's city Bethel was one of those in the lawgiver's mind because of its worship of the calf in Jeroboam's reign.[16]

[16]Note that just as we can infer for the law a link between a tradition in the Book of Kings and one in the Book of Joshua, so there is explicit textual evidence for such links.

The law against an Israelite's cutting himself when mourning the dead includes the assertion that Israelites are sons of Yahweh, a people separate from other nations. The law should be viewed in light of the event recorded in 1 Kings 18. The prophets of Baal tried to evoke a manifestation of life on the part of their gods by cutting themselves. But these gods do not have life, as Elijah demonstrated. The lawgiver is reminded of a comparable act among the Israelites by which they sought to make contact with the dead: the custom existing in both Israel and its neighbors of mourning the dead by cutting oneself and making bald the forehead.[17] That the rite was practiced in the surrounding culture and that the same verb (*gādad, hithpoʿel*) is used as in the rite involving the Baals suggests a similar intention: to bridge the gulf between the visibly living world and the supposed hidden other world where the gods and the dead reside. However that may be, the presentation of the prohibition at this point in the code is probably the result of the lawgiver's attempts to ensure that the Israelites in no way mirrored the idolatrous practices of the worshippers of Baal. Put in simpler terms, the view of the lawgiver is that just as the prophets of a foreign god vainly cut themselves for the dead (the Baals), so the Israelites should not cut themselves for the dead because their only contact with supernatural life is Yahweh. By juxtaposing the common mourning practice in Israel with the Canaanite religious practice, the Deuteronomist shows that he opposes the custom. This change in Israelite practice calls for an explanation.

Conceivably the Israelite rite of circumcision may also underlie the lawgiver's thinking. This view is supported by the affirmation that Israelites are sons of Yahweh—compare Jeremiah's "circumcise yourselves to Yahweh" (Jer 4:4)—and prompted by the lawgiver's recollection of the one required act of cutting the body in Israelite practice and its significance.

Law: Abominable food

[3]Thou shalt not eat any abominable thing. [4] These are the beasts which ye shall eat: the ox, the sheep, and the goat, [5] the hart . . . .[6] And every beast that parteth the hoof, and cleaveth the

[17]See Jer 16:6, 41:5, 47:5; Amos 8:10; Isa 3:24, 15:2, 22:12; Mic 1:16; Ezek 7:18.

cleft into two claws, and cheweth the cud among the beasts, that ye shall eat. [7] Nevertheless these ye shall not eat of them that chew the cud, or of them that divide the cloven hoof; as the camel, and the hare, and the rock badger; for they chew the cud, but divide not the hoof; therefore they are unclean unto you. [8] And the swine, because it divideth the hoof, yet cheweth not the cud, it is unclean unto you: ye shall not eat of their flesh, nor touch their dead carcase. [9] These ye shall eat of all that are in the waters: all that have fins and scales shall ye eat: [10] and whatsoever hath not fins and scales ye may not eat; it is unclean unto you. [11] Of all clean birds ye shall eat. [12] But these are they of which ye shall not eat: the eagle. . . . [19] And every creeping thing that flieth is unclean unto you: they shall not be eaten. [20] But of all clean fowls ye may eat.

[21] Ye shall not eat of any thing that dieth of itself: thou shalt give it unto the soujourner that is in thy gates, that he may eat it; or thou mayest sell it unto an alien: for thou art an holy people unto Yahweh thy God. Thou shalt not seethe a kid in his mother's milk. (Deut 14:3–12, 19–21)

Background: The house of Ahab punished by famine

[1] And Elijah the Tishbite, who was of the inhabitants of Gilead, said unto Ahab, As Yahweh God of Israel liveth, before whom I stand, there shall not be dew nor rain these years, but according to my word. (1 Kings 17:1)

[1] And it came to pass after many days, that the word of Yahweh came to Elijah in the third year, saying, Go, shew thyself unto Ahab; and I will send rain upon the earth. [2] And Elijah went to shew himself unto Ahab. And there was a sore famine in Samaria. (1 Kings 18:1, 2)

[25] And there was a great famine in Samaria; and behold, they besieged it, until an ass's head was sold for fourscore pieces of silver, and the fourth part of a cab of dove's dung for five pieces of silver. [26] And as the king of Israel was passing by upon the wall, there cried a woman unto him, saying, Help, my lord, O king. [27] And he said, If Yahweh do not help thee, whence shall I help thee? out of the barnfloor, or out of the winepress? [28] And the king said unto her, What aileth thee? And she answered, This woman said unto me, Give thy son, that we may eat him to day, and we will eat my son to morrow. [29] So we boiled my son, and did eat him: and I said unto her on the next day, Give thy son, that we may eat him:

> and she hath hid her son. [30] And it came to pass, when the king heard the words of the woman, that he rent his clothes; and he passed by upon the wall, and the people looked, and, behold, he had sackcloth within upon his flesh. [31] Then he said, God do so and more also to me, if the head of Elisha the son of Shaphat shall stand on him this day. (2 Kings 6:25–31)

The famines visited as a punishment for apostasy upon the house of Ahab both in his reign and that of his son Joram readily suggest problems relating to food. It is, for instance, during famine conditions that people are likely to consume food that ordinarily falls under a taboo. The most extreme example is that described in 2 Kings 6:24–31 when two mothers agreed to eat their sons and one son was duly boiled and eaten. From this background in the time of Ahab and his successor, the lawgiver takes up the topic of food that is permitted and food that is prohibited, and lays down rules that cover normal circumstances.[18]

The preceding laws in Deuteronomy 12 concern the Israelite's consumption of meat. For example, the lawgiver opposes consuming the blood of an animal. The dietary laws constitute another aspect of this concern. We noted in regard to the prohibition against consuming blood that the topic arose because of the Israelites' extreme state of hunger (1 Sam 14:24–35). Also noteworthy is the idea behind the rule against cutting oneself for the dead. An animal's blood is its "life" and an Israelite must not associate himself with it, just as he should not come into contact with any "life" he might attribute to the dead.

The latter law immediately precedes the dietary laws and concerns a customary practice among the Israelites, their habit of cutting their bodies in mourning. In regard to eating the Deuteronomist is also interested in what must have been customary practice: some food was not eaten as a matter of course, other food was, and he seeks to explain why this should be so. An obvious link with his mourning law is that bodily marks, for example, whether the hoof of an animal is cleft in two or not, constitute criteria in the matter.

Equally revealing is the wider prohibition against a relationship, as

[18]Interestingly, the topic of clean and unclean creatures arises in the similar context of God's visiting the flood upon the earth (Gen 7:1–5).

indicated by the marks on one's body, between the living and the dead. In the laws just preceding this mourning law other gods are not living ones; hence for an Israelite to go after them is to be in touch with the dead. Recall that the destruction of an idolatrous city is commemorated by its remains forming a "heap forever," a mark on the land that no life should spring up there again. By contrast, because of the human desire to eat slaughtered animals and other creatures, there has to be a physical contact between the living and the dead. This contact, which represents a concession to human weakness,[19] has to be controlled and is permitted or prohibited depending upon certain distinguishing bodily features. Outward signs play an important role in these laws and tie in with the interest in prophetic signs (for example, that of Aaron,) and the many signs to be found in the traditions about Elijah and Elisha. It is interesting to note that many of the signs involving these two prophets had to do with food: ravens (which are unclean) brought Elijah bread and meat (1 Kings 17:6); Elijah caused a jar of meal to last the length of the famine (1 Kings 17:16); an angel provided food under a broom tree that lasted him forty days and nights (1 Kings 19:4–8); Elisha miraculously rid food of poison (2 Kings 4:41). The point of these miracles is that in the midst of death Yahweh is seen to be very much alive. The most important sign of all, however, is the famine itself that occurred during Ahab's time, because it represents the outward mark of God's displeasure, an indication that he as the ultimate source of life was withholding it.

In addition to the listing of clean and unclean creatures, which may be based upon some previously existing list, there are the two prohibitions against eating the flesh of any animal dying a natural death and against seething a kid in its mother's milk (Deut 14:21). Both these rules exemplify the concern with avoiding wherever possible the overlapping of life and death. In that blood constitutes "life" and must be drained from the newly slaughtered creature (Deut 12:23), an animal that dies exhibits the undesirable mixing of "life" and death. This is true also, in a somewhat more subtle way, of a dead young kid that is

[19]See D. Daube, "Concessions to Sinfulness in Jewish Law," *JJS* 10 (1959):1–13; C. M. Carmichael, "A Common Element in Five Supposedly Disparate Laws," *VT* 29 (1979), 132, n. 7. The contact between life and death is minimized as much as possible in that creatures that kill and consume other creatures are not to be eaten. To eat them is to be in contact with death to a multiple degree.

cooked not in any milk—that might be acceptable—but in its mother's. That milk is in some ways comparable to its life blood in that it is the means of sustenance until its slaughter.[20]

An animal dying naturally would be a frequent occurrence during conditions of famine, indeed, very much a sign of the famine's existence. This observation is strengthened by the parallel rule in the Book of the Covenant about animal flesh that has been torn by beasts (Exod 22:31). We shall presently see that the kid law can also be linked to the lawgiver's focus upon famine.

The motivation for the Israelites to keep both the rule against mourning the dead by cutting themselves and shaving the forehead (Deut 14:1), and the rule against eating an animal dying naturally (Deut 14:21), is that "For thou art an holy people unto Yahweh thy God." This is expanded in verse 2, "And Yahweh hath chosen thee to be a peculiar people unto himself, above all the nations that are upon the earth." Each rule involves the undesirable mixing of life and death: blood (from the cut) and hair given up for the dead and blood undrained from animal flesh. As sons of Yahweh the Israelites must be conscious of life in some special way. Each rule involves a contrast between the Israelite and the foreigner: other texts indicate that Israel's neighbors practiced the custom of mourning proscribed in the rule, and in the motivation attached to the proscription reference is made to Israel's being different from other nations. The flesh of an animal dying naturally may be given to an alien in Israel's midst or sold to a foreigner, the implication being that a non-Israelite has no relationship with Yahweh and hence no need to be aware of the exclusive commitment to "life" entailed by an Israelite's allegiance to him.

If establishing rules about food is the lawgiver's response to his observation of the famine conditions imposed in the reign of the house of Ahab, the prohibited food in the final example, a kid boiled in its mother's milk, may have been prompted by the extreme example of the two mothers who boiled and ate the son of one of them (2 Kings 6:29). What is plainly abhorrent about the example is not just

[20]For a more detailed discussion, see my "On Separating Life and Death: An Explanation of Some Biblical Laws," *HTR* 69 (1976):1–7. The concern with keeping life and death apart is spelled out in the nonlegal parts of Deuteronomy, for example, in Deut 30:15–20.

that human beings consumed human flesh but that a mother who had given life to her child fed upon its boiled flesh. As is characteristic, what the lawgiver may have done is take stock of the extreme happening in the tradition and seek out an example that was in some important feature—the dramatic clash of life and death—reminiscent of it and that represented more common practice. By concentrating on the process of cooking and not upon eating what is cooked, the lawgiver draws attention to the mother and her offspring.

SUMMARY Saul forced David to leave his own people and was seen as encouraging him to worship non-Israelite gods. This is the first instance in the history of the kings when such an issue arose. Being so, it inspired the rule warning against interest in foreign gods when the Israelites were settled in the land. Just as the conflict between Saul and David made the latter vulnerable to the claims of alien gods, so the conflict between Rehoboam and Jeroboam prompted the latter to give up his allegiance to the worship of the invisible Yahweh at Jerusalem and to install the golden calves at Bethel and Dan. This development had its precedent in Moses' life when Aaron made the golden calf. Both these developments come under scrutiny in a number of laws.

In doing what he did Aaron usurped Moses' supreme authority in matters sacred and secular. The rule that Moses himself speaks requiring that no one add to or subtract from what he commands constitutes an assertion of this authority over such as Aaron or Jeroboam. Aaron was a prophet to Moses and performed signs and wonders before the people. His prophetic office was less authoritative than that of his brother's in that he heard from Yahweh by dreams, unlike Moses who heard directly. Aaron's influential, but not very clear, role in the idolatry of the golden calf prompts a rule about a prophet or dreamer of dreams who instigates Israelites to idolatry. Moses' brother, the brothers and companions of the Levites, were all culpable in the incident of the calf. The problem of close relatives' religious influence over their kin came into the open in later royal familes and led to the law on the subject. Counselors advised Jeroboam to install the golden calves in Bethel and Dan, where the inhabitants responded by worshipping them. The first example in Israelite history of a city that threatened the nation with the infection of idolatry was the Canaanite city of Jericho. The lawgiver applies the punishment that befell it and the Israelite Achan, who was infected, to any Israelite city that is led into idolatry by counselors in its midst.

The prophets of Baal cut themselves in the hope that their gods would give a sign that would attract the Israelites under Ahab's rule to serve them. Only Yahweh, however, gave such a sign: an indication that he was alive and that the Baals were dead. The Israelites, because they are the sons of Yahweh, are warned not to mirror Canaanite practices by cutting themselves when mourning their dead. In the apostate reign of the house of Ahab Yahweh showed his displeasure by causing famine. Rules are set down, for times when there is no famine, that distinguish between food that can be eaten and food that cannot.

CHAPTER 3

ACKNOWLEDGMENT OF YAHWEH'S SOVEREIGNTY

If the preceding rules owed much to a survey of traditions in which a failure to acknowledge Yahweh's authority has been uppermost, it is understandable why the lawgiver should continue to set out similar rules. A dominant interest of his is the clash between the deity's sovereignty and other religious authority, typically in the person of the king who embraces foreign gods. Issues that have arisen in this context, Elijah's clash with the prophets of Baal, the visitation of famine upon Israel because of their idolatrous ways, are taken up in the laws.

Law: Tithes

[22] Thou shalt truly tithe all the increase of thy seed, that the field bringeth forth year by year. [23] And thou shalt eat before Yahweh thy God, in the place which he shall choose to place his name there, the tithe of thy corn, of thy wine, and of thine oil, and the firstlings of thy herds and of thy flocks; that thou mayest learn to fear Yahweh thy God always. [24] And if the way be too long for thee, so that thou art not able to carry it; or if the place be too far from thee, which Yahweh thy God shall choose to set his name there, when Yahweh thy God hath blessed thee: [25] then shalt thou turn it into money, and bind up the money in thine hand, and

shalt go unto the place which Yahweh thy God shall choose: [26] and thou shalt bestow that money for whatsoever thy soul lusteth after, for oxen, or for sheep, or for wine, or for strong drink, or for whatsoever thy soul desireth: and thou shalt eat there before Yahweh thy God, and thou shalt rejoice, thou, and thine household, [27] and the Levite that is within thy gates; thou shalt not forsake him; for he hath no part nor inheritance with thee.

[28] At the end of three years thou shalt bring forth all the tithe of thine increase the same year, and shalt lay it up within thy gates: [29] and the Levite, because he hath no part nor inheritance with thee, and the sojourner, and the fatherless, and the widow, which are within thy gates, shall come, and shall eat and be satisfied; that Yahweh thy God may bless thee in all the work of thine hand which thou doest. (Deut 14:22–29)

Background: Famines in Samaria and Egypt, and Joram's and Joseph's agricultural policies

[1] Then spake Elisha unto the woman, whose son he had restored to life, saying, Arise, and go thou and thine household, and sojourn wheresoever thou canst sojourn: for Yahweh hath called for a famine; and it shall also come upon the land seven years. [2] And the woman arose, and did after the saying of the man of God: and she went with her household, and sojourned in the land of the Philistines seven years. [3] And it came to pass at the seven years' end, that the woman returned out of the land of the Philistines: and she went forth to cry unto the king for her house and for her land. [4] And the king talked with Gehazi the servant of the man of God, saying, Tell me, I pray thee, all the great things that Elisha hath done. [5] And it came to pass, as he was telling the king how he had restored a dead body to life, that, behold, the woman, whose son he had restored to life, cried to the king for her house and for her land. And Gehazi said, My lord, O king, this is the woman, and this is her son, whom Elisha restored to life. [6] And when the king asked the woman, she told him. So the king appointed unto her a certain officer, saying, Restore all that was her's, and all the fruits of the field since the day that she left the land, even until now. (2 Kings 8:1–6)

[20] And Joseph bought all the land of Egypt for Pharaoh; for the Egyptians sold every man his field, because the famine prevailed over them: so the land became Pharaoh's. [21] And as for the

> people, he removed them to cities from one end of the borders of Egypt even to the other end thereof. [22] Only the land of the priests bought he not; for the priests had a portion assigned them of Pharaoh, and did eat their portion which Pharaoh gave them: wherefore they sold not their lands. [23] Then Joseph said unto the people, Behold, I have bought you this day and your land for Pharaoh: lo, here is seed for you, and ye shall sow the land. [24] And it shall come to pass in the increase, that ye shall give the fifth part unto Pharaoh, and four parts shall be your own, for seed of the field, and for your food, and for them of your households, and for food for your little ones. [25] And they said, Thou hast saved our lives: let us find grace in the sight of my lord, and we will be Pharaoh's servants. [26] And Joseph made it a law over the land of Egypt unto this day, that Pharaoh should have the fifth part; except the land of the priests only, which became not Pharaoh's. (Gen 47:20–26)

Elisha, like his predecessor Elijah, represented the deity's rule, and a successor of Ahab, King Joram, represented opposition to it. He viewed Elisha as responsible for the famine, and in response to the incident (pertinent to the kid law preceding that concerning tithes) of mothers' consuming their children, sought to kill him (2 Kings 6:31). In another incident involving a mother and her son, Elisha counseled the woman to leave Israel because God had called for a famine that would last seven years. She left, and when she returned at the end of seven years she appealed to the king for her house and fields. The king, influenced by the account of Elisha's power exhibited on her behalf—he had on one occasion restored her dead son to life—responded positively to her appeal and added all the produce of the fields "from the day that she left the land until now." The direction might be puzzling, but it does raise the question of the availability of annual supplies of grain and their distribution.

If famine conditions inevitably direct attention to what kind of food people might eat during them, it is not surprising that attention might also turn to normal conditions, to what is ordinarily produced agriculturally. The switch from the food laws to the rules affecting tithes can be accounted for on this basis. This change of perspective is all the more likely because of the lawgiver's view that the deity controls nature. What the lawgiver has done, however, is characteristically to turn to the earliest example in Israelite history in which the issue of famine followed by measures affecting agricultural produce arose. In the story of Joseph the deity is understood to have brought the seven-year famine upon Egypt and upon Canaan, and to have inspired Joseph's measures in dealing with it. The rules about tithing are presented largely as a parallel to what Joseph did for the Egyptians. The contrast between the produce of the land of Egypt and that of Israel's land had already been the subject of comment in Deut 11:10–17. In these verses, moreover, there is a warning that famine may occur should Israel disobey the commandments and turn to other gods—exactly as described in the time of the house of Ahab.

Joseph's statute (*ḥōq*) concerning the land of Egypt required the Egyptians to give a fifth of their harvest to the pharaoh and to keep four-fifths for themselves. Only the priests were exempt from the requirement because they received a prescribed portion from the pharaoh. In the Israelite scheme, in which the deity's role has to be of a different order from the pharaoh's, Yahweh receives a tenth, half of what the pharaoh received, and this is consumed in a religious feast. The tithes, because of this sacred, joyous feasting, are the opposite of abominable food. They are presented at the chosen place in acknowledgment of the deity's sovereignty. Joseph's scheme of taxing the land's increase was on behalf of a king, the pharaoh. We have noted the frequent contrast in the laws between the demands of the Israelite god and those of some earthly authority.

There was most likely (cp., Gen 28:22; Amos 4:4) a custom of tithing known to the lawgiver even though there is no written law on it in the existing JE legislation. What can be claimed is that the Deuteronomist wrote his law up in response to a scrutiny of Joseph's scheme. One indication of this claim is that initially it confines itself to the increase (*tᵉbûʾāh*, as in Gen 47:24) of the seed of the field, as did Joseph's statute. Only latterly (in Deut 14:23) do we find that the firstlings of the herds and flocks (not a tenth of them) come under consideration too.

Only in regard to the tithes, and not for the Passover sacrifice, the feasts of weeks and booths (Deut 16:1–15), is it mentioned that if distance constitutes a handicap, one's produce may be converted into money and its equivalent bought at the central place. Consideration of this aspect may have been stimulated by the first episode in Israelite history in which brother Israelites interchanged money and food.

Although Joseph's brothers took money to the central source of food under his control in order to buy it for their home consumption, they ended up feasting with him (Genesis 43). Surprisingly the law permits the consumption of strong drink (*šēkār*). Underlying this permission may be the view that, without the accompanying deceit and tension, the merrymaking that results from the strong drink which Joseph and his brothers imbibe (Gen 43:34) would be a fine thing when their descendants later derived benefit from the abundance of their own land.

The Levites occupy the lawgiver's attention because they have no land to farm. Their lot in life depended upon the dues given to the deity. Their position within Israel was therefore analogous to the Egyptian priests whose portion came from the pharaoh. To be sure, they possessed lands, unlike the Levites. There is, however, a sense in which in substantive terms part of an Israelite's land is the deity's and, consequently, because a religious notion has practical effect, laid claim to by the priests.

A further indication that the Deuteronomist writes up the rules about tithing in the context of the Joseph story is seen in the institution of the triennial tithe. Every third year the land's produce is not to be consumed in celebratory fashion at the chosen place but is to be made available at the local places for those who are without land, the Levites, the alien, the fatherless, and the widow. Joseph's statute on behalf of the landless Egyptian population came out of the circumstances that prevailed following a famine, a context in which recognition of general need was uppermost. The rule about the third year release of the tithe is for those in particular need. We cannot say whether it reflects an existing practice or owes something to the JE legislation about the seventh year requirement to let the fields lie fallow for the sake of the poor (Exod 23:10, 11). One question that Joseph's ultimate scheme of taxing the land's produce readily prompts but does not address is what is to be done for the remaining disadvantaged in the populace. General need led to the statute, but it in turn did not take up the inevitably residual problem. The Deuteronomic rule covers this aspect for Israel.

Law: The release of debts every seven years

[1] At the end of every seven years thou shalt make a release. [2] And this is the manner of the release: Every creditor that lendeth

ought unto his neighbour shall release it; he shall not exact it of his neighbour, or of his brother; because it is called Yahweh's release. [3] Of a foreigner thou mayest exact it again: but that which is thine with thy brother thine hand shall release; [4] to the end that there be no poor with thee; for Yahweh shall greatly bless thee in the land which Yahweh thy God giveth thee for an inheritance to possess it: [5] only if thou carefully hearken unto the voice of Yahweh thy God, to observe to do all these commandments which I command thee this day. [6] For Yahweh thy God blesseth thee, as he promised thee: and thou shalt lend unto many nations, but thou shalt not borrow; and thou shalt reign over many nations, but they shall not reign over thee.

[7] If there be in thy midst a poor man of one of thy brethren within any of thy gates in thy land which Yahweh thy God giveth thee, thou shalt not harden thine heart, nor shut thine hand from thy poor brother: [8] but thou shalt open thine hand wide unto him, and shalt surely lend him sufficient for his need, in that which he wanteth. [9] Beware that there be not a base thought in thy heart, saying, The seventh year, the year of release, is at hand; and thine eye be evil against thy poor brother and thou givest him nought; and he cry unto Yahweh against thee, and it be sin unto thee. [10] Thou shalt surely give him, and thine heart shall not be grieved when thou givest unto him: because that for this thing Yahweh thy God shall bless thee in all thy works, and in all that thou puttest thine hand unto. [11] For the poor shall never cease out of the land: therefore I command thee, saying, Thou shalt open thine hand wide unto thy brother, to thy poor, and to thy needy, in thy land. (Deut 15:1–11)

Background: The Egyptians enslave the Israelites (after there arose a pharaoh "which knew not Joseph"), and give them valuables on their release

[21] And I will give this people favour in the sight of the Egyptians: and it shall come to pass, that, when ye go, ye shall not go empty: [22] but every woman shall borrow of her neighbour, and of her that sojourneth in her house, jewels of silver, and jewels of gold, and raiment: and ye shall put them upon your sons, and upon your daughters; and ye shall spoil the Egyptians. (Exod 3:21, 22)

[3] Speak now in the ears of the people, and let every man borrow of his neighbour, and every woman of her neighbour, jewels of silver, and jewels of gold. (Exod 11:3)

> [35] And the children of Israel did according to the word of Moses; and they borrowed of the Egyptians jewels of silver, and jewels of gold, and raiment: [36] and Yahweh gave the people favour in the sight of the Egyptians, so that they lent unto them. And they spoiled the Egyptians. (Exod 12:35, 36)

A common solution to this most puzzling of institutions is the rationalization that the release of debts in the seventh year is only a temporary suspension and not in fact a cancellation of them. Modern critics, assuming that the institution has to be interpreted in the light of historical reality, feel that a temporary suspension is the only plausible solution. Yet nothing in the law justifies such a watering down of its import.[1] Both the term used, *šᵉmiṭṭāh,* and the plain sense of the law indicate an actual remission of loans. An approach that starts out from a consideration of actual historical circumstances does not work for the Deuteronomic laws. Time and again we find that some idiosyncratic development in a tradition is taken up and institutionalized.

What accounts for this institution of "Yahweh's release" is the odd incident at the time of the exodus. Whatever the original incident's significance, the lawgiver notes that what appeared, especially from the Egyptian stance, to be loans to the Israelites—they asked for the articles in question—turned out to be gifts to them because their release from slavery then took place.[2] We might note that the very next law is about the release of Hebrew slaves in their seventh year of

[1]See S. R. Driver's criticism in *Deuteronomy* ICC (Edinburgh: T. and T. Clark, 1902), 179, 180. G. von Rad argues that verse 9 implies a total discharge of a debt (*Das fünfte Buch Mose, Deuteronomium* [Göttingen: Vandenhoeck and Ruprecht, 1964], 76). We cannot say if the release of debts by new monarchs in the ancient Near East was known to the Deuteronomist.

[2]D. Daube is probably correct to argue against understanding the significance of the original handing over of the articles as lending (*The Exodus Pattern in the Bible* [London: Faber and Faber, 1963], 55–61). The Septuagint, the Vulgate, and most modern versions all agree that the articles were lent. The fact that God is said to be behind the action suggests an out-of-the-ordinary one. My point is that the Deuteronomist, from his later perspective and with his aim of translating what happened into ordinary Israelite terms, came up with the notion of loans turning into gifts, and hence the cancellation of debts. He might have been aided in this task by the law in Exod 23:10, 11, about the release of agricultural produce every seventh year for the poor, especially if this law had already been associated with the rule about lending to the poor in Exod 22:25–27. On this association see my *Laws of Deuteronomy* (Ithaca: Cornell University Press, 1974), 63, 85.

service and the recollection of Israel's slavery in Egypt. Also noteworthy is the link with the preceding law and its background, wherein Yahweh enables the Hebrews to obtain food from the Egyptian granaries. Oddly (but recall the role of providence), these provisions also turned out to be gifts, because each time Joseph had put the money back in the sacks.

A strange institution is explained on the basis of a strange incident. Full weight can be given to its being termed Yahweh's release because of the emphasis in the exodus tradition that Yahweh had given the Israelites favor in the sight of the Egyptians. Details in the law become more meaningful in light of this background. There is concern about an underprivileged Israelite who is refused a loan because the seventh year is at hand. His fellow Israelite is not to harden his heart lest the one in need cry to God. We are reminded of the pharaoh's treatment of the Israelites, because his heart was hardened, and of their crying to God.[3]

Both the preceding institution of tithing and this one lay down first of all rules that cover a general state of affairs and then concentrate on conditions that affect the poor. This concern for the poor reflects the corresponding tradition: the inhabitants of Egypt were enslaved to the pharaoh, and Joseph under God's guidance arranged relief for them; the Israelites were enslaved in Egypt and God brought them relief.

Law: The release of Hebrew slaves in their seventh year

[12] And if thy brother, an Hebrew man, or an Hebrew woman,
be sold unto thee, and serve thee six years; then in the seventh year
thou shalt let him go free from thee. [13] And when thou sendest
him out free from thee, thou shalt not let him go away empty: [14]
thou shalt furnish him liberally out of thy flock, and out of thy
floor, and out of thy winepress: of that wherewith Yahweh thy God
hath blessed thee thou shall give unto him. [15] And thou shalt
remember that thou wast a bondman in the land of Egypt, and
Yahweh thy God redeemed thee: therefore I command thee this
thing to day. [16] And it shall be, if he say unto thee, I will not go

[3]Deuteronomic language is used throughout this section, not the vocabulary of the exodus story.

away from thee; because he loveth thee and thine house, because he is well with thee; [17] then thou shalt take an aul, and thrust it through his ear unto the door, and he shall be thy servant for ever. And also unto thy maidservant thou shalt do likewise. [18] It shall not seem hard unto thee, when thou sendest him away free from thee; for he hath been worth a double hired servant to thee in serving thee six years: and Yahweh thy God shall bless thee in all that thou doest. (Deut 15:12–18)

Background: The release of the Hebrews from Egyptian slavery (Exodus 3–12)

If the institution of the seventh year release of debts is largely inspired by reflection upon the valuables received by the Hebrew slaves just before they obtained their freedom from slavery, this law continues to focus on the same period of time. No doubt the lawgiver brings to its drafting his familiarity with the existing law in Exod 21:2–6, but the exodus story is the decisive context in accounting for its details. The concern, not found in the earlier law, with furnishing the slave liberally at the cessation of his service appears to be largely an attempt to parallel what God did for the departing Hebrew slaves in Egypt. The lawgiver institutionalizes what happened then and understandably substitutes gifts from flock, mill, and winepress for the silver and gold objects that the Egyptians had handed over.[4] In giving these gifts the Israelite is to remember that he himself had been a bondman in the land of Egypt. We must not forget that Moses is the author of these laws and, we are to believe, formulated them on the basis of what he and the people of Israel to whom he is talking had personally experienced. If God had done certain things on their behalf, then it seemed clear to them that they should imitate the example in whatever form was appropriate in their new location.

The two laws about the seventh year release of debts and the seventh year release of a slave are closely related in a way not previously realized. That one follows the other might lead us to expect such a connection. The exodus story and the deity's role in it account for this connection. Because Yahweh made the Egyptians grant favor

[4]The term *heʿenîq,* "to furnish," is literally "to make a necklace for" and may reveal the link between the law and the story because articles of jewellery appear to be what the Egyptians gave the Israelites.

to the Israelites, an Israelite creditor should cancel a debtor's loan every seventh year. Similarly, because Yahweh redeemed Israel from slavery, an Israelite master should release a slave in his seventh year of service. Historical circumstances have changed, however, and both rules are seen in the light of economic conditions prevailing when Israel acquires its land. The reason why an Israelite master might find it hard (Deut 15:18) to release his slaves is to be thought of as different from that which made it hard for the pharaoh (Exod 13:15). The reasoning appears to be related to the institution of the seventh year release of debts. A master is required to release a slave in his seventh year of service because, it is said, in order to mollify the master, the slave has worked for half the cost of a hired servant. A debtor who cannot pay off his loan becomes enslaved. Presumably this happens at a time before the seventh year cancellation of debts has effect. Similar considerations, however, should apply to his eventual release. A departure after six years generously cancels the outstanding debt owed to the creditor-master.

Law: Firstlings and the three annual feasts

[19] All the firstling males that come of thy herd and of thy flock thou shall sanctify unto Yahweh thy God: thou shalt do no work with the firstling of thy bullock, nor shear the firstling of thy sheep. [20] Thou shalt eat it before Yahweh thy God year by year in the place which Yahweh shall choose, thou and thy household. [21] And if there be any blemish therein, if it be lame, or blind, or have any ill blemish, thou shalt not sacrifice it unto Yahweh thy God. [22] Thou shalt eat it within thy gates: the unclean and the clean shall eat it alike, as the roebuck and as the hart. [23] Only thou shalt not eat the blood thereof; thou shalt pour it upon the ground as water.

[1] Observe the month of Abib, and keep the passover unto Yahweh thy God: for in the month of Abib Yahweh thy God brought thee forth out of Egypt by night. [2] Thou shalt therefore sacrifice the passover unto Yahweh thy God, of the flock and the herd, in the place which Yahweh shall choose to place his name there. . . .

[9] Seven weeks shalt thou number unto thee: begin to number the seven weeks from such time as thou beginnest to put the sickle

to the corn. [10] And thou shalt keep the feast of weeks unto Yahweh thy God with a tribute of a free will offering of thine hand. . . . in the place which Yahweh thy God hath chosen to place his name there. [12] And thou shalt remember that thou wast a bondman in Egypt: and thou shalt observe and do these statutes.

[13] Thou shalt observe the feast of tabernacles seven days, after that thou hast gathered in thy corn and thy wine. . . . in the place which Yahweh shall choose: because Yahweh thy God shall bless thee in all thine increase, and in all the works of thine hands, therefore thou shalt surely rejoice.

[16] Three times in a year shall all thy males appear before Yahweh thy God in the place which he shall choose; in the feast of unleavened bread, and in the feast of weeks, and in the feast of tabernacles: and they shall not appear before Yahweh empty: [17] every man shall give as he is able, according to the blessing of Yahweh thy God which he hath given thee. (Deut 15:19–16: 2, 9–13, 15–17)

Background: The slaughter of the Egyptian first-born of men and cattle for the purpose of releasing the Israelites to serve their God

[4] And Moses said, Thus saith Yahweh, About midnight will I go out into the midst of Egypt: [5] and all the firstborn in the land of Egypt shall die, from the firstborn of Pharaoh that sitteth upon his throne, even unto the firstborn of the maidservant that is behind the mill; and all the firstborn of beasts. [6] And there shall be a great cry throughout all the land of Egypt, such as there was none like it, nor shall be like it any more. [7] But against any of the children of Israel shall not a dog move his tongue, against man or beast: that ye may know how that Yahweh doth put a difference between the Egyptians and Israel. (Exod 11:4–7; cp., 12:29–32)

[18] And thou [Moses] shalt come, thou and the elders of Israel, unto the king of Egypt, and ye shall say unto him, Yahweh God of the Hebrews hath met with us: and now let us go, we beseech thee, three days' journey into the wilderness, that we may sacrifice to Yahweh our God. (Exod 3:18)

[23] And I say unto thee, Let my son go that he may serve me: and if thou refuse to let him go, behold, I will slay thy son. (Exod 4:23; cp., Exod 5:1, 3, 8:1, 8, 20, 25–29, 9:1, 13, 10:3, 7–9, 24–26, 12:25, 26, 31)

The exodus story continues to account for the presentation of the four laws following the one on the manumission of slaves. Because of their oppressive treatment of the Hebrews, the Egyptians had death visited upon their first-born of man and cattle in order to force them to release their slaves. In a law immediately following one addressed to Israelite masters about the release of their slaves, there is a rule requiring Israelites to slaughter all the firstling males of their herd and flock. This rule is then followed by the institution of the Passover, which commemorates the slaughter of the Egyptian first-born and the accompanying forced departure of the Hebrew slaves. Not all firstlings in Egypt were slaughtered on the extraordinary occasion of Israel's release from slavery. Yahweh distinguished between the Egyptian and the Israelite. The law addresses itself to the ordinary, future situation within Israel when another kind of distinction, between blemished and unblemished animals, is to apply.

What underlies the presentation of the two laws about firstlings and Passover, plus the subsequent two about the feast of weeks and the feast of booths, is again the dominant concern with acknowledging the deity's sovereignty by, as in the cultic laws in Deuteronomy 12, serving him in sacred feasts. The particular motivation in the exodus story is expressed in the recurring statement about how the Israelites are obliged to go and serve their god. There is a sense in which the Israelites exchange one master, the king of Egypt, for another, God.[5] We saw in regard to the tithes how the lawgiver first considered the pharaoh's tax before formulating his rule about the tax owed to the Israelite deity.

Each of the four laws about sacred feasting stipulates that it take place at the chosen place, the establishment so closely associated with the Israelite kings. We have noted how the rules in Deuteronomy 12 arose from a scrutiny of the cultic practices of Kings Saul, David, and Solomon with a view to establishing the deity's sovereignty over and against any conflicting claims they might have. By basing Moses' laws upon the experience of the exodus, the Deuteronomist could show that they provided the standards by which he judged events in the lives of the kings. A continuous linking of the history of the kings and the Mosaic period is a major characteristic of his legal material.

The element in the tradition that requires a statement about where

[5]See Daube, *The Exodus Pattern,* 42–46.

the various feasts should be celebrated is the emphasis on the Israelites' obligation to go and worship their God. Moses in the story of the exodus does not in fact address himself to where they will worship in the future; he does address this issue in the Deuteronomic laws.

The process that accounts for the presentation of the Deuteronomic laws is paralleled in the actual narrative of the exodus. We find inserted in the narrative rules about the firstlings and about an institutionalized Passover commemoration (Exod 12:14–20, 43–49, 13:2–16). The fact that the Deuteronomic law on firstlings has already been commanded (in Deut 12:6, 14:23) indicates that the law's fuller statement at this point in the code has been determined by the flow of events under scrutiny.

Laws: Local judges, Asherah, pillars, blemished sacrifice, idolatry within the gates, and the central tribunal

[18] Judges and officers shalt thou make thee in all thy gates, which Yahweh thy God giveth thee, throughout thy tribes: and they shall judge the people with just judgment. [19] Thou shalt not wrest judgment; thou shalt not respect persons, neither take a gift: for a gift doth blind the eyes of the wise, and pervert the words of the righteous. [20] Justice shalt thou follow, that thou mayest live, and inherit the land which Yahweh thy God giveth thee.

[21] Thou shalt not plant thee an Asherah, any tree, near unto the altar of Yahweh thy God, which thou shalt make thee. [22] Neither shalt thou set thee up any pillar which Yahweh thy God hateth.

[1] Thou shalt not sacrifice unto Yahweh thy God any bullock, or sheep, wherein is blemish, or any evilfavouredness: for that is an abomination unto Yahweh thy God.

[2] If there be found in thy midst, within any of thy gates which Yahweh thy God giveth thee, man or woman, that hath wrought wickedness in the sight of Yahweh thy God, in transgressing his covenant, [3] and hath gone and served other gods, and worshipped them, either the sun, or moon, or any of the host of heaven, which I have not commanded; [4] and it be told thee, and thou hast heard of it, and enquired diligently, and, behold, it be true, and the thing certain, that such abomination is wrought in Israel: [5] then shalt

thou bring forth that man or that woman, which have committed that wicked thing, unto thy gates, even that man or that woman, and shalt stone them with stones, till they die. [6] At the mouth of two witnesses, or three witnesses, shall he that is worthy of death be put to death; but at the mouth of one witness he shall not be put to death. [7] The hands of the witnesses shall be first upon him to put him to death, and afterward the hands of all the people. So thou shalt put the evil away from thy midst.

[8] If there arise a matter too hard for thee in judgment, between blood and blood, between plea and plea, and between stroke and stroke, being matters of controversy within thy gates: then shalt thou arise, and get thee up into the place which Yahweh thy God shall choose; [9] and thou shalt come unto the priests the Levites, and unto the judge that shall be in those days, and enquire; and they shall shew thee the sentence of judgment: [10] and thou shalt do according to the sentence, which they of that place which Yahweh shall choose shall shew thee; and thou shalt observe to do according to all that they inform thee: [11] according to the sentence of the law which they shall teach thee, and according to the judgment which they shall tell thee, thou shalt do: thou shalt not decline from the sentence which they shall shew thee, to the right hand, nor to the left. [12] And the man that will do presumptuously, and will not hearken unto the priest that standeth to minister there before Yahweh thy God, or unto the judge, even that man shall die; and thou shalt put away the evil from Israel. [13] And all the people shall hear, and fear, and do no more presumptuously. (Deut 16:18–17:13)

Background: Moses' involvement in the subject of sacrificial worship after the Israelites left Egypt

Moses informed Jethro about the Israelites' experience in Egypt and their deliverance by Yahweh. Acknowledging Yahweh above all other gods, "Jethro, Moses' father in law, took a burnt offering and sacrifices for God: and Aaron came, and all the elders of Israel to eat bread with Moses' father in law before God" (Exod 18:12). When Moses then proceeded to judge the people, Jethro criticized the procedure and suggested a better way by which some of the people themselves might participate. "So Moses hearkened to the voice of his father in law, and did all that he had said. And Moses chose able men out of all Israel, and made them heads over the people, rulers of thousands, rulers of hundreds, rulers of fifties, and rulers of tens. And they judged the people at all seasons: the hard causes they brought unto Moses, but every small matter they judged themselves" (Exod 18:8–26).

> [22] And Yahweh said unto Moses, Thus thou shalt say unto the children of Israel, Ye have seen that I have talked with you from heaven. [23] Ye shall not make with me gods of silver, neither shall ye make unto you gods of gold. [24] An altar of earth thou shalt make unto me, and shalt sacrifice thereon thy burnt offerings, and thy peace offerings, thy sheep, and thine oxen: in all places where I record my name I will come unto thee, and I will bless thee. [25] And if thou wilt make me an altar of stone, thou shalt not build it of hewn stone: for if thou lift up thy tool upon it, thou hast polluted it. (Exod 20:22–25)
>
> [4] And Moses wrote all the words of Yahweh, and rose up early in the morning, and builded an altar under the hill, and twelve pillars, according to the twelve tribes of Israel. [5] And he sent young men of the children of Israel, which offered burnt offerings and sacrificed peace offerings of oxen unto Yahweh. [6] And Moses took half of the blood, and put it in basons; and half of the blood he sprinkled on the altar. [7] And he took the book of the covenant, and read in the audience of the people: and they said, All that Yahweh hath said will we do, and be obedient. (Exod 24:4–7)

When Moses delayed to return from Mount Sinai, the people requested his substitute authority, Aaron, to make them gods to go before them in their journeyings. He had the people give him golden earrings from the male and female members of their families, and he fashioned the golden calf. The people spoke of the calf in terms of the gods that had brought them out of Egypt. Aaron built an altar and made the next day a feast to Yahweh. The latter beheld the development and sought to destroy the people. Moses interceded and directed their punishment. He chastised Aaron verbally and had the Levites slay "every man his brother, and every man his companion, and every man his neighbour." Some three thousand men died. As a result of the Levites' loyalty to Moses and Yahweh, they were to serve in a special capacity in the future (Exodus 32).

Critics invariably comment on how difficult it is to see any sense in the way in which these laws are set down. They speak of old rules—for example, the one about the Asherah in which there is no mention of the chosen place—that the Deuteronomist has incorporated in a rather haphazard fashion from sources not known to us. There is no need, however, for this rather demeaning assessment of his ability. These rules again illustrate his typical process of setting them down against a background of issues that arise in the traditions available to him.

The preceding rules about the various annual pilgrimages and the requirement that the males appear three times a year before God are found in the earlier JE legislation (Exod 23:14–17). The Deuteronomist presents his version of the rules in the context of the exodus narrative and with a view to having Moses anticipate the period of the kings when Jerusalem would be the chosen place for sacrifices. The feature in the tradition that invites his attention is the recurring reference to the Israelite's release from bondage that they might serve their God (Exod 3:18, 4:23, and so on). For the Deuteronomist Moses is thought of as taking not just a short-term interest in where this will occur, in the wilderness (Exod 3:18), but a long-term one too. The result is that not only is he concerned with Moses' anticipation of some future chosen place but also with those places and occasions in which he was involved with sacrifices after Israel's escape from Egypt. Once this concern is seen the five laws in question form an intelligible sequence in the Deuteronomist's scheme of presentation.

Local judges

We are not in fact told in the aftermath of the escape from Egypt, as the account in Exodus might have led us to expect, about Israel's sacrificing to their God in the wilderness. The first occasion we hear of sacrifices to the Israelite God is when Jethro, Moses' father-in-law, was informed about God's deliverance of the Israelites and, acknowledging his greatness above all other gods, "took a burnt offering and sacrifices for God" (Exod 18:12). It is in this context that Jethro proceeds to give counsel to Moses about delegating judicial authority to certain chosen men to aid him in the task of administering justice. Throughout his counsel Jethro stresses the need for God's approval of his suggestion and, in taking it up, Moses plainly views it as representing God's decision (Exod 18:23, 24). This aspect would be important for the Deuteronomist because his dominant concern has been to uphold the notion of God's rule. He therefore has Moses state in terms of Israel's future needs in the new land the formal nature of the institution of local judges at this point in the code,[6] that is, just after the formal requirement that all males appear before Yahweh three times each year for the purpose of acknowledging his sovereignty. It is perhaps worth noting that we are told how at Jethro's sacrifice Aaron and all the elders participated. The Deuteronomist would have observed how the sequence of events revealed a proper recognition of priorities, first the worship and then attention to the administration of justice.

The Asherah

Commentators are puzzled by the fact that the prohibitions about the Asherah, the pillar, and blemished animals appear after the rule about the local judges rather than following the rule about a case of idolatry to be dealt with by them. The explanation for the sequence is this: the lawgiver moves from the occasion of Jethro's sacrifices to the next context concerned with them, God's instruction to Moses at Sinai, to the next, Moses' ceremony when the Book of the Covenant was read, and finally, to the occasion of the sacrificing to the golden calf in Exodus 32. Each of these contexts inspires the construction of a rule.

After Jethro's sacrificial activity, God instructs Moses after the momentous occasion when he utters the decalogue (Exod 20:21–26). Alone, Moses approaches God who communicates to him first a rule against having gods of silver and gold along with him, and then an instruction to make an altar of earth and to sacrifice on it burnt offerings and peace offerings. God's instruction anticipates the future: he will cause his name to be remembered at certain places of worship. This episode marks the first time in the narrative of the exodus that formal, as against incidental, attention is given to places of worship for sacrificial purposes. The Deuteronomist looks back on this rule about the making of an altar of earth and views it from the perspective of his later time and experience. Because he has to show that Moses legislated against later idolatrous developments, he sets down a prohibition against planting "an Asherah, any tree, beside the

[6]It is not surprising that just as the rules about the annual feasts in Exodus 23 influence his formulation of these rules, so the words of Exod 23:8 about bribes are appropriated almost exactly in his formulation of the rule about administering justice.

altar of Yahweh thy God which thou shalt make thee." The prohibition is not an old rule but a deliberately archaic one so as to make it appear Mosaic. This is why it borrows the same language about the altar "which thou shalt make" and omits any reference to the chosen place. This omission would also have been determined by the prescience of Moses's rule, which concerns not only the eventual chosen place but all the intervening ones that were necessary before the chosen one could exist.

The rule in Exod 20:24 about the altar of earth evokes the potential problem of idolatry on two counts. First, the opening statement of the instruction to Moses is indeed about idolatrous objects, gods of silver and gold. It is therefore natural for the Deuteronomist to introduce the Canaanite object, the Asherah. Second, because earth is referred to as being used in the making of the altar he naturally recalls that Asherim were objects, trees or poles, planted in earth. In the other Deuteronomic contexts in which they are mentioned (7:5, 12:3), the fact that they can be trees is not brought out. That it is in this law suggests that this interest in earth and altars is significant.

Pillars

God's instruction to Moses continues with a warning against building an altar of hewn stone. The next Deuteronomic law prohibits the setting up of a stone pillar, a *maṣṣēbāh,* "which Yahweh thy God hates." The factor that prompts the law's formulation is not just this reference to a stone altar in Exod 20:25 but also the following occasion, involving the construction of an altar, in which we again hear of actual sacrificial activity on the part of the Israelites. Just after the instruction about the altars of earth and stone, Moses receives the body of rules, the Book of the Covenant, many of which are used by the Deuteronomist in compiling his own material. When Moses communicated them to the people they pledged their obedience. He then built an altar at the foot of the mountain and twelve pillars for the twelve tribes of Israel. Young men offered burnt offerings and sacrificed peace offerings of oxen to Yahweh. Moses took some of the blood and threw it upon the altar, read the Book of the Covenant to the people who responded affirmatively to it, and sprinkled some blood upon them by way of symbolizing the pact between the deity and them (Exod 24:1–8).

What catches the Deuteronomist's attention is that pillars are erected legitimately on that occasion. From later history, however, he knows about the idolatrous pillars of the Canaanites. Indeed, already inserted into the context of the giving of the rules of the covenant is a divine address that anticipates this future Canaanite menace and commands the Israelites to break their pillars in pieces (Exod 23:24). This speech comes just before the account of the erection of the altar and the twelve Israelite pillars. The prohibition against setting up a pillar "which Yahweh thy God hates" is, the Deuteronomist would have us understand, an indication that Moses was alert to the problem when he erected pillars himself. Note that, unlike the preceding prohibition proscribing the planting of all trees, this one rules out only "a pillar which Yahweh thy God hates."[7] That must mean there were pillars that were acceptable to him, for example, the twelve set up by Moses.

In order to understand the sequence of rules in Deut 16:18–17: 13, I am claiming that the Deuteronomist is especially interested in that material, ascribed to the source JE, in which matters pertaining to worship at altars arise. From the material in Exodus 24, which concludes with a notice about Moses being on the mountain forty days and forty nights, the Deuteronomist moves to the next incident involving Israelite worship at an altar: the matter of the golden calf, which arises because of Moses' delay upon the mountain (Exod 32:1). In between these two accounts is a body of material given over to the sacrificial system within Israel and generally agreed to be the product of the priestly school (P). It appears that both the Deuteronomist and the priestly school share an interest in the same section of JE material: both concentrate upon an incident of worship in Moses' time and present rules (Deut 16:22 and Exodus 25–31) that they claim to be from him.

Blemished sacrifice

The next rule that the Deuteronomist presents is a prohibition against sacrificing a blemished ox or sheep "for that is an abomination unto Yahweh thy God" (Deut 17:1). S. R. Driver, taking up from

[7]How A. D. H. Mayes (*Deuteronomy* NCBC [Grand Rapids: Eerdmans, 1981], 265) is able to make this statement refer to the Asherah also is beyond me.

A. Dillmann, infers from the context in which this rule is embedded, and from the use of the term "abomination," "that in the idolatrous sacrifices with which the author was familiar, no importance was attached to this point," namely, blemishes on the animals.[8] Driver is correct in noting the flavor of idolatry surrounding the rule, but the reason for this has to do less with some possible historical reality than with the recollection of the worship of the golden calf. That animal artifact was judged to be idolatrous. It gave God offense and was interpreted as a rejection of him. The question that this incident raises for the Deuteronomist is: in what other, later circumstances in Israelite worship might the people offend when it comes to relating to God through animals? The answer: blemished sacrificial animals. Recall how the incident of the sacrifice of the Egyptian first-born prompted the statement about the customary requirement for Israelite firstlings.

The golden calf represented a human creation that was endowed with divine power: it brought, the claim was, Israel out of Egypt. Such a representation was a distortion of the true created order of things, an attack upon the notion of Yahweh as creator and the power behind the exodus. Likewise, a defective animal would constitute an insult if it were offered to God, because it too would fail to acknowledge his worth as creator. What we find is the typical Deuteronomic logic: in the idiosyncratic circumstances of Exodus 32 a distortion of creation, an animal made out of gold, was an abomination; so too, in the ordinary circumstances of Israelite worship, are blemished animals. In both this prohibition and the preceding one against setting up a pillar which Yahweh hates, the object of condemnation belongs to categories, pillars and animals, that have a legitimate place in the worship of Yahweh.

Idolatry within the gates

A link can also be established between the next two laws—idolatry within the gates, the central tribunal—and the tradition about the golden calf. Perhaps the best way to appreciate this connection is to consider both these laws together and puzzle over why the one follows the other. It cannot be solely because one concerns a matter

[8]Driver, *Deuteronomy* ICC, 204.

within the gates, before the local judges, and the other a matter that is too difficult for local judges and consequently has to come before the priests and judge at the "place which Yahweh thy God shall choose." Even that distinction has to be traced to something of substance in the background to the two laws.

Both laws can be viewed as responses to the problems connected with the incident of the golden calf. It was the people themselves who decided upon idolatry, with their request to Aaron to make them gods, because Moses had apparently disappeared upon the mountain. Note that they were faced with a problem and that they had taken it to Aaron. This was what Moses himself had commanded when he took his leave of them to go up the mountain: "Behold, Aaron and Hur are with you, if any man have any matters to do, let him come unto them" (Exod 24:14). It happened in this instance that Aaron became party to their idolatry. The situation raises the question of the institution of problem solving that Jethro had counseled Moses about and that he had acted upon. Wherever possible matters were to be decided among the people themselves by means of certain men chosen to rule over smaller groups of them. Only intractable problems were to be brought before Moses. The Deuteronomist, thinking of this institution in relation to Exodus 32 and observing the problems there, has Moses then anticipate the situation at a time when the people will be settled in their towns throughout the land.

Idolatry, he decrees, should be put down within the towns. He speaks of a man or a woman transgressing his covenant, of serving other gods, or the sun or the moon or any of the host of heaven "which I [Moses] have not commanded." This is the only reference in the laws to the covenant and it appears to be a recollection of the events at Sinai. By the time of Exodus 32 the covenant with the people had been put into effect (Exod 24:8), just before Moses was to ascend the mountain for forty days and nights. The use of the first person in the laws is uncommon and is reminiscent of Deut 12:32, in which, it was argued, Moses asserted his authority over such as Aaron because of what had taken place with the calf. The same is true here. Moses had not commanded that their God should be represented by any visible image; that Aaron made such an image usurped Moses' religious authority. The reference in the law to other gods includes no indication that they were foreign, Canaanite, which suggests that the type of god in mind is like the golden calf. Recall too that the calf was given a plural designation, "These be thy gods" (Exod 32:4). The additional reference to the sun, moon, and the host of heaven again specifies created objects, albeit of another order from the man-made golden calf. In the other Deuteronomic context in which they are mentioned there is an unmistakable allusion to that incident (Deut 4:10–20). The sex of those who requested to worship other gods in Exod 32:1 is not stated, but males and females are both involved (v. 2). The law speaks of the man or woman "doing wickedness in the sight of Yahweh thy God." God had looked upon the people's idolatrous activity in Exodus 32. In his description of the incident in Deut 9:18 the Deuteronomist refers to their "doing wickedness in the sight of Yahweh."

Procedure for convicting and executing the idolaters is spelled out in the law, a necessity that could well be prompted by the far from clear or satisfactory method resorted to by Moses in Exodus 32. We find, as in the law, Israelites executing their brothers, companions, and neighbors, but it is not clear on what basis the executioners, the Levites, acted. Many of the people were killed but many were not, a fact that raises the question of proper procedure in coping with idolaters in the later, settled conditions of Israelite life.

Central tribunal

From the case of idolaters within the gates, the Deuteronomist switches to legal matters that the local jurisdictions cannot handle and that consequently come before a central authority, which is represented as already existing. In the specification of these matters—one kind of homicide and another, one kind of legal right and another, one kind of assault and another—idolatry is not included. The background in the exodus narrative explains the lawgiver's position. In Exodus 32 the Mosaic institution of having the people take some difficult problem to a recognized central authority—himself in Exod 18:22, 26, his replacements in Exod 24:14—was already in place. The problem, however, that arose and that was brought before Aaron, who was Moses' substitute authority, concerned a matter of religious allegiance to Yahweh, something that Jethro's counsel never envisioned and that defied the whole idea of the institution. The Deuteronomist, having Moses think ahead to the institution's later operation, lays down its proper role—concern with difficult legal problems.

The law cites the central authority as consisting of the Levitical priests and the judge. This arrangement is exactly analogous to the authority established in the aftermath of the making of the golden calf. Moses as judge doing Yahweh's bidding and the Levitical priests who demonstrated their loyalty to Yahweh represented supreme authority on that occasion. Moses, moreover, instituted a similar role for them to play in the future (Exod 32:29).[9] In that their role was in the service of Yahweh it would, in the Deuteronomic scheme of things, be viewed as operating at the chosen place in the land. In the incident of the golden calf Yahweh required them to exercise their duty even to the extent of the execution of their close relatives (Exod 32:27; cp., Deut 33:9). We might note the strict nature of the warning issued to the Israelites in the law: they must obey the decision of the Levitical priests and judge, no deviation from it "to the right hand or to the left," being permitted. Any failure to obey will meet with the penalty of death.

The incident of the golden calf is seen to have modified the nature of the institution of centralized authority as set up by Moses in Exod 18:24–26. Hard cases were to come before him and, in the event of his absence, before his approved substitutes (Exod 24:14). In light of Aaron's failure to fulfill Moses' function, the Levitical priests were appointed to be partners with Moses (and his successor) in, we can infer, the future workings of the institution. In laying down the institution as finally constructed by Moses, the Deuteronomist may have avoided the term *qāšeh,* "hard," used in reference to its initial construction (Exod 18:22, 26; Deut 1:17), because of the unacceptable problem that was brought before Aaron. Instead *pālā'* (*niphal*) "too difficult to decide" is used. This term, moreover, is often found in reference to Yahweh's extraordinary acts of judgment. This association would be particularly appropriate in light of Aaron and the people's failure to acknowledge Yahweh's true nature in Exodus 32.[10]

[9]Interpreters, because they seek a historical reality for it, have great difficulty in assessing the combined authority of the priests and the judge at the central sanctuary. They plainly do not take seriously the position in the text that Moses is the author of the laws and consequently fail to appreciate the sophisticated nature of this fiction.

[10]The Chronicler records (2 Chron 19:3, 5–10) how King Jehoshaphat in effect observed the laws set down in Deut 16:21 (the Asherah), 16:18–20 (appointment of

Law: The institution of kingship

[14] When thou art come unto the land which Yahweh thy God giveth thee, and shalt possess it, and shalt dwell therein, and shalt say, I will set a king over me, like as all the nations that are about me; [15] thou shalt in any wise set king over thee, him whom Yahweh thy God shall choose: one from among thy brethren shalt thou set king over thee: thou mayest not set a stranger over thee, which is not thy brother. [16] But he shall not multiply horses to himself, nor cause the people to return to Egypt, to the end that he should multiply horses: forasmuch as Yahweh hath said unto you, Ye shall henceforth return no more that way. [17] Neither shall he multiply wives to himself, that his heart turn not away: neither shall he greatly multiply to himself silver and gold. [18] And it shall be, when he sitteth upon the throne of his kingdom, that he shall write him a copy of this law in a book out of that which is before the priests the Levites: [19] and it shall be with him, and he shall read therein all the days of his life: that he may learn to fear Yahweh his God, to keep all the words of this law and these statutes, to do them: [20] that his heart be not lifted up above his brethren, and that he turn not aside from the commandment, to the right hand, or to the left: to the end that he may prolong his days in his kingdom, he, and his children, in the midst of Israel. (Deut 17:14–20)

Background: The people's request for a king, Abimelech's kingship, and Solomon's reign

[4] Then all the elders of Israel gathered themselves together, and came to Samuel unto Ramah, [5] and said unto him, Behold, thou art old, and thy sons walk not in thy ways: now make us a king to judge us like all the nations. [6] But the thing displeased Samuel, when they said, Give us a king to judge us. And Samuel prayed unto Yahweh. [7] And Yahweh said unto Samuel, Hearken unto the voice of the people in all that they say unto thee: for they have not rejected thee, but they have rejected me, that I should not reign over them. [8] According to all the works which they have done since the day that I brought them up out of Egypt even unto this day, wherewith they have forsaken me, and served other gods, so do they also unto thee. [9] Now therefore hearken unto their voice: howbeit yet

---

judges in the cities and exhortation to observe justice), and Deut 17:8–13 (appointment of Levitical priests along with heads of families in Jerusalem to judge controversial cases).

protest solemnly unto them, and shew them the manner of the king that shall reign over them. (1 Sam 8:4–9)

[1] And Abimelech the son of Jerubbaal went to Shechem unto his mother's brethren, and communed with them, and with all the family of the house of his mother's father, saying, [2] Speak, I pray you, in the ears of all the men of Shechem, Whether is better for you, either that all the sons of Jerubbaal, which are threescore and ten persons, reign over you, or that one reign over you? remember also that I am your bone and your flesh. [3] And his mother's brethren spake of him in the ears of all the men of Shechem all these words: and their hearts inclined to follow Abimelech; for they said, He is our brother. [4] And they gave him threescore and ten pieces of silver out of the house of Baal-berith, wherewith Abimelech hired vain and light persons, which followed him. [5] And he went unto his father's house at Ophrah, and slew his brethren the sons of Jerubbaal, being threescore and ten persons, upon one stone: notwithstanding yet Jotham the youngest son of Jerubbaal was left; for he hid himself. [6] And all the men of Shechem gathered together, and all the house of Millo, and went, and made Abimelech king, by the oak of the pillar that was in Shechem. (Judg 9:1–6)

[14] Now the weight of gold that came to Solomon in one year was six hundred threescore and six talents of gold. . . . [18] Moreover the king made a great throne of ivory, and overlaid it with the best gold. . . . [21] And all king Solomon's drinking vessels were of gold, and all the vessels of the house of the forest of Lebanon were of pure gold. . . . [27] And the king made silver to be in Jerusalem as stones. . . . [28] And Solomon had horses brought out of Egypt. (1 Kings 10:14, 18, 21, 27, 28)

[3] And he [Solomon] had seven hundred wives, princesses, and three hundred concubines: and his wives turned away his heart. [4] For it came to pass, when Solomon was old, that his wives turned away his heart after other gods: and his heart was not perfect with Yahweh his God, as was the heart of David his father. [5] For Solomon went after Ashtoreth the goddess of the Zidonians, and after Milcom the abomination of the Ammonites. [6] And Solomon did evil in the sight of Yahweh, and went not fully after Yahweh, as did David his father. [7] Then did Solomon build an high place for Chemosh, the abomination of Moab, in the hill that is before Jerusalem, and for Molech, the abomination of the children of Ammon. [8] And likewise did he for all his strange wives, which burnt incense and sacrificed unto their gods. (1 Kings 11:3–8)

The Deuteronomists's concern with true and false sources of authority continues with this law that, while upholding the legitimacy of the institution of kingship in Israel, is primarily directed at controlling any potential for apostasy. We can clearly observe the transition from the law on the supreme tribunal to this one.

This law clearly exemplifies the lawgiver's focus upon literary traditions and formulation of his rule on the basis of a reading of them. It begins with a reference to the people's request in the time of Samuel to have a king like the surrounding nations (1 Sam 8:5).[11] The context in which the request came and Samuel's response to it both tie in with the Deuteronomist's focus in his preceding laws. The reason why a request for a king arose was the behavior of Samuel's sons as judges in Beersheba. They had been perverting justice and taking bribes (1 Sam 8:1–3; cp., Deut 16:18–20). Because their justice was lacking in the town (or towns; cp., 1 Sam 7:16, 17), all the elders of Israel took the problem to the supreme authority, Samuel himself, "a prophet like unto Moses," with their request for a king. His response is distinctly reminiscent of Moses' reaction to the people's asking in Exodus 32 for gods to lead them. Both view the initiatives as tantamount to rejecting God as their leader. Indeed, the indication is that there is a common Deuteronomic redaction of both these traditions, and that the earlier episode of Exodus 32 has been in mind in the writing up of the later one.[12] This influence shows in God's speech to Samuel when he mentions the people's apostasy from the day that he brought them out of Egypt, how "they have forsaken me and served other gods" (1 Sam 8:8). The concern with local judges, with the supreme tribunal, and especially with the problems raised by the events of Exodus 32 informed the preceding laws. It is worth noting that two important developments relating to kingship are associated with Exodus 32: the people's approach to Samuel and Jeroboam's fateful installation of the golden calves at Bethel and Dan.[13]

[11]The supposed tension in the law between the people's request for a king and the fact that Yahweh ultimately chooses him (see Mayes, *Deuteronomy* NCBC, 271) simply reflects the traditions in Samuel about the request of the people and Yahweh's selection of Saul.

[12]J. Coert Rylaarsdam points out the link in substance between 1 Sam 8:5 and Exodus 32 (*Exodus* IB 1 [New York: Abingdon, 1952], 1064).

[13]For the Deuteronomic redaction of both these traditions, see P. Kyle McCarter (*I Samuel* AB [New York: Doubleday, 1980], 157, 161) and J. Gray (*I and II Kings*

The Deuteronomist has to have Moses respond positively to the anticipated request for a king for the simple reason that kingship became a fact of life in Israel. He views it, however, in a way that is colored by Moses' first experience of a leader's idolatry, namely, Aaron's in Exodus 32. This underlying concern with the issue of apostasy in the Israelite king comes out in three different notices in the law.

First is the surprising statement that a brother be appointed king and not a foreigner. As D. Daube has shown,[14] the background to this requirement is the tradition in Judg 9:1–6 about Gideon's son, Abimelech, by his Canaanite concubine from Shechem. Shechem was at this time under Israel's rule, and Abimelech proposed to their citizens that it was better that he and not his seventy half-brothers should reign over them. The Shechemites responded favorably to his request because they were his mother's relations: "He is our brother." By proceeding to slay his seventy half-brothers, Jotham excepted, Abimelech showed that he was king over all Israel. His father had previously been offered hereditary rule but had declined it, asserting instead that Yahweh should rule over them (Judg 8:22, 23). The Deuteronomist focuses on this tradition for two reasons: it is the first example in Israelite history when the request for a king arose; and he is consistently interested in tracing later developments back to their beginnings, or to parallel episodes. He would also have noted that Abimelech was part foreign, that his mother's kinsmen gave him their allegiance, and that they were Canaanites. If the development had been allowed to stand, Canaanite religious influence would have been increasingly prevalent. Moses, anticipating such undesirable developments, sets out a requirement to counter them.

Second is the allusion to Solomon's multiplying horses, wives, silver, and gold in the warning that the Israelite king should not multiply any of these. The lawgiver's reason for making the allusion is the recognition that Solomon's apostasy was attributable directly to his

---

[Philadelphia: Westminster, 1963], 293–94). The structural parallel (see my *Laws of Deuteronomy*, 104, 105), between the law in Deut 12:20–28, involving a request to eat meat, and the law on the king, is accounted for by the fact that the request to eat meat arises from a tradition about Saul's kingship.

[14]Daube, "One from among your brethren shall you set king over you," *JBL* 90 (1971):480–1.

foreign wives and indirectly to all his dealings with foreign nations, for example, his importing horses from Egypt and trading them abroad to their rulers (1 Kings 10:28, 29).[15]

Third is the requirement that the king should always have before him the book of the law that the Levitical priests possessed. Their loyalty to Yahweh during the incident of the golden calf gave them a special standing alongside Moses, one that was incorporated into the preceding institution of the supreme tribunal. By keeping the king ever alert to the contents of the book of the law, we can infer, they ensure his avoidance of idolatrous ways.

Law: The Levitical priests and their revenues

[1] The priests the Levites, and all the tribe of Levi, shall have no part nor inheritance with Israel: they shall eat the offerings of Yahweh made by fire, and his inheritance. [2] Therefore shall they have no inheritance among their brethren: Yahweh is their inheritance, as he hath said unto them. [3] And this shall be the priest's due from the people, from them that offer a sacrifice, whether it be ox or sheep; and they shall give unto the priest the shoulder, and the two cheeks, and the maw. [4] The firstfruit also of thy corn, of thy wine, and of thine oil, and the first of the fleece of thy sheep, shalt thou give him. [5] For Yahweh thy God hath chosen him out of all thy tribes, to stand to minister in the name of Yahweh, him and his sons for ever. [6] And if a Levite come from any of thy gates out of all Israel, where he sojourned, then he may come with all the desire of his mind unto the place which Yahweh shall choose; [7] and he shall minister in the name of Yahweh his God, as all his brethren the Levites do, which stand there before Yahweh. [8] They shall have like portions to eat, beside his wages for the fatherly offices. (Deut 18:1–8)

Background: The king's exactions from the people, the exactions of the sons of Eli, and the fatherly office of the sojourning Levite

[10] And Samuel told all the words of Yahweh unto the people that asked of him a king. [11] And he said, This will be the manner

[15]Isaiah (2:6, 7) links the Israelite's acquisition of silver, gold, horses, and chariots with their apostasy. Deut 8:11–20 contains a similar association between such acquisitions and apostasy.

> of the king that shall reign over you. . . . [14] And he will take your fields, and your vineyards, and your oliveyards, even the best of them, and give them to his servants. [15] And he will take the tenth of your seed, and of your vineyards, and give to his officers, and to his servants. . . . [17] He will take the tenth of your sheep: and ye shall be his servants. (1 Sam 8:10, 11, 14, 15, 17)

> [12] Now the sons of Eli were sons of Belial; they knew not Yahweh. [13] And the priest's custom with the people was, that, when any man offered sacrifice, the priest's servant came, while the flesh was seething, with a fleshhook of three teeth in his hand; [14] and he struck it into the pan, or kettle, or caldron, or pot; all that the fleshhook brought up the priest took for himself. So they did in Shiloh unto all the Israelites that came thither. [15] Also before they burnt the fat, the priest's servant came, and said to the man that sacrificed, Give flesh to roast for the priest; for he will not have sodden flesh of thee, but raw. [16] And if any man said unto him, Let them not fail to burn the fat presently, and then take as much as thy soul desireth; then he would answer him, Nay; but thou shalt give it me now: and if not, I will take it by force. [17] Wherefore the sin of the young men was very great before Yahweh: for men abhorred the offering of Yahweh. (1 Sam 2:12–17)

A sojourning Levite came to Mount Ephraim, to the house of Micah which possessed its own household gods. "And Micah said unto him, Dwell with me, and be unto me a father and a priest, and I will give thee ten shekels of silver by the year, and a suit of apparel, and thy victuals. So the Levite went in" (Judg 17:10). When the tribe of Dan was seeking a permanent settlement, some of its members came upon the Levite and sought his counsel. Later when they came with a military force to establish a place for themselves, they removed the religious objects from Micah's house and constrained the Levite to go with them and "be to us a father and a priest." The comment (Judg 17:6, 18:1) on the developments that took place was, "In those days there was no king in Israel, every man did that which was right in his own eyes" (Judges 17, 18).

The role of the priests as guardians of the laws of Moses is cited in the preceding rule about the people's request for a king. This following rule concerns what is due the priests from the people. The lawgiver's focus is again the same tradition that motivated the formulation of the law about the king, namely, Samuel's response to the people's request for one. In his response Samuel listed the various exactions that the king would demand of the people, for example, the best of their fields, vineyards, olive orchards, and flocks. This emphasis on the king's revenues prompts the lawgiver to consider those due to the Levites (for example, the firstfruits of corn, wine, oil and the fleece of the sheep), presumably because of the status accorded them in relation to the king by the Deuteronomist.

Another tradition pertinent to the law comes from the time when Samuel was first established as a prophet (1 Sam 3:20). At that time the sons of Eli were acting as priests but were abusing their privilege in what they took from the sacrifices offered by the people. Their servants would, for example, take forks and thrust them into the container where meat was being cooked, taking whatever they could. This account of what is referred to as the custom of the priests (*mišpaṭ hakkōhanîm* [1 Sam 2:13]) raises the issue what the proper arrangement should be. This the Deuteronomist takes up with his, "And this shall be the *mišpaṭ hakkōhanîm*," laying out exactly what parts of the animal they should be given, in contrast to the arbitrary appropriation resorted to by the sons of Eli.

In the judgment against their father for not stamping out the abuses, reference is made to the recognition of his ancestors during the Egyptian bondage, how in time they were to serve at God's altar and to receive for their services all the offerings by fire from the people (1 Sam 2:28). In his law the Deuteronomist opens with a comparable general statement about the special position of the tribe of Levi, noting that as priests they were entitled to Yahweh's fire offerings. The judgment against Eli's house continues with predictions about the calamity that will befall it and about God's raising up a faithful priest who will take his position beside the future king. This judgment is by an unnamed prophet and is thoroughly Deuteronomic in character. It can therefore be aligned to what lies behind the presentation of the rules involving the Levites, their role with the king, their standing alongside the supreme prophet Moses, the sustained interest in sources of authority. The latter interest is about to culminate in the law of the prophet.

Provision is made in the law for those Levites who, having no inheritance in Israel, are sojourners in the towns and who may decide to come to the chosen place. If they do, they are to receive the same privileges accorded to those Levites already serving there. This is in addition to what they receive from a certain kind of sale they make or earnings they possess: *l^ebad mimkārā(y)w ʿal-hāʾābôt.* The nature of this reference has been a major puzzle. Driver, in his discussion of the problem, indicates that the phrase can be literally rendered, "besides his sellings according to the fathers," and is usually understood to mean, "apart from what he has realized by selling the possessions belonging to him in virtue of his family descent." He also cites Dillmann's explanation, "besides what he has realized by selling the dues (tithe, etc.) rendered to him at his home by particular families."[16] Driver finds both explanations questionable.

The background to this part of the law is again a tradition, probably the earliest non-Deuteronomic one about the Levites as priests, that was available to the Deuteronomist and that he, as Moses, had to take account of because of the requirement that was to come into effect regarding the central sanctuary. Indeed in the tradition in Judges 17 and 18, a redactor makes a link between the unsatisfactory cultic arrangements in these times, and the time when there will be a king in Israel—when, it is implied, a higher cultic order will prevail, presumably such as obtained at Solomon's temple. The notices in Judg 17:6, 18:1, about the need for a king, almost certainly reflect the hand of the Deuteronomist. In any event, in his law he contemplates the position of the type of Levite who is mentioned in Judges 17 and 18. He was a sojourner (Judg 17:7, 9; cp., 19:1), as in the description of the Levite in the law, and he took up residence in the family of Micah. In issuing the invitation, Micah requested that he become to him "a father and a priest." In return for his services he was to receive certain payments (Judg 17:10; cp., 18:4 in which there is reference to Micah's hiring him). He was eventually to change his service and become "a father and a priest" to the tribe of Dan (Judg 18:19).

The puzzling phrase in the law becomes intelligible in the light of the description of this Levite's priestly office. He is referred to as a "father" and, person and office often being identical in Hebrew, the meaning of *ʾābôt* will be, "fatherly, priestly offices." The other term, *mkr,* is sufficiently flexible to mean, in this phrase, "wages." The sojourning Levite in question sold his services and received payment in return. The selling is also an acquisition.[17] In the law then the

[16]Driver, *Deuteronomy* ICC, 217, 218.

[17]I am indebted to Professor Chaim Rabin of the Hebrew University, Jerusalem, for his guidance on the linguistics of this difficult phrase. He pointed out to me, for example, the striking interchangeability of the verbs "to buy" and "to sell" in Arabic.

reference is to those Levites who were employed in a manner similar to Micah's Levite, and who in leaving this employment would be in possession of the wages they had received from it. A suitable translation might read: "Apart from his wages for having the fatherly offices." It would have been necessary for the Deuteronomist to have viewed the revenues of these sojouring Levites in the light of the notion that the tribe had "no part nor inheritance with Israel" (Deut 18:1). He presumably judges that there is no conflict.

SUMMARY From the deity's visiting famine upon the house of Ahab, which prompted rules about the consumption of food, the lawgiver switches to the deity's provision of food in the aftermath of the famine in Joseph's time. This was the first example in Israelite history which was given an institutionalized form, albeit in an Egyptian setting. It prompts the presentation of the equivalent institution of tithing within Israel. Egyptian history dominates a succession of laws. From the deity's causing the Hebrews to be fed from the Egyptian stores, the lawgiver turns to a comparable situation when Yahweh caused the Egyptians to give the oppressed Hebrews favor in the form of articles of silver and gold. The lawgiver again drafts a rule in which what happened then is given an institutionalized form within Israel, namely, the release of debts every seven years. Just after receiving these articles the Hebrews were released from their slavery in Egypt. A law sets down the conditions, including the provision of items for departing slaves, that govern the release of Hebrew slaves within Israel. The Hebrews were redeemed from slavery in Egypt in order that they might serve their god. Four feasts, two of which (firstlings and Passover) recall what took place in Egypt, are set down for this purpose.

After the departure from Egypt a series of events involving sacrificial worship took place. Each occasion in turn prompts a rule. First, Jethro's sacrificing was followed by his counsel about spreading the burden of judging the people by appointing men to aid Moses in the task. A rule on the subject is set down. Next, at Sinai Yahweh instructed Moses about making an altar of earth so that sacrifices might be offered. Moses, alert to later developments, prohibits the planting of an Asherah, any tree, beside Yahweh's altar. On the same occasion Yahweh instructed Moses about altars of stone, and just after the receiving of this and other instructions in the Book of the Covenant,

Moses communicated them to the people and built an altar and twelve pillars to mark the event. Again anticipating further negative developments, Moses prohibits the erection of stone pillars of the Canaanite variety. The next incident involving Israelite worship was that of the golden calf, an animal artifact imbued with religious associations and opposed by Yahweh. In regular Israelite worship an animal that is in any way defective is not acceptable to Yahweh.

The people first promoted the idolatry of the calf when they approached Aaron with the problem of Moses' disappearance. They took the problem to Aaron because Moses had appointed him to handle difficult problems in his absence, but their request to make gods to lead them was inappropriate. Moses, anticipating later, settled conditions, first deals with idolatry breaking out among the people in the local towns. He then restates the rule about the kinds of problems, legal not religious, that are too hard for the people to deal with among themselves and that have to be taken to the central authority. In reaction to the difficulty of having legal problems solved in one of the towns in Samuel's time, the elders of Israel took the matter to Samuel as the central authority. Their request for a king as a solution met with the same negative response as the people's request to Aaron to make them gods to lead them. Yahweh's authority was being rejected. Kingship was nonetheless instituted at that time. Earlier in the time of the judges Abimelech's attempt, the first ever, to be king had been rejected, partly because of his Canaanite background. Later in Solomon's reign problems of apostasy again came to the fore. Alert to these historical developments the Deuteronomist composes his law on Israelite kingship. The Levitical priests, as guardians of the law and because of their loyalty to Yahweh in the incident of the calf, are given a special role in directing the ways of the king. When the request for a king was made to Samuel he warned the people about the exactions a king would impose upon them. The priests were also to receive exactions from the people, and a problem involving wrongful ones had arisen earlier in Samuel's life. A law sets down what the position should be. It also addresses itself to the earnings of the Levites when they were "fathers" to Israelite families in the time of the judges.

CHAPTER 4

CONFRONTATIONS BETWEEN PROPHET AND KING

A cursory glance at the law code indicates how much the topic of idolatry appears and reappears. This repetition simply reflects the theme of idolatry that runs through the Deuteronomic redaction of the histories of the judges and the kings. Indeed the recurring concern in the laws is much greater than actually appears, for it not only emerges in rules plainly dealing with the topic. The same histories that earned the Deuteronomic redactor's anti-idolatrous judgment turn up issues nonidolatrous in character but nonetheless linked to an Israelite ruler's apostate ways. In the traditions in the Books of Samuel and Kings the conflicts between prophet and prophet and, even more pronounced, between prophet and king bring out the issues. These in turn engage the lawgiver's attention.

Laws: Nonlegitimate sources of authority and the authority of the prophet

[9] When thou art come into the land which Yahweh thy God giveth thee, thou shalt not learn to do after the abominations of those nations. [10] There shall not be found in thy midst any one that maketh his son or his daughter to pass through the fire, or that useth divination, or a soothsayer, or an augur, or a witch, [11] or a charmer, or a consulter with familiar spirits, or a wizard, or a

necromancer. [12] For all that do these things are an abomination unto Yahweh: and because of these abominations Yahweh thy God doth drive them out from before thee. [13] Thou shalt be perfect with Yahweh thy God. [14] For these nations, which thou shalt possess, hearkened unto observers of times, and unto diviners: but as for thee, Yahweh thy God hath not suffered thee so to do. [15] Yahweh thy God will raise up unto thee a prophet from the midst of thee, of thy brethren, like unto me; unto him ye shall hearken; [16] according to all that thou desiredst of Yahweh thy God in Horeb in the day of the assembly, saying, Let me not hear again the voice of Yahweh my God, neither let me see this great fire any more, that I die not. [17] And Yahweh said unto me, They have well spoken that which they have spoken. [18] I will raise them up a prophet from among their brethren, like unto thee, and will put my words in his mouth; and he shall speak unto them all that I shall command him. [19] And it shall come to pass, that whosoever will not hearken unto my words which he shall speak in my name, I will require it of him. [20] But the prophet which shall presume to speak a word in my name, which I have not commanded him to speak, or that shall speak in the name of other gods, even that prophet shall die. [21] And if thou say in thine heart, How shall we know the word which Yahweh hath not spoken? [22] When a prophet speaketh in the name of Yahweh, if the thing follow not, nor come to pass, that is the thing which Yahweh hath not spoken, but the prophet hath spoken it presumptuously: thou shalt not be afraid of him. (Deut 18:9–22)

Background: Deviant influences upon the kings and the succession of prophets in the time of the kings

[8] And Saul disguised himself, and put on other raiment, and he went, and two men with him, and they came to the woman by night: and he said, I pray thee, divine unto me by the familiar spirit, and bring me him up, whom I shall name unto thee. (1 Sam 28:8; cp., 2 Kings 17:17)

[5] For Solomon went after Ashtoreth the goddess of the Zidonians, and after Milcom the abomination of the Ammonites. . . . [7] Then did Solomon build an high place for Chemosh, the abomination of Moab, in the hill that is before Jerusalem, and for Molech, the abomination of the children of Ammon. (1 Kings 11:5, 7)

[22] And it came to pass, when Joram saw Jehu, that he said, Is it peace, Jehu? And he answered, what peace, so long as the whore-

doms of thy mother Jezebel and her witchcrafts are so many? (2 Kings 9:22)

[6] But he [Manasseh] made his son pass through the fire, and practised soothsaying, and augury, and dealt with familiar spirits and wizards: he wrought much wickedness in the sight of Yahweh to provoke him to anger. (2 Kings 21:6; cp., 2 Kings 16:3; 17:17; 23:10)

[18] And all the people saw the thunderings, and the lightnings, and the noise of the trumpet, and the mountain smoking: and when the people saw it, they removed, and stood afar off. [19] And they said unto Moses, Speak thou with us, and we will hear: but let not God speak with us, lest we die. (Exod 20:18, 19)

[29] And it came to pass at that time when Jeroboam went out of Jerusalem, that the prophet Ahijah the Shilonite found him in the way; and he had clad himself with a new garment; and they two were alone in the field: [30] and Ahijah caught the new garment that was on him, and rent it in twelve pieces: [31] and he said to Jeroboam, Take thee ten pieces: for thus saith Yahweh, the God of Israel, Behold, I will rend the kingdom out of the hand of Solomon, and will give ten tribes to thee. (1 Kings 11:29–31)

The lawgiver's concern in the preceding law about the revenues of the Levites is in a way a diversion from his overriding interest in laying out rules delineating the true order of religious authority within Israel.[1] This aim continues to be manifest in the joint presentation of the rules: first, against forms of divination and magic that might influence an Israelite; and second, the requirement ("unto him shall ye hearken," as against those heathen sources of authority) that an Israelite obey the prophet who has Moses' authority invested in him. The preceding laws about the king and the central tribunal were a response to the problems that arose in the related narratives of Exodus 32 and 1 Samuel 8, about the people's rejection of God as their ruler. The influence of foreign, superstitious practices upon the kings of Israel and Judah is also cause for considering further examples of declension from God's rule. One indication of the close relationship between the law on the king and this one on the practices of many of

[1]Even the concern with secular authority, for example, the administration of justice within the gates, was, we saw, given a religious basis. Jethro's counsel on the subject was from God.

them is that both have the same opening statement: "When thou art come into the land which Yahweh thy God giveth thee" (Deut 17:14, 18:9). The practices in question first appeared with Solomon ([1 Kings 11:7] the worship of Molech, which involved passing children through fire), and continued from his time according to the notices, some of them Deuteronomic, about the ways of the kings ([2 Kings 16:3, 17:17, 21:6, 23:10] the worship of Molech; [1 Sam 28:8; 2 Kings 17:17] divination; [2 Kings 21:6] soothsaying; [2 Kings 17:17, 21:6] observing omens; [2 Kings 9:22] sorcery; [1 Sam 28:8, 9; cp., Isa 8:19; 2 Kings 21:6, 23:24] consulting with a ghost or a familiar spirit, necromancy).

In the law Moses warns how the nations that practice what God abominates are being driven out of the land. What is really on his mind is the expulsion of the Israelites in the time of King Hoshea. The Deuteronomist attributes the expulsion to the fact that the king and his predecessors imitated these nations' practices (2 Kings 17). By having Moses address himself to the issue within the context of his own historical experience, the Deuteronomist can claim to have the authority to judge the kings in the terms that he does in 2 Kings 17 and that are also to be inferred in his law.

Just as the relationship between supposed supernatural agencies and the kings has engaged the lawgiver's attention, so that between prophets, men of God, and the kings comes under his scrutiny in the law about the true and false prophet. Typically, because of the setting of the laws, he cites the historical incident at Horeb when the people requested Moses to stand between them and God (Exod 20:19; Deut 5:23–31). The order of Moses-like prophets that is to be established is, in turn, based upon the history of the succession of prophets who tried to check the deviant ways of the kings.[2] Samuel with Saul and the unnamed prophet who confronted Ahab are examples. The statement that whoever does not obey God's words spoken by the prophet, "it will be required of him," could well have someone like Saul or

[2]The prophets are brother Israelites. This seems an unnecessary description but it may have been prompted by the exclusion of a prophet and diviner (Num 22:7) like the foreigner Balaam. He had a vision of Israel's future king (Num 24:7) and felt constrained to speak only those words put into his mouth by Yahweh (Num 22:18, 25, 28, 23:12). However, he worshipped at the high places of Baal (Num 22:41), and was eventually put to death because, it is implied, he had a hand in Israel's apostasy to the Baal of Peor (Num 31:8, 16).

Ahab in mind, who suffered the consequences of the failure to heed such words (1 Sam 13:13, 14; 1 Kings 20:42). The divinatory practices that Saul had recourse to were condemned in the preceding rule. Elijah (with Ahab) is another example. His journey to Horeb on food that lasted him forty days and nights and his hearing God's voice upon the mountain makes him very much a prophet like Moses (1 Kings 19:4–18). In his contest with the prophets of Baal he spoke in God's name and was proved right. The prophets, who spoke in the name of other gods and who by cutting themselves tried to have their gods act, died. In the law this kind of prophet is executed and so too is the prophet who speaks a word that God has not commanded him. This latter type specifies the criterion for distinguishing between a true and a false prophet, namely, his capacity to be right in his prediction.

A line of prophets in the time of the kings demonstrated this capacity, and it is they who have provided the type of the true Israelite prophet. Samuel successfully predicted thunder and rain at a wheat harvest as a sign of God's wrath at the people's request for a king (1 Sam 12:16–18). Nathan's prophecy that the sword would not depart from King David's house proved accurate (2 Sam 12:10). Ahijah's pronouncement over King Jeroboam came true (1 Kings 11:29–39). An unnamed prophet correctly forecast by the use of a sign the destruction of Jeroboam's newly established altar at Bethel (1 Kings 13:1–5). This same prophet died shortly after because he heeded the words, which turned out to be false even though spoken in God's name, of an old prophet of Bethel. The latter incident would have encouraged the Deuteronomist to address himself to the problem of determining a false prophetic message from a true one. The tradition that permitted him to address it is found in 1 Kings 22:5–40. The prophet Micaiah spoke about the pending death of Ahab and about the lying spirit that had been put into the mouth of the four hundred prophets consulted by Ahab. Both sides spoke in the name of Yahweh. Micaiah's words were proved true because they came to pass. One of the duped prophets, Zedekiah, on the other hand, made horns of iron and informed Ahab, "With these thou shalt push the Syrians, until thou hast consumed them" (1 Kings 22:11). That success was not to befall Ahab. The criterion that emerges from this prophetic tradition for judging a false prophet is, as the law has it, "When a prophet speaketh in the name of Yahweh, if the thing follow not, nor come to pass, that is the thing which Yahweh hath not spoken" (Deut 18:22).

Driver points out how narrowly focused the law is in regard to the criterion for distinguishing between true and false prophecy. No consideration is given to the fulfillment of a prediction alleged falsely to have been uttered in the name of Yahweh, nor to the nonfulfillment of a prediction uttered truly in his name because a moral change for the better has occurred, or because of effectual intercession.[3] Driver does note that the case of the fulfillment of a sign or wonder done in the interest of (but note, not in the name of) other gods has been dealt with in Deut 13:2. The point is, however, that the Deuteronomist has confined himself to those issues that have been raised by certain traditions. Aaron's claim to have thrown some gold into the fire and produced a golden calf had suggested the case of a sign carried out in the interest of other gods. Likewise, the narrower focus in Deut 18:22 results from the lawgiver's concentration upon the conflict between Micaiah and the four hundred prophets, all speaking in the name of Yahweh, who had dealings with King Ahab.

Events in Ahab's reign, because they involve confrontation between prophet and king, dominate the presentation of the following laws: cities of asylum for the manslayer; removal of boundary marks; false witness; and protection of certain individuals from death in war (Deut 19:1–20:9). The prophetic activities that come under scrutiny for the purpose of laying out laws on the topics that arise are: the unnamed prophet's judgment upon Ahab for sparing Benhadad's life; Elijah's judgment upon Ahab for taking Naboth's ancestral land and causing the latter's death by means of false witness; and Micaiah's fulfilled prophecy about God's use of war to engineer Ahab's death (1 Kings 20:30–22:36). The events are idiosyncratic, and the lawgiver attempts to probe beyond the peculiar elements and bring out the more general issue. In concentrating upon the relationship between prophet and king, he continues to display his interest in the authority of the Moses-like prophet and in the related notion of God's sovereignty.

[3]Driver, *Deuteronomy* ICC (Edinburgh: T. and T. Clark, 1902), 230. He cites Jeremiah's words on this type of prediction that is not in the end acted upon (Jer 18:7–10; cp., Jer 26:19).

Law: Cities for the protection of the manslayer

[1] When Yahweh thy God hath cut off the nations, whose land Yahweh thy God giveth thee, and thou succeedest them, and dwellest in their cities, and in their houses; [2] thou shalt separate three cities for thee in the midst of thy land, which Yahweh thy God giveth thee to possess it. [3] Thou shalt prepare thee a way, and divide the territories of thy land, which Yahweh thy God giveth thee to inherit, into three parts, that every slayer may flee thither. [4] And this is the case of the slayer, which shall flee thither, that he may live: Whoso killeth his neighbour ignorantly, whom he hated not in time past; [5] as when a man goeth into the wood with his neighbour to hew wood, and his hand fetcheth a stroke with the ax to cut down the tree, and the head slippeth from the helve and lighteth upon his neighbour, that he die; he shall flee unto one of those cities, and live: [6] lest the avenger of the blood pursue the slayer, while his heart is hot, and overtake him, because the way is long, and smite him in life; whereas he was not worthy of death, inasmuch as he hated him not in time past. [7] Wherefore I command thee, saying, Thou shalt separate three cities for thee. [8] And if Yahweh thy God enlarge thy territory, as he hath sworn unto thy fathers, and give thee all the land which he promised to give unto thy fathers; [9] if thou shalt keep all these commandments to do them, which I command thee this day, to love Yahweh thy God, and to walk ever in his ways; then shalt thou add three cities more for thee, beside these three: [10] that innocent blood be not shed in thy land, which Yahweh thy God giveth thee for an inheritance, and so blood be upon thee. [11] But if any man hate his neighbour, and lie in wait for him, and rise up against him, and smite him in life that he die, and fleeth into one of these cities: [12] then the elders of his city shall send and fetch him thence, and deliver him into the hand of the avenger of blood, that he may die. [13] Thine eye shall not pity him, but thou shalt put away the guilt of innocent blood from Israel, that it may go well with thee. (Deut 19:1–13)

Background: Ahab spares Benhadad's life and his own death as retribution for his offense against Naboth (1 Kings 20–22)

[35] And a certain man of the sons of the prophets said unto his neighbour in the word of Yahweh, smite me, I pray thee. And the man refused to smite him. [36] Then said he unto him, Because

> thou hast not obeyed the voice of Yahweh, behold, as soon as thou art departed from me, a lion shall slay thee. And as soon as he was departed from him, a lion found him, and slew him. [37] Then he found another man, and said, Smite me, I pray thee. And the man smote him, so that in smiting him he wounded him. [38] So the prophet departed, and waited for the king by the way, and disguised himself with ashes upon his face. [39] And as the king passed by, he cried unto the king: and he said, Thy servant went out into the midst of the battle; and, behold, a man turned aside, and brought a man unto me, and said, Keep this man: if by any means he be missing, then shall thy life be for his life, or else thou shalt pay a talent of silver. [40] And as thy servant was busy here and there, he was gone. And the king of Israel said unto him, So shall thy judgment be; thyself hast decided it. [41] And he hasted, and took the ashes away from his face; and the king of Israel discerned him that he was of the prophets. [42] And he said unto him, Thus saith Yahweh, Because thou hast let go out of thy hand a man whom I appointed to utter destruction, therefore thy life shall go for his life, and thy people for his people. (1 Kings 20:35–42)

The narratives about Ahab are highly sophisticated, in part because a scheme of exact retaliation is applied to his offenses. As a result, interrelated features in the narratives have caused the lawgiver to take up the topic of cities of refuge for a manslayer. In response to a prophet's direction Ahab was able to overcome the apparently overwhelming military might of the Aramean Benhadad. The final rout took place in the city of Aphek where he took refuge and appealed to Ahab to spare his life on account of some brotherly tie between them. His request was granted and he was let go in return for promising to hand back cities that had previously belonged to Israel (1 Kings 20:34), one of which was Ramoth-gilead, a city that in times past had been set apart for a manslayer seeking to save his life (Deut 4:41–43). As it turned out this particular city was not given over. Ahab was eventually to attempt to acquire it, but he died in the course of the battle, an outcome interpreted as retribution for his culpability in the killing of Naboth and his failing to destroy Benhadad.

Ahab's release of Benhadad brought condemnation upon him by way of a strange event that was intended to mirror the wrongfulness of his action. One prophet asked another to strike him. Remarkably, for refusing to do so he was killed. He had disobeyed the "voice of

Yahweh" and a lion had carried out the punishment. A second prophet accepted the invitation and struck and wounded him. Ahab, illogically at first sight, is represented as both the prophet who asked to be struck and the prophet who refused to strike. This dual representation anticipates, first, Ahab's self-condemnation when confronted with the story about the man who was negligent in guarding the prisoner of war and, second, his eventual demise.

The prophets represent proper values, have divine approval, and are of the order of Moses. The Deuteronomist is therefore taken up with this story about a leading Israelite who exercised his authority and freed a man who deserved to die. It prompts him to explore that aspect of the incident relevant to normal Israelite life. Hence the concern of the law with the question of whether to provide protection to the most common example in ordinary life of one liable to a sentence of death, namely, a manslayer. This concern is preceded by statements about Israel overcoming its enemies and acquiring their territory and cities. Three of these are to be set apart as cities of refuge for manslayers. The presentation of the rule about the manslayer is therefore set in the broader context described in the narrative.

In that Ahab made a wrong decision to spare Benhadad's life, and in that he is about to add to his offense by acquiring Naboth's vineyard, he himself is sentenced to death; the result is that the lawgiver's focus for exploring the issue of the protection or the disposal of a life switches to him. The bewildering interplay of events among the sons of the prophets heralds this switch and has possibly contributed to some statements in the Deuteronomist's law. In response to Ahab's wrongful sparing of Benhadad's life, there followed an example of someone intentionally wounding someone else though he felt no enmity toward him. No blame attached to him for having done so. The action was a prophetic sign involving a topsy-turvy state of affairs and raises the issue of what should happen in normal circumstances when someone deliberately strikes someone else.[4] It raises the question of motivation in particular. Ordinarily, one is punished for striking someone intentionally and not punished if the action is unintentional. The considerable attention that is given in the law to the

[4]The assault in the story led to injury, not death as in the law. It should be noted, however, that the action is intended to convey a message about Ahab's failure to put Benhadad to death.

manslayer's motivation is illumined by this background. It is, for example, discussed in terms of death by striking. The matter, moreover, is gone into in some detail: "Whoso killeth his neighbour ignorantly, whom he hated not in time past," and then follows a carefully worded description of a possible illustration of an accidental death involving the use of an ax.[5]

The attention in the law to the number of cities to be designated as places for the reception of manslayers is also illumined by aspects of the Ahab narrative. He was killed in attempting to take back one of these cities, Ramoth-gilead, and his death interpreted as his just desert for what happened to Naboth. J. Gray has pointed out that God's pursuit of Ahab in the person of his spokesman Elijah is such that, "Ahab apparently regards Elijah as the avenger of blood who pursues his victim relentlessly."[6] The Deuteronomist, whose hand is detectable in the story, may have observed that the avenger, the deity, killed him in the very act of attempting to repossess an Israelite city of asylum. A heavenly court, as reported by the prophet Micaiah, had sentenced him (1 Kings 22:19–23). The city would have been won if Ahab had been obedient to the commandments. In the law three more cities of refuge are to be added to those already existing on just this condition, that the commandments be honored.

The opening statement of the law about Yahweh cutting off the nations is identical to that which opens Deut 12:29. The similar backgrounds of these two laws are remarkable: one king (or future king in the case of David) spares the life of another (Saul in 1 Sam 26:21–24). In each instance the one showing clemency was involved in military victories against other peoples.

The Deuteronomist presumably had before him the rule in the Book of the Covenant about Yahweh's appointing a place for someone who has slain a man by accident (Exod 21:12–14). That rule also

[5]Interestingly, on another occasion during the reign of the house of Ahab, the sons of the prophets were involved in an incident in which the head of an ax accidentally flew off (without injuring anyone) (2 Kings 6:1–7).

[6]J. Gray, *I and II Kings* (Philadelphia: Westminster, 1963), 393. On the Deuteronomic redaction of the story, see 383–85. In his sources the Deuteronomist would probably have been aware of the description "avenger of blood" (Deut 19:6) from the story concocted by the wise woman of Tekoa and designed, like the prophet's story to Ahab about the prisoner of war, to pressure a king to pronounce judgment upon his situation (2 Sam 14:11).

states that the willful murderer has to be taken from Yahweh's altar and put to death. Presupposed is the existence of a number of places in the land with sanctuaries. The implication is that one of, or perhaps even some of, these places was to be set apart for the unintentional manslayer. In light of the Deuteronomist's ideal of the one exclusive sanctuary, his rule must express Moses' eventual aim to designate cities, not sanctuaries. What the customary practice was in the Deuteronomist's time is difficult to evaluate. The notices in Deut 4:41–43 and in Josh 20:3–6 (this section being ascribed to the Deuteronomist) suggest that there may have been such cities of refuge already in existence.

Law: Removal of boundary marks

> [14] Thou shalt not remove thy neighbour's landmark, which they of old time have set in thine inheritance, which thou shalt inherit in the land that Yahweh thy God giveth thee to possess it. (Deut 19:14)

Background: Ahab appropriates Naboth's vineyard

> [1] And it came to pass after these things, that Naboth the Jezreelite had a vineyard, which was in Jezreel, hard by the palace of Ahab king of Samaria. [2] And Ahab spake unto Naboth, saying, Give me thy vineyard, that I may have it for a garden of herbs, because it is near unto my house: and I will give thee for it a better vineyard than it; or, if it seem good to thee, I will give thee the worth of it in money. [3] And Naboth said to Ahab, Yahweh forbid it me, that I should give the inheritance of my fathers unto thee. (1 Kings 21:1–3)

Ahab's offense was not just a result of his culpability in respect to Naboth's death, which enables him to take possession of his vineyard, but his attempt to obtain that vineyard in the first place. The negotiations that took place between them were straightforward and businesslike: Ahab would offer money or another and better vineyard so that he could acquire Naboth's because it was conveniently located beside his palace. Naboth refused the offer on the ground that it was his ancestral property. He indicated that it would go against the divine order of things for him to do so, "Yahweh forbid it me, that I should give the inheritance of my fathers unto thee" (1 Kings 21:3). The question arises about the merit of this claim, and the Deuteronomist has moved to support it with his rule prohibiting the removal of a neighbor's landmark, "which they of old time have set in thine inheritance." From the perspective of the period of the kings this statement has reference to the time of Moses.

The lawgiver continuously links activity in the history of the kings to Moses' own time in an attempt to demonstrate that Moses had implicitly laid down rules on any matter that arose after his time. We therefore find an account of how Moses had carefully designated boundaries and had given instruction about their inviolability being respected. He had set apart three cities of asylum east of the Jordan for the inheritance of the Reubenites, Gadites, and Manassites (Deut 4:41–43). Before that he had allotted to these tribes their territories, divisions, and boundaries (Deut 3:12–17). He had forbidden Israel not to move against the land of certain countries because it had been allotted to them by God (Deut 2:4, 5, 9, 18, 19). The similar terms used in the two laws of asylum and the neighbor's landmark—the territory (*g^e^bûl*) that God gives as an inheritance (*hiph. nāḥal*); removing the territory (*g^e^bûl*) that the first generation in the land established as an inheritance (*naḥ^a^lāh*)—reflect this Deuteronomic account of Moses's activity.

Law: False witness

[15] One witness shall not rise up against a man for any iniquity, or for any sin, in any sin that he sinneth: at the mouth of two witnesses, or at the mouth of three witnesses, shall the matter be established. [16] If a false witness rise up against any man to testify against him defection; [17] then both the men, between whom the controversy is, shall stand before Yahweh, before the priests and the judges, which shall be in those days; [18] and the judges shall make diligent inquisition: and, behold, if the witness be a false witness, and hath testified falsely against his brother; [19] then shall ye do unto him, as he had thought to have done unto his brother: so shalt thou put the evil away from thy midst. [20] And those which remain shall hear, and fear, and shall henceforth commit no more any such evil in thy midst. [21] And thine eye shall not

> pity; life shall go for life, eye for eye, tooth for tooth, hand for hand, foot for foot. (Deut 19:15–21)

Background: False witness against Naboth

> [7] And Jezebel his wife said unto him, Dost thou now govern the kingdom of Israel? arise, and eat bread, and let thine heart be merry: I will give thee the vineyard of Naboth the Jezreelite. [8] So she wrote letters in Ahab's name, and sealed them with his seal, and sent the letters unto the elders and to the nobles that were in his city, dwelling with Naboth. [9] And she wrote in the letters, saying, Proclaim a fast, and set Naboth on high among the people: [10] and set two men, sons of Belial, before him, to bear witness against him, saying, Thou didst blaspheme God and the king. And then carry him out, and stone him, that he may die. [11] And the men of his city, even the elders and the nobles who were the inhabitants in his city, did as Jezebel had sent unto them, and as it was written in the letters which she had sent unto them. [12] They proclaimed a fast, and set Naboth on high among the people. [13] And there came in two men, children of Belial, and sat before him: and the men of Belial witnessed against him, even against Naboth, in the presence of the people, saying Naboth did blaspheme God and the king. Then they carried him forth out of the city, and stoned him with stones, that he died. (1 Kings 21:7–13)

The lawgiver continues to make judgments upon Ahab's reign when he examines the circumstances surrounding the death of Naboth. Naboth was judicially executed but the event constituted extreme lawlessness on the part of the authorities. The local court that should have protected him was itself involved in the false charge that had been brought against him. To enable Ahab to acquire Naboth's vineyard his wife Jezebel sought out two "sons of Belial" to accuse Naboth of cursing God and the king. She had the elders and nobles of Naboth's city choose the false accusers and accept their charges. This was done and Naboth died.

Once the Deuteronomic law is seen as a response, like Elijah's, to this perversion of justice, much in it is illumined. The local courts, for example, are not to be involved in a case involving false witness. Such a case has to go before the central tribunal. The usual and understandable explanation is that such a case comes under the category of difficult ones that have to be brought before this central authority

(Deut 17:8). There is, however, no inherent reason why a local court might not attempt to try it. The law on procedure for taking a case to the central authority mentions that the difficulty arises within the gates. An implication is that the local court considered it and then found it too complex for them to handle. No such local attempt at adjudication is cited in the law concerning the malicious witness. The reason is not that any such dispute is automatically judged too complex for the local courts, but the facts of the story in 1 Kings 21:8–13. The local officials were all involved in the false charge against Naboth. Moses is therefore thought of as assuming such local corruption and legislating for it. Hence the puzzling fact that a case of false witness apparently automatically goes to the central tribunal. The incident with Naboth was seemingly such a shocking one that the Deuteronomic legislator, in dealing with the topic of false testimony, can not rid his mind of the collusion between the false accusers and the local officials of Naboth's city. As a result, anyone who knew that two or three people were laying false charges against him would have recourse to a hearing denied to Naboth. The lawgiver's awareness that Naboth was denied recourse to an impartial tribunal helps to explain why the law focuses upon an attempted crime rather than upon an accomplished one.

The law begins with a statement that one witness cannot testify against a man, but only two or three. It then proceeds to consider false witness. This initial statement may be a response to the information in 1 Kings 21:9 that two witnesses testified against Naboth. In that what followed their testimony required negative judgment by the lawgiver, this first step may also have been scrutinized with a view to passing judgment on its worthiness in a situation free of corruption. In establishing two witnesses against Naboth, Jezebel and the local dignitaries were procedurally at least conforming to proper practice. A restatement of the correct form would have countered any doubts about Jezebel's lawlessness in this matter too. The rule's generalizing language, false witness "against a man for any iniquity, or for any sin," is prompted by the need to include offenses other than the one under consideration.

The false witness in the law testifies against the other of "defection" (*sārāh*). The term is elsewhere used only for defection from God in a religious sense (Deut 13:5; Isa 1:5, 31:6, 59:13; Jer 28:16,

29:32). Driver points out that this context appears to be an exception in that the Deuteronomist intends a more general sense, defection from law and right.[7] Again, however, the influence of the narrative provides clarification: Naboth was accused of cursing God. To be sure, once the law is isolated from its background in the story a broader meaning may have to be read. The false witness is described as "a witness of violence," in the same language used in the law on the subject in the Book of the Covenant (Exod 23:1). We have seen that wherever possible the Deuteronomist links his formulations to laws already in his time regarded as Mosaic.

The punishment for the false witness is to be the same as the one he would have brought upon his victim if he had succeeded with his charge: "life for life, eye for eye, tooth for tooth, hand for hand, foot for foot." In the story much care is taken to show that Ahab, upon whom the responsibility was laid for Naboth's death, was treated in a way that closely paralleled the treatment of Naboth. Indeed the detailed attention to retaliation is remarkable.

Ahab wrongly appropriates Naboth's land. He then meets his death attempting to appropriate land, the city of Ramoth-gilead, that rightly belongs to Israel. His entitlement to it, however, is conditional upon his worthiness in observing the commandments. Since he offended in acquiring Naboth's land, he will be opposed in acquiring Ramoth-gilead. Lies and deception were used against Naboth, and they are similarly used in bringing about Ahab's death. The elders of Jezreel were involved in the deception against Naboth; so too are certain established prophets involved in the deception against Ahab. The actions in each case have a judicial setting, an early court trafficking in lies in the case of the elders, and a heavenly one in the case of the prophets who come under its influence in speaking lies to Ahab about the successful outcome of the battle. Both are killed while playing uncharacteristic roles. "Proclaim a fast, and set Naboth on high among the people" (1 Kings 21:9). While enjoying this high position Naboth is accused of cursing God and the king.[8] He dies for

[7]Driver, *Deuteronomy* ICC, 235. The apparent anomaly that it takes two witnesses in any case (v. 15), but that only "a false witness" is referred to (in v. 16), is resolved when we take into account what is going on in the narrative. Jezebel was the main false witness, but she organized two others in the court proceedings. The law is written with her example in mind.

[8]On Naboth's honored place see the remarks of Gray, *I and II Kings,* 391.

this offense. Ahab dresses incognito as a common charioteer in going into battle. He chooses this low position with a view to escaping death for it is known that the enemy will only go after the king. He should be safe, in a way perhaps that the honored Naboth should have been against any hostility within his community, but a stray arrow strikes him. The certain man who drew his bow at a venture was deviating from orders because the king alone was to be killed. Recall the role of the sons of Belial, a description synonymous with deviant conduct: both they and the archer are nameless individuals. The precise detail of Ahab's retribution for his offense seems to have inspired the Deuteronomic use of the precise formula of the *jus talionis*. If so, the link between the story and the law suggests that its expression in Deut 19:21 is not to be understood literally, at the level of the practical administration of justice.

Law: Precautions against certain individuals dying in war

> [1] When thou goest out to battle against thine enemies, and seest horses, and chariots, and a people more than thou, be not afraid of them: for Yahweh thy God is with thee, which brought thee up out of the land of Egypt. [2] And it shall be, when ye are come nigh unto the battle, that the priest shall approach and speak unto the people, [3] and shall say unto them, Hear, O Israel, ye approach this day unto battle against your enemies: let not your hearts faint, fear not, and do not tremble, neither be ye terrified because of them; [4] for Yahweh your God is he that goeth with you, to fight for you against your enemies, to save you. [5] And the officers shall speak unto the people, saying, What man is there that hath built a new house, and hath not consecrated it? let him go and return to his house, lest he die in the battle, and another man consecrate it. [6] And what man is he that hath planted a vineyard, and hath not yet profaned it? let him also go and return unto his house, lest he die in the battle, and another man profane it. [7] And what man is there that hath betrothed a wife, and hath not taken her? let him go and return unto his house, lest he die in the battle, and another man take her. [8] And the officers shall speak further unto the people, and they shall say, What man is there that is fearful and faint-hearted? let him go and return unto his house, lest his brethren's heart melt as well as his heart. [9] And it shall be, when the officers have made an end of speaking unto the people, that they shall make captains of the armies to lead the people. (Deut 20:1–9)

Background: Ahab dies in battle; Saul attempts to have David killed in battle; Gideon directs the fainthearted

> [20] And Yahweh said, Who shall deceive Ahab, that he may go up and fall at Ramoth-gilead? And one said on this manner, and another said on that manner. [21] And there came forth a spirit, and stood before Yahweh, and said, I will deceive him. [22] And Yahweh said unto him, Wherewith? And he said, I will go forth, and I will be a lying spirit in the mouth of all his prophets. And he said, Thou shalt deceive him, and prevail also: go forth, and do so. (1 Kings 22:20–22)

> [20] And Michal Saul's daughter loved David: and they told Saul, and the thing pleased him. [21] And Saul said, I will give him her, that she may be a snare to him, and that the hand of the Philistines may be against him. . . . [25] And Saul said, Thus shall ye say to David, The king desireth not any dowry, but an hundred foreskins of the Philistines, to be avenged of the king's enemies. . . . [27] Wherefore David arose and went, he and his men, and slew of the Philistines two hundred men; and David brought their foreskins, and they gave them in full tale to the king, that he might be the king's son in law. And Saul gave him Michal his daughter to wife. (1 Sam 18:20, 21, 25, 27)

> [2] And Yahweh said unto Gideon, The people that are with thee are too many for me to give the Midianites into their hands, lest Israel vaunt themselves against me, saying, Mine own hand hath saved me. [3] Now therefore go to, proclaim in the ears of the people, saying, Whosoever is fearful and afraid, let him return and depart early from mount Gilead. And there returned of the people twenty and two thousand; and there remained ten thousand. (Judg 7:2, 3)

Benhadad should have been put to death at the conclusion of the fighting he unsuccessfully waged against the Israelites. Ahab offended by not doing so. This offense was followed by the putting to death of a man who should not have died. In the law granting exemption from war service for certain Israelites, the concern in regard to three such individuals is that they should not face death in battle. This issue arises from the focus upon the means by which a leading Israelite, King Ahab himself, met death in battle. The lawgiver continues his exploration of confrontations between prophet and king. God, by means of his prophet, caused Israel to go against its enemies so that one of them, its leader, might die. Note the concern with the death in battle of a single Israelite. The Deuteronomist has thought about this strange episode, has noted the use of war for the purpose of bringing vengeance upon Ahab for the perversion of justice against Naboth, and has raised the contrasting, more reasonable issue: in going against their enemies, are there Israelites who should be saved from the prospect of death in war?

The three singled out are the Israelite who has built a new house but has not "consecrated" it, the one who has planted a vineyard and not "profaned" it (eaten the fruit), and the one who has betrothed a woman but not yet taken her. In regard to each of them the fear is expressed, "lest he die in the battle." We can pinpoint why these three categories are singled out, the first two from reflection upon Ahab's situation and the third from reflection upon a comparable event in the time of a predecessor of his, King Saul.[9] Ahab's death in battle fulfilled Elijah's prophecy that his house would not be established, that it would be obliterated like his evil predecessor's, Jeroboam's (1 Kings 21:22). In the notice about his demise there is even a reference to an ivory house that he had built (1 Kings 22:39). His death would also have meant that although he had newly acquired Naboth's vineyard he did not live to make use of it. The lawgiver simply strips Ahab's situation of its exceptional, wrongful elements in order to come up with his contrasting examples. This contrast is echoed in the narrative, in the description of the forthcoming battle scene: "I [Micaiah] saw all Israel scattered upon the hills, as sheep that have not a shepherd: and Yahweh said, These have no master: let them return every man to his house in peace" (1 Kings 22:17).

The unusual term *ḥānak,* "to consecrate" (the man's house), is used in reference to God's house, the temple, in Solomon's dedication of it (1 Kings 8:63). The reason for its use in the law is linked to the fact that there is a close relationship between the notion of God's establishing his house and the notion of his establishing the king's house—Saul's, David's, Solomon's, Jeroboam's, and Ahab's—in the sense of hereditary rule. At the level of the ordinary Israelite there will be present the idea that a man setting up his house enters into a God-given inheritance.

Use of the term *ḥālal,* "to profane" (the man's vineyard), can be

[9]Needless to say, I am not thereby excluding by this explanation the possibility that the rules had a reality in customary usage.

explained by observing that Ahab had profaned Naboth's ancestral vineyard by acquiring it. Note how God profaned (*ḥālal*) his inheritance (Israel) by giving it over to Babylon (Isa 47:6). The view that a man's vineyard is his inheritance from God is fundamental to the story about Naboth and Ahab. Moreover, the idea of profaning it is actually brought out. When Ahab asked Naboth for it the latter exclaimed, "*ḥālîlah*," literally, "To profaneness!" at the thought of his giving it over. By recalling this aspect, the lawgiver would readily focus upon the idea that in taking for the first time the fruit of his vineyard an Israelite profaned it by the mere fact that he makes use of something inherently sacred.

The Deuteronomist is typically alert to comparable developments in the traditions available to him. A parallel to the use of war in order to deny an Israelite his inheritance in the land is found in 1 Sam 18:17–27. Saul attempted to have David killed in battle by offering his daughter Michal on condition that he bring back one hundred foreskins of the Philistines. The category in the law of the man who is exempt from war service because he has betrothed a wife but not yet taken her is the product of a negative reaction to the circumstances surrounding David's betrothal to Michal.

More evidence that the Ahab narrative has determined the shape and substance of the legal material in Deut 20:1–9 comes from observing the shared interest in the overwhelming military might of Israel's enemies. Ahab faced an army of thirty-three kings and had to bow to their power without even putting up a fight. The way, however, in which Benhadad intended to realize the terms of the treaty forced upon Ahab was too humiliating to be gone along with, and Israel resisted. A prophet informed Ahab that despite the tremendous disparity in numbers God would fight for Israel and give them the victory. This happened. A second battle ensued and again the overwhelming might of the enemy is stressed by the narrator. Instead of the kings who led in the first battle, commanders took their place and an army was mustered like the first one, "horse for horse, and chariot for chariot" (1 Kings 20:25). The scene was such that Israel was "like two little flocks of kids; but the Syrians [Arameans] filled the country" (1 Kings 20:27). A prophet's prediction that God would deliver this great multitude (including Benhadad himself) into Israel's hands again proved accurate.

The opening words of the law portray a situation identical to the one Ahab faced: "When thou goest out to battle against thine enemies, and seest horses, and chariots, and a people more than thou, be not afraid of them: for Yahweh thy God is with thee." The use of the term "people" and not "army" has nothing to do with theological notions of the nature of Israel's army, as A. D. H. Mayes thinks,[10] but with Benhadad's boast about all the people that will follow him against Israel (1 Kings 20:10).

Wherever he can, the Deuteronomist links activity in the time of the kings to Moses' own time. He does it again in this issue of Israel's confronting enemies, indicating the link with his language. In the law the people assembling for war are urged by the priest not to be afraid. The phrase used is the one the Deuteronomist uses in his description of the time when the fathers of the Israelite tribes spied out the valley of Eshcol, and returned and discouraged the people from entering (Deut 1:29). Their fear then stemmed from the daunting nature of the Amorite enemy. The spies "melted" the hearts of their fellow Israelites with their depiction of the enemy (Deut 1:28). The law exempts from military service the man who is fearful and liable to "melt" the hearts of his comrades. The verb *māsas* only occurs in these two contexts in Deuteronomy.

The reason for returning to this episode in Moses' own time is not just the link with the topic of the enemy's overwhelming might. There is an even more specific reason. The Eshcol incident was used by Moses to rebuke those tribes, Reuben, Gad, and Manasseh, when he had to raise with them the subject of military exemption (Num 32:1–32). These tribes had many cattle (Num 32:1; cp., Deut 3:19, "I know that ye have much cattle") and had requested to settle in the good cattle land of Jazer and Gilead. Ahab eventually died, it might be noted, while seeking to repossess for Israel a city of this region, Ramoth-gilead. Moses interpreted the request as opting out of military duty and an attempt, similar to the earlier one at Eshcol, to discourage the tribes from seeking to possess the land west of the Jordan. In his account of this JE narrative Moses is reported as communicating to the people, "Ye shall not fear them [the enemy]: for Yahweh your God he shall fight for you" (Deut 3:22).[11] This exhor-

[10]*Deuteronomy* NCBC (Grand Rapids: Eerdmans, 1981), 292.

[11]For the Deuteronomist's use of the JE material, see S. R. Driver, *Deuteronomy* ICC, 59, and my *Laws of Deuteronomy* (Ithaca: Cornell University Press, 1974), 119–21.

tation is very similar to his statement in the law: "For Yahweh your God is he that goeth with you, to fight for you against your enemies, to save" (Deut 20:4). Noteworthy is the switch in the law from the use of the second-person singular to the second-person plural. The reason is that the second-person plural reflects the use of the "You" form in Numbers 32 and Deut 1:19–46, 3:18–22, where Moses addressed the people directly, as against the "Thou" form in 1 Kings 20, where a prophet (like Moses) addressed Ahab singly on behalf of all the people. This linguistic variation is indeed, as critics have commonly claimed, an indication of composite sources, but the variation does not suggest, as they might think, evidence that an old law has been subject to Deuteronomic reshaping.[12] Rather, the entire law belongs to the original redactive process by which it and all the others have been produced.

Although the language of the exemption granted to the Israelite who is fearful and fainthearted seems to reflect Moses' words about the damage done by the discouraging report of the spies in Deut 1:28, there is an actual example in Judg 7:3 of men made to return home before a battle because of their fear. Gideon, in a direction from the deity, proclaimed: "Whoever is fearful and afraid, let him return and depart from mount Gilead." Twenty-two thousand responded. That this precedent is incorporated into Deut 20:1–9 is suggested by the fact that Gideon was a member of the half tribe of Manasseh (Judg 6:15), and we have just seen that on an earlier occasion Moses considered a request from it, and from the tribes Reuben and Gad, for release from battle duty.

Law: Those subject to death among Israel's enemies

[10] When thou comest nigh unto a city to fight against it, then proclaim peace unto it. [11] And it shall be, if it make thee answer of peace, and open unto thee, then it shall be, that all the people that is found therein shall be forced labour for thee, and they shall serve thee. [12] And if it will make no peace with thee, but will make war against thee, then thou shalt besiege it: [13] and when Yahweh thy God hath delivered it into thine hands, thou shalt smite every male thereof with the edge of the sword: [14] but the women,

[12]To be more precise: there could have been a preexisting law, but the language of the Deuteronomic formulation is *not* an indication of its existence.

> and the little ones, and the cattle, and all that is in the city, even all the spoil thereof, shalt thou take unto thyself; and thou shalt enjoy the spoil of thine enemies, which Yahweh thy God hath given thee. [15] Thus shalt thou do unto all the cities which are very far off from thee, which are not of the cities of these nations. [16] But of the cities of these people, which Yahweh thy God doth give thee for an inheritance, thou shalt save alive nothing that breatheth: [17] but thou shalt utterly destroy them; namely, the Hittites, and the Amorites, the Canaanites, and the Perizzites, the Hivites, and the Jebusites; as Yahweh thy God hath commanded thee: [18] that they teach you not to do after all their abominations, which they have done unto their gods; so should ye sin against Yahweh your God. (Deut 20:10–18)

Background: Ahab's enemies and the Amorite enemy in Moses' time

Benhadad, the king of Aram, along with thirty-two other kings, besieged Samaria and sent in messengers to propose peaceful terms to Ahab. They were accepted. It was only after a complicating factor introduced by Benhadad, to the effect that he would have his messengers enter Ahab's houses to fetch his pledge, that Ahab renounced the peace treaty and resolved to fight (1 Kings 20:1–12).

> [26] And I [Moses] sent messengers out of the wilderness of Kedemoth unto Sihon king of Heshbon with words of peace, saying, [27] Let me pass through thy land: I will go along by the highway, I will neither turn unto the right hand nor to the left. [28] Thou shalt sell me food for money, that I may eat; and give me water for money, that I may drink: only I will pass through on my feet; [29] as the children of Esau which dwell in Seir, and the Moabites which dwell in Ar, did unto me; until I shall pass over Jordan into the land which Yahweh our God giveth us. [30] But Sihon king of Heshbon would not let us pass by him: for Yahweh thy God hardened his spirit, and made his heart obstinate, that he might deliver him into thy hand, as appeareth this day. [34] And we took all his cities at that time, and utterly destroyed the men, and the women, and the little ones, of every city, we left none to remain: [35] only the cattle we took for a prey unto ourselves, and the spoil of the cities which we took. (Deut 2:26–30, 34, 35; cp., Num 21:21–32)

From the narrower, more unusual concern with those who should not have to face the prospect of death in battle (in contrast to the equally narrow and extremely unusual interest in the death of a side's leader in battle), the lawgiver turns his attention to the question of who among Israel's enemies should be killed in warfare. It is no surprise to find that he concentrates first on the relationship between Ahab and his enemy Benhadad, and then on Israel's Amorite and Canaanite enemies. Issues raised in regard to these groups were integrated into the preceding law. It is useful to remember that Benhadad should eventually have been put to death as an enemy of Israel and that Ahab offended by not doing so. His offense is looked at once again in order to explore it in a wider context.

Because Israel accepted the position at the time, the Deuteronomist judges that Benhadad's initial move to besiege a city of Israel is an appropriate one for Israel to adopt: "When thou comest nigh unto a city to fight against it, then proclaim peace unto it." If the offer is accepted forced service is to be exacted of the other party, as Benhadad did to Ahab and his subjects. If the offer is declined the siege is to proceed and all the males are to be slaughtered. Ahab's decision not to go through with the peace treaty resulted in a reversal of fortune for Benhadad. This reversal, predicted and directed by Yahweh's prophet (1 Kings 20:13, 14), would have encouraged the Deuteronomist to view Benhadad's initial hold over Israel differently, and consider what Israel might do in a comparable situation. During the course of two battles, all the males, with the wrongful exception of Benhadad (and possibly some of his servants), were killed (1 Kings 20:21, 29, 30, 33). The outcome of this fighting determines the thrust of that section of the Deuteronomic law on the subject of Israel's having to proceed hostilely against the "cities which are very far off from thee, which are not of the cities of these nations." Benhadad and his fellow monarchs would, if Israel chose to besiege their cities (as happened in the inconclusive attack upon Ramoth-gilead [1 Kings 22:1–4, 29]), fall into this category of nation-cities whose population is not liable to total extermination.

The other category, "the cities of these people, which Yahweh thy God doth give thee for an inheritance," is subject to complete destruction. As in his preceding law, the Deuteronomist turns from the period of the kings back to Moses' own time and to the accounts about

Israel's battles then with the Amorites and Canaanites (Deut 2:26–3:11; Num 21:21–35). These groups lived on the east side of the Jordan and in the case of the Amorite king, Sihon of Heshbon, a peace proposal was put to him by Moses. The response was negative, because Yahweh had determined it to be so (Deut 2:30), and all the inhabitants of the city were destroyed.[13] In the law, as in the comparable material in Deut 7:1–5, Moses is seen to be thinking of the cities on the west side of the Jordan where the main part of the Israelite nation will eventually settle. These he wants to be subject not to a peace treaty but to automatic destruction, because Yahweh had indicated that this was his intention. Scrutiny of the abortive peace treaties between Benhadad and Ahab and between Moses and Sihon leads the Deuteronomist to formulate the joint laws about dealing with cities far and near. Indeed, these two episodes illustrate well how the Deuteronomist proceeds in constructing his rules, in particular, how he evaluates Yahweh's role.

We noted in the preceding law the switch from the "Thou" form to the "You" form that occurs when the Deuteronomist returns to the earlier Mosaic period. The same switch is observable here. The "Thou" form, which is the dominant, preferred form in the legal material, gives way again to the "You" form in Deut 20:18. "You" is found, for example, in the comparable expressions of concern in Deut 7:4, 5.

Law: An enemy's fruit trees not to be the object of killing

> [19] When thou shalt besiege a city a long time, in making war against it to take it, thou shalt not destroy the trees thereof by forcing an ax against them: for thou mayest eat of them, and thou shalt not cut them down. Are the trees in the field men that they should be besieged by thee? [20] Only the trees which thou knowest that they be not trees for food, thou shalt destroy and cut them down; and thou shalt build bulwarks against the city that maketh war with thee, until it be subdued. (Deut 20:19, 20)

[13]The interdependent relationship between Deut 2:26–35 and Num 21:21–35 is revealing. The Deuteronomic account makes explicit what is implicit in Numbers—for example, the mention of the peace proposal. It is precisely this process that is often at work in a law's relationship to its influencing tradition.

Background: The siege of Moab and the destruction of its trees

After Ahab's siege of the city of Ramoth-gilead, which ended in his death, the next incident involving an Israelite siege of an enemy is the attack on Moab, which had rebelled against Israel (2 Kings 1:1, 3:5). Elisha, Elijah's successor as prophet, was consulted about prospects of victory after the combined armies of Israel, Judah, and Edom were faced with conditions of drought. To show no doubt that it was the deity who would be responsible for any victory, he predicted that the dry streambeds would become pools of water. He further predicted that they would conquer fortified cities, and in doing so they should fell all the good trees, stop up all the springs of water, and heap stones upon good pieces of land. The water duly came; the Moabites, thinking that the kings had fought one another, mistook the sun-struck water for blood, and were attacked, pursued, and overwhelmed. The Israelites proceeded to do what Elisha had directed—for example, they felled every good tree (2 Kings 3).

After the preceding interest in what constitutes the proper object of killing in warfare, it is somewhat less puzzling to find a rule in which the concern is that the Israelites do not destroy an enemy's fruit trees when they are involved in the siege of a city. We have come to expect two things, first, that a law should fit into a context already formulated by what precedes it, either in the substance of the previously presented law or in the influencing narrative, or in both of these; and, second, it should issue from a response to something that is found in a tradition. The law about the fruit trees proves to be no exception. In regard to the former expectation, the tradition that has come under scrutiny in the preceding law prohibited the Israelites from contending with the Moabites in battle and taking their land (Deut 2:9). In later Israelite history such a battle did take place, and it is not surprising that the Deuteronomist is interested in this development, especially since he continuously looks back and forth between the period of the kings and the time of Moses. It is equally noteworthy that in scrutinizing this later battle he is interested in one aspect only, namely, the Israelites should not have contended with the Moabites' fruit trees.

The role of the prophets has been a recurring feature in the lawgiver's attention to the histories. A prophet also plays a role in the narrative behind the fruit tree law. In response to Elisha's directions, the lawgiver apparently reacts to an irrational element in them. The Israelites faced conditions of drought. To be sure, a miracle had overcome them and they were rescued from a bad situation. What the Deuteronomist has probably noted, however, is that by felling every good tree they were denying themselves a source of food, in effect creating adverse conditions similar to those they had been saved from. He therefore presents a law that takes stock of this contradictory situation and in a spirit of practical wisdom—in part determined by the recognition that supernatural help cannot always be expected—calls for a distinction between fruit-bearing and non-fruit-bearing trees. The former should not be cut down, the latter, for the purpose of building siege works, should. The rhetorical statement in which the trees are personified, "Are the trees in the field men that they should be besieged by thee,"[14] ties in with the Deuteronomist's previous sensitivity about who should and who should not be destroyed in war.

The formulation of this rule aptly illustrates the Deuteronomist's interest in wisdom teaching. The process has been first to note the strange development in the story and then to construct a rule about trees in warfare that addresses itself to some practical aspect of warfare. Wisdom teaching about the importance of distinguishing between life and death underlies its construction.

SUMMARY Prophetic activity in relation to the kings dominates a series of laws. The influence of deviant practices designed to make contact with the supernatural was constant throughout the history of the kings. A rule proscribes an exhaustive list of such practices. Throughout this history there appeared prophets who were regarded as legitimate representatives of the divine will, who made predictions in the name of Yahweh that came to pass. At the same time other prophets attempted to do this but their predictions failed. Ahab's reign illustrated the situation well and informs the rule distinguishing between true and false prophets. A prophet by means of a sign caused Ahab to condemn himself for releasing Benhadad who deserved to die. Ahab had released him on the basis of the promise that certain cities, one of which was a city of refuge for manslayers, would be

[14]This reading requires a minor alteration in the Masoretic vocalization which, as Driver (*Deuteronomy* ICC, 240) points out, yields no sense.

restored to Israel. In the end this city was not won back and Ahab died at heaven's hand in the attempt to force its restoration, because he had come under a sentence of death. The lawgiver uses the incident to clarify the law about how the cities of refuge function in regard to manslayers and to state on what basis new cities might be added.

Ahab's attempt to acquire Naboth's vineyard, though gone about in a businesslike fashion, nonetheless offended custom. This customary rule is spelled out. Jezebel resorted to false witness, and involved the local dignitaries for the purpose of condemning Naboth and permitting Ahab to acquire his vineyard. This incident, condemned by the prophet Elijah, has dictated that a case of false witness come before the central tribunal and not before any local court. The extraordinary incident in which the deity, according to the prophet Micaiah, used a battle to encompass the death of Ahab, because of his offense against Naboth, raises the issue of Israelites who should be singled out so as to avoid death in battle. At Ahab's death his house was not established, in part because he had profaned Naboth's vineyard by acquiring it. Israelites singled out for military exemption include the one who has not yet established his house and the one who has not yet profaned his vineyard by acquiring its fruit. At an earlier period King Saul tried to bring about the death of David in battle by having him betrothed to his daughter and requiring that he pay one hundred foreskins for her. This incident is behind the exemption granted to the man who has betrothed a woman but not yet taken her.

Benhadad's terms of peace to Ahab, which included an obligation on the part of the latter to do forced service, were first accepted by Ahab. In putting the treaty into effect Benhadad offended, and in the subsequent fighting that was directed by a prophet, Ahab defeated the armies of the many nation-cities involved. Benhadad's initial procedure is laid out in a law as the one to be adopted by Israel in its dealings with cities distant from Israel. For those cities that Israel intend to conquer and occupy, Moses bases the rule as to whether their inhabitants should live or die on his own experience with them on the east side of the Jordan. Their inhabitants, with the exception of the Ammonites, Edomites, and Moabites, were destroyed, because despite efforts to make peace it turned out that Yahweh intended their destruction. The law requires that the cities on the west side of the Jordan should be similarly destroyed. In the siege subsequent to that which Ahab laid against Benhadad, the Israelites under Elisha's direction went against the Moabites. In doing so they felled every tree, despite the fact that a miracle had been needed to overcome conditions of drought. A law takes up the subject of besieging an enemy and concentrates on the practical matter of saving trees that can provide a source of food, and cutting down those that can be used to build siege works.

CHAPTER 5

MISDIRECTED HOSTILITY

The sages—for example, those in the Book of Proverbs—teach the need to purge confusion by means of the capacity to make proper distinctions. The influence of wisdom counsel on Deuteronomy is considerable and an interest in appropriate distinctions shows up in Deuteronomy. The concern with killing that is improper because it represents a failure to identify the true object of enmity is carried over into the law that follows about the man found slain in the field or, rather, into the scrutiny of the tradition that prompts this narrow focus. In the pursuit of the Moabites, Israel, so the Deuteronomist judged, should not have cut down all their trees. It was an inappropriate thing to do because some of them, the fruit trees, could have provided a source of food and hence sustained life should the siege have been a long one. The Deuteronomist in a number of laws then concentrates upon occasions when people were, from one perspective or another, inappropriately treated as objects of enmity, switching his interest from confrontations between prophet and king. In his use of traditions the Deuteronomist first explores an incident from the time of the kings (involving David, whose betrothal to Michal was mentioned earlier), before turning to the earliest example of the problem back in the time of the ancestor Jacob.

Law: The man found slain in the field

[1] If one be found slain in the land which Yahweh thy God giveth thee to possess it, lying in the field, and it be not known who hath slain him: [2] then thy elders and thy judges shall come forth, and they shall measure unto the cities which are round about him that is slain: [3] and it shall be, that the city which is next unto the slain man, even the elders of that city shall take an heifer, which hath not been wrought with, and which hath not drawn in the yoke; [4] and the elders of that city shall bring down the heifer to a valley with running water, which is neither ploughed nor sown, and shall break the heifer's neck there in the valley: [5] and the priests the sons of Levi shall come near; for them Yahweh thy God hath chosen to minister unto him, and to bless in the name of Yahweh; and by their word shall every controversy and every stroke be tried: [6] and all the elders of that city, that are next unto the slain man, shall wash their hands over the heifer whose neck was broken in the valley: [7] and they shall answer and say, Our hands have not shed this blood, neither have our eyes seen it. [8] Be merciful, O Yahweh, unto thy people Israel, whom thou hast redeemed, and set not innocent blood in the midst of thy people. And the blood shall be forgiven them. [9] So thou shalt put away the guilt of innocent blood from thy midst, when thou shalt do that which is right in the sight of Yahweh. (Deut 21:1–9)

Background: Joab slays Amasa and casts his body into a field

[1] And there happened to be there a man of Belial, whose name was Sheba, the son of Bichri, a Benjaminite: and he blew a trumpet, and said, We have no part in David, neither have we inheritance in the son of Jesse: every man to his tents, O Israel. [2] So every man of Israel went up from after David, and followed Sheba the son of Bichri: but the men of Judah clave unto their king, from Jordan even to Jerusalem. . . . [4] Then said the king to Amasa, Assemble me the men of Judah within three days, and be thou here present. [5] So Amasa went to assemble the men of Judah: but he tarried longer than the set time which he had appointed him. [6] And David said to Abishai, Now shall Sheba the son of Bichri do us more harm than did Absalom: take thou thy lord's servants, and pursue after him, lest he get him fenced cities, and escape us. [7] And there went out after him Joab's men, and the Cherethites, and the Pelethites, and all the mighty men: and they went out of Jerusa-

> lem, to pursue Sheba the son of Bichri. [8] When they were at the great stone which is in Gibeon, Amasa went before them. And Joab's garment that he had put on was girded unto him, and upon it a girdle with a sword fastened upon his loins in the sheaf thereof; and as he went forth it fell out. [9] And Joab said to Amasa, Art thou in health, my brother? And Joab took Amasa by the beard with the right hand to kiss him. [10] But Amasa took no heed to the sword that was in Joab's hand: so he smote him therewith in the fifth rib, and shed out his bowels to the ground, and struck him not again; and he died. So Joab and Abishai his brother pursued after Sheba the son of Bichri. [11] And one of Joab's men stood by him, and said, He that favoureth Joab, and he that is for David, let him go after Joab. [12] And Amasa wallowed in blood in the midst of the highway. And when the man saw that all the people stood still, he removed Amasa out of the highway into the field, and cast a cloth upon him, when he saw that every one that came by him stood still. [13] When he was removed out of the highway, all the people went on after Joab, to pursue after Sheba the son of Bichri. (2 Sam 20: 1, 2, 4–13)

From one pursuit of an enemy the lawgiver turns to another that similarly involved a misperception of who constituted an enemy worthy of destruction. The Deuteronomist would have noted that just as an Israelite should not have regarded trees as enemies, so more seriously in this instance, Joab should not have confused war and peace. Sheba was the enemy to be destroyed, not Amasa. Joab was avenging Amasa's role in the earlier rebellion against David that Joab crushed but that Amasa survived. Already in a separate tradition the nature of Joab's wrongdoing is spelled out. He had, according to David on his deathbed, "shed the blood of war in peace" (1 Kings 2:5). The Deuteronomist pays particular attention to what befell Amasa's body. For him the unburied corpse signifies an offense: it lies upon the land that has been given as an inheritance to Israel and therefore constitutes a repellent mixture of death in the midst of life.

A noteworthy and puzzling feature of the law is its narrow interest in the blemish caused by a slaying. The opening statement indicates this focus: "If one be found slain in the land which Yahweh thy God giveth thee to possess it, lying in the field." The interest is not in the unknown assailant but in a ceremonial procedure leading up to a prayer that God might remove the stain of innocent blood. The ceremony of slaughtering a heifer, one that has not been worked and that has not pulled in the yoke, at a place in the land which has not been plowed or sown and which is beside a perpetually flowing stream, is designed to imitate the dramatic and shocking contrast between the dead man and the life-giving land that is Israel's. Both the heifer and the piece of land where it is slaughtered are characterized by their untapped vitality.[1]

The link between the story and the law clarifies much, including, as indicated, the focus upon the slain man. The story's opening statement contains the term *ḥālal,* "to slay, pierce," which refers to a specific mode of dying—typically, for example, by the sword, as in Joab's slaying of Amasa.[2] In the story we know who did the killing and that it was a wrongful one. In the law it is not known who did the killing, but the presumption is, and it need not have been, that the homicide is a wrongful one, that innocent blood was shed.[3] The lawgiver can only take up a suggested case from the story, but he nonetheless incorporates elements that are found in the story. He thinks of the body of Amasa that was thrown into a field. So far as the story relates the corpse simply remained there. It is this development the lawgiver chooses to concentrate upon. Joab did eventually die for his offenses, including his killing of Amasa, but nothing was done about the killing at the time. To reflect upon a parallel example likely to occur in circumstances different from those of the civil war in David's time, the lawgiver has to invent an unknown assailant. Had the killer been known, his judicial execution would have expiated the shedding of innocent blood and obviated the need for the ceremony involving the heifer. That approach would not have enabled the lawgiver to focus on the horror of the slain body juxtaposed with the land.

The prayer of forgiveness to be recited at the ceremony requests

[1]For details, see my "A Common Element in Five Supposedly Disparate Laws," *VT* 29 (1979):129–34. The priests attend the ceremony not because of the ritual involved but because they represent central authority. They are present because the body was found outside the local towns, and thus they may be needed to mediate a possible dispute over which town is responsible for expiating the blood-guilt.

[2]In the law the term *hrg* is used also. It is the term used in 1 Kings 2:32, when Joab slays Amasa by the sword.

[3]It is this bias in the law that has confused critics and caused them to see the ceremony of the heifer as an attempt to represent the punishment of the unknown murderer. See my "Disparate Laws," 131.

that innocent blood be not laid upon the people of Israel. This was David's and then Solomon's fear about their house, because of Joab's deed (1 Kings 2:5, 31).

In the arrangement of material in 2 Samuel 20, 21, the story of Amasa's end is followed by the account of how David sought to expiate the blood-guilt that was upon Saul and his house because Saul had killed the Gibeonites. The latter requested that seven of Saul's sons be put to death. The request was granted and they were duly slaughtered. David's need to have this act of expiation was because the land had been affected by the blood-guilt (2 Sam 21:1). What is expressed in the law on the slain man is precisely the concern of the story about David and the Gibeonites. This shared feature supports the view that the Deuteronomist is working upon the story of Amasa's death in his law. It probably also indicates that he is responsible for placing one story after the other.[4] We shall see that the law on the hanged man (Deut 21:22, 23) reflects upon the fact that the hanging corpses of Saul's sons in turn affected the land.

Law: The female captive

> [10] When thou goest forth to war against thine enemies, and Yahweh thy God hath delivered them into thine hands, and thou hast taken them captive, [11] and seest among the captives a beautiful woman, and hast a desire unto her, that thou wouldest have her to thy wife; [12] then thou shalt bring her home to thine house; and she shall shave her head, and pare her nails; [13] and she shall put the raiment of her captivity from off her, and shall remain in thine house, and bewail her father and her mother a full month: and after that thou shalt go in unto her, and be her husband, and she shall be thy wife. [14] And it shall be, if thou have no delight in her, then thou shalt let her go whither she will; but thou shalt not sell her at all for money, thou shalt not treat her oppressively, because thou hast humbled her. (Deut 21:10–14)

Background: Laban's pursuit of Jacob

> [25] Then Laban overtook Jacob. . . . [26] And Laban said to Jacob, What hast thou done, that thou hast stolen away unawares

[4]Interpreters have difficulty relating the material in 2 Samuel 21 to the preceding narrative. See H. P. Smith, *Samuel* ICC (Edinburgh: T. and T. Clark, 1904), 373.

> to me, and carried away my daughters, as captives taken with the sword? [27] Wherefore didst thou flee away secretly, and steal away from me; and didst not tell me, that I might have sent thee away with mirth, and with songs, with tabret, and with harp? [28] and hast not suffered me to kiss my sons and my daughters? thou hast now done foolishly in so doing. [29] It is in the power of my hand to do you hurt: but the God of your father spake unto me yesternight, saying, Take thou heed that thou speak not to Jacob either good or bad. [30] And now, though thou wouldest needs be gone, because thou sore longedst after thy father's house, yet wherefore hast thou stolen my gods? [31] And Jacob answered and said to Laban, Because I was afraid: for I said, Peradventure thou wouldest take by force thy daughters from me. [32] With whomsoever thou findest thy gods, let him not live: before our brethren discern thou what is thine with me, and take it to thee. For Jacob knew not that Rachel had stolen them. . . . [48] And Laban said, This heap is a witness between me and thee this day. Therefore was the name of it called Galeed; [49] and Mizpah; for he said, Yahweh watch between me and thee, when we are absent one from another. [50] If thou shalt humble my daughters, or if thou shalt take other wives beside my daughters, no man is with us; see, God is witness betwixt me and thee. (Gen 31:25–32, 48–50)

Like the tradition behind the law on the slain man, the one that generates a statement about an Israelite's acquisition of a foreign woman in war also concerns a pursuit and a complaint that, in this instance, two women were being treated like enemies in war. This common feature explains why the lawgiver moves, bewilderingly as it may first appear, from the one topic to the other.

Israel's relations with the Arameans went back, long before Ahab's with Benhadad, to Jacob's with Laban. Like Ahab and Benhadad there was hostility between them, as evidenced by Laban's cheating Jacob and the latter's response. Jacob sought to acquire Laban's daughter, Rachel, as a wife but he was duped into taking her sister, Leah, as well. Treated as a hired servant, he eventually rebelled and decided to return to his ancestral land. When he announced this decision to Rachel and Leah, they criticized their father for denying them "part or inheritance" in his house (Gen 31:14). When Sheba rebelled against King David he had announced his dissatisfaction in the same terms (2 Sam 20:1).

Laban's comparison of Jacob's action to the taking of women in war has inspired the law about an Israelite's acquisition of a captive woman as a wife. The Deuteronomist chooses to take up the topic in less idiosyncratic circumstances. Two other factors are relevant. In keeping with his preceding interest in misplaced enmity (the fruit trees and a fellow soldier), the Deuteronomist notes the nature of Laban's complaint: it was inappropriate for his daughters to be driven off "like captives of the sword." Again, the daughters' complaint that their inheritance has been denied them is a subject that becomes a dominant one in succeeding laws.

Elements of the story cast light on what is stated in the law. The remarkable reference about the Israelite's beholding among the captives a woman "beautiful in form" (*yᵉpat-tōʾar*) has someone like Rachel in mind. The expression is found in the Pentateuch solely in regard to Rachel (Gen 29:17) and to the woman in the law. Only someone like the Aramean Rachel could be taken as a captive in accord with the preceding rules about who of the enemy should or should not be killed in war. For places "far off" such as Aram the women were to be spared (Deut 20:14). The captive woman has to mourn her parents even though they may well be alive. When Rachel and Leah left their parental home it is understood that they were likely never to see their kin again. Laban acknowledged that Jacob longed to return to his father's house (Gen 31:30), but if he had not been so concerned about the theft of his household gods, he might well have asked for some sympathy for himself.

Rachel's motivation for taking the gods is not made clear. Most likely she simply wished to maintain contact with her homeland. Her possession of the gods may well be what prompted the directions in the law about how the captive shall symbolically sever contact with her past: put off the raiment of her captive state, shave her head, pare her nails, bewail her parents for a month.[5] The Deuteronomist would certainly have found an Aramean woman's possession of family gods unacceptable in his time.

A strong indication that the details of the story have influenced the writing up of the law is to be seen in the consideration given to the

[5]For a possible parallel from Mari in which hair and clothing are removed during a rite symbolizing severance from homeland, see M. Du Buit, "Quelques contacts bibliques dans les archives royales de Mari," *RB* 66 (1959):576–77.

possibility of the union not working out. Laban sought to make Jacob agree that in their subsequent life with him his daughters would not be "humbled" (*ʿinnāh*). Because he would not be there to protect his daughters' rights, Laban sought assurance that Jacob would not take any wives in addition to Rachel and Leah (Gen 31:50). No doubt he wanted to be sure that if Jacob sought to rid himself of them he would not, in keeping with his action of treating them like captives, regard them as slaves to be sold. Their father would not be around to protect their rights. Laban's concern finds expression in the law: the captive woman is judged to be "humbled" (*ʿinnāh*) should her Israelite husband grow to dislike her and rid himself of her. In the event of this happening she must not be sold for money.[6]

Law: The right of the first-born son

> [15] If a man have two wives, one beloved, and another hated, and they have born him children, both the beloved and the hated; and if the firstborn son be her's that was hated: [16] then it shall be, when he maketh his sons to inherit that which he hath, that he may not make the son of the beloved firstborn before the son of the hated, which is indeed the firstborn: [17] but he shall acknowledge the son of the hated for the firstborn, by giving him a double portion of all that he hath: for he is the first-fruits of his strength; the right of the firstborn is his. (Deut 21:15–17)

Background: Jacob's problem with his first-born

> [31] And when Yahweh saw that Leah was hated, he opened her womb: but Rachel was barren. [32] And Leah conceived, and bare a son, and she called his name Reuben: for she said, Surely Yahweh hath looked upon my affliction; now therefore my husband will love me. (Gen 29:31, 32)

> [22] And it came to pass, when Israel dwelt in that land, that Reuben went and lay with Bilhah his father's concubine: and Israel heard it. (Gen 35:22)

[6] I have tried to show that the Deuteronomist may well have looked at comparable elements in other traditions about the patriarchs' wives before drafting the law. Similarly, he may have been guided by the rules relating to wives in Exod 21:4, 8, 11. See my *Women, Law, and the Genesis Traditions* (Edinburgh: Edinburgh University Press, 1979), 22–30.

> [3] Reuben, thou art my firstborn, my might, and the first-fruits of my strength, the excellency of dignity, and the excellency of power: [4] Unstable as water, thou shalt not excel; because thou wentest up to thy father's bed; then defiledst thou it: he went up to my couch. (Gen 49:3, 4)

The law on the fruit trees was prompted by the tradition about the king of Moab's rebellion against Israel when in the subsequent pursuit of the Moabites all the good trees were destroyed; the law on the slain man by the tradition about Sheba's rebellion when Joab in pursuit of him slew his fellow pursuer, Amasa; and the law on the female captive by the episode about Jacob's rebelling against Laban when in the subsequent pursuit Laban accused him of taking his daughters as if they were captives of the sword. A common element that emerges in the relationship between each law and its tradition is the focus upon misplaced enmity. It was inappropriate to treat fruit trees as enemies, to avenge in peace blood shed in war, and to treat Laban's daughters, Rachel and Leah, as captives.

The law on the right of the first-born son is similarly taken up with this topic of misdirected hostility, in particular, Jacob's dislike of Leah and the question whether it might have carried over to Reuben, his first-born son by her, even if he had not offended in lying with his concubine. Indeed it looks as if, in line with the preceding laws and traditions, the Deuteronomist has set up the topic by seeing Reuben's offense as tantamount to his rebellion against Jacob (recall Absalom's action with his father's concubines [2 Sam 16:22]), and then asking whether he was denied the right of the first-born because of his offense, or whether in fact hatred of the mother was the dominant influence. The fact that the right was conferred upon Joseph, the son of the loved wife, Rachel, and not upon another son born to Leah suggests bias. If so, the Deuteronomist perceives Jacob's confusion over what merits antagonism and what does not as an invitation to exploration.

An accompanying, more direct concern is the preservation of an inheritance. This topic emerges initially in Sheba's complaint and then in Rachel's and Leah's complaint that they were being denied "part and inheritance" in what belonged to them.

The link between the law and the story is an especially clear one. It brings out, moreover, the reason why the law exists in the first place. We might ask why in the entire code the lawgiver only presents one explicit case of a problem within a family about inheritance rights, a case that is decidedly narrow in scope (where a man has two wives, one hated, the other loved, and the first-born son is by the former).

Reuben forfeits his first-born status apparently because he lay with his father's concubine (Gen 35:22). Jacob openly condemns his offense when he gathers his sons together before his death (Genesis 49). This is the appropriate occasion for a father to acknowledge the standing of his eldest son, and it is not surprising that Reuben is the first addressed by Jacob and that this recognition is accorded him as a matter of fact: "Reuben, thou art my firstborn, my might, and the first-fruits of my strength" (v. 3). Jacob, however, then refers to the offense and strikes a negative note about Reuben's future. In particular, the implication seems to be that as a first-born his specially endowed procreative powers will not manifest themselves as they should because of his sexual misdeed.[7] Jacob's chief blessing is reserved for Joseph (Gen 49:22–26). Already in a previous scene (in Genesis 48) Jacob confers upon Joseph's sons Ephraim and Manasseh the renown of his own name and that of his great ancestors, Abraham and Isaac (vv. 15, 16). The Chronicler spells out the situation unambiguously when citing Reuben's descendants: "The sons of Reuben the firstborn of Israel, for he was the firstborn; but because he polluted his father's couch, his birthright was given to the sons of Joseph the son of Israel" (1 Chron 5:1).

Reuben's loss of his birthright seems straightforward enough. For the Chronicler and, apparently, for Reuben's father, his sexual misconduct is determinative. Yet questions remain that complicate the matter. One obvious question is why, if Reuben's offense ruins his status, the blessing was then conferred upon Joseph? Why were his older brothers passed over? Is it because of their antagonism to Joseph and Jacob's eventual knowledge that they had wrongfully sold him to Egypt? Possibly, but there is a further complicating factor. Of

[7]That Reuben as the first-born has an abundance of procreative strength is probably implied in the phrase *yeter ʿāz*. The succeeding verbal form *ʾal-tôtar* then describes how this power is denied him because he misused it. In Moses' corresponding speech to Reuben in Deut 33:6 the reference also seems to address this consequence: "Let Reuben live, and not die, but let his men be few." The RSV's "Nor let his men be few" is unwarranted, as S. R. Driver (*Deuteronomy* ICC [Edinburgh: T. and T. Clark, 1902], 395) shows.

the older sons who were passed over, some are offspring of Jacob's hated wife, Leah. None comes from his loved wife, Rachel. But Joseph, who receives the birthright, is Jacob's firstborn son by her. Is it then Jacob's attitude to his two wives that is also influencing his decisions? We cannot form a judgment based upon the traditions in Genesis,[8] and the Chronicler's reading of the record is only one possible interpretation. In regard to Reuben's position this interpretation is convincing, but conveniently glosses over the question of the other sons' claims.

The lawgiver, who is alert to such issues, has reflected upon the matter. He raises the question—which might be hypothetical rather than a reflection of a confirmed judgment upon Jacob's decision to choose Joseph, although it is probably the latter—about what a man might do should he be married to two wives, one of whom he hates, the other whom he loves, and whose first-born son is by the former: Reuben's situation exactly. Even the language he uses is taken from the Genesis material: "the first-fruits of his strength" (Gen 49:3). Only the Deuteronomist puts aside such considerations as Reuben's misconduct and the brothers' hostility toward Joseph. As a good lawyer should, he seeks to bring out one particular issue and to clarify it. His judgment is that should the first-born son have been the offspring of the disliked wife (in the law as in the tradition she has not been divorced by the husband), he is still to be given the double share of the father's inheritance. Conceivably this double portion, rather than representing customary practice, may be the lawgiver's interpretation of what Jacob actually did to Joseph in settling the prime inheritance upon him: Jacob took two of Joseph's sons and gave each a blessing. This double bounty for the future well-being of Joseph's line emerges as the significant aspect of the primary blessing upon him.

[8]These traditions address the fact that Jacob's first-born does not come from his loved wife—see, for example, the account of Rachel's barrenness and her elder sister's fertility. The substitution of the elder daughter Leah was regarded as punishment for having usurped his elder brother's place. That she is granted children before Rachel is viewed as compensation for Jacob's hatred of her. In other words, that she becomes pregnant before her younger sister does suggest Jacob attained his brother's position fraudulently and implies that he will experience a problem involving the right of the first-born.

Law: The rebellious son

[18] If a man have a stubborn and rebellious son, which will not obey the voice of his father, or the voice of his mother, and that, when they have chastened him, will not hearken unto them: [19] then shall his father and his mother lay hold on him, and bring him out unto the elders of his city, and unto the gate of his place; [20] and they shall say unto the elders of his city, This our son is stubborn and rebellious, he will not obey our voice; he is a glutton, and a drunkard. [21] And all the men of his city shall stone him with stones, that he die: so shalt thou put evil away from thy midst; and all Israel shall hear, and fear. (Deut 21:18–21)

Background: Isaac and Rebekah's problem with Esau

[29] And Jacob sod pottage: and Esau came from the field, and he was faint: [30] and Esau said to Jacob, Feed me, I pray thee, with that red, red stuff; for I am faint: therefore was his name called Edom. [31] And Jacob said, Sell me this day thy birthright. [32] And Esau said, Behold, I am at the point to die: and what profit shall this birthright do to me? [33] And Jacob said, Swear to me this day; and he sware unto him: and he sold his birthright unto Jacob. [34] Then Jacob gave Esau bread and pottage of lentiles; and he did eat and drink, and rose up, and went his way: thus Esau despised his birthright. (Gen 25:29–34)

[32] And Isaac his father said unto him, Who art thou? And he said, I am thy son, thy firstborn Esau. [33] And Isaac trembled very exceedingly, and said, Who? where is he that hath taken venison, and brought it me, and I have eaten of all before thou camest, and have blessed him? yea, and he shall be blessed. [34] And when Esau heard the words of his father, he cried with a great and exceeding bitter cry, and said unto his father, Bless me, even me also, O my father. [35] And he said, Thy brother came with subtilty, and hath taken away thy blessing. [36] And he said, Is not he rightly named Jacob? for he hath supplanted me these two times: he took away my birthright; and, behold, now he hath taken away my blessing. (Gen 27:32–36)

[34] And Esau was forty years old when he took to wife Judith the daughter of Beeri the Hittite, and Bashemath the daughter of Elon the Hittite: [35] which were a bitterness of spirit unto Isaac and to Rebekah. (Gen 26:34, 35)

> [46] And Rebekah said to Isaac, I am weary of my life because of the daughters of Heth: if Jacob take a wife of the daughters of Heth, such as these which are of the daughters of the land, what good shall my life do me? [1] And Isaac called Jacob, and blessed him, and charged him, and said unto him, Thou shalt not take a wife of the daughters of Canaan. [2] Arise, go to Padan-aram, to the house of Bethuel thy mother's father; and take thee a wife from thence of the daughters of Laban thy mother's brother. . . . [6] When Esau saw that Isaac had blessed Jacob, and sent him away to Padan-aram, to take him a wife from thence; and that as he blessed him he gave him a charge, saying, Thou shalt not take a wife of the daughters of Canaan; [7] and that Jacob obeyed his father and his mother, and was gone to Padan-aram; [8] and Esau seeing that the daughters of Canaan pleased not Isaac his father; [9] then went Esau unto Ishmael, and took unto the wives which he had Mahalath the daughter of Ishmael Abraham's son, the sister of Nebajoth, to be his wife. (Gen 27:46–28:2, 6–9)

Jacob's disposal of the birthright raises the important question of when a son might be denied it. The tradition that brings out the issue even more forcibly is the one about Esau's loss of his birthright to Jacob. The Deuteronomist, in his law of the rebellious son, casts a critical eye on what happened there, and rather than repeat his concern about the rights of a first-born he raises the question: when does a son, any son, deserve to be cut off altogether by his parents? To pursue the matter the lawgiver explores Esau's situation. He is *not* judging what happens there, although it is almost certain that his judgment would be that Esau should not have lost his birthright.

Like the preceding law of the first-born, this law too has had to contend with the complicating factor of ambivalent parental attitudes toward sons. "Isaac loved Esau, because he ate of his game; but Rebekah loved Jacob" (Gen 25:28). It is the mother's love for Jacob, and her antagonism toward Esau, that is behind Jacob's cheating him out of his birthright. Consistent with the preceding laws and their background, this one too reveals an interest in unjustified antagonism. Although the Deuteronomist would certainly have opposed the injustice to Esau, he is nonetheless interested in following up Rebekah's apparent objections to Esau. After all, the tradition itself leaves him without his birthright and such a loss requires the active participation of both his mother and his father. Moreover, as it is written, the record is biased against him. It is this bias that prompts the lawgiver to ask the larger, more extreme question: when can the almost inalienable right of a son to life, and to all that that entails, be taken away? To be clear about the relationship between the law and the story we should recall the parallel relationship for the preceding law and its narrative background. Reuben deserved to lose the primogeniture because of his sexual misdeed. The lawgiver noticed, however, that even if he had not offended he might still have lost it because of Jacob's antagonism toward his mother. In a comparable approach to Esau's situation, the lawgiver notes that his mother's favoritism to his brother unjustly deprived Esau of the primogeniture. He also notes, however, unacceptable traits in Esau's conduct and concentrates on an extreme example of these in regard to a son's standing in a family: Esau's situation turned into an offense.

The Deuteronomist uses suggestions in the story to build up a case against a son. In the law the son is stubborn and rebellious. He does not obey the voice of his father or the voice of his mother. He is also a glutton and a drunkard. These behavioral traits, though not an extrapolation from Esau's conduct, are nonetheless suggested by certain aspects of it. At one stage he marries two Hittite women who made life "bitter for Isaac and Rebekah" (Gen 26:35).[9] When she complains to Isaac about being weary of her life because of them, and warns that she will simply give up should Jacob take such a woman, Isaac commands him not to marry a Canaanite woman (Gen 27:46–28:1). Esau then observes how his brother resolved to obey his father and his mother in the matter (Gen 28:6, 7), and he too decides to please. Avoiding marriage to another Canaanite woman, he takes instead an Ishmaelite wife. The issue of obedience to both a father and a mother is clearly brought out in the tradition. Not that we would judge, or that the Deuteronomist has judged, Esau to be diso-

[9]This notice and the similar one in Gen 27:46–28:1 are commonly assigned to P, see E. A. Speiser, *Genesis*, AB (New York: Doubleday, 1964), 202. The former is said to be inserted into a whole that is essentially the work of J (*Genesis* AB, 203), the latter to belong to a section, Gen 27:46–28:9, that is all P (*Genesis* AB, 215). There are, however, no compelling arguments for attributing these particular verses about marriage to P. J. Skinner has to admit that Rebekah's initiative in Gen 27:46 is "more in the spirit of JE than of P" (*Genesis* ICC [New York: Scribner's, 1910], 375), and he is open to the doubts of other commentators about assigning this verse to P (see his note on 375). That Reuben took Bilhah and Jacob took Rachel and Leah influenced, respectively, the two preceding rules.

bedient; that is not the point. The history is used to illuminate the subject and to sharpen the focus on the question of a son's confirmed disobedience to his parents. Esau had caused distress by marrying certain women who were unacceptable to his parents. When, however, he takes another wife he avoids giving them more distress. His motivation even appears to be the commendable one that like Jacob he wishes to heed his parents' wishes. The allegation of willful, stubborn behavior cannot be brought against him. The possibility of such willfulness, however, surfaces readily in a scrutiny of his activities. It is therefore likely that the type of the son who is stubborn (*sôrēr*), by repeating actions that cause his parents anguish, has come to the Deuteronomist's mind after looking at the history in this way.[10] In addition, the reference to the bitterness of spirit (*mōrat rûaḥ*) caused by Esau's initial act (marrying the Hittite women) has probably prompted the lawgiver to think of the related sort of son who is rebellious (*mōreh*),[11] who does not conform to his parents' wishes.

The further characteristics of this type of disobedient son, his gluttony and drunkenness, can also be derived by thinking of Esau and extending to its limit a specific trait of his. The tradition depicts in a negative light his appetite for meat dishes. He is a hunter. He seems to have an inordinate craving for meat. When one day he comes in after an unsuccessful hunt, he requests of Jacob that he be allowed to eat some of the "red, red stuff" that Jacob is cooking (Gen 25:30). Indeed the word he uses (*lāʿaṭ*, "to gulp") connotes the desperate, primitive nature of his appetite, and it is in connection with this request that his name is changed to the "red one," Edom. The tradition itself pronounces judgment upon him for losing his birthright in the manner that he did,[12] and his craving for food and drink seems to inform that judgment. After swearing away his birthright to Jacob he

[10]*srr* in Isa 30:1 refers to rebellious children; in Isa 65:2 to people who choose bad ways, following their own devices.

[11]Needless to say, the linguistic link (if link there be) is not etymological but one of sound and association of ideas: what causes parents bitterness of spirit—a son who is rebellious.

[12]It should not be forgotten, however, that Jacob was exploiting and tricking him. See the analysis by D. Daube, *Studies in Biblical Law* (Cambridge: Cambridge University Press, 1947), 193–98. Whether the Deuteronomist saw the trickery involved is difficult to say. Daube underlines the narrator's emphasis upon Esau's appetite for food. In the law the gluttony is mentioned first, perhaps to reflect the story.

eats, drinks, rises and goes off; and the narrator appends the words, "So Esau despised his birthright" (Gen 25:34).

To repeat: Esau is *not* as described in the law. He is not a stubborn and rebellious son, who is also a glutton and a drunkard.[13] His father would rightly have given him his birthright. Perhaps we can go so far as to say that he was potentially disreputable. In other words, just as a Reuben removed of his blemish showed up in the preceding law, so a hypothetical Esau is depicted in this one. Its careful formulation has to be seen against the background of his conduct. To contrast the condemned son with Esau, the lawgiver spells out such requirements as the failure to obey the voice of his father and the voice of his mother. Esau had certainly been obedient to his father's requests for game. The son in the law must also be chastised, and only after such warning, if he persists in his disobedience, can or should the parents proceed against him—in contrast to Esau, who seems to have seen the light in deciding not to marry another Canaanite woman. The lawgiver's basic aim has been to observe Esau's wrongful loss of his birthright and lay out the conditions when such a loss might be justified.[14]

Law: The hanging corpse

> [22] And if a man have committed a sin worthy of death, and he be put to death, and thou hang him on a tree: [23] his body shall not remain all night upon the tree, but thou shalt in any wise bury him that day; (for he that is hanged is accursed of God;) that thy land be not defiled, which Yahweh thy God giveth thee for an inheritance. (Deut 21:22, 23)

Background: Saul's sons

> [1] Then there was a famine in the days of David three years, year after year; and David enquired of Yahweh. And Yahweh answered, It is for Saul, and for his bloody house, because he slew the Gi-

[13]Philo would not agree. He does see him as disobedient to parents and indulgent to bodily appetites (*De Virtutibus* 38.208).

[14]For further comments on this law and the preceding one, see my "Uncovering a Major Source of Mosaic Law: The Evidence of Deut 21:15–22:5," *JBL* 101 (1982):506–11.

beonites. [2] And the king called the Gibeonites, and said unto them; (now the Gibeonites were not of the children of Israel, but of the remnant of the Amorites; and the children of Israel had sworn unto them: and Saul sought to slay them in his zeal to the children of Israel and Judah.) [3] Wherefore David said unto the Gibeonites, What shall I do for you? and wherewith shall I make the atonement, that ye may bless the inheritance of Yahweh? [4] And the Gibeonites said unto him. . . . [6] let seven men of his sons be delivered unto us, and we will hang them up unto Yahweh in Gibeah of Saul, whom Yahweh did choose. And the king said, I will give them. . . . [9] And he delivered them into the hands of the Gibeonites, and they hanged them in the hill before Yahweh: and they fell all seven together, and were put to death in the days of harvest, in the first days, in the beginning of barley harvest. [10] And Rizpah the daughter of Aiah took sackcloth, and spread it for her upon the rock, from the beginning of harvest until water dropped upon them out of heaven, and suffered neither the birds of the air to rest on them by day, nor the beasts of the field by night. [11] And it was told David what Rizpah the daughter of Aiah, the concubine of Saul, had done. [12] And David went and took the bones of Saul and the bones of Jonathan his son from the men of Jabesh-gilead, which had stolen them from the street of Beth-shan, where the Philistines had hanged them, when the Philistines had slain Saul in Gilboa: [13] and he brought up from thence the bones of Saul and the bones of Jonathan his son; and they gathered the bones of them that were hanged. [14] And the bones of Saul and Jonathan his son buried they in the country of Benjamin in Zelah, in the sepulchre of Kish his father: and they performed all that the king commanded. And after that God was intreated for the land. (2 Sam 21:1–4, 6, 9–14)

[29] And the king of Ai he hanged on a tree until eventide: and as soon as the sun was down, Joshua commanded that they should take his carcase down from the tree, and cast it at the entering of the gate of the city, and raise thereon a great heap of stones, that remaineth unto this day. (Josh 8:29)

From a law about the wrongful denial of inheritance rights to a first-born son, to one in which a son legitimately loses his rights because his conduct requires his execution, the lawgiver moves to an aspect of the death penalty itself. If after the sentence has been carried out the body is exposed to public view (presumably as a deterrent to others), it must be removed and buried before nightfall. Not to do so would defile the land,[15] "which Yahweh thy God giveth thee for an inheritance" (v. 23). How do we account for this shift of topic? The answer is the lawgiver's interest in a tradition in which just such a problem arose. Equally to the point, and this is what brought him to this particular tradition in the first place, is the fact that those executed, the sons of Saul, furnish an example of sons wrongly forfeiting their lives and their place in the land. If in the previous law a son had to die because he offended his parents (he was stubborn and rebellious), in this law the focus is on a parent who offended (in his time Saul had been judged guilty of rebellion and arrogant stubbornness [1 Sam 15:23]), but his sons were the ones executed because of his conduct. We have observed law after law in which the background narratives present examples of misdirected antagonism.

According to the tradition in 2 Samuel 21, Saul had wrongly sought to destroy—misplaced enmity again—the Amorite group, the Gibeonites, with the consequence that famine was visited upon the land of Israel. The guilt of bloodshed upon Saul and his house required expiation before the famine could be lifted: "Wherewith shall I make the atonement, that ye may bless the inheritance of Yahweh" (David to the Gibeonites, v. 3). An interesting parallel to a feature of the Jacob-Esau story is worth noting in passing. Saul's slaughter of the Gibeonites was wrong, because of a longstanding league between them and the Israelites, even though the original covenant was achieved by deception (Joshua 9). As an Amorite group they should have been destroyed by Israel. Just as in regard to Jacob's acquisition of his special status, so here too a benefit retained its validity, even though obtained fraudulently.[16]

To expiate Saul's offense the Gibeonites requested that David hand over seven of Saul's sons. He duly complied. No doubt an element of political expediency entered into David's response. His house was

[15]Presumably because "the eyes of Yahweh thy God" are always upon this land (Deut 11:12), to bless it and give it increase. Should any blemish appear upon it (and a hanged man is "accursed of God"), these eyes will turn away, as they do when they behold uncleanness in the army camp (Deut 23:9–14). On the emphasis in Deuteronomy on the blemish left by wrongs, see D. Daube, "To be found doing wrong," *Studi in onore di Edoardo Volterra,* Pubblicazioni della Facolta di iurisprudenza dell' Universita di Roma 41 (Milan: Giuffrè, 1969), 3–13.

[16]The validity appears to be based on the notion that the words of the agreement, like those of the blessing, once uttered, are beyond recall. They have entered the realm of the numinous.

now in possession of the monarchy and with the death of so many of Saul's sons (some of them were grandsons), the threat from this royal family would be greatly lessened. They were put to death in the first days of the barley harvest, presumably on the understanding that their deaths would satisfy the deity and the famine would cease. But that did not happen. Another problem arose: the sight of the exposed bodies offended the deity. The famine did not end until the corpses—plus the bones of Saul and Jonathan, who had been hanged by the Philistines in a public place in Beth-shan—were buried in the family sepulchre in their tribal allotment. "And after that God was intreated for the land" is the concluding statement of the story (v. 14). It is again interesting to note in passing that just as parental love (and hate) played an important role in the stories about Isaac and Rebekah with Jacob and Esau, and Jacob and Rachel with Reuben and Joseph, so here a mother's love for her sons has a decisive influence, this time in the recognition of a problem. The loving office she, Rizpah, performs for their dead bodies first brought to David's attention the need for their burial to end the defilement of the land.

The continuing exposure of the bodies of those executed, in the pursuit of redressing wrongdoing, and the ensuing defilement of the land is very much the concern, and a narrow one at that, of the law about the hanging corpse. The problem has been picked up from the tradition about Saul's sons. By linking the law and the tradition we can illuminate further the law's content. From the Deuteronomic point of view Saul's sons did not deserve to die. It was their father who had been judged guilty of an offense that merited death. According to his law on individual responsibility (Deut 24:16), the sons should not have been held culpable too. This is why the lawgiver, unnecessarily in terms of legal drafting, states, "And if a man have committed a sin worthy of death, and he be put to death, and thou hang him on a tree."[17] In a legal code a statement such as, "And if a man be put to death, and thou [then] hang him on a tree," should be sufficient, it being understood that the authorities will not put a man

[17]The exposure of the bodies in the tradition may not be by hanging but by some other way not entirely clear to us. The exposure of Saul and Jonathan in their time was by hanging. It is important to remember that the laws seek to describe conventional, not idiosyncratic practices. If executed criminals were displayed in Israelite society with some degree of regularity, then I presume that hanging was the standard procedure.

to death unless he has committed a capital offense. The reference to the *mišpaṭ māwet* is necessary here because it should not have applied to the sons of Saul,[18] just as the reference to the *mišpaṭ habbᵉkōrāh* is necessary in Deut 21:17 because it was being ignored in Jacob's dealings with his sons. Confusion about what properly deserves condemnation results in these references to *mishpatim*. The lawgiver has been heeding his own advice: "That which is altogether just shalt thou follow" (Deut 16:20).

To minimize the harmful effect of a judicial execution, the Deuteronomic rule is that the malefactor's corpse be buried before nightfall. This rule is also found in another tradition, which has, it is generally agreed, undergone some Deuteronomic redaction. Just before the Gibeonites had tricked the Israelites into concluding a covenant with them (Joshua 9), another Amorite group, the inhabitants of Ai, had been destroyed by Joshua. Its king had been hanged on a tree until evening, when Joshua commanded that his body be taken down and buried (Josh 8:29). This fate would doubtless have befallen the Gibeonite chiefs, had their deception not been successful, and is probably pertinent to the nature of their request about Saul's sons. Either Joshua's command is a genuine part of the tradition, or it has been introduced into it by the Deuteronomist.[19] Whatever its origin the important point is that the rule in question is associated with Joshua and, so the Deuteronomist would believe, came originally from Moses. As successor to Moses' high office, Joshua had been the recipient of his laws. The event that immediately followed the hanging and burial of the king of Ai was the building of an altar on Mount Ebal upon which Joshua wrote a copy of the Mosaic legislation.

The Deuteronomist is himself setting forth the laws of Moses. He does so, not by producing judgments that really do come from that legendary lawgiver but by creating them himself. For example, he

[18]The expression "a judgment of death" occurs in the homicide law in Deut 19:6. It is probably too restrictive to interpret the reference in the law of the hanged man to an offense involving bloodshed. If, however, the meaning is so confined, the link between the tradition and the law is all the closer because Saul's offense was that he shed blood.

[19]The same consideration applies to the tradition in Josh 10:22–27: Joshua's execution of the five Canaanite kings, the display of their hanging bodies until evening, and their burial. For the view that we are dealing with the Deuteronomic redactor, see M. Weinfeld, *Deuteronomy and the Deuteronomic School* (Oxford: Clarendon, 1972), 167, n.3.

formulates the law about the hanged man on the basis of a critical scrutiny of the tradition in 2 Samuel 21. By including a rule, however, that can be associated with Joshua, he is able to turn the matter around and make the assumption that Joshua's command was based upon some such law about a hanged corpse as he is presenting and that it came from Moses. What motivates him is the need to understand why David had his problem: why the land continued to be unproductive even after the Gibeonites had executed Saul's sons. The law, understandably designed to describe more conventional circumstances, nonetheless becomes a means of judging the shortcomings and failures described in the tradition.

Law: Straying animals

[1] Thou shalt not see thy brother's ox or his sheep go astray, and hide thyself from them: thou shalt in any case bring them again unto thy brother. [2] And if thy brother be not nigh unto thee, or if thou know him not, then thou shalt bring it unto thine own house, and it shall be with thee, until thy brother seek after it, and thou shalt restore it to him again. [3] In like manner shalt thou do with his ass; and so shalt thou do with his raiment; and with all lost thing of thy brother's, which he hath lost, and thou hast found, shalt thou do likewise: thou mayest not hide thyself. [4] Thou shalt not see thy brother's ass or his ox fall down by the way, and hide thyself from them: thou shalt surely help him to lift them up again. (Deut 22:1–4)

Background: The cattle of the Reubenites and Gadites

[1] Now the children of Reuben and the children of Gad had a very great multitude of cattle: and when they saw the land of Jazer, and the land of Gilead, that, behold, the place was a place for cattle; [2] the children of Gad and the children of Reuben came and spake unto Moses, and to Eleazar the priest, and unto the princes of the congregation, saying, . . . [5] if we have found grace in thy sight, let this land be given unto thy servants for a possession, and bring us not over Jordan. [6] And Moses said unto the children of Gad and to the children of Reuben, Shall your brethren go to war, and shall ye sit here? [7] And wherefore discourage ye the heart of the children of Israel from going over into the land which Yahweh

> hath given them? [8] Thus did your fathers, when I sent them from Kadesh-barnea to see the land. . . . [16] And they came near unto him [Moses], and said, We will build sheepfolds here for our cattle, and cities for our little ones: [17] but we ourselves will go ready armed before the children of Israel, until we have brought them unto their place: and our little ones shall dwell in the fenced cities because of the inhabitants of the land. [18] We will not return unto our houses, until the children of Israel have inherited every man his inheritance. [19] For we will not inherit with them on yonder side. Jordan, or forward; because our inheritance is fallen to us on this side Jordan eastward. [20] And Moses said unto them, If ye will do this thing, if ye will go armed before Yahweh to war, [21] and will go all of you armed over Jordan before Yahweh, until he hath driven out his enemies from before him, [22] and the land be subdued before Yahweh: then afterward ye shall return, and be guiltless before Yahweh, and before Israel; and this land shall be your possession before Yahweh. [23] But if ye will not do so, behold, ye have sinned against Yahweh: and be sure your sin will find you out. [24] Build you cities for your little ones, and folds for your sheep; and do that which hath proceeded out of your mouth. [25] And the children of Gad and the children of Reuben spake unto Moses, saying, Thy servants will do as my lord commandeth. [26] Our little ones, our wives, our flocks, and all our cattle, shall be there in the cities of Gilead: [27] but thy servants will pass over, every man armed for war, before Yahweh to battle, as my lord saith. (Num 32:1, 2, 5–8, 16–27)

The odd use of language in this law indicates that, despite the manifest difference in subject matter, the law on straying animals follows the law about the hanging corpse. In the latter the deity, seeing the dead man, will look away and consequently withhold his blessing from Israel. Contrariwise, an Israelite, seeing a straying beast, is not to yield to the temptation to "hide himself" from it by way of avoiding service to his fellow Israelite.

In 2 Samuel 21 the assistance of the Gibeonites was sought, because of the famine in the midst of Israel, in order that they might confer a blessing upon "the inheritance of Yahweh" (v. 3). But in expiating the blood-guilt upon Saul's house, another problem arose—the sight of the dead bodies offended the deity. The fact that the Gibeonites were able to aid the Israelites at all was owing to the relationship they managed to establish at the time when Israel was conquering the land. Like their fellow Amorites before them, Sihon the king of Heshbon, and Og king of Bashan, they should have been destroyed (Josh 9:10). Their destruction then would not have involved confusion as to who was, and was not, an enemy. Their city and land should have been given to the Reubenites, Gadites, and the half-tribe of Manasseh. As it was, these latter tribes came to possess Heshbon and Bashan (Josh 13:15–31 and Num 32:33–42). An incident in Numbers 32 involving the Reubenites and Gadites, at the time when they were laying claim to these places, inspires the construction of the law on straying animals. As in the effort of the Gibeonites on behalf of the Israelites, so again assistance with one problem led to the uncovering of another one. The lawgiver's method of focusing upon a problem because it has come to light in the shadow of another is highlighted in the law of the first-born. Reuben's offense in lying with his father's concubine is seen to have obscured Jacob's reason for conferring the right of primogeniture upon Joseph.

In Numbers 32 the descendants of Jacob's sons, Reuben and Gad, are cattlemen who wish to inherit the land east of the Jordan. This request results in a dispute. It is the time of the conquest of the land, and Moses views their appeal as tantamount to opting out of a clear duty to proceed against an enemy for the purpose of securing the land west of the Jordan. Indeed, he further views it as a covert act of hostility against their fellow Israelites ("And wherefore discourage ye the heart of the children of Israel from going over into the land which Yahweh hath given them" [Num 32:7]). In line with the preceding laws and traditions, the notion (albeit of a more subtle kind) of misdirected enmity can still be observed. The Reubenites and Gadites respond to the objection by agreeing to continue in arms until their brother Israelites have secured their promised inheritance. In the resolution of this problem, the Deuteronomist sees the seeds of a new problem. By taking up arms to secure their brothers' land they are leaving their own new land unprotected and, in particular, their own prize possession, their cattle, unattended and therefore liable to wander off or be seized by others.[20] This development did not in fact

[20]Israel's failure to obey the commandments will, Moses predicts, result in the loss of all their possessions and the land that had been given to them (Deuteronomy 28). They will not simply lose their animals, but their enemies will actively take them (Deut 28:31). Such a possibility comes to mind in the context of the situation involving the Reubenites and Gadites in Numbers 32. Moreover, if the Israelites obey Moses, providence, it is implied, will protect them from such an outcome, as presumably happened in Numbers 32.

take place. Its peacetime analogue, however, comes to the Deuteronomist's mind because the laws are designed for the time when Israel will inherit the land and acquire possessions in it. The tradition in Numbers 32 concerns precisely this time and brings out, for anyone reflecting on it, the need for brother Israelites to help one another out, to reciprocate so that a brother's inheritance is made secure. The Reubenites and Gadites did go on to help out their fellow Israelites, and hence it was reasonable to imagine how Moses could have raised the question as to when a reciprocal service might be rendered to them in the future. In that they possessed many animals their brothers could help in protecting them.

A problem that suggests itself when the Deuteronomist scrutinizes a tradition—rather than one that is actually raised in the history itself—appears in a law. In less exceptional circumstances than a time of military need, the lawgiver is prompted to ask what an Israelite should do when he comes upon another's straying animals. The answer: he should not ignore them but should return them to his brother. The law, reflecting the tradition, uses the term "brother" in a broad sense, because it goes on to consider what should be done when the owner of the animal is not personally known to the finder.

Another motivation for constructing the law would be the Mosaic law on straying animals in Exod 23:4, 5: "If thou meet thine enemy's ox or his ass going astray, thou shalt surely bring it back to him again. If thou see the ass of him that hateth thee lying under his burden, and wouldest forbear to help him, thou shalt surely help with him." Its bias in favor of helping the lost and broken-down beasts of one's personal enemy would have provoked the question why Moses did not legislate for the more conventional, neutral situation of animals belonging to one's fellow. The tradition about his dealings with the cattlemen, his brothers, the Reubenites and the Gadites, would have indicated that he had indeed addressed himself to it. What is interesting about the Exodus version of the rule is its concern with confusing the object of hostility. Its intent is to ensure that one's enmity against someone is not carried over to his animals.[21]

[21]For a common misunderstanding of the significance of this rule see my "A Time for War and a Time for Peace: The Influence of the Distinction upon Some Legal and Literary Material," *JJS* 25 (1974):56–58.

SUMMARY While pursuing Sheba, Joab wrongfully slew Amasa, whose body was cast into a field. The problem of the corpse found in the field, where the assailant is unknown, is legislated for. In Laban's pursuit of Jacob he accused him falsely of taking his daughters, Rachel and Leah, as captives of the sword. The issue of an Israelite's treatment of a captive woman is the subject of a law. Jacob's hostility to Leah appears to have influenced his attitude to her children by him. Reuben, their first-born, lost his primogeniture. This issue is probed in a law, because, although Reuben deserved to lose it, he might have lost it even if he had not offended. Rebekah's love for Jacob led to Esau's loss of primogeniture. Esau, like Reuben, did offend his parents but not to the extent that he deserved to lose his birthright. The issue of a son who offended like Esau, but to an extreme degree, is the subject of a law. Saul's wrongful hostility against the Gibeonites caused them unjustly to take revenge on his sons, whose exposed corpses affected the land. A comparable problem within the sphere of the legitimate exercise of justice is dealt with. The assistance rendered to the Israelites by the Gibeonites led to the problem. After acquiring their inheritance, which should have included the land of the Gibeonites, the Reubenites and Gadites assisted their brother Israelites, but in doing so left their many cattle unprotected. A law requires Israelites to be of service to one another by protecting animals that have strayed.

CHAPTER 6

JUSTIFIED AND UNJUSTIFIED MILITARY ENGAGEMENT

From an interest in hostility that was wrongly directed we move, in the tradition that has prompted the Deuteronomic version of a rule about straying animals, to the fault of failure to engage in hostility at all. Moses had addressed himself to the particular instance of this fault in the tradition in Numbers 32 and resolved the matter then. What he does in his laws is first to take up the legitimate concern that lay behind Reuben and Gad's initial abstention from military service, namely, their attachment to their cattle. He consequently saw scope for focusing upon some future fault of an Israelite who abstained from helping out his fellow Israelites whose cattle have wandered or broken down. It is in his next law on transvestism that he takes up again the issue of avoiding military service.

Law: Transvestism

[5] The woman shall not wear that which pertaineth unto a man, neither shall a man put on a woman's garment: for all that do so are abomination unto Yahweh thy God. (Deut 22:5)

Background: The military service of the Reubenites and Gadites (Num 32:16–27; see p. 156)

> [4] And Deborah, a prophetess, the wife of Lapidoth, she judged Israel at that time. [5] And she dwelt under the palm tree of Deborah between Ramah and Beth-el in mount Ephraim: and the children of Israel came up to her for judgment. [6] And she sent and called Barak the son of Abinoam out of Kedesh-naphtali, and said unto him, Hath not Yahweh God of Israel commanded, saying, Go and draw toward mount Tabor, and take with thee ten thousand men of the children of Naphtali and of the children of Zebulun? [7] And I will draw unto thee to the river Kishon Sisera, the captain of Jabin's army, with his chariots and his multitude; and I will deliver him into thine hand. [8] And Barak said unto her, If thou wilt go with me, then I will go: but if thou wilt not go with me, then I will not go. [9] And she said, I will surely go with thee: notwithstanding the journey that thou takest shall not be for thine honour; for Yahweh shall sell Sisera into the hand of a woman. And Deborah arose, and went with Barak to Kedesh. (Judg 4:4–9)

> [15] And the princes of Issachar were with Deborah; even Issachar, and also Barak: he was sent on foot into the valley. For the divisions of Reuben there were great thoughts of heart. [16] Why abodest thou among the sheepfolds, to hear the bleatings of the flocks? For the divisions of Reuben there were great searchings of heart. [17] Gilead abode beyond Jordan. (Judg 5:15–17)

The law about lost animals is extended, from what is after all a rather narrow base, to include any lost thing belonging to one's Israelite brother. An obvious point is that the law is concerned with goods that do not belong to the person finding them but that nonetheless because of the circumstances, may remain temporarily in his possession. The law that follows is about possessions that even temporarily should never be attached to a person: no woman shall put on anything that belongs to a man and no man shall put on a woman's garment. That the move from the one law to the next is not so haphazard as might appear is also suggested by the mutual concern with a person's wrongfully concealing himself. An Israelite who comes upon his brother's broken-down or straying animal, or anything belonging to him, is not "to hide himself." This notion appears to be carried over into the transvestite law. The links between them are attributable to the fact that the tradition in Numbers 32 continues to be under review.

Although the male Reubenites and Gadites decided to continue in arms at Moses's behest, they were obviously reluctant to do so. The women and children, as well as the many cattle, would be vulnerable while they were on war duty. Their families were to stay within fortified cities "because of the inhabitants of the land" (v. 17), while their cattle would presumably remain outside. Moses raises the possibility that some of the men might try to avoid conscription in order, no doubt, to remain with their families and cattle. After they had agreed to take up arms, Moses warned them that should they seek to avoid their obligation they would be sinning against Yahweh and "your sin will find you out" (Num 32:23). Although not to be interpreted as what Moses is actually hinting at in the story, a transvestite ruse constitutes an example of secret sinning in this context of avoiding military service and would, in the words of the law, be properly described as "an abomination to Yahweh." Moreover, the first part of the law also suggests that the substitution of women for male warriors could be a ruse by which a community might appear to be fulfilling an agreement similar to the one made with Moses. Noteworthy in this regard is that the description of the female dressing up uses language of a decidedly military flavor. "No woman shall put on the gear of a warrior [*kᵉlî-geber*]" is an accurate translation.[1] An interest in this type of deliberate confusion in the context of war is consistent with the focus upon confusion over objects worthy of enmity (fruit trees, Amasa, Laban's daughters, Reuben, Esau, Gibeonites, other Canaanites) in so many of the Deuteronomist's preceding laws and their traditions. Except that in this instance the focus is upon those proceeding (or not) to fight, rather than upon those fought against.

As for the notion of disguise itself, we have just observed the lawgiver's awareness of its role in the example of the Gibeonites. In order to make an agreement with the Israelites—for, we might note, the purpose of avoiding military engagement—they dressed in such a way as to suggest that they had been on a long journey (Josh 9:2–15). An interest in a comparable ruse is therefore hardly surprising; the

[1]See F. Brown, S. R. Driver, and C. A. Briggs, *Hebrew and English Lexicon of the Old Testament* (Oxford: Clarendon, 1907), 149, 150, 479.

lawgiver sees its relevance in Moses' concern about the Reubenites and Gadites opting out of the agreement he had made with them.

The topic of women in the army does not arise directly from the tradition in Numbers 32. It contains, however, certain statements that, strictly interpreted, do raise the issue. In Num 32:16–27 the Reubenites and the Gadites answer Moses' complaint about their opting out of Israel's military effort. They propose that they will build enclosures for their animals and cities for their little ones (*ṭap*) east of the Jordan, but that they will take up arms on behalf of their kinsmen to help them secure their inheritance on the west side. Moses agrees to this offer and commands them (v. 24), "Build you cities for your little ones, and folds for your sheep; and do that which hath proceeded out of your mouth." Absent from these statements is any reference to their wives. To be sure, the Reubenites and Gadites respond to Moses's command, perhaps unnecessarily because it was their proposal in the first place, with the words (vv. 26, 27), "Our little ones, our wives, our flocks, and all our cattle, shall be there in the cities of Gilead; but thy servants will pass over, every one armed for war, before Yahweh to battle, as my lord saith." It is conceivable, though unlikely, that this statement represents a clarification of the preceding ones because of the possible confusion about whether wives were to remain behind or were to bear arms like the men. Common sense suggests that their remaining behind was implied all long.[2] For an understanding of the tradition itself the obscurity is more apparent than real. Its relevance, however, to the manner in which the Deuteronomist constructs his laws is clear. A careful reading of the tradition raises the topic of the position of women in a time of war.[3] It does so, not so much by what is said but by what is unsaid, or, more accurately, by a combination of both. As we have seen, this is precisely the way that this lawgiver brings out a problem. When the Reubenites and Gadites spell out their agreement with Moses and mention what had presumably been taken for granted, namely, that their wives would remain behind, this declaration becomes the cue for

[2]There are other examples where a reference to little ones has to be extended to include women, for example, 2 Sam 15:22, "So Ittai the Gittite passed on, with all his men and all the little ones who were with him." The setting is David's retreat from Jerusalem in the face of Absalom's uprising. Cp., too, Exod 10:10, 24.

[3]Cp. how in Num 31:15, 17, Moses raises the issue of Israel's treatment of female captives.

the Deuteronomist to consider when women might in fact turn up in the army. The possibility that one party to the agreement might proceed to deceive the other reinforces this consideration, especially when there lies before the Deuteronomist the example of the Gibeonites, whose own dilemma was bound up with the claims of the Reubenites and Gadites to their land.

Another related tradition would also have spurred the lawgiver's interest. In the Song of Deborah, in Judg 5:15–17, the Reubenites, along with the Gadites, too, it appears,[4] are rebuked for not participating in the war against the Canaanites. In this regard there is a close parallel to the objection Moses had raised with them. That the problem resurfaced in a later generation would incline the lawgiver to reflect upon the topic of military participation. His interest, moreover, would focus on the fact that in this history Deborah is the central figure, initiating the war against the enemy and actually accompanying the Israelite army. From the Deuteronomic point of view, this tradition has a quite specific link to the one in Numbers 32, and it dramatically raises the question about the presence of women within the army. In addition, it also celebrates how the woman, Jael, usurped the military glory of the Israelite commander by killing the Canaanite general, Sisera, with a workman's hammer (Judg 4:9, 5:26). Deborah's stature in Israelite lore would have been such that confusion might arise in the minds of later Israelites about the mixing of the sexes, or of sex roles, during military activity.

Although the terms *kᵉlî* and *geber* are indeed capable of a narrow military meaning, they can also be given the more general meaning that is adopted in the versions, for example, the AV's "The woman shall not wear that which pertaineth unto a man." In that the lawgiver is legislating for peacetime conditions, the latter meaning is probably the one intended. The wartime incident in Numbers 32 prompts his initial thinking on the subject, but in so far as the choice of language permits it, there is a move from the particular to the general. Such a procedure is well illustrated in the preceding law about lost possessions.

[4]The reference in verse 17 is to Gilead, Gad's tribal location. The Peshitta reads Gad. The interest in Reuben (or the Reubenites) underlying so many of the laws seems clear. Much reflection must have been occasioned by the fact that he was Israel's firstborn and yet lost the renown of this position. Israel's prime inheritance could have been his.

Law: Sparing a mother bird

[6] If a bird's nest chance to be before thee in the way in any tree, or on the ground, whether they be young ones, or eggs, and the dam sitting upon the young, or upon the eggs, thou shalt not take the dam with the young: [7] but thou shalt in any wise let the dam go, and take the young to thee; that it may be well with thee, and that thou mayest prolong thy days. (Deut 22:6, 7)

Background: Sheba's rebellion and the wise woman of Abel of Bethmaacah

[1] And there happened to be there a man of Belial, whose name was Sheba, the son of Bichri, a Benjaminite: and he blew a trumpet, and said, We have no part in David, neither have we inheritance in the son of Jesse: every man to his tents, O Israel. [2] So every man of Israel went up from after David, and followed Sheba the son of Bichri: but the men of Judah clave unto their king from Jordan even to Jerusalem. [There follows Joab's murder of Amasa.] [14] And he [Joab] went through all the tribes of Israel unto Abel, and to Bethmaachah, and all the Berites: and they were gathered together, and went also after him. [15] And they came and besieged him in Abel of Bethmaacah, and they cast up a bank against the city, and it stood against the outmost wall: and all the people that were with Joab battered the wall, to throw it down. [16] Then cried a wise woman out of the city, Hear, hear; say, I pray you, unto Joab, Come near hither, that I may speak with thee. [17] And when he was come near unto her, the woman said, Art thou Joab? And he answered, I am he. Then she said unto him, Hear the words of thine handmaid. And he answered, I do hear. [18] Then she spake, saying, They were wont to speak in old time, saying, They shall surely ask counsel at Abel: and so they ended the matter. [19] I am one of them that are peaceable and faithful in Israel: thou seekest to destroy a city and a mother in Israel: why wilt thou swallow up the inheritance of Yahweh? [20] And Joab answered and said, Far be it, far be it from me, that I should swallow up or destroy. [21] The matter is not so: but a man of mount Ephraim, Sheba the son of Bichri by name, hath lifted up his hand against the king, even against David; deliver him only, and I will depart from the city. And the woman said unto Joab, Behold, his head shall be thrown to thee over the wall. [22] Then the woman went unto all the people in her wisdom: and they cut off the head of Sheba the son of Bichri,

> and cast it out to Joab. And he blew a trumpet, and they retired from the city, every man to his tent. And Joab returned to Jerusalem unto the king. (2 Sam 20:1, 2, 14–22)

A longstanding view interprets the bird's nest law more or less at face value. It is seen as urging sensitive feelings toward birds: one should be regardful of the relationship between a mother bird and its young, the latter should be enjoyed as food but the mother bird should go free. Biblical laws sometimes confine themselves to the inculcation of moral values, in this instance, it is thought, respect for a parent, animal primarily, but by extension human too. Moreover, since laws are expected to have some practical bearing, it can be observed that the freeing of the mother bird means that she can produce more young and therefore more food. This conventional interpretation, however, leaves one wondering about the trivial nature of the supposed practical concern on the part of the lawgiver. The law presupposes a chance encounter with a nest. What possible point would there be in urging that many months hence the mother bird might supply a further source of food? If the intention of the law is more to reinforce respect for parents, it is something of a jolt to note in this context how the law finds the slaughter of the young quite acceptable. Its position in the code likewise indicates no such interest.

The law is manifestly interested in the question of what to kill and what not to kill; in particular, the view is that killing in a selective way means that an important life is preserved. It is, the lawgiver implies, necessary to kill something. In the context of the law recognition of this necessity is linked to a man's desire to acquire some food. From this viewpoint the law contains matters of profound moment, but their expression is distressingly insignificant.

The preceding two laws have had as background a tradition about problems that arise in times of military need: animals liable to get into difficulties and the position of women. The law about a chance encounter with a bird's nest while one is "on the way" turns out to be about seizing birds as if they were enemies to be attacked. It also involves a tradition in which a woman's power in a military confrontation proves decisive. The law's language provides the initial clues. The Hebrew verb (*niphal qārāh*) used to speak of the encounter commonly occurs in contexts of hostility, actual or potential.[5] When Absalom met (*niphal qārāh*) the servants of David violence was to be expected (2 Sam 18:9). When Amalek met (*qārāh*) Israel "on the way" it was a hostile encounter: "Remember what Amalek did unto thee on the way, when ye were come forth out of Egypt: How he met thee on the way, and smote the hindmost of thee, even all that were feeble behind thee, when thou was faint and weary; and he feared not God" (Deut 25:17, 18). Pursuing further the language of the bird's nest law, we find a prohibition against taking "the mother with the children." In the two other contexts in which this same idiomatic phrase is found, the slaughter of mother and children in a violent confrontation is alluded to. Jacob anticipated violence from his brother, the more so when his messengers reported that Esau was coming to meet him (*qārāh* again) and added that he was accompanied by four hundred men (Gen 32:6). Jacob prays for deliverance, "for I fear him, lest he will come and smite me, and the mother with the children" (Gen 32:11). In the siege of Betharbel "the mother with the children" were dashed in pieces (Hos 10:14).[6] Significantly, battle sieges are often likened to the plundering of a bird's nest. Edom, or the city of Bozrah in particular, might make its nest as high as the eagle's, but, the deity threatens, it will be destroyed nonetheless (Jer 49:16). The Assyrian conquest of other peoples is described in terms of their having plundered nests (Isa 10:14). An attack on Moab is said to have left but a few scattered nestlings, a remnant of Moabites (Isa 16:2).

The use of language associated with military sieges suggests that the lawgiver is seeking to distinguish between such sieges and raids

[5]David Daube drew attention to the fact that this verb occurred in the Old Testament in connection with a preponderance of adverse meetings or happenings: "The casual tends to be *casus,* obstruction, frustration" (*Suddenness and Awe in Scripture* [London: Robert Waley Cohen Memorial Lecture, Council of Christians and Jews, 1963], 6–10).

[6]Cp. also 2 Kings 8:12 (Elisha to Hazael), "I know the evil that thou wilt do unto the children of Israel: their strongholds wilt thou set on fire, and their young men wilt thou slay with the sword, and wilt dash their children, and rip up their women with child." Also 2 Kings 15:16: Menahem sacked Tappuah (Tiphsah) and ripped up all the women in it who were with child. The duration of the Trojan war for nine years was predicted by the seer Calchas after he observed a serpent consume eight young birds and then their mother (Apollodorus, *Epitome* 3.15; Homer, *Iliad* 2.299–330).

upon birds' nests. He would have someone who comes upon a nest not proceed in such a way that he imitates the worst excesses of real military sieges; indeed he would have him refrain from perceiving the encounter as one of warlike confrontation. This is a strange concern on the part of a lawgiver. That we are correct in picking it up from the law's formulation is confirmed by noting his identical reaction in one of the preceding laws. In contemplating procedure for a siege upon a city, he confines himself solely to the consideration that fruit trees should not be axed in preparing siege works (Deut 20:19, 20). Only non-fruit-bearing trees should be used. He goes out of his way to underline the point by asking: "Are the trees in the field men that they should be besieged by thee?" So too, in the law of the bird's nest, he does not wish to have a nestful of birds, mother and young, rifled as if they constituted an enemy under siege. The theme of misplaced enmity, so common in the preceding laws, again shows up. More accurately, and consistent with the topic underlying the two preceding rules about unjustified avoidance of military engagement, the lawgiver is concerned with justifying avoidance of it.

There is a difference between the two nature laws: one is about actual involvement in warfare, the other about peacetime activity. In one a city is to be captured but a source of food for the besiegers is not to be damaged; in the other a mother bird is to be saved from destruction but her young may be taken for food. The contrasting parallel between the mother and the city, the latter to be taken because war is in progress, the former to be saved because it is not, proves most interesting.

The law about the bird's nest, like the one about the fruit trees, owes its origins to a military siege. King David, whose affections were often misplaced, could not overcome his grief at the death of his upstart son, Absalom, who had sought to overthrow him. On hearing the news that he had been killed during the course of the revolt against him, he retired to his private chamber, but in going he was heard to exclaim: "O my son Absalom, my son, my son Absalom! would God I had died for thee, O Absalom, my son, my son!" (2 Sam 18:33). Strange, from his fellow countrymen's standpoint, that the death of a wicked offspring should evoke such profound grief when the result achieved was the reestablishment of the father's kingdom; as strange in its way as his excessive expression of grief before the death of the love child by the beautiful Bathsheba, and his total lack of grief immediately afterwards (2 Sam 12:15–23). On each occasion those outside the family were bewildered by his conduct, and in regard to Absalom's death they reacted by defecting on a large scale, because they perceived that the king was weak in the face of his son's challenge.

One man, Sheba, son of Bichri, a Benjaminite, who is judged harshly in the tradition about him in 2 Samuel 20, initiated a potentially disastrous revolt against David. All the men of Israel followed him, while only the men of Judah remained loyal to David. The latter ordered the revolt to be crushed, and the decisive moment came when Sheba took up position in the city of Abel of Bethmaacah. Joab, the most ferocious of David's military commanders, arrived (having just carried out the wrongful slaying of his fellow commander, Amasa, 2 Sam 20:4–13), and set up siege works against the city. About to break down the wall and achieve access, he was stopped by the call of a woman from inside the city. No name is given her but she is described as wise, and she takes the initiative in this military confrontation. The preceding transvestite law was very much interested in the activity of women in a time of war. This woman does become involved in a military situation but she proves to be a different kind of warrior. She refers to Abel's reputation for wisdom in times past and pleads with Joab not to destroy a city in Israel. Her formulation is what particularly interests us: "I am one of them that are peaceable and faithful in Israel; thou seekest to destroy a city and a mother in Israel; why wilt thou swallow up the inheritance of Yahweh?" (2 Sam 20:19). Joab aggressively denies such an intention ("Far be it from me, far be it, that I should swallow up or destroy!") and requests that Sheba alone be given up. Her response is immediate: "Behold his head shall be thrown to thee over the wall." She approaches all the people "in her wisdom" and accomplishes the beheading of Sheba—and the saving of her city.[7]

[7]For a parallel to the wise woman whose name is not recorded, cp. Eccles 9:13–16: "This wisdom have I seen also under the sun, and it seemed great unto me: There was a little city, and few men within it; and there came a great king against it, and besieged it, and built great bulwarks against it. Now there was found in it a poor wise man, and he by his wisdom delivered the city; yet no man remembered that same poor man. Then said I, wisdom is better than strength: nevertheless, the poor man's wisdom is despised, and his words are not heard."

Commentators and lexicographers note the peculiar use of the term "mother" in the woman's address to Joab. They claim that it points to a geographical idea: a mother city whose neighboring settlements or villages are thought of as her offspring, who in times of distress seek protection in her midst.[8] But there is no reference to the inhabitants of such settlements seeking refuge in Abel of Bethmaacah. The plain meaning of the text, as well as perhaps the fact that it is a woman who speaks, suggests the simpler notion, namely, that this city in Israel is compared to a mother, and its inhabitants to her children. In addressing Joab she is appealing to a fellow Israelite to avoid wholesale destruction of the city and its inhabitants, that is, the slaughter of the "mother with the children." The agreement to kill only one of its temporary inhabitants, Sheba, prevents the terrible consequence of war. Sheba himself does not belong to that city in Israel, and hence he is not a "child" of that "mother." He is nonetheless a member of the larger group, the children of Israel. There is then, from this wider perspective, a sense in which it was considered necessary to kill an Israelite son so that a "mother" in Israel could go free. A situation of war, and a civil one at that, had been transformed into one of peace with the sacrifice of Sheba's life.[9]

The lawgiver focuses on the wisdom of the woman's action (alluded to three times in the tradition, vv. 16, 18, 22), and notes how, because of the selective killing, the overall result was the survival of a group of Israelites and their place in the land, in the woman's words, the preservation of the "inheritance of Yahweh." He too is concerned with this preservation. His laws are designed for the time when the Israelites will have entered their inheritance, the land, and when they will dwell securely because the deity will have rid it of enemies. Such civil strife as is recorded in the Sheba incident will be unthinkable in

[8]See L. Koehler and W. Baumgartner, *Lexicon in Veteris Testamenti Libros* (Leiden: Brill, 1958), 59, 159.

[9]Observe how in the tradition behind the fruit trees law the king of Moab caused hostilities to cease by sacrificing his eldest son (2 Kings 3:27). Socrates, under sentence of death, but considering an offer of freedom, pictures the city and the laws pleading with him: "Are you intending, as far as in you lies, to destroy us and with us the whole city? You must know that the city cannot continue if the decisions of its courts are to be set at nought by any private individual." He goes on to point out that the city and its laws are the author of his being; through them his father married his mother and gave birth to him. See *Crito*, 50, and J. W. Jones, *Law and Legal Theory of the Greeks* (Oxford: Clarendon, 1956), 1.

that time of peace and rest from enmity. To maintain this God-given tranquillity, the Deuteronomist's laws communicate measures that will ensure that even in regard to the responses necessitated by the human appetite for food—its acquisition is one peacetime activity he thinks of as potentially like military action—nothing resembling war will take place. Noting the resolution of the confrontation between Joab and Sheba, he fashions his food law. That is why there is inherent in it the view that an Israelite should not proceed against a nestful of birds as if it were an enemy to be attacked and destroyed. In his mind is Joab's standing before the city of Abel and already involved in the beginnings of a siege. The necessity to kill for the sake of satisfying one's appetite is acknowledged, but the mother bird must not be killed. Slaughtering her young is permitted but nothing more. This discriminating course of action will have its reward, in the words of the law, "that it may go well with thee and that thou mayest live long." The wise woman's action achieved precisely this end: her city continued to live on.[10] The promise in the law to those who observe it seems incongruous for such a trivial matter as obtaining a source of food in the form of the young of birds; it is—unless we take into account how this lawgiver proceeds in constructing his laws.

In light of the link between the Sheba story and the bird's nest law, it is noteworthy that both open with the use of *qārāh* in the *niphal* form of the verb: "And there chanced to be there a man of Belial, whose name was Sheba" (2 Sam 20:1); "If a bird's nest chance to be before thee in the way" (Deut 22:6). Although the verb is neutral in each instance, the use of the expression, "a man of Belial," conveys that there is trouble brewing, just as there are hints in the language and meaning of the law to suggest matters more fearful than an attack upon a bird's nest.

It is most illuminating to look at other events in David's reign in the light of the Sheba incident, the woman's wisdom, and the law of the bird's nest. Like Sheba, David too once happened to be the object of destruction when he took refuge in the city of Keilah (1 Sam 23:1–14). The entire place inevitably faced his same fate. He learned, however, that its rulers, who owed him much because he had rescued the city from a Philistine attack, would in fact deliver him over to his

[10]Until Tiglath-pileser captured it and carried its people captive to Assyria (2 Kings 15:29).

pursuer, Saul. He escaped before the siege could be mounted. As Sheba had concluded that he and his fellow Israelites had no future with the reigning monarch, David, in their time, so the latter had been forced to conclude that King Saul was his enemy and that he and his followers had best live the lives of renegades. The indication is that both Sheba and David were bent on toppling the throne. Sheba in Israelite, or perhaps, more accurately, Judean tradition, was condemned; David, a Judean, was considered heroic. Similarly, it was wise of the woman to have Sheba executed; the deity saw to it that David escaped unharmed. On another occasion when Saul sought to track David down he was defeated by the superior stratagem of David and his men. Addressing the king from a distant hill, David complained about how Saul was depriving him of "the inheritance of Yahweh," that is, excluding him from his rightful place in the land (1 Sam 26:19). He pleaded for his life and asked why the king of Israel was pursuing him "as one doth hunt a partridge in the mountains" (v. 20).

When David was living the life of a freebooter, in forced exile from King Saul and building up support to become king himself, he and his men exacted payment from a wealthy sheepfarmer, Nabal by name, "Folly" in translation (1 Samuel 25). In return for not visiting harm upon Nabal's shepherds and flocks, David requested some food from him on the occasion of a sheep-shearing festival. The request was foolishly denied. Foolish because David's message of peace to Nabal and his house carried with it the threat of violence should the request find no favor. David and four hundred of his men moved against Nabal to destroy him and his household.

A wise woman, in the person of Nabal's wife, Abigail ("And she was a woman of good understanding, and of a beautiful countenance" [1 Sam 25:3]) took the initiative in confronting this tyrannical threat. Laden with supplies of food she appealed to David not to shed blood but expressed the wish that evil befall her husband nonetheless. David and his men accepted her fare and refrained from their hostile intentions. Abigail returned to her house and found her husband in a drunken state; she told him nothing at this time. She, like the wise woman in regard to Sheba, nonetheless perceived the need to have him out of the way. In the morning, "when the wine had gone out of Nabal" (1 Sam 25:37), she told him what had transpired. He had a stroke and died some ten days later. She had a hand in his death. Like the other wise woman she did not do the actual killing. We are however informed not just that he died but that God, no doubt acting for her, smote him. Like Sheba, Nabal too was condemned as a worthless fellow, a son of Belial (1 Sam 25:17, 25). Moreover, like Joab against the city of Abel, David had proceeded against his fellow countrymen, sons of Israel. Abigail's wisdom, acknowledged by David, consisted in saving the larger group, the many members of her household, at the expense of one member's death and, equally important, in restraining David from shedding any blood. His intended attack upon the household was, despite the motive of vengeance, primarily for the purpose of procuring some food. In supplying him with it, Abigail prevented him from engaging in an unnecessary warlike act. Such a desirable consequence is the aim of the law on the bird's nest, just as it is for the following law about blood on a new house, where the background is again a concern with blood-guilt on David's house.

Another major event in David's life that brings out issues similar to those underlying Sheba's death and the taking of the young of birds is Absalom's revolt against his father. The biblical writer views it from two perspectives. The wider one relates the revolt to David's retribution for his offense against Uriah the Hittite. Recall that David had Uriah, one of his finest warriors, put in the forefront of a battle against the Ammonites, making his death inevitable. By ensuring Uriah's death, David had hoped to cover up his adultery with his wife, Bathsheba, who had become pregnant because of it. David's despicable action resulted in a particularly humiliating death for her soldier husband. It is likened to the ignominious end of the upstart King Abimelech. In a siege against the city of Thebez he had gone too close to its wall and a woman dropped a millstone on his head. (Abimelech's improper rule had begun when he slaughtered seventy of his brothers upon one stone [Judg 9:5].) Rather than have it said that a woman slew him he had his armor bearer run him through (v 54).

Uriah's death is specifically compared to what happened to Abimelech beside the wall. The reason for the comparison is not too clear. A possibility is that a woman—namely, Uriah's unfaithful wife—is to be thought of as ultimately responsible for his death. Such causal thinking is present in the text. It was the defenders of the city of Rabbah who killed Uriah. But Joab had deliberately placed him in the front line. Joab, in turn, was carrying out written instructions in the matter. David had recourse to the stratagem because he had to make it appear that Bathsheba was pregnant by her own husband. He had not been able to get Uriah to lie with her when he had brought him home from the war for this very purpose. Uriah's death was therefore required to make it appear that he had conceived life in the normal way of things. As proof that he had given life, his had to be taken away! The incident provides a powerful illustration of how, for some biblical writers, wrongdoing is characterized as a dramatic mixing of life and death.[11] In any event, Bathsheba's pregnancy had to be linked to a dead Uriah.[12] Retribution was to come in the form of the sword's never departing from David's own house (2 Sam 12:10), which now included a new wife, Bathsheba. His callous use of a war situation to rid himself of someone who had become an inconvenience to him eventually brought punishment in the form of domestic chaos. That his son takes up the sword against him has to be viewed in the light of this drama of retribution.

Absalom's revolt was not successful. He ended up dying in a humiliating fashion himself. Fighting took place in the wood of Ephraim and, incredibly (trees can be men of war),[13] "the wood devoured more people that day than the sword devoured" (2 Sam 18:8). Absalom, for example, riding upon a mule, was taken by the animal "under the boughs of a great oak, and his head caught hold of the oak, and he was taken up between the heaven and the earth; and the mule that was under him went away" (v. 9). Suspended there, he was run through with three darts by Joab, David's commander.

Events might not have turned out this way if Absalom had followed the direction of Ahithophel, a professional advisor whom he consulted just after his bloodless coup d'état. Ahitophel's instruction was the same as the wise woman's of the city of Abel: kill one man, in this

[11]See my "On Separating Life and Death: An Explanation of Some Biblical Laws," *HTR* 69 (1976): 1–7; and "A Common Element in Five Supposedly Disparate Laws," *VT* 29 (1979): 129–142.

[12]The child eventually dies and its death is viewed as a punishment for the adultery. It follows that a child died so that a mother could go free.

[13]And not just by way of a ruse as in Malcolm and MacDuff's attack upon Dunsinane Castle (*MacBeth* 5.4–6).

instance King David himself, and peace would prevail in Israel because all the people who had accompanied David would join with the rest of the nation in giving their allegiance to Absalom (2 Sam 17:1–3). Like the woman, Ahithophel agreed to take the initiative in carrying out the killing. Absalom liked the advice but sought the view of another professional aide, Hushai, who had appeared in Absalom's court as a defector from David's camp. In fact, he was there to work against Absalom. Hushai considered the weakness of Ahithophel's recommendation to lie in his underestimation of David's strength. He likened David to a mother bear that had been robbed of her cubs (2 Sam 17:8; cp., Prov 17:12), the latter being a reference to the people whom David had been ruling over before Absalom's coup. Put in these terms, Hushai conveyed the daunting task of taking on such a fierce enemy. As a result Absalom rejected Ahithophel's counsel, and Ahithophel committed suicide. Having sought to kill David as the head of Absalom's own house and the house of Israel, he returned to his own home, set it in order, and hanged himself (2 Sam 17:23).

In overturning Ahithophel's counsel Hushai concentrated on Absalom's initial act of aggression against his father and its consequence. The difference between this assessment of what Absalom had done and what Joab was counseled to do against Sheba is interesting. By having Sheba killed, Joab would not be involved in a warlike action against a "mother" in Israel, the city of Abel. Motherhood in this figure symbolizes peace: a mother and her children will be preserved intact. Absalom, on the other hand, having engaged in an act of war against the king of Israel by causing the people to come under his rule, was now faced with an enemy described as a mother bear robbed of her children. No killing has taken place but motherhood in this instance signifies enmity, a mother deprived of her still living offspring. The need to kill is acknowledged as an inevitable consequence of this situation, and Hushai advises Absalom to proceed to battle in his own person (2 Sam 17:11). David, informed through spies of developments, likewise prepares for battle. Despite his wish to accompany his troops in person, he is persuaded to the contrary (2 Sam 18:2). Pathetically he requests of his commanders: "Deal gently for my sake with the young man, even with Absalom" (v. 5). The civil war breaks out and thousands of Israelites are killed, but with Absalom's death it comes to an end. The result is that at the general figurative level a mother is reunited with her children, although many have perished. At the level of the particular, a father has been re-established in his kingdom but only because his son has been killed.

In terms of the broader perspective of divine providence at work, this child had to be killed because peace could only be restored to David's house once he had suffered for causing the death of Uriah in battle. Absalom's death on the battlefield is David's punishment. He unwittingly acknowledges this fact when he laments: "Would God I had died for thee, O Absalom, my son, my son!" His unrealistic request that Absalom not be slain in the conflict contrasts with his calculated disposal of Uriah in the siege of Rabbah. What is interesting for our purposes is that divine wisdom (or rather the elevated and frightening view of those who have interpreted the history) requires not the death of David himself but that of his offspring. The implication is that chaos and the total destruction of war are avoided by the preservation of the parent and the slaughter of the young.

It clearly emerges in the traditions about David that there is much preoccupation with the topic of whom to kill and whom not to kill.[14] For example, David found himself in conflict over this issue with his military men, the sons of Zeruiah, Joab and Abishai (2 Sam 3:37–39). The fact that so many experiences arose that put the issue of selective killing to the test would be cause for reflection, and it in turn would achieve proverbial expression. One aspect of wisdom is its capacity to gain from human experience ways of achieving benefit for as many people as possible. This aspect is prominent in the wisdom revealed by the wise woman of Abel of Bethmaacah, by Abigail, and in the wisdom implied in the Deuteronomist's law of the bird's nest. In biblical material wisdom is defined as the knowledge of good and evil and the capacity to discriminate between them. This definition is well illustrated in the incidents cited above.

Law: Blood on a new house

> [8] When thou buildest a new house, then thou shalt make a parapet for thy roof, that thou bring not bloods upon thine house, if any man fall from thence. (Deut 22:8)

[14]This has been noted by D. M. Gunn, *The Story of King David, JSOT* Supplement Series 6 (Sheffield: Sheffield University Press, 1978), 39, 40.

Background: David establishes his house and Solomon removes blood from it

> [1] Now the days of David drew nigh that he should die; and he charged Solomon his son, saying. . . . [5] Moreover thou knowest also what Joab the son of Zeruiah did to me, and what he did to the two captains of the hosts of Israel, unto Abner the son of Ner, and unto Amasa the son of Jether, whom he slew, and shed the bloods of war in peace, and put the bloods of war upon his girdle that was about his loins, and in his shoes that were on his feet. [6] Do therefore according to thy wisdom, and let not his hoar head go down to the grave in peace. (1 Kings 2:1, 5, 6)

> [29] And it was told King Solomon, Joab has fled unto the tabernacle of Yahweh; and, behold, he is by the altar. Then Solomon sent Benaiah the son of Jehoiada, saying, Go, fall upon him. . . . [31] and bury him; that thou mayest take away the innocent bloods, which Joab shed, from me, and from the house of my father. [32] And Yahweh shall return his blood upon his own head, who fell upon two men more righteous and better than he, and slew them with the sword, my father David not knowing thereof, to wit, Abner the son of Ner, captain of the host of Israel, and Amasa the son of Jether, captain of the host of Judah. [33] Their bloods shall therefore return upon the head of Joab, and upon the head of his seed for ever: but upon David, and upon his seed, and upon his house, and upon his throne, shall there be peace for ever from Yahweh. [34] So Benaiah the son of Jehoiada went up, and fell upon him, and slew him: and he was buried in his own house in the wilderness. (1 Kings 2:29, 31–34)

Like the law of the bird's nest, this one about building a parapet upon the roof of a new house is sensitive about blood.[15] The erection of the parapet is to ensure that no blood comes upon the house. It makes sense to concentrate on this aspect of the law rather than upon any legal notions of negligence, for the fact that no sanction is mentioned should anyone fall from the roof, owing to the failure to erect the structure, suggests that such notions are irrelevant to the lawgiver's concern.

Like the preceding law the parapet law is also inspired by reflection

[15] I suppose too there is a link between a nest built upon a tree and a parapet added to the roof of a house in the sense that maximum protection is afforded to the occupants. In some of the texts noted previously where the reference was to the human world a bird's nest was synonymous with safety.

upon a matter in the traditions about David. After Sheba's rebellion was quelled, his reign entered its final stage. As the first leader in Israel to be guaranteed hereditary rule (2 Sam 7:11, 16, 18, 19, 25–27),[16] he had to establish his house. After a struggle his successor proved to be his son Solomon, and David laid upon him the obligation to rid his house of the blood that was thought to adhere undesirably to it. In his farewell address to Solomon he first urged that his successor keep the law of Moses (1 Kings 2:3). His next request was the quite specific one that his military commander Joab not be allowed to die in peace. He recalled how, in killing the two captains, Abner and Amasa, Joab "set bloods of war in peace." The reference is to Joab's avenging in a situation that did not call for military confrontation blood that had been shed in war by these military men (2 Sam 3:22–39, 17:25–18:8, 20:4–13). Amasa's murder belongs to the story of Sheba's rebellion (pertinent to the preceding law on the bird's nest) and had prompted the formulation of the law concerning the slain man. Also noteworthy is the fact that the three laws preceding this one on the new house have been taken up with the topic of justified or unjustified military engagement.

After David died Solomon found occasion to put Joab to death, and he justified it on the grounds that the bloods that Joab had shed without cause would now be removed from him and his father's house (1 Kings 2:31). Peace and rest from enemies prevailed for Solomon, and he proceeded to build a new house, one that represented the Davidic kingship. Observing this development, the Deuteronomist comes up with his law to ensure that no "bloods be set" upon a new house—the same language as in 1 Kings 2:5 about the effects of Joab's action upon David's house. The specific direction, that one should erect a parapet on the roof to prevent a fall, is attributable to the fact that problems in the ordinary circumstances of peacetime are addressed. The exceptional problems that had confronted the founding of David's house inspire a more conventional parallel. The lawgiver asks himself how blood(s) might come upon a new house in a normal day-to-day situation. One obvious source of trouble is where a house is not provided with a parapet.[17]

[16]Many critics attribute this particular prophetic part of the Samuel tradition to a Deuteronomic redactor. Should this view be correct, it would be added proof that the lawgiver produced his laws during a process of redaction similar to the one that has shaped the Book of Samuel itself.

[17]Commentators point out how much human activity took place on rooftops.

The Deuteronomist would have had no difficulty in suggesting that such a law could easily have come from Moses. The law is about a new house that, in terms of the setting of the entire legislation, will be built upon the new land after the Israelites come into their inheritance. Of interest is the fact that just before David commanded Solomon to rid his house of blood, he had urged his son and successor to keep the laws of Moses (1 Kings 2:1–6). The Deuteronomist could easily have drawn the inference that David's concern about blood was based upon a law similar to the one he formulates. In drafting it his view would have been that in a time of peace and rest from enemies the presence of blood was disturbing and too reminiscent of what occurred in war.

A law about the building of a new house already appears in Deut 20:5: the warrior who has built one but not yet dedicated (*ḥānak*) it is exempted from battle duty so that he can do so. The concern is that he might die before establishing his house. David, conscious of his coming death, had taken steps to ensure the sanctity of his prospective house. We already noted that the only other comparable use of the term *ḥānak* occurs in 1 Kings 8:63(=2 Chron 7:5), in reference to Solomon's dedication of God's house. The building of it had proceeded apace with that of Solomon's new house (1 Kings 9:1).

The common background in traditions relating to David and the establishment of his dynasty largely accounts for the setting down together of the laws on the bird's nest and the new house. The interest in "mother with children" was dominant in the former, the slaughter of both being prohibited. In the law's background was reflection upon what can happen in human hostilities when real mothers and children are victims. Underlying the law on the new house is the tradition about the succession of Solomon and the building of his new house. It is interesting to observe that before Solomon succeeded to the throne his mother (Bathsheba) and he were in danger of their lives because of Adonijah's temporary rise to power (1 Kings 1:12, 21; cp., 2 Sam 14:16). In other words, a mother with child was almost destroyed, which would have destroyed Solomon's house.

Perhaps too, if Bathsheba and Solomon had been slain, David's house would have come to an end. Adonijah's supremacy was born of opportunism and with Joab around it might have been short-lived. Already David's family had been reduced to a shadow of its former existence. Amnon and Absalom were dead. Michal, the daughter of

Saul, who had loved him and who had become his wife, had grown to despise him. No offspring came of their union (2 Sam 6:23). His ten concubines, with whom his son Absalom had lain, were treated as widows by him (2 Sam 20:3). About his other sons born to him in Hebron (2 Sam 3:2–5), the traditions record nothing more.

SUMMARY Reuben and Gad were seen to be at fault in not proceeding against Israel's enemies. Even when they agreed to fight, Moses feared that they might secretly sin in the matter. The problem of transvestism is viewed as one such example of avoiding military service. Joab was urged by a woman not to proceed militarily against a "mother" in Israel, an Israelite city. To do so would have destroyed "mother with children," the city and its inhabitants. He was encouraged, however, to proceed against one of its "children," Sheba. A literal analogue in peacetime is the permission to kill the inhabitants of a nest, the young of birds, but not the mother bird. On two other occasions Joab did offend by proceeding militarily against Abner and Amasa. The "bloods" he had shed remained a problem for David's house (in a symbolic sense), and their removal was vital for the establishment of Solomon's house (both symbolic and actual). This specific historical problem about "bloods" on a house is translated into a comparable problem: when an Israelite builds his new house in the new land he should prevent the spilling of "bloods" by the erection of a parapet upon its roof.

CHAPTER 7

PROBLEMS OF PEDIGREE

The lawgiver's interest in the establishment of David's house also appears in the law prohibiting the sowing of mixed seeds in a vineyard. It is not surprising that we can detect this concern with the future of the house in Solomon's time or with its origin back in the time of Judah and Jacob. Hereditary rule, as we noted, appears in Israel for the first time with David. Before him leadership was of a charismatic kind and was thus almost bound to be nonhereditary in character. Succession is a prominent feature of the material in Samuel and Kings. Apart from the dominant concern in these books with David's dynasty, Saul's failure to establish his claim to hereditary rule is prominent. This is both explicit (1 Sam 13:13, 14) as well as implicit in the traditions about David's relations with surviving members of Saul's family. Samuel appointed his sons as judges over Israel, presumably to carry on his work. Such a succession was abortive because his sons were corrupt. Indeed, it was their conduct that led to the request for the institution of kingship in Israel (1 Sam 8:1–5). The traditions also record the breakup of the priestly dynasty to which Eli belonged. Its downfall is attributed to the corruption of Eli's sons (1 Sam 2:27–36; 1 Kings 2:26, 27). The lawgiver's awareness of David's lineage is all the more to be expected. In a series of preceding laws and their traditions, the topic of inheritance rights (Rachel and Leah's, Reuben's, Esau's, Saul's sons', the Reubenites and Gadites', Sheba's) was a major one.

Solomon, despite his great merit and accomplishments, threatened his own succession with almost total breakdown. His fault lay in the marriages he contracted with foreign women. The problem is first hinted at in connection with the building of his new house and that of the deity's. He married the pharoah's daughter and brought her to Jerusalem while he was building both of these structures. This was also a time when people were still sacrificing on hilltop shrines because God's house was not built (1 Kings 3:1, 2). Eventually, after the successful completion of the construction projects, the link between foreign wives and the apostasy of the people and Solomon came to the fore, and engulfed him in crisis after crisis. The end result was a grievous division of his kingdom with one son, Rehoboam, managing to retain leadership of the tribe of Judah. David's dynasty was salvaged but the threat of its disappearance was very real.

One of Solomon's foreign wives was Naamah the Ammonitess. She was responsible for turning his attention to Milcom and Molech "the abominations of the Ammonites" (1 Kings 11:4, 5, 7). His successor, Rehoboam, was born to her. It is a truly remarkable fact that this half-Israelite, half-Ammonite product is the only son attributed to Solomon (two of his daughters are given incidental mention in 1 Kings 4:11, 15). Why is there no mention of the presumably myriad offspring who came of his unions to seven hundred wives and three hundred concubines? The silence can probably be interpreted as an extension of the negative attitude toward these foreign unions (1 Kings 11:1, 2). The product of a foreign marriage was mixed seed.

Solomon belonged to the tribe of Judah, and the problem he had maintaining his line—in particular, establishing rule over all the tribes of Jacob—is very closely paralleled in the situation of his eponymous ancestor, Judah. The Deuteronomist has noted two parallels between them. The mention of only one son of Solomon is a reminder of the precarious position Judah found himself in with his progeny; and both men produced children of mixed seed.[1] There is more in the traditions about Judah's fragile situation, and the Deuteronomist turns his attention to Judah's plight when he sets down his law prohibiting the sowing of two kinds of seed in the Israelite vine-

[1]Solomon and Judah are juxtaposed for genealogical purposes in 1 Chron 3:10–4:1.

yard. Judah's situation, in fact, is pertinent to an understanding of all three laws about forbidden mixtures (vineyard, plowing with an ox and an ass, wool and linen).

The clue to the construction of these rules lies in recognizing that lawmaking of the kind in question is akin to the composition of proverbs. If, as is claimed, sayings and proverbs are sometimes condensed stories, then these laws constitute a marvelous example of the process.[2] We are able to observe, in a way that is rarely available to inquirers in any body of literature,[3] how these apparently odd constructions represent clever, allusive, proverbial-type commentary upon certain happenings in the patriarchal narratives. The link between law and wisdom is well recognized. Especially in early legal development, before the formalization of courts and court procedure, the dispensers of justice often use folk wisdom to establish judgment in a case. Sometimes a proverb that has no background in law is used to express an important legal principle. Writing in 1659, James Howell states, "In our Common Law there are some Proverbs that carry a kind of authority with them, as that which began in Henry the Fourth's time, He that bulls the cow must keep [take care of] the calf."[4] Biblical law codes themselves incorporate statements that are also found in collections of proverbs. The laws about removing a neighbor's landmark, and about correct weights and measures are illustrations in point (Deut 19:14, 25:13–16; Prov 23:10, 11:1, 16:11, 20:23). The statement in Lev 19:32, "Thou shalt rise up before the hoary head, and honour the face of the old man, and fear thy God," is one of a series of laws, but it could equally well come from a collection of proverbs.

By way of illuminating events in the human world, proverbs often

[2]See A. Taylor, *The Proverb* (Cambridge, Mass.: Harvard University Press, 1931), 27–32; also *The Disciplina Clericalis of Petrus Alfonsi,* trans. and ed. Eberhard Hermes (English translation by P. R. Quarrie), The Islamic World Series (Berkeley and Los Angeles: University of California Press, 1977), 23: "Such proverbs are basically stories which have either been shrunk or expanded." It should be remarked that while the connection between fables and proverbs is well-known ("The grapes are sour" from Aesop's *The Fox and the Grapes*), the dependence of some proverbs upon narratives can often only be assumed because the latter no longer exist.

[3]"Rarely indeed is one permitted to sit in at the birth of a proverb." *The Home Book of Proverbs, Maxims and Familiar Phrases,* ed. Burton Stevenson (New York: Macmillan, 1948), vi.

[4]Cited by Taylor, *The Proverb,* 91.

refer to activity in the plant and animal one. This is exactly what is going on in the laws against mixtures in Deuteronomy. They are not to be understood literally, unlike those in Lev 19:19 (breeding cattle with a different kind, sowing a field with two different kinds of seed, wearing a garment of two kinds of stuff). The reason for this major divergence is probably that the Levitical legislator no longer understood their real meaning. We shall return to this difference later, after explaining the inspiration behind the construction of the Deuteronomic laws. The fundamental observation is that their author is inspired by the sayings ascribed to Jacob in Genesis 49. In that material Jacob is depicted on his deathbed with his sons assembled before him. Looking back on their lives, especially as they affected him, he evaluates their conduct and predicts their future. The sayings he utters are characteristically cryptic, and employ language that is full of wordplays and comparisons of his sons to animals. In Deuteronomy, so we are to understand, Moses too is about to leave life and is looking back on the experience of the nation Israel. He also makes judgments about matters that arose in the past and issues laws that address themselves to similar problems in the future. He is interested in the doings of the sons of Israel and that means he pays attention to some of the very things that Jacob commented upon in regard to his sons' deeds. To be sure, what Moses accomplishes is of a much broader scope. Nonetheless, now and again interest and comment overlap. This occurs precisely when the lawgiver resorts to figurative language. It is an interesting phenomenon: he employs allusive language whenever he seeks to focus on a specific event or person. Otherwise, as we have come to expect, he formulates a rule for the more typical circumstances in which some problem that is found in a tradition needs to be regulated.

Jacob condemned his first-born son's act of lying with one of his concubines. But how does he express himself in the matter? "Thou [Reuben] wentest up to thy father's bed; then thou defilest it—he went up to my couch" (Gen 49:4). If taken literally the implied meaning is that Reuben lay with his father and did something he should not have done. The real meaning is, however, that he lay with his father's wife (possibly in his father's bed but that does not necessarily follow from this allusive statement). The Deuteronomist also focuses on the subject of a man's relationship with his father's wife. In a two-part law he first prohibits a man from taking his father's wife, presumably in the sense that this kind of marriage (after the father is dead or even before because he is willing to release her to a son) is not to be permitted. In the second part he too is interested in Reuben's specific offense, namely, lying with the woman while she is still bound to the father. Like Jacob, he also chooses to express his condemnation in a deliberately cryptic and misleading way: "Nor shall he uncover his father's skirt" (Deut 22:30). Literally this statement means a son shall not interfere with his father; figuratively it refers to, and this is the intended meaning, lying with the father's wife. One reason for this mode of expression, apart from the imitation of the style in Genesis 49, is that in the culture in question the suggestion of uncovering a father's nakedness is as powerfully shaming as the fact of having intercourse with one of his wives.

Law: Mixed seed in a vineyard

[9] Thou shalt not sow thy vineyard with two kinds of seed: lest the whole yield be rendered taboo: the seed which thou hast sown and the produce of the vineyard. (Deut 22:9)

Background: Judah's sons

[1] And it came to pass at that time, that Judah went down from his brethren, and turned in to a certain Adullamite, whose name was Hirah. [2] And Judah saw there a daughter of a certain Canaanite, whose name was Shuah; and he took her, and went in unto her. [3] And she conceived, and bare a son; and he called his name Er. [4] And she conceived again, and bare a son; and she called his name Onan. [5] And she yet again conceived, and bare a son; and called his name Shelah: and he was at Chezib, when she bare him. [6] And Judah took a wife for Er his firstborn, whose name was Tamar. [7] And Er, Judah's firstborn, was wicked in the sight of Yahweh; and Yahweh slew him. [8] And Judah said unto Onan, Go in unto thy brother's wife, and marry her, and raise up seed to thy brother. [9] And Onan knew that the seed would not be his; and it came to pass, when he went in unto his brother's wife, that he spilled it on the ground, lest that he should give seed to his brother. [10] And the thing which he did displeased Yahweh: wherefore he

slew him also. [11] Then said Judah to Tamar his daughter in law, Remain a widow at thy father's house, till Shelah my son be grown: for he said, Lest peradventure he die also, as his brethren did. And Tamar went and dwelt in her father's house. [12] And in process of time the daughter of Shuah Judah's wife died; and Judah was comforted, and went up unto his sheepshearers to Timnath, he and his friend Hirah the Adullamite. [13] And it was told Tamar, saying, Behold, thy father in law goeth up to Timnath to shear his sheep. [14] And she put her widow's garments off from her, and covered her with a vail, and wrapped herself, and sat at the entrance to Enaim, which is by the way to Timnath; for she saw that Shelah was grown, and she was not given unto him to wife. [15] When Judah saw her, he thought her to be an harlot; because she had covered her face. [16] And he turned unto her by the way, and said, Go to, I pray thee, let me come in unto thee; (for he knew not that she was his daughter in law.) [She negotiates payment of a kid for her services and receives a pledge of his personal insignia. He is unable, however, to hand over the kid because she can not be found.] [24] And it came to pass, about three months after, that it was told Judah, saying, Tamar thy daughter in law hath played the harlot; and also, behold, she is with child by whoredom. And Judah said, Bring her forth, and let her be burnt. [25] When she was brought forth, she sent to her father in law, saying, By the man, whose these are, am I with child: and she said, Discern, I pray thee, whose are these, the signet, and bracelets, and staff. [26] And Judah acknowledged them, and said, She hath been more righteous than I; because that I gave her not to Shelah my son. And he knew her again no more. [27] And it came to pass in the time of her travail, that, behold, twins were in her womb. [28] And it came to pass, when she travailed, that the one put out his hand: and the midwife took and bound upon his hand a scarlet thread, saying, This came out first. [29] And it came to pass, as he drew back his hand, that, behold, his brother came out: and she said, How has thou broken forth? this breach be upon thee: therefore his name was called Perez. [30] And afterward came out his brother, that had the scarlet thread upon his hand: and his name was called Zerah. (Gen 38:1–16, 24–30)

[8] Judah, thou art he whom thy brothers were praising: thy hand was on the neck of thine enemies; thy father's children were bowing down before thee. [9] Judah was a lion's whelp: from the prey of my son thou didst come up: he stooped down, he couched as a lion, and as a lion; who was rousing him? [10] The sceptre was

> not departing from Judah, nor the ruler's staff from between his legs, until Shelah would go in [to Tamar]; and unto him would be the obedience of the peoples. [11] Binding his ass unto the vine, and the son of the she-ass unto the choice vine, he washed his cloak in wine, and his robe in the blood of grapes. [12] Dull were the eyes from wine, but white were the teeth from milk. (Gen 49:8–12)

If understood literally, the prohibition against sowing two kinds of seed in a vineyard poses some puzzling questions. First and foremost is, what is wrong with such a practice? There is even evidence in Isa 28:24–29 (the reference is to fields, but recall the extent of the prohibition in Lev 19:19),[5] that it might have been the normal, and one might add the sensible, thing to do. A far from insignificant problem is the reference to two seeds (*kil'ayim*), and not to a plural number. It is no solution, especially in light of the rather arresting term, *kil'ayim,* to argue that the specification really stands for many.[6] There is, moreover, something ambiguous about what the two refer to—presumably to vines and one other seed. Yet in that the vineyard is not a new one, the more natural meaning would be that the vines are already there and two kinds of (other) seed are not to be added. This solution does not appear to be the right one, however. The lawgiver spells out the results of the mixed sowing: the seed that has been sown and the yield of the vines. There is, we shall see, a deliberate ambiguity involved in the formulation.

Another major problem in a literal reading is why the sanction attached to the law is conditional in nature: "lest the whole yield be forfeited." Most commentators, taking the law at face value, interpret the term *qādaš,* "to be forfeited, to render holy," as signifying that the resultant mixed crop may be removed by the priests to the sanctuary. An obvious objection to this view, and it underlines the difficulty of accepting the law in a literal sense, is why sometimes the priests will opt for forfeiture while other times they will not. Surely, if there is something wrong with sowing mixed seed, the harvest should always be subject to forfeiture by the sacred officials. The fact is that no such right or duty is to be attributed to them. The term *qādaš* should not be extended to embrace some priestly power. One more difficulty

[5]In Cant 1:14 the vineyards of En-gedi contain Henna plants.
[6]The AV translates, "divers seeds."

in accepting the prohibition on its own terms is that the lawgiver feels the need to spell out what appears to be redundant detail. Instead of its being sufficiently clear to state that the entire harvest (*m^e lēʾāh*) will be rendered taboo, he goes on to state: "the seed that thou hast sown and the yield of the vineyard."

All these difficulties disappear once we give up a literal interpretation of the law and view it as a cryptic judgment upon Judah's dilemma over the perpetuation of his line, as described in Genesis 38, and as already commented upon by Jacob in Gen 49:8–12. The lawgiver's interest in Judah's lineage in the context of the Book of Genesis should occasion no surprise in light of the manifest importance ascribed to the family of Abraham, Isaac, and Jacob. Elsewhere in biblical literature, Israel, Jacob's family in the widest sense, is thought of as God's vineyard (Ps 80:8, 14; Isa 5:2; Jer 2:21, 6:9; Hos 10:1 and so on). The representation suggests the notion of Israel's self-conscious grandeur, because the vine is regarded as a noble plant, and its abundant blossoming from small beginnings, because the vine grows so well. Things can go wrong. This people can be like the vine of Sodom, which produces bitter grapes only (Deut 32:32). Instead of being a cultivated vine, Israel can turn into a degenerate, wild one (Isa 5:2; Jer 2:21). It is also vulnerable to destructive forces (for example, Israel is referred to as a vine in Ezek 15:2, 6, and Jer 12:10). This vulnerability is the focus of Jacob's comment upon Judah's attempt to have his sons reproduce by Tamar. When he refers to Judah's binding first one and then another ass to the vine (Gen 49:11), he is alluding to the damage that these animals will do to the vine.

The vine in this saying refers to Jacob-Israel. With the birth of twelve sons to him, Jacob had proved to be a fruitful vine. Alas, at the point in time to which he is referring in this particular part of the saying, he had just lost his favorite son, Joseph. Now on his deathbed, all his sons, including Joseph, are before him, and he knows how Judah, as the instigator of Joseph's sale into slavery, was duly paid back for his misdeed.[7] He began to experience what it was like to lose sons. First Er and then Onan died in their attempt, arranged by Judah, to add to the line of Israel. As Jacob chose to reflect upon the

[7]Judah's initiative was motivated by his desire to become the leading member of the family. On this aspect see my *Women, Law, and the Genesis Traditions* (Edinburgh: Edinburgh University Press, 1979), 60.

matter, two asses tied to a vine would tread in a destructive way. The grapes would be crushed and their juice would run. Jacob thinks of Judah's washing his garment in this flow of liquid—the blood of grapes, he calls it. Such an odd action with his clothing is only intelligible if it is viewed as a symbolic one that Jacob imagines Judah engaged in by way of acknowledging the death of his two sons. No ordinary, customary gesture of mourning is meant. Rather Jacob sees the gesture as mirroring what he himself had to go through: he had been forced to acknowledge that the bloodstained coat of his son Joseph signified that he had died by the action of some animal. That beast turned out to be Judah himself, and Jacob had commented upon the fact in the preceding part of the saying when he referred to Judah as the lion that had come up from "the prey of my son" (*miṭṭerep b^e^nî* [Gen 49:9]). Judah's action with his covering (*l^e^bûš*) has in fact its own symbolical meaning. A man's garment or covering is, figuratively speaking, his wife.[8] The reference to Judah's washing it by treading upon it in the juice of the grapes alludes not just to the deaths of Er and Onan in association with the Israelite vine, but to their origin from Judah's union with the daughter of Shuah. They constituted a branch of his father's vine. To wash one's garment in the juice of grapes is to acknowledge that the "grapes" produced by one's wife have perished.[9]

The comparison of Judah's sons to asses, as opposed to their father the lion, is both clever and precise. It reflects their ethnic identity and hence a concern about the purity of the Israelite line. Canaanites are, from the Israelite point of view, properly (and nastily) comparable to asses. According to Israelite genealogical lore the Canaanite descendants of Ham were under a curse such that servitude to the Israelites would be their lot in life (Gen 9:18–27). Interestingly, the curse causing offense occurred in the midst of the first vineyard ever associ-

[8]Discussed in the following law prohibiting a mixture of wool and linen.

[9]In Robinson Jeffers's freely adapted version of *Medea* by Euripides (New York: Samuel French, 1946), Jason asks Medea about her bloodstained hands (she has just killed their two sons), and she replies, "The wine I was pouring for you spilled on my hand—Dear were the little grapes that were crushed to make it; dear were the vineyards" (act 2). Note too how the activity of gleaning grapes is a figure for the destruction of human beings in Judg 8:2 (the slaying of the two Midianite princes) and 8:13; and Rev 16:18. For the sexual symbolism of the vineyard in the Song of Songs and in Near Eastern material, see M. H. Pope, *Song of Songs* AB (New York: Doubleday, 1977), 323–26.

ated with an ancestor of Israel. An implication of the story is that because Ham looked upon his father's nakedness and observed the place of his virility, Ham (Canaan) was rendered unfit to participate in the perpetuation of Noah's lineage.

If the thought is not already entertained by those who recorded the story, it is not difficult to see that later Israelite interpreters would think of the offense as leading to Canaanite exclusion from, metaphorically speaking, the Israelite vineyard. However that may be, if animal comparisons were sought in order to describe the relationship of subservience of one group to the other, the ass as the proverbial beast of burden is the appropriate one. And such comparisons were indeed sought. In Genesis 34 the names of the head of the Caananite group, the Hivites, and his son, Hamor and Shechem (ass and ass's shoulder) respectively, reveal the Israelite attitude. Equally revealing is Jacob's low opinion of his son Issachar in Gen 49:14, 15. He too is compared to an ass (*ḥamôr*) who, bowing his shoulder (*šekem*), became a slave to others, probably to Canaanites. In Genesis 38, Judah, in Canaan, married a native woman and, figuratively speaking, produced three "asses" by her, Er, Onan, and Shelah.[10] It is the first two of these three sons who are in mind in Jacob's describing their relationship to the Israelite vine. The first ass mentioned—*ʿîrōh* (his ass)—by a wordplay characteristic of the author of these sayings, is Er (*ʿēr*); the second is the *benî ʾatōnô* (the son of his she-ass), Onan—Judah's son by his Canaanite "she-ass." Their union with Tamar was for the purpose of producing progeny for Judah's line, hence Jacob's, and, overall, for the growth of the Israelite vine. Real asses destructively tread upon real vines. That picture is conveyed in Jacob's remarks about them. The reality he is referring to, however, is the sexual treading they carried out upon Tamar,[11] which resulted in their deaths and, more significant in the wider perspective of the perpetuation of Judah's line, in the failure to produce offspring, to cause the vine to grow and increase.

Like Jacob, Moses also is understood to have commented adversely upon Judah's involvement with the Canaanites. In his view the Isra-

[10] J. R. Emerton traces a Canaanite character to Genesis 38 before the story was included in the Book of Genesis, "Judah and Tamar," *VT* 29 (1979): 403–15.

[11] On this kind of treading see my "'Treading' in the Book of Ruth," *ZAW* 92 (1980): 248–66.

elite vineyard should not be sown with hybrid seed. He reflects upon Judah's attempt to increase his stock by sending Er and then Onan into Tamar. His seed, each son, was half-Israelite, half-Canaanite, two in one, *kil'ayim*. This is the explanation for the use of a dual and not a plural form in specifying the number of seeds that should not be sown in the vineyard. The entire law is meant to be read as a figurative comment upon Judah's problem. No extension of meaning is intended other than perhaps a warning to the original recipients of the law that they too might find that contracting a marriage with a Canaanite woman could lead to problems. It should be stressed, however, that the main point of the law is the specific judgment it makes upon Judah's family life. Once this is appreciated, and the model of Jacob's judgment is kept in mind, every aspect of the law is illuminated. The reference to what might happen should mixed seed be sown—namely, that it could become holy (*tiqdaš*)—is explained by the lawmaker's observation of what befell Er and Onan. The deity struck both of them down. This happened, moreover, in connection with their sowing activity. Perhaps this is not so pointedly stated in the case of Er ("And Judah took a wife for Er his first-born, whose name was Tamar. And Er, Judah's first-born, was wicked in the sight of Yahweh; and Yahweh slew him" [Gen 38:6; cp., Genesis Rabba 85]), but it is certainly so in Onan's case. To be sure, his offense was disloyalty to his family and perhaps also his deceit of his father, but the later reflection that the deity caused Onan to do what he did because he was opposed to the sowing of mixed seed in the Israelite vineyard should not be excluded.[12]

"To render holy" should be understood as referring to divine action. The conditional nature of the law's sanction excludes the possibility that the term refers to removal by sacred officials. The deity might or might not remove from earthly existence the results of the sowing. The lawgiver cannot know for certain whether such removal will be forthcoming. In any event, this conditional clause ("lest . . .") is based upon the observation that Judah's third son, Shelah, did not go into Tamar, and whether he too might have done what Onan did and suffered a similar fate remains unknown. Even more to the point,

[12]Recall how the writer of the Joseph story records that God caused Joseph's brothers to sell him into slavery (Gen 45:4–8). Note, too, that in Jer 12:3 God planted wicked Israelites.

Judah himself produced two sons, Perez and Zerah, by Tamar, who is surely a Canaanitess herself, and they too duly constituted mixed seed, *kil'ayim*. In that the lawgiver knew that the line of Judah had continued beyond these two sons,[13] he could only infer that sometimes the deity was moved to interfere in such undesirable unions themselves or in their products, or in both. A parallel to the meaning of *qādaš* in the law is found in Jer 12:3. In referring to wicked Israelites who had been planted by the deity and had taken root, Jeremiah requests that they be extirpated by him, that is, that like sheep they be set apart (*hiph. qādaš*) for sacrifice, rendered taboo. Plainly, removal by the deity, without any earthly assistance, is in Jeremiah's mind.

We can also explain why the lawgiver is deliberately ambiguous about the relationship between the double seed and the vine. They are in fact overlapping entities. Er and Onan are half-Israelite vine, half-Canaanite plant. When Judah had them give of their seed to the Israelite vineyard (the line of Abraham, Isaac, Jacob, and Judah) through a union with Tamar, whose name means a palm tree, neither the seed that was sown nor the vine produced anything on that occasion. The vineyard itself, however, continued to exist because it was larger than Judah's immediate family. The mixed seed included the vine and was to be grafted onto the existing vine of Jacob. Probably the thought is acknowledged by the lawgiver that uniting such a mixture with a Canaanite palm tree (*tāmār*) was not going to produce the fruit of the vine. Certainly the picture projected is of a vineyard that contains plants other than the vine which threaten the vine's growth. It is just possible that the breach birth that Tamar eventually experienced, and that was intended to be remembered in the name Perez, signified either to the narrator of the story or to later thinkers the precarious nature of the union between Judah, who would be regarded as pure vine, and Tamar, the palm tree.[14]

By spelling out in an apparently unnecessary way that the entire yield of the vineyard means the seed that has been sown and the produce of the vineyard, the lawgiver accurately conveys what happened to Judah's sowing with his sons. Both they as the mixed seed,

[13]Cp. the genealogies in Num 26:20, 21;1 Chron 2:4–6, 9:4, 6.

[14]On the failure of the thistle to contract a marriage for his son with the cedar's daughter, see 2 Kings 14:9.

and the seed that was sought through their union with Tamar, came to nothing. She conceived by neither and both died. Jacob himself, in Gen 49:8–12, chose to express Judah's problem with his lineage in terms of animals mixing with vines. The Deuteronomist limits himself to the incompatible mixing of plants. Either way of thinking works well for the purpose intended, namely, to focus upon the problem of interbreeding. The switch to the mixing of plants was probably encouraged by the fact that Tamar's name meant a palm tree. To expand a little: if the model of Jacob's saying influenced the Deuteronomist, he had three possible modes of figurative expression to choose from—animals and plants, Jacob's choice; animals and animals; or, the one he chose, plants and plants. In that a vine was already used in reference to the activities of Judah's sons in Gen 49:11, the significance of Tamar's name would probably incline him to concentrate solely on the mixing of plants. It is in his next law, against plowing with an ox and an ass together, that he resorts to figurative meaning involving animals only.

Law: Plowing with an ox and an ass

[10] Thou shalt not plow with an ox and an ass together. (Deut 22:10)

Background: Shechem's seduction of Dinah

[1] And Dinah the daughter of Leah, which she bare unto Jacob, went out to see the daughters of the land. [2] And when Shechem the son of Hamor the Hivite, prince of the country, saw her, he took her, and lay with her, and humbled her. [3] And his soul clave unto Dinah the daughter of Jacob, and he loved the damsel, and spake kindly unto the damsel. [4] And Shechem spake unto his father Hamor, saying, Get me this damsel to wife. [5] And Jacob heard that he had defiled Dinah his daughter: now his sons were with his cattle in the field: and Jacob held his peace until they were come. [6] And Hamor the father of Shechem went out unto Jacob to commune with him. [7] And the sons of Jacob came out of the field when they heard it: and the men were grieved, and they were very wroth, because he had wrought folly in Israel in lying with Jacob's daughter; which thing ought not to be done. [8] And

Hamor communed with them, saying, The soul of my son Shechem longeth for your daughter: I pray you give her him to wife. [9] And make ye marriages with us, and give your daughters unto us, and take our daughters unto you. [10] And ye shall dwell with us: and the land shall be before you; dwell and trade ye therein, and get you possessions therein. [11] And Shechem said unto her father and unto her brethren, Let me find grace in your eyes, and what ye shall say unto me, I will give. [12] Ask me never so much dowry and gift, and I will give according as ye shall say unto me: but give me the damsel to wife. [13] And the sons of Jacob answered Shechem and Hamor his father deceitfully, and said, because he had defiled Dinah their sister: [14] and they said unto them, We cannot do this thing, to give our sister to one that is uncircumcised; for that were a reproach unto us: [15] but in this will we consent unto you: If ye will be as we be, that every male of you be circumcised; [16] then will we give our daughters unto you, and we will take your daughters to us, and we will dwell with you, and we will become one people. [17] But if ye will not hearken unto us, to be circumcised; then we will take our daughter, and we will be gone. [Hamor and Shechem take the proposition to the men of their city and all the males agree to undergo circumcision.] [25] And it came to pass on the third day, when they were sore, that two of the sons of Jacob, Simeon and Levi, Dinah's brethren, took each man his sword, and came upon the city boldly, and slew all the males. [26] And they slew Hamor and Shechem his son with the edge of the sword, and took Dinah out of Shechem's house, and went out. [27] The sons of Jacob came upon the slain, and spoiled the city, because they had defiled their sister. [28] They took their sheep, and their oxen, and their asses, and that which was in the city, and that which was in the field, [29] and all their wealth, and all their little ones, and their wives took they captive, and spoiled even all that was in the house. [30] And Jacob said to Simeon and Levi, Ye have troubled me to make me to stink among the inhabitants of the land, among the Canaanites and the Perizzites: and I being few in number, they shall gather themselves together against me, and slay me; and I shall be destroyed, I and my house. [31] And they said, Should he deal with our sister as with an harlot. (Gen 34:1–17, 25–31)

[5] Simeon and Levi are brothers; weapons of violence are their swords. [6] O my soul, come not into their council; unto their assembly, mine honour, be not thou united: for in their anger they slew a man, and by their goodwill they hamstrung an ox. [7] Cursed be their anger, for it was fierce; and their wrath, for it was

cruel. I will divide them in Jacob, and scatter them in Israel. (Gen 49:5–7)

This prohibition neglects to state that an Israelite should not plow *his field* with an ox and an ass together. If the rule as formulated, without the reference to the field, is to be understood literally, this meaning is obviously implied. The omission, however, invites comment, especially in light of the explicit, seemingly unnecessary detail in the preceding law. The omission is in fact one indication that a figurative meaning is sought and that the emphasis is upon the relationship between the ox and the ass. How can an ox plow an ass, or an ass an ox? The answer lies in the figurative sense of plowing and the representation intended by the two animals in question. Plowing, like sowing, readily lends itself to the notion of sexual intercourse.[15] The ass has a Canaanite reference, the ox, an Israelite. Before passing on to the meaning intended, it should also be noted that a further indication that a literal meaning is excluded comes from observing that an ox and an ass can indeed be harnessed to a plow.[16] If so, what then would be the point of the prohibition? If it is somehow awkward to plow with the two, the farmer will find out soon enough. He hardly needs a prohibition on the matter.[17]

In Jacob's saying about Judah he used the ass in alluding to Judah's half-Canaanite sons, Er and Onan, and he did so precisely in regard to their sexual activity, their unions with Tamar. It is in his preceding comments, however, about Simeon and Levi, that animal imagery involving both the ass and the ox comes into play. In condemning Simeon and Levi for their savage treatment of all the male Sheche-

[15]See Pope, *Song of Songs,* 323–24.

[16]See S. R. Driver, *Deuteronomy* ICC (Edinburgh: T. and T. Clark, 1902) 253.

[17]In deciding that a statement should be read as originally intending a figurative meaning, we must be able to point to an oddity either in its formulation—for example, the omission of certain words that might be expected—or in its apparent meaning. The legal proverb, "He that bulls the cow must keep the calf," indicates that a figurative sense is intended: we are meant to wonder why the natural order of things does not prevail, namely, why the cow does not keep its calf. Note too in this saying the ambiguous use of "to keep." Both senses, to possess and to maintain, are attested in early English. In John 4:7 Jesus' request of the Samaritan woman for a drink, *Dós moi pieĩn,* the water (*húdōr*) is understood. The result is that a bold figurative meaning is achieved, quite different from the literal. See my "Marriage and the Samaritan Woman," *NTS* 26 (1980): 336.

mites, Jacob expresses his complaint in characteristically allusive fashion: in their anger they had killed a man and in their "goodwill" they had hamstrung an ox (Gen 49:6). The man killed is Hamor, who stands for all the Hivites or Shechemites, and the parallel reference to the ox that still lives but is hamstrung is to Jacob's family. Jacob is referring to the fearful incident recounted in Genesis 34. His sons' action, which they took to be a desirable one, of slaughtering this Canaanite clan had on the contrary the baneful effect of rendering their own people vulnerable to revenge at the hands of other Canaanite groups.[18] As Jacob puts it, these two sons had brought trouble on him by making him odious to the inhabitants of the land, to the Canaanites and the Perizzites. His military strength would be impaired because his numbers were few and any attack upon his family would lead to its destruction (Gen 34:30). The ox, domestic or wild, is sometimes used to suggest Israel's military stance (Deut 33:17; Num 23:22, 24:8; cp., Num 22:4; 1 Kings 22:11; Amos 6:12, 13), and the image of one that has been hamstrung is a singularly appropriate reference to their handicap in the face of their Canaanite enemies.[19] Even the choice of the word "to hamstring" (*ʿiqqēr*) is inspired by the fondness for wordplays exhibited throughout all of the sayings in Genesis 49.[20] It takes up Jacob's complaint in Gen 34:30 about the trouble that his sons had brought upon him (*ʿākar*). Quite apart from the general use of animal comparisons in Genesis 49, a specific influence upon the choice of the ox in the saying about Simeon and Levi is the contrast that has to be drawn between the man, Hamor, who was slain and the ox, Israel, that was hamstrung. The name in the background, Hamor (ass), readily suggests a corresponding animal comparison for the other party.

If Jacob in Genesis 49 reflected negatively upon his sons' extreme action in slaughtering the collective group, the Hivites, or alternatively the innocent Hamor, the father of the guilty Shechem,[21] the

[18]Jacob is being ironical when he refers to the "favor, goodwill" (*rāṣôn*) done to the house of Israel by Simeon and Levi.

[19]Hamstringing an animal is something that occurs in military activity apparently to frustrate the opposition's capacity to continue to operate. Joshua, among whose enemies were the Hivites, and David both did it to their enemies' animals (Josh 11:6, 9; 2 Sam 8:4; 1 Chron 18:4).

[20]Cp. the play upon the name Ekron, *ʿeqrôn tēʿaqēr* (Zeph 2:4).

[21]See my analysis (in chapter 10) of the law on individual responsibility (Deut 24:16).

Deuteronomist reflects adversely upon the main issue that gave rise to it. This issue is Shechem's seduction of Jacob's daughter, Dinah, and the subsequent attempt to forge a link between the Israelites and these Canaanites. The son of the ass, Hamor, had plowed the daughter of the ox, Jacob, and this had led to the possibility of a much broader alliance between the two ethnic groups, which, because of his fierce views on the subject, invited condemnation by the Deuteronomist. In Deut 7:1–5 he explicitly prohibits such alliances and mentions Hamor's group, the Hivites. The arrangement in Genesis 34 was in fact vitiated because of the extermination by Simeon and Levi of the male Hivites. What did take place, however, was that the remaining Hivite women and their children were incorporated into Jacob's family (Gen 34:29, 35:1–4). This raises the possibility that Israelite men might take Canaanite women, the very thing the lawgiver reflected negatively upon in his preceding vineyard law. Judah had "plowed" such a woman and she had produced three sons, each of them mixed seed that Judah had then tried to use in sowing the Israelite vineyard. If an ox plows an ass, figuratively speaking, this can lead to a mixed breed. In this light, the law comes very close in meaning to the prohibition against sowing mixed seed in an Israelite vineyard.[22] Its formulation is inspired by the specific example of the plowing that took place between Dinah and Shechem, but the lawgiver's attention turns to the influx of the Hivite women into Jacob's family and the possibilities that that suggested, and Judah's example of a marriage between an Israelite and a Canaanite. It is again important to emphasize that the law should not be viewed as a general condemnation, along the lines of Deut 7:1–5, of Israelite-Canaanite unions. Such a view is not wrong; it distorts, however, the perspective necessary to appreciate these figurative laws, namely, as cryptic comments upon historical developments during the formative beginnings of the Israelite nation.

Law: Wearing wool and linen

[11] Thou shalt not put on *šaʿaṭnēz*: wool and linen together. (Deut 22:11)

[22]And even closer, I might add, to the Levitical injunction against breeding two different kinds of animals (Lev 19:19).

Background: Judah and Tamar (Gen 38, 49:8–12)

The prohibition, "Thou shalt not put on *šaʿaṭnēz*, wool and linen together," is also linked to the preceding prohibitions in that it is meant to be understood figuratively, has a sexual import, and focuses negatively on Judah's relationship with Tamar. Clothes are attached to the body, and their intimate personal ("persona" may originally have meant a mask)[23] associations can occasion no surprise. Biblical illustrations of this fact are readily available. To spread a garment over a woman to cover her nakedness, as the deity, who is construed as a human lover, did for the nubile woman, Jerusalem (Ezek 16:8), has a symbolical meaning. At the level of male-female relationships the man is betrothing her and intends to put her on as his new garment in a reciprocal action by which he will cover his own nakedness. Ruth's request of Boaz when lying at his feet on the threshing floor is distinctly comparable. She is suggesting that she will become his new garment, that is, his wife, just as her action of uncovering his feet and lying at them conveys the similar sexual suggestion of becoming his new "shoes" to be put on his genital "feet."[24] The Koran's statement, "They [wives] are raiment for you and ye are raiment for them," accurately describes the biblical position.[25] A biblical example of a wife being referred to as his garment (*lebûšô*) occurs in Mal 2:16. The text is problematic but this identification is fairly assured. The context is about the cruelty of divorcing a wife.

The most persuasive evidence of the figurative significance of the clothing in the law comes from its context. In a preceding law the subject of a man's dressing as a woman, that is, putting on (*lbš*) her garment in a literal sense,[26] comes up. The two laws that follow the one we are discussing both involve clothing. The tassels law is about wearing a garment with certain attachments that symbolically declare

[23]Gellius, *Attic Nights,* 5.7.

[24]For the symbolism, see my "Treading." The verb *lbš*, "to put on," is frequently given a figurative sense, for example, putting on beauty, strength, shame.

[25]Q. 2:187. Cp. too, "Behold not everybody's beauty, and sit not in the midst of women. For from garments cometh a moth, and from women wickedness" (Sir 42:12, 13).

[26]The switch from the literal to the figurative characterizes this lawgiver's methods. In his levirate law (Deut 25:5–10) a woman symbolically interferes with a man's genitals in order to disgrace him. The next law concerns a woman who grabs a man's genitals in a fight.

that the (male) wearer is not given to lust. In the succeeding law the production of a bloodstained cloth provides evidence that a woman was a virgin on her wedding night. After a number of other sex laws there is the direct equation of a wife to a garment: "A man shall not take his father's wife, nor shall he uncover his father's skirt" (22:30). The latter text alone is sufficiently important to encourage us to be alert to a figurative sense for the foreign garment referred to in Deut 22:11.

If we attempt to give the law literal sense we are confronted with some difficult problems. All commentators are agreed that its meaning is obscure. Indications are, moreover, that wool and linen were worn together, for example, in such important garments as the priestly robes, breastpiece, and ephod.[27] In its context, just preceeding a series of sex laws and immediately after two laws concerned with the sexual activities of Judah's sons and Jacob's daughter, an originally intended figurative meaning about similar patriarchal matters is likely. The levirate law in Deut 25:5–10 is derived from reflection upon Tamar's problem in Genesis 38. One conclusion that follows from the integral relationship between that law and narrative is the not surprising negative attitude on the part of the Deuteronomist to her having to resort to harlotry. Recall that she put off her widow's garments and dressed herself as a prostitute. The latter's clothing advertises her profession, and other evidence indicates that her finery would typically be made of linen because of its luxurious quality. The emphasis on Tamar's clothing is explained by the fact that she had to conceal her identity from Judah as well as attract him to her. On both counts she was successful. Judah, on his way to gather his annual supply of wool, lay with her. The law condemns Judah's involvement with her as a harlot.

If we understand that the Deuteronomist's use of a garment figuratively represents a woman, then it is easy to see how this episode would lead him to construct a prohibition against putting on a certain kind of clothing, namely, that associated with harlotry. The prominence, moreover, given to clothing both in the story of Genesis 38 and in Jacob's saying in Genesis 49:11 (do not forget its role in Joseph's

[27]See *Interpreter's Dictionary of the Bible*, ed. G. A. Buttrick (New York: Abingdon, 1962), s.v. "cloth."

problems in Genesis 37 and 39) would encourage him to compose a proverbial-type law. Inspired by the poetical constructions of Jacob in Genesis 49, he would note the parallel activities of Judah and Tamar and how they coincided, under the latter's direction, in their sexual encounter. Judah's wife died, but after the widower was comforted he sought to engage in what was a festival occasion, woolgathering at Timnah. Tamar, seeking a child by Judah, put off her widow's garb and disguised herself in clothes that would bring pleasure to Judah's wandering eye. This interplay between wool and linen, Judah's going for one but being attracted to the other, has, in part, generated the law: already wearing wool himself he should not then have put on linen. An additional impetus for the prohibition comes from Gen 49:11. Jacob had used imagery about clothing and grapes to convey Judah's action of mourning the sons who had come from his "covering" (*l^ebûšô*), his wife. This description of his activity with wine is followed by an allusion to his wine pleasure at the place *ʿênayim* ("red are the eyes [*ʿênayim*] from wine"),[28] the place where he went into Tamar. By tuning in to this language, the Deuteronomist would readily switch from the funeral use of a garment to its sexual use in order to give his cryptic judgment upon Judah's contact with the prostitute.

The way in which he chooses to express his judgment reflects certain associations that are attached to wool and linen in the wider culture. Linen in particular arouses sensual appetites. In an interesting parallel to Tamar's activity Judith seduced Holofernes by putting off her widow's garb, anointing her face with perfume, binding her hair with a headband, and dressing in "a linen gown to beguile him" (Jth 16:8). The luxuriousness of the harlot city in Rev 18:16 is manifest in her linen garment. In Hos 2:5 Israel, the harlot, receives wool and linen from her lovers. Probably the former is for her ordinary clothing while the latter is for attracting the lovers. Rahab seems to have had a plentiful source of linen because she hid the Israelite spies among the stalks of flax on her roof (Jos 2:6). The wanton in Prov 7:16 covers

[28]Wine is not mentioned in the story itself, but Jacob has good reason to think Judah is inebriated—he was en route to a festival and he failed to recognize his daughter-in-law when lying with her. Her veil is not sufficient to explain his failure to recognize her. The reference, however, is probably more metaphorical in character—it alludes to his drinking the wine of love. On the link between the two in Cant 5:1, see Pope, *Song of Songs* 501–9; cp., Prov 5:15, "Drink waters out of thine own cistern."

her couch with Egyptian linen in order to lure her lovers. By contrast, the ordinariness of wool, its common use, perhaps the nature of the material itself, would neutralize any sensual associations. Interesting in this regard is the contrast drawn between wool and linen material in Isaiah's reference to the sins of the harlot Jerusalem: "Though they are red like crimson [scarlet stuff or robes], they shall become like wool" (Isa 1:18, 21).[29]

In the law the material referred to by the foreign word *šaʿaṭnēz* does not refer to a combination of wool and linen, but to a luxurious linen garment (probably of foreign origin like the Egyptian linen of Prov 7:16) that a prostitute might wear.[30] The reason it has been interpreted to mean a mixed stuff is because the law is taken at its literal, face value. Once, however, the figurative sense is seen as an interpretive possibility the wool represents the addressee (Judah in particular, but any descendant of his could be intended), and the linen takes up the reference to the *šaʿaṭnēz*, and hence to the prostitute: "Thou [Judah/Israel] shalt not put on *šaʿaṭnēz* [a prostitute], wool [the Israelite] and linen [the prostitute] together." In other words, the addressee ("Thou") and the *šaʿaṭnēz* are paralleled by the wool and the linen, respectively. The use of a strange, foreign word is itself a device to direct the hearer to wider, human associations.

Although the law has an obvious allegorical character, this should not be emphasized. The lawgiver is not dependent upon a tradition of allegorical interpretation.[31] The identifications he makes are inspired by the example of Jacob's language in Genesis 49 and certain features of the narratives he is interested in. Some of the law's aspects already bear meaningful overtones in these narratives, others do not. It would therefore be quite misleading to argue that an ox or wool, especially the latter, was to be equated with an Israelite because such identifications were standard, well-recognized ones. The literary cleverness of the authors of the sayings and the laws is the primary feature. To

[29]Cp., Jer 4:30, Jerusalem (represented by the figure of a woman) will put on (*lbš*) crimson (robes) and other fine things in a vain attempt to attract her lovers.

[30]On the conjectured Egyptian origin of *šaʿaṭnēz*, see T. O. Lambdin, "Egyptian Loan Words in the Old Testament," *JAOS* 73 (1953): 155. The suggested meaning (to do with cutting) does not connote a mixing of two materials. Zephaniah (1:8) predicts punishment for those who have put on (*lbš*) foreign attire.

[31]His procedure, however, should be compared with such parables as Jothan's (Judg 9:7–15) and Nathan's (2 Sam 12:1–6).

avoid an overly artificial reading of the law it is best to concentrate on its close connection with the narrative in Genesis 38.

It is obviously noteworthy that the three laws on mixtures can each be interpreted similarly. Their common background in judging patriarchal matters merits further comment. The law on clothing follows the one on the ox and the ass. The latter takes up the issue of Shechem's appropriation of Dinah, which from Simeon and Levi's point of view meant that he had treated her like a harlot (Gen 34:32). The link to Tamar's harlotry that emerges in the clothing law is therefore a clear and direct one. It is typical of the lawgiver to range over traditions that share common features. In this regard all three laws can be seen to apply to Judah. He it was who sowed his vineyard with mixed seed, who in marrying a Canaanite woman in the first place provided an example of an ox plowing an ass, and whose intercourse with Tamar, because he failed to recognize her, could be said to take the form of his putting on a certain kind of finery, a prostitute.

It is especially appropriate, because of a prostitute's anonymity, to make use of the sexual associations of clothing in speaking of a man's contact with her. A man's desire for a prostitute is the subject of the proverb: "Can a man carry fire in his bosom and his clothes not be burned" (Prov 6:27). In regard to Judah an additional factor is noteworthy. The transvestite law prohibits a man's disguising himself in a woman's clothing. This lawgiver often switches from a literal meaning to a figurative one, or vice versa. One stimulates the other. Tamar's disguise and Judah's subsequent intercourse with her combine to suggest the notion of Judah's covering himself with her "clothing." This idea is also suggested by the fact that Tamar would not have removed her clothes when giving herself to Judah. It is also interesting to observe that from Tamar's side she required a male of Judah's family to "spread his skirt" over her because she had a legitimate claim to it.

The proverbial element in these laws has to be kept in mind. Two of them are especially short and pithy in nature; if we paraphrase them in terms of the stories from which they issue an artificial aspect emerges. This awkwardness is common to all abbreviated forms of speech, proverbs, wit, and the like. The statement, "Clothes make the man," if given an extended paraphrase, degenerates into something banal and silly. The German, "neuer Arzt-neuer Friedhof," has, in the words of T. Boman,[32] the logical content: "When a new and inexperienced doctor replaces the older one, so many people will die that a new cemetery will become necessary." As Boman points out, this is a position no reasonable person would maintain, but when the idea is expressed in an abbreviated form its measure of truth can be accepted. The same observations hold for an understanding of the coming together of wool and linen as Judah on his way to his sheep shearing and encountering the disguised Tamar in her harlot's finery.[33]

The parallel rules in Lev 19:19

"Thy cattle thou shalt not breed with two kinds; thy field thou shalt not sow with two kinds, and a garment of two kinds, *šaʿaṭnēz*, shall not come upon thee."

Each of the three Deuteronomic laws can be viewed as arising from reflection upon matters relating to the patriarch Judah: the sowing, plowing, and putting on all bear similar sexual meanings. As we have repeatedly indicated, the inspiration for their construction is Jacob's cryptic comments upon his son's activities (Genesis 49). Another factor is that the judgments in question stand in condemnation of Judah and that, from a political point of view, such criticism of a revered ancestor is often best expressed less directly. It is a reasonable assumption that the original recipients of these pronouncements belonged to the Judean community that traced its origin to this particular patriarch. While it might be fine for this special group openly to condemn patriarchal actions, it was prudent for them to conceal their criticism from the wider community. However that may be, it seems clear that the Deuteronomic laws were addressed to a group who surveyed the ancient traditions of their nation and who understood the hidden references in these figurative laws. Any other audience, not knowing their source, would readily lose their original significance. It appears that the Levitical lawgivers constituted such a group. They no longer understood their allusions and gave them a literal meaning

[32]T. Boman, *Hebrew Thought Compared with Greek* (London: SCM, 1960), 35, n. 2.

[33]John Dover Wilson points out how disguised characters in Shakespearian comedy provide opportunity for all kinds of veiled allusion, double meaning, dramatic irony, and subtlety of dialogue (*Shakespeare's Happy Comedies* [Evanston, Ill.: Northwestern University Press, 1962], 28).

that was to become the standard way of evaluating them throughout Jewish legal history. We might compare how certain proverbs lose their meaning because the historical incidents upon which they were based are forgotten, or no longer recognized.[34]

Sense was made of the prohibition against plowing with an ox and an ass together by seeing the figurative force of "to plow," and applying it generally to two different kinds of animal (*behēmāh*). A more inclusive construction was also made of the prohibition against sowing a vineyard with mixed seed. The limitation to a vineyard was viewed as puzzling probably because in practice fields were more likely, or just as likely, to be sown with different seeds (such is apparently the case in Isa 28:25). Hence the prohibition was applied to fields, with vineyards presumably included.[35] The threatened sanction in the Deuteronomic law made no sense because a mixed sowing gave rise to no more problems than a single one. Consequently, any reference to the results of sowing mixed seed was omitted from the law's formulation. The clothing prohibition also underwent changes because the same generalizing tendency and pursuit of a literal meaning were at work. Just as the specific references to the ox, the ass, the vineyard were altered by introducing wider categories, so the particular mention of wool and linen was dropped and replaced by the general notion of a garment of two kinds (of stuff). The literal meaning was more firmly secured by reformulating. Instead of, "Thou shalt not put on *šaʿaṭnēz,* wool and linen together," we find: "A garment of two kinds, *šaʿaṭnēz,* shall not come upon thee." The metonymy was no longer understood.[36] It now meant a garment of

[34]"As a rule, the meaning of an historical allusion cannot long remain generally intelligible" (Taylor, *The Proverb,* 83). Again, certain proverbs undergo a change in emphasis because the historical background is lost. Taylor plausibly argues that this has occurred for the saying, "A fair exchange is no robbery" (93).

[35]A.D.H. Mayes draws attention to the use of the verb "to sow" rather than "to plant" in reference to the vineyard, *Deuteronomy* NCBC (Grand Rapids: Eerdmans, 1981), 308. He asserts that the rule in Lev 19:19 is "undoubtedly original" because "to sow" is more appropriate when speaking of a field. The point is, however, that at the figurative level a man sows seed in a woman (e.g., Lev 12:2; Num 5:28), he does not plant it. Apart from being unaware of the figurative meaning of the law, Mayes overlooks the much more formal and systematic character of the material in Lev 19:19, itself telling evidence of secondary development.

[36]Just as those not familiar with western culture, and even those who are, might not understand such terms as: brown shirt, blue-collar worker, bluestocking, bobby-soxer, hard-hat, redcoat, sans culotte, zoot suiter.

two kinds, and wool and linen together would constitute but one example. Each of the three laws was similarly formulated: the object of the prohibition—animals (the collective *beḥēmāh*), field, garment—was placed at the head of the sentence, and the term *kil'ayim* introduced into each. What meaning was attributed to them in this new form it is impossible to say. The role of priestly interpretation of divine statutes ("My statutes ye shall keep" is the injunction appended to the three laws) should be borne in mind because the emphasis of such interpretation may be upon their sacred, mysterious content. A failure to comprehend their original meaning would encourage the notion of an arcane dimension.

SUMMARY Judah's problem in having his half-Israelite, half-Canaanite sons perpetuate his line, the line of Jacob/Israel, is addressed in the proverbial-type law against planting mixed seeds in a vineyard. His marriage to a Canaanite woman is likewise reflected in the rule against plowing with an ox and an ass together, because this injunction takes up the earlier problem of intermarriage between Jacob's family and that of Hamor. Judah's solution to the problem of the continuance of his family, his intercourse with the attractively dressed prostitute at Enaim when he was on his way to a sheep-shearing festival, is the focus of the rule against the mixing of wool and linen.

CHAPTER 8

SEXUAL MATTERS IN PATRIARCHAL TIMES

In the series of sex laws in Deut 22:9–22:30 it is noteworthy that every one of them can be shown to owe its inclusion to traditions in the Book of Genesis, from those about Abraham and Sarah to the one about Joseph and Potiphar's wife. The first four (mixed seed, ox and ass, wool and linen, tassels) are Deuteronomic creations that are based entirely upon elements in the patriarchal traditions. The others are additionally dependent upon the Deuteronomist's knowledge of customary law, or upon his familiarity with such rules as that about the seduction of an unbetrothed girl in Exod 22:16, 17.

Law: Tassels on an Israelite's covering

[12] Thou shalt make thee tassels upon the four corners of thy cloak, wherewith thou coverest thyself. (Deut 22:12)

Background: Joseph's "adultery" with Potiphar's wife

[7] And it came to pass after these things, that his master's wife cast her eyes upon Joseph; and she said, Lie with me. [8] But he refused, and said unto his master's wife, Behold, my master wotteth not what is with me in the house, and he hath committed all that he

> hath to my hand; [9] there is none greater in this house than I; neither hath he kept back any thing from me but thee, because thou art his wife: how then can I do this great wickedness, and sin against God? [10] And it came to pass, as she spake to Joseph day by day, that he hearkened not unto her, to lie by her, or to be with her. [11] And it came to pass about this time, that Joseph went into the house to do his business; and there was none of the men of the house there within. [12] And she caught him by his garment, saying, Lie with me: and he left his garment in her hand, and fled, and got him out. [13] And it came to pass, when she saw that he had left his garment in her hand, and was fled forth, [14] that she called unto the men of her house, and spake unto them, saying, See, he hath brought in an Hebrew unto us to mock us; he came in unto me to lie with me, and I cried with a loud voice: [15] and it came to pass, when he heard that I lifted up my voice and cried, that he left his garment with me, and fled, and got him out. [16] And she laid up his garment by him until his lord came home. [17] And she spake unto him, according to those words, saying, The Hebrew servant which thou hast brought unto us, came in unto me to mock me: [18] and it came to pass, as I lifted up my voice and cried, that he left his garment with me, and fled out. [19] And it came to pass, when his master heard the words of his wife, which she spake unto him, saying, After this manner did thy servant to me; that his wrath was kindled. [20] And Joseph's master took him, and put him into the prison, a place where the king's prisoners were bound: and he was there in the prison. (Gen 39:7–20)

The law requiring an Israelite to place tassels on the four corners of his covering contrasts with the preceding laws in that it involves the notion of a compatible combination rather than an incompatible one. It is a positive injunction, not a prohibition. No clue to its meaning is found in its formulation. Yet the fact that it is a positive command compels one to look for a symbolical meaning. Fortunately a clue is furnished in a later, more expanded statement of the law in Num 15:37–41: the tassels are for looking upon and remembering all the commandments.[1] This general meaning takes care of the positive nature of the law, but it obscures the particular significance that one would expect to find attributed to what is, after all, a detail of dress.

[1]Biblical proverbs (Prov 1:9, 3:3) about clothing oneself with virtue and wisdom come to mind.

The lawgiver goes on to state in a negative vein that the Israelite should not follow after his heart and eyes "after which ye go a whoring." The verb is *zānāh*, "to commit fornication." It is this specific connection between dress and wrongful sexual desire that supplies the law's original significance and links it to the preceding *šaʿaṭnēz* law. Its origin again lies in the Deuteronomist's reflection upon patriarchal incidents.

The role of clothing in the Joseph story is pronounced. His special coat was a mark of his father's esteem for him and a symbol of his brothers' envy. They eventually stripped him of it, and to convey to their father that he had been destroyed by a wild beast, they dipped it in some blood and presented it as evidence of his death. Joseph, however, was not dead but had been sold, on Judah's instigation, and had become a head servant in the Egyptian Potiphar's house. A garment again becomes a crucial element in the continuing history of Joseph's humiliation. As a servant in Potiphar's house he, like Judah, became the object of a non-Israelite woman's sexual advances. Unlike Judah, he resisted. Judah's action came under negative review in the *šaʿaṭnēz* prohibition; Joseph's passiveness is commended in the tassels law. His garment, removed from him by the scheming wife of Potiphar, constituted proof that he had tried to seduce her. He was convicted and cast into prison. Given that Joseph, whose virtue is made a point of in the narrative, was innocent yet stood condemned because a woman possessed his garment, the Deuteronomist asks: how can an Israelite's garment outwardly indicate that he is not given to adulterous intent? The tassels are to be put upon an Israelite's garment precisely for this purpose, to remind him that like Joseph he should be virtuous in matters of sexual morality, that he "should not follow after his heart and eyes to commit fornication," as Judah did in possessing the *šaʿaṭnēz*, Tamar.[2] Obviously the lawgiver is not thinking of any legal significance that the tassels may have in a situation comparable to Joseph's. In his adultery law (Deut 22:22) he cites a criterion, namely, the discovery of the man and the woman together, that would nullify the kind of evidence furnished by Potiphar's wife.

[2]In *Babylonian Menahoth* 44a, we find the story of the disciple who, about to have intercourse with a harlot, was stopped by the tassels of his garment miraculously striking him on his face. Impressed, she became a proselyte and married him. I am indebted to Dr. Jacob J. Petuchowski of Hebrew Union College, Cincinnati, for drawing my attention to this passage.

Only in symbolical fashion and only in regard to a mental state can the tassels represent male innocence in the face of false charges of sexual misconduct.

That we are probing in the right direction for the origin of the tassels law is supported by analysis of the law that immediately follows. This time, instead of a false charge of sexual misconduct against an Israelite male, we have the contrasting case where an Israelite woman is wrongfully accused. Her new husband slanders her by claiming that she was not a virgin on her wedding night, that she had engaged in acts of harlotry prior to her marriage. Her innocence, unlike Joseph's, is established by a garment, in her case the blood-stained virginity sheet (*b^e^tûlîm*). It constitutes a token of her freedom from harlotry, just as the tassels on the male garment are supposed to communicate his. The latter has symbolical force only, the former legal.

The Deuteronomist is, not surprisingly, alert to recurring issues in patriarchal history. It happens that Joseph's problem has a precedent in Genesis 20. Abimelech, king of Gerar, sought what he perceived to be a legitimate relationship with Abraham's sister, Sarah. She herself had let him think that she was free to become his wife. From the deity's point of view, that is, one that represents either a universal or an Israelite community standard, he was in fact attaching himself to a married woman and committing adultery (Gen 20:3). He rightly protested his innocence and successfully fought his condemnation. Nonetheless we find him paying Abraham as Sarah's brother a thousand pieces of silver as "a covering of the eyes" (*k^e^sût ʿênayim*) to all her acquaintances. The implication appears to be that their eyes will be blind to any sexual misconduct on her part, or inflicted on her.[3] The term *k^e^sût*, "covering," is used figuratively and is linked to the notion of concealing sexual impropriety. The lawgiver, observing this development but interested in the innocent male's side of things, pursues a contrary significance for an Israelite's actual covering (*k^e^sût*): it should declare, by means of the tassels attached to it, that he is not

[3]The text is difficult. The final word is either (with AV) *w^e^nōkāḥat*, "And [or thus] she was reproved," or (with RSV) *w^e^nōkaḥt*, "And thou art set right." If the text refers to Sarah's justification, such a reading does not account for the fact that she participates in Abraham's stratagem. That the innocent Abimelech has to make a payment is less puzzling in light of the well-recognized view that even unwitting tresspass must not go unpunished.

given to wrongful sexual desire. It is the association between this term and the subject of sexual wrongdoing in Gen 20:16 that accounts for its use in the law, rather than the term *beged* as in the Joseph story (and in the law in Num 15:38).[4]

Law: The wedding night cloth

> [13] If any man take a wife, and go in unto her, and hate her, [14] and bring trumped-up charges against her, and bring up an evil name upon her, and say, I took this woman, and when I came to her, I found her not a maid: [15] then shall the father of the damsel, and her mother, take and bring forth the tokens of the damsel's virginity unto the elders of the city in the gate: [16] and the damsel's father shall say unto the elders, I gave my daughter unto this man to wife, and he hateth her; [17] and lo, he hath brought trumped-up charges against her, saying, I found not thy daughter a maid; and yet these are the tokens of my daughter's virginity. And they shall spread the cloth before the elders of the city. [18] And the elders of that city shall take that man and chastise him; [19] and they shall amerce him in an hundred shekels of silver, and give them unto the

[4]There may exist indications that the language of Genesis 38 has influenced the tassels law. The expression "to cover oneself with" (*piʿel* of *kāsāh* with *b*) is found only in the tassels law and in Gen 38:14 (but possibly also in Jon 3:6). The sexual significance of each covering is uppermost. Judah identified the woman as a harlot "for she had covered her face" (v. 15). In the law, as David Daube pointed out to me when he kindly read my analysis, the covering is enormously emphasized by the addition of the verb to the noun: "He is to be totally enwrapped, and thus totally free from any shaming suspicion." The term for tassels, *gᵉdīlîm* (only in Deuteronomy), may be related to the verb *gādal,* "to become strong." In the law these cords are for the purpose of proclaiming a man's control of his desires, his strength to resist illicit sex. The Deuteronomist's use of the term may owe something to his reflection upon the Tamar story. The reason why she prostituted herself was because Shelah had matured sexually, *gādal* (Gen 38:11, 14) but had not been sent into her. That Shelah's sexual maturity (which is not put to the test) is followed by Joseph's (which is) may well be an important link between the two traditions and the law. The Hebrew word *gᵉdīlîm* is a cognate to terms in Aramaic and Arabic that denote plaited cords or hair, but proof of its ultimate relationship to a verb meaning "to become strong" is hard to establish. See, however, G. R. Driver's observations (kindly drawn to my attention by John Emerton) on the possible semantic link between Semitic words for "strong" and those to do with "twisting" in, "L'interprétation du texte masorétique à la lumière de la lexicographie hébraïque," *ETL* 26 (1950):343. In the parallel Num 15:38 law the term for the cords is *pᵉtîlîm.* Again it is interesting to note that Judah handed his *pᵉtîlîm* to Tamar by way of pledging that he would pay for her services (Gen 38:18, 25). They can indeed, on reflection, be viewed as betokening his lust. In other words, a later interpreter would readily choose to ascribe this significance to them.

father of the damsel, because he hath brought up an evil name upon a virgin of Israel: and she shall be his wife; he may not put her away all his days. [20] But if this thing be true, and the tokens of virginity be not found for the damsel: [21] then they shall bring out the damsel to the door of her father's house, and the men of her city shall stone her with stones that she die: because she hath wrought folly in Israel, to play the whore in her father's house: so shalt thou put evil away from thy midst. (Deut 22:13–21)

Background: Jacob's marriage to Leah instead of to Rachel

[15] And Laban said unto Jacob, Because thou art my brother, shouldest thou therefore serve me for nought? tell me, what shall thy wages be? [16] And Laban had two daughters: the name of the elder was Leah, and the name of the younger was Rachel. [17] Leah was tender eyed; but Rachel was beautiful and well favoured. [18] And Jacob loved Rachel; and said, I will serve thee seven years for Rachel thy younger daughter. . . . [20] And Jacob served seven years for Rachel; and they seemed unto him but a few days, for the love he had to her. [21] And Jacob said unto Laban, Give me my wife, for my days are fulfilled, that I may go in unto her. [22] And Laban gathered together all the men of the place, and made a feast. [23] And it came to pass in the evening, that he took Leah his daughter, and brought her to him; and he went in unto her. . . . [25] And it came to pass, that in the morning, behold, it was Leah: and he said to Laban, What is this thou hast done unto me? did not I serve with thee for Rachel? wherefore then has thou beguiled me? [26] And Laban said, It must not be so done in our country, to give the younger before the firstborn. [27] Fulfil her week, and we will give thee this also for the service which thou shalt serve with me yet seven other years. [28] And Jacob did so, and fulfilled her week: and he gave him Rachel his daughter to wife also. . . . [30] And he went in also unto Rachel, and he loved Rachel rather than Leah, and served with him yet seven other years. [31] And when Yahweh saw that Leah was hated, he opened her womb: but Rachel was barren. (Gen 29:15–18, 20–23, 25–28, 30, 31)

The law about the man who falsely accuses his bride of not being a virgin on her wedding night and how she, or rather her parents, disprove the allegation by producing the bloodstained wedding night cloth, provides a matter that contrasts with what happened to Joseph. His garment in his female accuser's possession falsely convicted him of a sexual offense against her (and her husband). In the law about the slandered bride the case in question has been inspired by yet another patriarchal narrative: Jacob's marriage to Leah instead of to Rachel. The deliberate mix-up occurred on the wedding night. Laban, so we can assume, took advantage of the cover of darkness, as well as Jacob's probable inebriation from the nuptial festivities, to carry out the substitution. There is a sense in which Leah seduced Jacob, and this aspect parallels Potiphar's wife's attempted seduction of Joseph, which inspired the preceding tassels law. In each instance the man had not wished to be sexually involved with the woman.

From our point of view we might have expected Jacob to seek to dismiss Leah by divorcing her. That step, however, he never took. At the time this would have been an unwise move on his part. He was totally dependent upon her father for his livelihood. Moreover, a negative action toward her on his part would inevitably have met with Laban's refusal to give Jacob the wife he really wanted, Rachel.

The story has its own special features—without them it would never have survived. Typically, our lawgiver attempts to sketch a less idiosyncratic situation than Jacob's, and he seeks to concentrate on the bridegroom's possible reaction to finding himself on the day after the consummation of a marriage bound to a woman he does not want. The lawgiver imagines the husband resorting to slander in order to hit back at the girl's father. That a situation, admittedly a rare one, could arise where a man found himself legally tied to a woman he did not love seems likely, not just in legend, but in actual life. In biblical law we know of no formal, written contracts entered into by the bridegroom and his prospective father-in-law,[5] so that a man might find himself being presented with one daughter when he had been sure that it was her sister he had spoken about. Likewise, the substitution Laban resorts to could have been managed easily precisely because of banqueting activity typical of wedding nights. Our lawgiver, to be sure, does not state the circumstances that might prompt a man's slander, but some such parallel to Jacob's situation seems plausible. The indication is that in each instance of disappointment (easily observed in Jacob's quarrel with Laban) the man's anger is directed against not just his newly acquired wife but the father also. In the law he is in possession of the wedding night sheet. The implica-

[5]Z. W. Falk, *Hebrew Law in Biblical Times* (Jerusalem: Wahrmann, 1964), 152–53.

tion is that his own reputation is at stake, that he, along with the girl's mother, is responsible for the bride's chaste state before marriage. The fact too that the slanderer has to pay the girl's father a considerable sum of money indicates that the attack on his daughter's reputation is aimed at him also. The sum represents twice what appears to be the recognized bride price for virgins (Deut 22:29). Jacob had paid double the price for the woman he wanted (Gen 29:30).

While it is true that the lawgiver gives hypothetical consideration to what a man in Jacob's position might have done after taking a wife he did not want, he is also inspired to construct a parallel to Joseph's case, only one that involves the woman. The false accusation about the bride's previous misconduct is probably primarily inspired by the lawgiver's interest, in his preceding law, in Potiphar's wife's fabricated story about Joseph's misconduct with her. Her reports about him to others and to her husband (Gen 39:14, 15, 17, 18) could well be described, in the language of Deut 22:14, as *ʿalîlōt dᵉbārîm,* "caprices of words, trumped-up charges." In Gen 39:17, "She spoke to him [her husband] according to these things [*dᵉbārîm*]," that is, she told him the same made-up story about Joseph's evil deeds that she had told the men of her household in verses 14, 15.

There is a second part to the law that concerns a truthful allegation about a bride not being a virgin on her wedding night. For her thereby proven past misconduct she suffers the supreme penalty: she is stoned to death at the door of her father's house. In accounting for this consequence, we need go no further perhaps than seeing it as an understandable extension intended to contrast with the first part of the law. We have also come to see, however, that the lawgiver tends to look through the eyes of Moses at what occurred in Israelite history and to let the circumstances of such occurrences suggest issues that require legislation. Three incidents involving women in the Book of Genesis are possibly pertinent to the case of the woman who has engaged in premarital sex.

It is first noteworthy that Leah was not the bride Jacob wanted because of some defect to do with her eyes (Gen 29:17). It is natural to focus upon a bride whose worth is suspicious. The more serious defect of lack of virginity would justify the lawgiver's attention.

A second story, which has played an important role in the preceding ox and ass law and which may also be pertinent to the matter of the unchaste bride, is found in Genesis 34: Dinah's seduction by the foreign prince, Shechem. She did not end up married to him, and we hear nowhere about a subsequent marriage of this sole daughter of Jacob by the wife (Leah) who was forced upon him. It is again the kind of element in a tradition that could have given rise to fairly straightforward speculation on the part of the lawgiver. Suppose, he might have asked, Dinah had eventually married one of her people; then it is clear that she would have gone into the marriage as a nonvirgin. Thinking about her position and contemplating the assumption that she might not reveal her previous experience, he would be led to the case formulated in the second part of the law. It is noteworthy that the same phrase that is applied to Shechem in condemning his sexual misconduct with Dinah is applied to the woman's premarital activity in the law.[6] Shechem "had wrought folly in Israel by lying with Jacob's daughter" (Gen 34:7), and the girl "has wrought folly in Israel by playing the harlot in her father's house" (Deut 22:21). Later in the story (v. 31) Shechem's offense is said to have been that he had treated Dinah as a harlot.

A third story invites reflection along the same lines, namely, that of Sarah's sexual adventures with the pharaoh (Gen 12:10–20) and with Abimelech (Genesis 20). In each instance the male conceived a desire for Sarah and sought to make her his wife. The pharaoh consummated the union but had to break it off, while Abimelech found out about her true status before having intercourse with her. Both times Sarah had let the man think that she was Abraham's sister when in fact she was his wife. Again, depending upon the angle from which the situation is viewed, a woman enters a marriage as a nonvirgin and deliberately tries to conceal her past history. Given the features common to each of the above three stories, it is not surprising that Moses is assumed to have set out a law that covered the more likely, less dramatic development of a previously unmarried girl who, on her wedding night, is found to have engaged in prior sexual activity.

Law: Adultery

[22] If a man be found lying with a woman married to an husband, then they shall both of them die, both the man that lay with

[6]This lawgiver's use of contrast is invariably noteworthy. The man's slander against his new wife recalls the slander by Potiphar's wife against Joseph. Shechem's folly inspires the Deuteronomist's interest in a parallel female folly.

the woman, and the woman: so shalt thou put away evil from Israel. (Deut 22:22)

Background: Joseph's "adultery" (Genesis 39), and Sarah's deception

[11] And it came to pass, when he [Abram] was come near to enter into Egypt, that he said unto Sarai his wife, Behold now, I know that thou art a fair woman to look upon: [12] therefore it shall come to pass, when the Egyptians shall see thee, that they shall say, This is his wife: and they will kill me, but they will save thee alive. [13] Say, I pray thee, thou art my sister: that it may be well with me for thy sake; and my soul shall live because of thee. [14] And it came to pass, that, when Abram was come into Egypt, the Egyptians beheld the woman that she was very fair. [15] The princes also of Pharaoh saw her, and commended her before Pharaoh: and the woman was taken into Pharaoh's house. [16] And he entreated Abram well for her sake: and he had sheep, and oxen, and he asses, and menservants, and maidservants, and she asses, and camels. [17] And Yahweh plagued Pharaoh and his house with great plagues because of Sarai Abram's wife. [18] And Pharaoh called Abram, and said, What is this that thou hast done unto me? why didst thou not tell me that she was thy wife? [19] why saidst thou, She is my sister? and I have taken her to me to wife: now therefore behold thy wife, take her, and go thy way. (Gen 12:11–19)

[2] And Abraham said of Sarah his wife, She is my sister: and Abimelech king of Gerar sent, and took Sarah. [3] But God came to Abimelech in a dream by night, and said to him, Behold, thou art but a dead man, for the woman which thou hast taken; for she is a man's wife. [4] But Abimelech had not come near her: and he said, Yahweh, wilt thou slay also a righteous nation? [5] Said he not unto me, She is my sister? and she, even she herself said, He is my brother: in the integrity of my heart and innocency of my hands have I done this. [6] And God said unto him in a dream, Yea, I know that thou didst this in the integrity of thy heart; for I also withheld thee from sinning against me: therefore suffered I thee not to touch her. [7] Now therefore restore the man his wife; for he is a prophet, and he shall pray for thee, and thou shalt live: and if thou restore her not, know thou that thou shalt surely die, thou, and all that are thine. (Gen 20:2–7)

A law about adultery is to be expected at this point. Interest in false accusations about sexual misconduct, against Joseph by a woman, and against a bride by her husband, dominated the two preceding laws. Joseph's alleged offense was in fact adultery.

We have seen that the lawgiver readily switches his attention to incidents that present similar problems. This switch is all the more necessary in this instance because the example in Joseph's case was only one of attempted adultery. It happens that Sarah's relationship with the pharaoh and with Abimelech raises the question of actual adultery, especially the woman's role in it. It was Sarah who did not let on to these men (like Potiphar's wife and the slanderous husband she is deceitful) that she was in fact another man's wife. In Genesis 12 divine wrath falls upon the pharaoh and his household because of his taking her. In Gen 20:3 God comes to Abimelech in a dream by night and informs him, "Behold, thou art a dead man, for the woman which thou has taken, for she is a man's wife." In both stories penalties focus upon the male. Nothing is said about the woman's involvement. Yet it was Sarah who encouraged the adulterous development because she deliberately concealed the fact of her marital status. Anyone reflecting upon what was taking place, if not sidetracked by the motivation underlying Abraham and Sarah's deception, namely, Abraham's fear for his life, would want to attach blame to Sarah. It is therefore no surprise to find that the law is especially interested in making clear that both the man and the woman are equally culpable. It is the lack of awareness in the Genesis traditions of Sarah's culpability that explains the expanded formulation of the law: "If a man be found lying with a woman married to an husband, even both of them shall die, the man that lay with the woman, and the woman." It is surely suggestive of the link between the law and the tradition in Genesis 20 that the technical designation, "a man's wife" (*beʿūlat-baʿal*), only occurs in biblical literature in these two places.[7]

[7]The formulation, "If a man be found lying with a woman," can be attributed to the lawgiver's reaction to the false evidence furnished by Potiphar's wife: the couple must be caught in flagrante delicto. What connection there was between this supposedly idealistic Mosaic view of adultery and societal practice in the Deuteronomist's time is impossible to judge. For a quite different understanding of the significance of "found" in the rule, see D. Daube, "To be found doing wrong," *Studi in onore di Edoardo Volterra,* Pubblicazioni della Facolta di iurisprudenza dell' Universita di Roma 41 (Milan: Giuffrè, 1971), 3–13.

Law: Seduction of a betrothed woman

[23] If a damsel that is a virgin be betrothed unto an husband,
and a man find her in the city, and lie with her; [24] then ye shall
bring them both out unto the gate of that city, and ye shall stone
them with stones that they die; the damsel, because she cried not,
being in the city; and the man, because he hath humbled his neighbour's wife: so thou shalt put away evil from thy midst. [25] But if a
man find a betrothed damsel in the field, and the man force her, and
lie with her: then the man only that lay with her shall die: [26] but
unto the damsel thou shalt do nothing; there is in the damsel no sin
worthy of death: for as when a man riseth against his neighbour,
and slayeth him, even so is this matter: [27] for he found her in the
field, and the betrothed damsel cried, and there was none to save
her. (Deut 22:23–27)

Background: The evidence against Joseph (Genesis 39)

The law about first the seduction of a betrothed woman within a city and then the seduction of one in the open country can be explained in terms of concerns that have arisen in the immediately preceding laws and the traditions that have influenced them. The Joseph story raises the topic of illicit intercourse, attempted against the woman's will. From Potiphar's point of view Joseph had attempted to commit adultery with his wife. Moreover, acceptance of the fact was not just an arbitrary favoring of her account. Not only did she possess Joseph's garment, but she had immediately called to the men of her household and claimed that she had cried out with a loud voice when Joseph had approached her (Gen 39:14). Her testimony is not trivial. In the law the failure of a betrothed woman to cry out, if her seducer happens to lie with her in a city, condemns her. The Deuteronomist reflects upon this aspect of the Joseph story, ignoring the complication of the woman's lies.

The question arises as to why the law addresses itself to the case of a betrothed woman and not to a woman already married. The answer is clear: in the case of a betrothed woman, a virgin, it is vitally important that, if she really has been seduced, she cry out with a loud voice so that she is heard, whether or not the hearer comes upon them in the act or after it. The law is formulated so as to avoid stating that they are found together. Unlike a married woman, the betrothed woman's virginity is at stake. Should she not make this seduction known, then when it comes to the consummation of her relationship with the man she is betrothed to, he can justifiably accuse her, with terrible consequences for her, of having played the harlot. In other words, it is the law prescribing the fate of the nonvirginal bride that determines for the lawgiver why there must be a rule formulated about the seduction of a betrothed virgin.

Potiphar's wife claimed that she had cried out with a loud voice, but the inference is that she had not been heard. The lawgiver looks at this possibility and wonders when it might have validity. Again he has to focus on a betrothed virgin, not on a woman already married, because although the legal status of each is almost identical (he refers to the betrothed girl who has been violated as the seducer's neighbor's wife), that she is no longer a virgin after being seduced constitutes objective evidence that intercourse has indeed taken place. For her to be in the clear requires that her seduction, unlike the one that Potiphar's wife alleged, take place well away from human habitation, namely, "in the field" (v. 25).

In support of his decision the lawgiver introduces the analogy of a man who is murdered in a setting where his cries would go unheeded. It is difficult to see the need for such an analogy. The reason for holding the woman innocent is plain enough. If, however, the presentation of the rule has been influenced by an evaluation of the evidence against Joseph's alleged act, it is at least interesting to note that Joseph too furnished an example of someone almost murdered in a setting where it was unlikely in the normal course of events that anyone would have come to his aid (Gen 37:17–20).[8]

Law: Seduction of an unbetrothed woman

> [28] If a man find a damsel that is a virgin, which is not betrothed, and lay hold on her, and lie with her, and they be found; [29] then the man that lay with her shall give unto the damsel's father fifty shekels of silver, and she shall be his wife; because he hath humbled her, he may not put her away all his days. (Deut 22:28, 29)

[8]Cp. how in the rule about the nonvirginal bride the language used to describe Shechem's folly is applied to the Israelite woman in the law.

Background: The seduction of Dinah (Genesis 34; see pp. 193, 194)

Dinah's seduction by Shechem is the focus of the law about the violation of an unbetrothed virgin. It may well be that reflection upon the possibility that she had contributed to her own seduction plays into why the lawgiver concentrates on the guilt or innocence of the betrothed girl in the law we have just been looking at. A noticeable feature of the narrative in Genesis 34 is that Dinah was not in the midst of her group, where a cry from her would have brought rescue from Shechem's advances. She had gone out to see the "daughters of the land" when he beheld her and seduced her (vv. 1, 2). If she had been betrothed to one of her own kind we might ask whether or not she was to be held responsible for what occurred, and the issue of where the seduction took place would acquire significance.

That the law concerning the unbetrothed virgin is prompted by reflection upon this same Genesis story seems especially clear. The unexpected, dramatic turn of events that takes place—Shechem's father had entered in good faith into negotiations with Jacob's family in hopes of concluding a marriage between his son and Jacob's daughter, only to end up destroyed by the sword along with his son and all the males of his clan—leaves the question: what should happen when a man has seduced a virgin? The Deuteronomist puts aside the complication about the Canaanite status of Shechem—he has already dealt with it in his ox and ass law—and probes the issue within an Israelite context. The reason given for the injunctions in the law is that the man had humbled (*ʿinnāh*) the woman. Shechem humbled (*ʿinnāh*) Dinah (Gen 34:2).

In Israelite legal tradition there already existed in the Deuteronomist's time a law on the subject (Exod 22:16, 17: "And if a man entice a maid that is not betrothed, and lie with her, he shall surely endow her to be his wife. If her father utterly refuse to give her unto him, he shall pay money according to the bride-price for virgins." A seducer pays a bride price (*mōhar*) to the girl's father and she becomes his wife. The father, however, may refuse to give his daughter to him, and if so, the seducer pays a bride price equivalent to the going rate for virgins. In Genesis 34 Shechem requests of Jacob and his sons that Dinah be given to him in marriage and that whatever bride price (*mōhar*) they wish he will pay. As it turned out, Shechem was refused the woman he seduced. The Deuteronomist, because of both the existing law and the story, concentrates on why the girl's family refuses, and uncovers a less dramatic and idiosyncratic reason than the one in the story. He would readily note that a father could take advantage of the situation by pressing the seducer to pay a very high bride price, one that is in excess of the usual rate for a virginal daughter. In other words, the most likely reason in ordinary circumstances for a father to refuse a suitor's offer is to maximize his financial gain. If he does not get the high bride price out of the man, he will still collect from him the regular price and will then be free to arrange another marriage—and another bride price—for his daughter. The Deuteronomic rule closes this loophole. The seducer must marry the girl he has violated, her father cannot withhold his daughter, and the bride price is fixed at the sum of fifty shekels of silver.

Another major reason why this lawgiver wants a marriage to be created is that the man has treated the girl as a harlot and this dishonor to her must be undone. If it were not—if no marriage took place—then she might marry another man and find herself accused of playing the harlot, as spelled out in the law about the nonvirginal bride. An indication of the importance the lawgiver places upon the formation of a marriage between the seducer and the woman comes out in his denial of divorce to him. He cannot put her away all his days (v. 29). Where the lawgiver requires the marriage and does not permit her father to prevent it, he also has to ensure that the man does not contract it and then slip out of it by moving to divorce her. Perhaps another detail that causes him to think about the permanency of such unions is the fact that Dinah did not end up married to another man. He may draw the implication that because of what happened to her she was in fact barred from any future marriage. It was her misfortune that her seducer should have been an uncircumcised Hivite.

That Potiphar's wife took hold (*tāpaś*) of Joseph's garment indicates that she wanted to seduce him: "Lie with me" (Gen 39:12). In the law a man's taking hold (*tāpaś*) of a woman (and not seizing her as in verse 25) is the preliminary to his lying with her (Deut 22:28). The law states that the pair of them must be caught in the act for guilt to be established. The example of Potiphar's wife's false but successful story about Joseph's seduction of her points to the need for such a requirement. Without it, a woman in collusion with her father could exploit a man, especially under the existing law in Exod 22:16, 17).

Law: A forbidden relationship with a father's wife

[30] A man shall not take his father's wife, nor uncover his father's skirt. (Deut 22:30)

Background: Reuben lies with Jacob's concubine

[22] And it came to pass, when Israel dwelt in that land, that Reuben went and lay with Bilhah his father's concubine: and Israel heard it. (Gen 35:22)

[4] Thou [Reuben] wentest up to thy father's bed; then defiledst thou it: he went up to my couch. (Gen 49:4)

The Deuteronomist follows up his interest in the sexual offense done to Jacob's first and only daughter by a scrutiny of Jacob's first-born son's misconduct with his concubine. The law that is prompted by reflection on the incident has a double statement. First, it prohibits a man's taking his father's concubine, probably out of concern for what might typically occur after a father dies: a son, especially the first-born, would almost as a matter of course take his father's concubines, or the younger ones at least. Commentators think that this might have been ancient Israelite practice. In any event, we have found that what occurs in a tradition causes the lawgiver to switch his attention to the more usual circumstances in which a similar issue might arise.

The second part of the law is more tantalizing. It resorts to figurative language: "Nor shall he uncover his father's skirt." We have seen previously, in the laws about the ox and ass, mixed seed, wool and linen, that such language is specifically directed toward certain incidents in patriarchal history. That is, contrary to what the lawgiver normally does when he seeks the more conventional parallel to what he finds in the tradition, in these laws he concentrates on the special event itself. Moreover, we have also seen that the figurative language is in large measure either an imitation of, or inspired by, similar language in Jacob's farewell address to his assembled sons before his death (Genesis 49). The prohibition against uncovering the father's skirt fits the pattern established for these other figurative laws. It is a condemnation of Reuben's action. The realistic language is an attempt to convey the wrongfulness of the deed. The first part of the law, which concerns a man who takes his father's wife, refers to a formal, long-term arrangement. This second part concentrates on Reuben's intercourse with Bilhah. Since the misconduct occurs within a family, the law on adultery does not apply.

To convey why his behavior is offensive the lawgiver compares it to the act of a son deliberately uncovering his father's nakedness—a very shaming act in this culture (and presumably in all others). In Hebrew tradition the shame of a son's deliberately looking upon his father's nakedness seems to be the sole point of the story of Noah's drunkenness (Gen 9:20–27). In the law, a man's wife is his skirt, and for a son to lie with her means that figuratively he has removed his father's covering and put it on himself. In a literal sense he uncovers his stepmother's nakedness, in a figurative, his father's. Indirect language is used to describe Reuben's offense in Gen 49:4: "Thou wentest up to thy father's bed; then defiledst thou it: he went up to my couch." The uninitiated is left guessing what the offense might be, although undoubtedly a sexual one is hinted at. Similarly, the lawgiver's reference to uncovering the father's skirt is also indirect. In each instance there is no plain reference to the woman, to Jacob's concubine, Bilhah.

From both the point of view of language and meaning, the uncovering of the father's skirt in the law is decidedly reminiscent of, is a parallel to, the approach to the father's bed in Jacob's address. Neither statement is to be understood in a strict sense. In the lawgiver's statement the literal implication is that the son is exposing his father's nakedness; in Jacob's statement that the son is lying with his father. The unquestionable figurative significance of the language in Jacob's utterance confirms the same figurative sense in the law:[9] the allusion is to a father's wife.

The double nature of this law is further noteworthy. A general prohibition against taking one's father's wife in a formal, institutionalized sense, no doubt after his death, is followed by the specific condemnation of a man who has intercourse with his father's concubine while he is still alive. It may well be that the Deuteronomist understood that in Jacob's time it was customary for a son to acquire his father's concubines after he died, and that Reuben's offense was to

[9]Contrary to the view of A. Phillips, "Uncovering the father's skirt," *VT* 30 (1980): 38–43.

lie with the concubine before his father had died. As already indicated, the matter was a family affair; the law of adultery did not apply; certain rules about forbidden degrees of affinity did not exist; and lawmakers simply looked away from such matters. In Gen 35:22 we read that Israel heard about Reuben's intercourse with Bilhah. No action was taken against him at that time. Only when Jacob contemplates death and the question of his sons' inheritance rights did he speak against Reuben's conduct and deny him the right of primogeniture. Whether this denial meant that Reuben was prevented from acquiring any of Jacob's concubines after his death we cannot say. The point is that the Deuteronomist reckoned that if a son could inherit a father's wives, he might be tempted to relate to them sexually before his inheritance was due. Thus he legislates against both matters simultaneously.

SUMMARY The attempted seduction of the Hebrew servant Joseph by Potiphar's wife highlighted his virtue. Although she possessed his garment, he was innocent of any adulterous intent. The lawgiver is prompted to construct a directive that all Israelite males should by means of tassels on their clothing indicate their commitment to sexual probity. Leah seduced the betrothed Jacob on his wedding night. He, angered because he found himself having to take her as a wife, hit back at her father who had been behind the stratagem, by adopting a hateful attitude toward her. The lawgiver constructs a law in which a man gives expression to his hatred against a new wife by accusing her and, by implication, her father of presenting him with a nonvirgin on his wedding night; but the wedding night cloth proves her sexual probity. Three women in Genesis, Leah, Dinah, and Sarah, but especially the latter, suggest grounds for considering the case of a female who enters a marriage without informing her new husband of her previous sexual experience. This situation comes under review in the second part of the law about the nonvirginal bride. Both Potiphar's wife and Sarah escaped censure for their adulterous activity, while the men involved all suffered consequences. The bias of the adultery law that insists upon penalties for both the man and the woman stems from these narratives. The claim by Potiphar's wife that she had cried out with a loud voice when sexually assaulted by Joseph raises the issue of when this claim might constitute a valid defense. The lawgiver chooses to deal with the issue in the case of a betrothed woman because her loss of virginity in such an incident could have serious repercussions for her. Shechem seduced Dinah and then sought to marry her by having his father negotiate terms with her father. Nothing worked out because of their Canaanite status. The lawgiver takes up the issue and sets out procedure for a comparable seduction within an Israelite context. Reuben seduced his father's concubine and this prompts a prohibition of such unions.

CHAPTER 9

FOREIGN RELATIONS AND ISRAEL'S EXPANSION

The existence of a link between the sex laws and the Genesis material is further indicated by the fact that the Book of Deuteronomy itself, Moses' farewell address to the assembly of the sons (children) of Israel, is modeled upon Jacob's (Israel's) parting words to the assembly of his sons in Genesis 49, as noted earlier. A specific link between the sayings of Jacob and the laws of Moses is all the more to be expected. What is of great interest at this point in the code is that there follows a succession of laws about who is to be admitted into, and who is to be excluded from, Israel's assembly, which is referred to by the idealized name of the assembly of Yahweh. This designation reflects the notion that when Jacob's name was changed to Israel, Yahweh was promising him and his descendants that they would prosper and greatly increase in numbers. In the laws that follow interest in the history of this national entity, especially during times when the Israelites were threatened with the loss of their special identity or their very existence at the hands of external groups, is pronounced. An obvious, fundamental aspect of this notion of Israel as a group is the question of the perpetuation of its line of descent through offspring. The fact that the preceding laws were about sexual relations suggests that a concern with procreation is likely to follow, either in the laws themselves or in the related narratives.

Law: Exclusion of eunuchs from Yahweh's assembly

> [1] He that is wounded in the stones, or hath his privy member cut off, shall not enter into the assembly of Yahweh. (Deut 23:1)

Background: The circumcision of the Hivites (Genesis 34; see pp. 193, 194)

Reuben was Jacob's first-born, the one through whom the line of descendants should have proved most prominent. He was the first fruit of his father's virility (Gen 49:3). The misuse, however, of his sexual potency in lying with his father's concubine offends and the importance of his line is consequently diminished. Jacob wished to deny him his abundant physical strength (Gen 49:4), and Moses' comparable pronouncement upon him in his farewell speech was: "Let Reuben live, and not die, but let his men be few" (Deut 33:6). If the deity's blessing of fertility is crucial to the strength and future of Jacob and his sons, it is not surprising that the topic of how a line cannot be continued at all will come to mind. This concern is expressed in the law (following the one about Reuben's offense) that excludes the eunuch from Yahweh's assembly. The man whose testes have been crushed or whose penis is cut off cannot produce offspring, and his condition is therefore incompatible with Yahweh's blessing upon a line. The reason, however, for raising this particular topic is not to highlight the contrast between a eunuch and a man who is richly endowed with procreative strength but to reflect upon the related topic of the abortive pact between the Hivites and the Israelites in Genesis 34. In the context of how the lawgiver moves from one item to the next, note how Jacob's pronouncement upon Reuben is immediately followed by his harsh judgment upon Simeon and Levi for what they did to the Hivites (Gen 49:5–7).

In Genesis 34 a group attempted to associate—marital arrangements and commercial transactions—with Jacob and his sons. In effect they sought to enter Jacob's assembly. Two of his sons, Simeon and Levi, fiercely opposed the idea. Their sister had been ravished by the prince of the Hivites and he was uncircumcised. As a means of getting even with him and his fellow Canaanites they tricked all the males of the clan into becoming circumcised. In the aftermath of this painful operation these two sons of Jacob fell upon them with their swords and killed all the males. Jacob reacted angrily against their deed and feared that his own group would be cut down. It was already in his assessment few in number (Gen 34:30). As we shall see, foreign groups that sought to diminish Israel's numbers were judged unworthy of association with Yahweh's assembly. Simeon and Levi's action and their motivation for it consequently invited further evaluation, especially because Jacob excluded them from his assembly (Gen 49:6). The Deuteronomist takes a contrary view of their conduct (cp., Jth 9:2) and concentrates on their opposition to the desire of the Hivites to join the Israelites.

He perceives Simeon and Levi's perspective to be totally antagonistic to any relationship between a Canaanite group and Israel. The Hivites had wanted to contract marriages; these would lead to births; and Jacob's assembly would be increased by such mixed seed. To counter this increase these two sons of Israel made use of circumcision in a deliberately ambiguous way. They gave the Hivites to believe that by undergoing it they would be welcome to associate with their group. Their aim was the opposite. By taking advantage of the pain caused by the operation they saw to it that no association would take place.[1] The lawgiver, who does not need to spend any time in support of this antagonism to a Canaanite group, instead focuses upon the contrasting element to association involved in the ruse to attack the Hivites. Ordinarily this form of genital mutilation, circumcision, signifies inclusion in Israel's, or better, Yahweh's, assembly, but in this instance it was used to facilitate forcible exclusion from it. Is there any form of genital mutilation, the lawgiver asks, which would in fact exclude someone from entering the assembly whose destiny it is to increase in size? Possibly, since his attention has been focused on a foreign group, the Hivites, the lawgiver is thinking of a certain type of eunuch apparently more common in the surrounding cultures than in Israel. The foreign eunuch whose penis has been removed cannot undergo circumcision, the sign of covenanting into Israel's assembly, and in addition the rite would hardly be appropriate for someone

[1]Except that the surviving women and children were, after certain purification acts (Gen 35:2–4), absorbed into Jacob's group. The text does not raise the question of whether or not Simeon and Levi opposed this incorporation.

whose testes have been crushed. However that may be, the primary reason for excluding the eunuch is that he cannot participate in the blessing of fertility that is upon Israel.

Law: Exclusion of the bastard, Ammonite and Moabite

> [2] A bastard shall not enter into the assembly of Yahweh; even to his tenth generation shall he not enter into the assembly of Yahweh. [3] An Ammonite or Moabite shall not enter into the assembly of Yahweh; even to their tenth generation shall they not enter into the assembly of Yahweh for ever; because they met you not with bread and with water in the way, when ye came forth out of Egypt; and because they hired against thee Balaam the son of Beor, of Pethor of Mesopotamia, to curse thee. [5] Nevertheless Yahweh thy God would not hearken unto Balaam; but Yahweh thy God turned the curse into a blessing unto thee, because Yahweh thy God loved thee. [6] Thou shalt not seek their peace nor their prosperity all thy days for ever. (Deut 23:2–6)

Background: Lot's daughters, and Ammon's and Moab's treatment of Israel at the time of the Exodus

> [31] And the firstborn [daughter] said unto the younger, Our father is old, and there is not a man in the earth to come in unto us after the manner of all the earth: [32] Come, let us make our father drink wine, and we will lie with him, that we may preserve seed of our father. [33] And they made their father drink wine that night: and the firstborn went in, and lay with her father; and he perceived not when she lay down, nor when she arose. [The younger daughter proceeds similarly]. [36] Thus were both the daughters of Lot with child by their father. [37] And the firstborn bare a son, and called his name Moab: the same is the father of the Moabites unto this day. [38] And the younger, she also bare a son, and called his name Ben-Ammi: the same is the father of the children of Ammon unto this day. (Gen 19:31–38)

> [19] And when thou [Israel] comest nigh over against the children of Ammon, distress them not, nor meddle with them: for I will not give thee of the land of the children of Ammon any possession; because I have given it unto the children of Lot for a possession. . . . [26] And I sent messengers out of the wilderness of Ked-

> emoth unto Sihon king of Heshbon with words of peace, saying, [27] Let me pass through thy land: I will go along by the highway, I will neither turn unto the right hand nor to the left. [28] Thou shalt sell me food for money, that I may eat; and give me water for money, that I may drink: only I will pass through on my feet; [29] as the children of Esau which dwell in Seir, and the Moabites which dwell in Ar, did unto me; until I shall pass over Jordan into the land which Yahweh our God giveth us. (Deut 2:19, 26–29)

> [4] And Moab said unto the elders of Midian, Now shall this assembly lick up all that are round about us, as the ox licketh up the grass of the field. And Balak the son of Zippor was king of the Moabites at that time. [5] He sent messengers therefore unto Balaam the son of Beor to Pethor, which is by the river, in the land of Amaw, to call him, saying, Behold, there is a people come out from Egypt: behold, they cover the face of the earth, and they abide over against me: [6] come now therefore, I pray thee, curse me this people; for they are too mighty for me: peradventure I shall prevail, that we may smite them, and that I may drive them out of the land: for I wot that he whom thou blessest is blessed, and he whom thou cursest is cursed. (Num 22:4–6)

Although much store is set by the capacity to reproduce, because of Yahweh's blessing of fertility upon Israel, it does not follow that all that comes from the womb will automatically be included in Yahweh's assembly. The manner in which certain conceptions take place will render the resulting produce unacceptable. Such, we are meant to understand, is Moses' judgment after he had scrutinized the activities of Lot's daughters in Gen 19:30–38. They, fearing that their father's line would not continue because of the dearth of males upon the earth, made him drunk and lay with him in turn. The ancestors of the Moabites and Ammonites were the products of these unions. If the Deuteronomist condemns Reuben for uncovering his father's skirt, that is, lying with his father's wife, it is not at all surprising that he would similarly condemn Lot's daughter's uncovering, literally this time, their father's skirt. It is also noteworthy that just as Simeon and Levi caused the Hivites to be off their guard by encouraging them to undergo circumcision, so Lot's daughters achieved a similar result by getting him drunk. In each instance, someone resorts to a ruse, and each time the ruse's focus is genital.

The motive for these girls' action was to preserve offspring for their father's line. The Deuteronomist has noted that, because Lot and Abraham were kinsmen, a continuing relationship between their descendants, that is, between the Moabites and the Ammonites on Lot's side and the sons of Jacob-Israel on Abraham's side, was to be expected and welcomed. In other words, if Lot's line had developed normally, probably through intermarriage with Abraham's family, there would have been no question about Lot's descendants being admitted into Jacob's or Yahweh's assembly. As it was, the unions by which Lot's daughters reproduced were unacceptable. The impropriety of the two unions affects their outcome, not just the immediate generation but each succeeding one. The law prohibiting the bastard admission into the assembly condemns the product of an incestuous union and arises from a scrutiny of the particular case of Lot's daughters. The point of the prohibition is that to produce children by such unions is not an acceptable way to increase the size of the assembly. Bountiful numbers are an indication of divine blessing, but some increases are incompatible with the legal and moral conditions under which this blessing operates.

That future generations of Moabites and Ammonites are to be excluded from Yahweh's assembly follows from the prohibition that denies admission to a bastard's descendants. The two generations belonging to Moses' time behave in a way that is antagonistic to the very idea of the assembly, namely, they deliberately attempt to prevent its expansion. They therefore provide evidence that they should never be associated with it. No doubt this finding reinforces the decision to exclude a bastard's line for all time. Their offending conduct, according to the lawgiver, is that they did not meet the journeying Israelites with bread and water at the time when they were coming forth from Egypt,[2] and that they hired the diviner Balaam to curse Israel. Not to furnish provisions to a group passing through desert wastes is an act of enmity that suggests a desire to see the group perish. Likewise, when the king of Moab saw how numerous this

[2]The "You" form intrudes: "because they met you not with bread and with water in the way, when ye came forth out of Egypt." Moses is speaking, and he is referring, it is implied, to the time mentioned in Deut 2:19. We have seen before that the "You" form is frequently used when Moses refers back to this period. It appears that the Moabites are not to be condemned for their failure to provide food (Deut 2:29). Nothing is said about the Ammonites in the matter and this omission may be the basis for their condemnation.

company was—the term used in Num 22:4 is *qāhāl* ("assembly")—he hired Balaam to utter a curse with a view to cutting them down in size and driving them out of his land (Num 22:6). That Yahweh turned the curse into a blessing means that he wished to preserve this mighty assembly and make it prosper in its future life. Balaam's oracles delivered on this occasion make reference to Israel's numbers and future expansion (Num 23:10, 24:6, 7).

Law: Admission of the Edomites and Egyptians

> [7] Thou shalt not abhor an Edomite; for he is thy brother: thou shalt not abhor an Egyptian; because thou wast a sojourner in his land. [8] The children that are begotten of them shall enter into the assembly of Yahweh in their third generation. (Deut 23:7,8)

Background: Edom denies permission to let Israel pass through its land; Esau welcomes Jacob; Egyptian policies toward Israel

> [14] And Moses sent messengers from Kadesh unto the king of Edom, Thus saith thy brother Israel, Thou knewest all the travail that befell us. [15] Then our fathers went down into Egypt, and we dwelt in Egypt a long time; and the Egyptians vexed us, and our fathers, [16] and when we cried unto Yahweh, he heard our voice, and sent an angel, and hath brought us forth out of Egypt: and, behold, we are in Kadesh, a city in the uttermost of thy border: [17] Let us pass, I pray thee, through thy country: we will not pass through the fields, or through the vineyards, neither will we drink of the water of the wells: we will go by the king's high way, until we have passed thy borders. [18] And Edom said unto him, Thou shalt not pass by me, lest I come out against thee with the sword. (Num 20:14–18)

> [1] And Jacob lifted up his eyes, and looked, and, behold, Esau came, and with him four hundred men. . . . [3]And he passed over before them [the women and the children], and bowed himself to the ground seven times, until he came near to his brother. [4] But Esau ran to meet him, and embraced him, and fell on his neck, and kissed him: and they wept. (Gen 33:1, 3, 4)

> [17] And Pharaoh said unto Joseph, Say unto thy brethren, This do ye; lade your breasts, and go, get you unto the land of Canaan;

> [18] and take your father and your households, and come unto me: and I will give you the good of the land of Egypt, and ye shall eat the fat of the land. (Gen 45:17, 18)
>
> [8] Now there arose up a new king over Egypt, which knew not Joseph. [9] And he said unto his people, Behold, the people of the children of Israel are more and mightier than we: [10] come on, let us deal wisely with them; lest they multiply, and it come to pass, that, when there falleth out any war, they join also unto our enemies, and fight against us, and so get them out of the land. [11] Therefore they did set over them taskmasters to afflict them with their burdens. And they built for Pharaoh treasure cities, Pithom and Raamses. [12] But the more they afflicted them, the more they multiplied and grew. And they were grieved because of the children of Israel. . . . [15] And the king of Egypt spake to the Hebrew midwives. . . . [16] When ye do the office of a midwife to the Hebrew women, and see them upon the stools; if it be a son, then ye shall kill him. . . . [22] And Pharaoh charged all his people, saying, Every son that is born ye shall cast into the river, and every daughter ye shall save alive. (Exod 1:8–12, 15, 16, 22)

The lawgiver presents two laws counseling against an attitude of abhorrence toward the Edomites and Egyptians, and permitting offspring of their third generation to enter the assembly; he formulates them in regard to how Israel as a group fared at the hands of these two nations. The period of their exclusion from the assembly dates from the Israelite settlement in the new land—Moses' laws speak to this time—and refers to those generations of Edomites and Egyptians who might be living in the land at the same time as the first three generations of Israelite settlers. They are the immediate successors (and might even include some) of those Edomites and Egyptians who during Moses's lifetime actively sought to diminish Israel's numbers. During the wilderness period, after the exodus from Egypt, the Israelites sought to pass through Edomite territory but were denied permission (Num 20:14–18). A renewed request to pass through a central highway and to pay for any water they might need was also denied and followed by a military attack. It is the generations of Edomites living at that time who obviously invite abhorrence.[3] That

[3]The term *tā'ab,* "to abhor," is used because the offense in the background is directed against Yahweh's preservation of his people—a religious offense.

the exclusion from the assembly is, however, lifted for the children of the third generation reflects a basically positive attitude toward the Edomites as a group, which is attributed to the fact that the Edomite is a brother to the Israelite. Particularly in the lawgiver's mind is the occasion when the original Israel (Jacob) had to traverse the land of the original Edom (Esau).

Just as the lawgiver's attitude toward the later generations of Moabites and Ammonites is fixed by the attitude toward the very first generation,[4] so too the positive evaluation of the Edomites that eventually prevails is determined by the fact that Jacob, fleeing from his angry father-in-law, was well received by his blood brother, Esau. Genesis 31 and 32 recount how Jacob and his family survived Laban's wrath because Yahweh had turned it into a blessing (Gen 31:29, 55); afterwards, Jacob expected Esau to attack him for cheating him out of his birthright. Again, however, Yahweh's blessing was upon this family, the original assembly of Israel. After a strange nocturnal encounter with a divine messenger, when Jacob won a blessing from the messenger, the fearful encounter with Esau, in which the loss of "mother with children" (Gen 32:11) was anticipated never transpired. Instead a friendly, helpful Esau sought Jacob's comfort and well being. He even suggested that some of his people might join Jacob's to help out (Gen 33:15). In other words, the narrative itself mentions the incorporation of the Edomites into Jacob's assembly. Esau's affirmation of Jacob's existence was a brotherly act, and this fraternal relationship transcends any temporary reverses, such as were revealed at the time of the desert journeys.

Similar observations can be made about the attitude toward the Egyptians. The three generations following upon those held responsible for the oppression of the Israelites, when there was a deliberate attempt to reduce their numbers (Exodus 1), are excluded from the assembly. However, because Jacob's family had previously sojourned in Egypt at the invitation of the pharaoh at that time (Gen 45:16–20), and had prospered and increased, this kindly treatment determines that children born to the third generation of Egyptians after the settlement in the land may enter Yahweh's assembly. In Moses' unsuccessful request for permission from the king of Edom for his brother

[4]To be sure, the reverse has occurred: a later dislike of Ammon and Moab has been retrojected into the past.

Israel to pass through his country, he referred to Israel's experience with the Egyptians. Israel had gone down to Egypt, had dwelt there a long time, and had then experienced oppression (Num 20:14–21). The expansion of Jacob and his family during their sojourn in Egypt, which was followed by the Egyptian policy that sought to contract numbers, is implicit in this account. The link between Edom and Egypt in this tradition has been carried over into the two laws that exclude each nation for a time from the assembly and then admit them.

After the sex laws in Deut 22:9–30 there is a series of laws dominated by the notion of Israel as a group living under the favor and guidance of its god Yahweh. In particular, the focus has been upon aspects of procreation, a topic that follows appropriately from rules about sexual relations. The initial sex laws take up undesirable unions between Israelites and Canaanites. The assembly series is similarly concerned with relations between foreign groups and Israel. The first such law concerns the Canaanite group, the Hivites. It, however, only played a background role because the Canaanites could not be considered for any association with Israel as a religious community.[5] This was not so for the other groups whose merits for an association had to be judged on nonreligious grounds. Noting the different generations that belong to these groups, the Deuteronomist evaluates their different traditions. Characteristically, he scrutinizes not just a single tradition but a number of related ones.

Law: Cleanliness in the army camp

> [9] When thou goest forth against thine enemies and are in camp, then keep thee from every evil thing. [10] If there be in thy midst any man, that is not clean by reason of uncleanness that chanceth him by night, then shall he go abroad out of the camp, he shall not come within the camp: [11] but it shall be, when evening cometh on, he shall wash himself with water: and when the sun is down, he shall come into the camp again. [12] Thou shalt have a place also without the camp, whither thou shalt go forth, [13] and thou shalt

[5]Note how the prohibitions against mixed seed and plowing with an ox and an ass rule out even the association that did take place when the Hivite women and children were absorbed into Jacob's family.

have a stick with thy weapon; and it shall be, when thou sittest down outside, thou shalt dig therewith, and shalt turn back and cover that which cometh from thee: [14] for Yahweh thy God walketh in the midst of thy camp, to deliver thee, and to give up thine enemies before thee; therefore shall thy camp be holy: that he see no nakedness of a thing in thee, and turn away from thee. (Deut 23:9–14).

Background: Jacob confronts God's army

[1] And Jacob went on his way, and the angels of God met him. [2] And when Jacob saw them, he said, This is God's army: and he called the name of that place Mahanaim. [3] And Jacob sent messengers before him to Esau his brother. . . . [6] And the messengers returned to Jacob, saying, We came to thy brother Esau, and also he cometh to meet thee, and four hundred men with him. . . . [9] And Jacob said, O God of my father Abraham. . . . [11] Deliver me, I pray thee, from the hand of my brother, from the hand of Esau: for I fear him, lest he will come and smite me, and the mother with the children. [12] And thou saidst, I will surely do thee good, and make thy seed as the sand of the sea, which cannot be numbered for multitude. [13] And he lodged there that same night; and took of that which came to his hand a present for Esau. . . . [24] And Jacob was left alone; and there wrestled a man with him until the breaking of the day. [25] And when he saw that he prevailed not against him, he touched the hollow of his thigh; and the hollow of Jacob's thigh was out of joint, as he wrestled with him. . . . [28] And he said, Thy name shall be called no more Jacob, but Israel: for thou has striven with God and with men, and hast prevailed. . . . [30] And Jacob called the name of that place Peniel: for I have seen God face to face, and my life is preserved. [31] And as he passed over Penuel the sun rose upon him, and he halted upon his thigh. [32] Therefore the children of Israel eat not of the sinew of the hip which is upon the hollow of the thigh, because he touched the hollow of Jacob's thigh on the sinew of the hip. (Gen 32:1–3, 6, 9, 11–13, 24, 25, 28, 30–32)

When we turn to the law about cleanliness in the army camp we again have to wonder why it follows the laws about the assembly. Linking like material with like so far as subject matter is concerned does not seem appropriate. Once more, however, the strategy of turning to a tradition about Israel's past effectively demonstrates a wholly intelligible link between this law and the preceding ones. In fact, a clue from a reading of the laws alone confirms that a link exists. The two about Edom and Egypt indicate that there can be exclusion from the assembly for a while and then admittance. In the law about the army camp a man may be excluded from it for a time before he is again admitted. The nexus does not seem overly significant. Once, however, the law is also linked to the tradition in Genesis 32 about Jacob's finding himself in the midst of God's army camp a fuller connection emerges. Having scrutinized in the preceding law Israel's confrontation with Edom after the exodus (Num 20:14–18), the lawgiver returns to the incident in Genesis 32, because it is the first example of Israel's preparing to confront a potential enemy. Num 20:14 refers to this period of time by recalling the trouble Jacob had with Laban before meeting up with Esau.[6]

Jacob and his family were fleeing from Laban the Aramean. The latter had caught up with them but, because of divine interference, had desisted from harming Jacob. Jacob's troubles were not over, however. His brother, Esau, had a score to settle with him and Jacob anticipated a fearful encounter. During the preparation for meeting this hurdle, the pollution-causing event at Mahanaim ("two camps") occurred. On an earlier occasion (Gen 28:10–22) Jacob had accidentally stumbled upon sacred ground, and in recognition of this pollution a pillar was built and oil poured on it. That place he had called Bethel ("house of God"). The momentous nature of each occurrence comes out in the fact that at Bethel the promise of the land of Canaan was given to him and at Mahanaim his own name was changed to Israel.

The Deuteronomist notes how the original Israel happened to find himself in the midst of God's camp; how he was opposed during the night by one of its warriors who by touching his thigh made him unclean; how this opposition turned to support of Jacob, just as the diviner Balaam's attempted curse of Israel's assembly turned into a

[6]The words to Edom in Num 20:14, "Thus saith thy brother Israel, 'Thou knewest all the travail that befell us,'' refer to the previous time they met, namely, following Jacob's flight from Laban, and not to Israel's troubles in Egypt, as is commonly thought. The following words, "And our fathers went down into Egypt," carry on the sequence of Israel's historical experiences in a manner similar to the account in Deut 26:5–10. See my analysis in *The Laws of Deuteronomy* (Ithaca: Cornell University Press, 1974), 248–51.

blessing; and how God's army must have fought on his behalf to overcome Esau's hostility and cause the latter to treat him well. The lawgiver produces a rational parallel to the legend while at the same time retaining the theological dimension. He takes up the aspect of a warrior's nocturnal bodily uncleanness in the military camp. It must be undone by his leaving and remaining outside all night, only to return after ablution at sunset the next evening. This contrasts with Jacob's experience of noctural uncleanness: he remains in camp and receives a divine blessing, followed next morning by success in the face of Esau's expected enmity. The law implies that the army encampment is sacred space. Indeed we are told that God walks in its midst. The additional implication—and this is what ties the law so closely to the immediately preceding ones—is that these Israelite warriors are Yahweh's assembly, which, if proper rules are followed, will be delivered from its enemies, its numbers preserved, ready to prosper again and increase. In this regard the law presents a close parallel to the Genesis tradition. Jacob had appealed to the deity for deliverance from his enemy. He feared a terrible loss in numbers, the slaying of "mother with children." His appeal was based on Yahweh's promise at Bethel that his descendants would become so many that they could not be numbered (Gen 28:13–15, 32:12). The *hiphil* form of the verb *nāṣal,* "to deliver," is used both in this appeal (v. 11) and in the law (in the promise that Yahweh will deliver Israel from its enemies).

Presumably what prompted the law in the first instance is the uncleanness that came to be associated with Jacob's presence in God's military camp. In one line of development that was actually incorporated in the tradition, this uncleanness was given symbolic expression in the prohibition about not eating that part of an animal equivalent to the spot on Jacob's thigh touched by the divine warrior. The Deuteronomic law represents another line of development prompted by a concern more closely related to the thrust of the narrative, namely, the preservation of Jacob's family, the incipient assembly of Yahweh.

Law: The fugitive slave

[15] Thou shalt not deliver unto his master the servant which is escaped from his master unto thee: [16] he shall dwell with thee, in

thy midst, in that place which he shall choose in one of thy gates, where it is good for him: thou shalt not oppress him. (Deut 23:15, 16)

Background: The slave Jacob in flight from Laban

[20] And Jacob stole away unawares to Laban the Aramean, in that he told him not that he fled. . . . [25] Then Laban overtook Jacob. . . . [26] And Laban said to Jacob, What hast thou done, that thou hast cheated me, and carried away my daughters, as captives taken with the sword? [27] Wherefore didst thou flee away secretly, and cheatest me; and didst not tell me, that I might have sent thee away with mirth, and with songs, with tabret, and with harp? [28] and hast not suffered me to kiss my sons and my daughters? thou hast done foolishly in so doing. [29] It is in the power of my hand to do you hurt: but the God of your father spake unto me yesternight, saying, Take thou heed that thou speak not to Jacob either good or bad. (Gen 31:20, 25–29)

[3] And Jacob sent messengers before him to Esau his brother unto the land of Seir, the country of Edom. [4] And he commanded them, saying, Thus shall ye speak unto my lord Esau; Thy servant Jacob saith thus, I have sojourned with Laban, and stayed there until now: [5] and I have oxen, and asses, flocks, and menservants, and womenservants: and I have sent to tell my lord, that I may find grace in thy sight. (Gen 32:3–5)

[4] And Esau ran to meet him, and embraced him, and fell on his neck, and kissed him: and they wept. [5] And he lifted up his eyes, and saw the women and the children; and said, Who are those with thee? And he said, The children which God hath graciously given thy servant. (Gen 33:4, 5)

Jacob's good fortune in being delivered first from Laban's hostile intent and then from Esau's is attributed to providential interference. In its outcome this fortune took the form of a welcoming, helpful attitude on the part of Esau toward his brother. Jacob had expected the opposite. He described himself as a slave who was on his way, not to a brother, but to a master. He had, moreover, recently fled from his servitude under Laban, an experience that had been oppressive and had also required the deity's interference (Gen 31:41, 42). Having escaped from an oppressive foreign master, Jacob was fearful of his reception at the hands of a new one. Certain facts lent special features to his situation. He was related both by marriage and on his mother's side to his first master, Laban, and he was a brother to the second one, Esau. He anticipated ill-treatment from this latter master in the terrible extreme of death. The lesser evil of being returned to his first master as a runaway slave is not raised in the narrative.

It is the Deuteronomist who, in his law concerning the escaped slave, puts aside the special features of the narrative and raises the issue of what to do with a slave who has run off from one master and seeks refuge with an Israelite one. The law does not state that the first master is foreign and that the receiving Israelite is appealed to as a new master. Realistically this situation has to be inferred. It is again clear that the law's formulation owes much to deliberation by the lawgiver on Jacob's position. There is an obvious sense in which Laban was a foreign master, an Aramean. When Jacob appealed to Esau, as slave to master, Esau responded as the brother he in fact was. He did not treat the suppliant as a slave but rather left him free to do as he wished, to settle wherever he chose. All of this background is relevant to an understanding of why the Israelite in the law is thought of not as a master but rather as a brother, one who will let the escaped slave settle where he wishes. Esau's fraternal kindness is the model.[7] Another obscurity is cleared up by noting the links between the law and the tradition. An escaped slave is not likely to have the wherewithal to settle wherever he chooses. The lawgiver seems happily unaware of this down-to-earth consideration, but he probably has Jacob in mind. Jacob had arrived in Esau's domain with great possessions.

This slave, Jacob, the original Israel, who had prospered under a foreign master, who had acquired wives and children, whose company (*maḥaneh* [Gen 33:8]) had been well received by Esau, the original Edom, is viewed as the forerunner of the later nation of Israel, Yahweh's assembly. This broader perspective has to be borne

[7]Those who quote (for example, M. Weinfeld, *Deuteronomy and the Deuteronomic School* [Oxford: Clarendon, 1972], 272–73), the positions in ancient Near Eastern law codes and state treaties seem to imply that the Deuteronomist knowingly takes a position opposite to these. This enables these scholars to extol the enlightened Israelite stance. More likely, however, is the simpler assumption that such extra-biblical material is irrelevant to Deuteronomic formulations. Weinfeld links the law's counsel to a wisdom background, which is another matter and much more pertinent.

in mind in accounting for the appearance of the law on the runaway slave at this point in the code.

Law: Cult prostitutes

[17] There shall be no cult prostitute of the daughters of Israel, nor cult prostitute of the sons of Israel. [18] Thou shalt not bring the hire of a harlot, or the price of a dog, into the house of Yahweh thy God for any vow: for even both these are abomination unto Yahweh thy God. (Deut 23:17, 18)

Background: Jacob's vow, and later Canaanite influence upon the Israelites

[31] And they [Simeon and Levi] said, Should he deal with our sister as with an harlot? [1] And God said unto Jacob, Arise, go up to Bethel, and dwell there: and make there an altar unto God, that appeared unto thee when thou fleddest from the face of Esau thy brother. [2] Then Jacob said unto his household, and to all that were with him, Put away the strange gods that are among you, and be clean, and change your garments: [3] and let us arise, and go up to Bethel; and I will make there an altar unto God, who answered me in the day of my distress, and was with me in the way which I went. [4] And they gave unto Jacob all the strange gods which were in their hand, and all their earrings which were in their ears; and Jacob hid them under the oak which was by Shechem. [5] And they journeyed: and the terror of God was upon the cities that were round about them, and they did not pursue after the sons of Jacob. [6] So Jacob came to Luz, which is in the land of Canaan, that is Beth-el, he and all the people that were with him. [7] And he built there an altar, and called the place El-beth-el: because there God appeared unto him, when he fled from the face of his brother. (Gen 34:31, 35:1–7).

[15] When Judah saw her [Tamar], he thought her to be an harlot; because she had covered her face. [16] And he turned unto her by the way, and said, Go to, I pray thee, let me come in unto thee; And she said, What wilt thou give me, that thou mayest come in unto me? [17] And he said, I will send thee a kid from the flock. And she said, Wilt thou give me a pledge, till thou send it? [18] And he said, What pledge shall I give thee? And she said, Thy signet, and

thy bracelets, and thy staff that is in thine hand. And he gave it her, and came in unto her, and she conceived by him. . . . [20] And Judah sent the kid by the hand of his friend the Adullamite, to receive his pledge from the woman's hand: but he found her not. [21] Then he asked the men of that place, saying, Where is the cult prostitute that was at Enaim by the wayside? And they said, There was no cult prostitute in this place. . . . [24] And it came to pass, about three months after, that it was told Judah, saying, Tamar thy daughter in law hath played the harlot; and also, behold, she is with child by harlotry. (Gen 38:15–18, 20, 21, 24)

[24] And there were also male cult prostitutes in the land: and they did according to all the abominations of the nations which Yahweh cast out before the children of Israel. (1 Kings 14:24; cp., 1 Kings 15:12, 22:46; 2 Kings 23:7)

The experience of Jacob and his group after their reception by Esau comes under scrutiny in the law prohibiting female and male cultic prostitutes among the daughters and sons of Israel, in particular, proscribing any payment derived from such prostitution to be paid into the house of God by way of fulfilling a vow. In the preceding laws interest has been shown by the lawgiver in the opposition of Moab, Ammon, Edom, and Egypt to Israel's attempts to enter the land of Canaan. Such opposition went counter to God's promise at Bethel that Jacob and his descendants would become its possessors. The first time Jacob acquired a piece of this land was just after his kindly treatment by his brother Esau, when he bought it from the Canaanite group, the sons of Hamor, and built an altar on it with the name, El-elohe-Israel (God, the God of Israel). There followed the incident in which a daughter of Israel, Dinah, was seduced by the Canaanite prince, Shechem. In the eyes of her brothers, Simeon and Levi, she was treated as a harlot by him. This incident led to the first major involvement of the Israelites with the Canaanites: the deliberately abortive attempt to forge a link between the two groups, the mass slaughter of all the newly circumcised male Hivites, and most noteworthy, the influx of the remaining females into Jacob's group.

Israel's relationships with foreign groups have dominated the background to the cluster of laws at this point in the code, as well as the interest in Israel's numbers. One topic that arises concerns which groups should be admitted into Yahweh's assembly and which excluded. The incorporation of female Canaanites is obviously a matter of interest in light of later Israelite-Canaanite history. The Deuteronomist was bound to focus attention on it, especially because the event coincided with Jacob's religious duty to fulfill his vow at the house of his God, that is, at Bethel.

Jacob himself was alert to the problem. The presence of foreign gods among his extended household had to be removed, and a purifying ritual and a change of garments had to be undergone, before he would proceed to visit Bethel and build an altar there (Gen 35:1–7). The vow he had made when he fled from an angry Esau—"If God will be with me, and will keep me in this way that I go, and will give me bread to eat, and raiment to put on, so that I come again to my father's house in peace, then shall Yahweh be my God: and this stone, which I have set for a pillar, shall be God's house; and of all that thou shalt give me I will surely give the tenth unto thee" (Gen 28:20–22)—was able to be fulfilled, because the deity had been with him during his time with Laban, his meeting with Esau, and his purchasing land out of his wealth near Shechem in Canaan. The change of garments is perhaps an acknowledgment that Jacob and his household had indeed raiment to put on. In any case, this tradition, like the law, is specifically concerned with payment to God's house in connection with the fulfillment of a vow and recognizes that impure worship, service to foreign gods, is incompatible with such payment.

The law is more specific, focusing on the payment from cultic prostitution. The reason for this is that Canaanite cult prostitutes had an effect on Israelite history. Jacob's son Judah married a Canaanitess and as a wife for his son, Er, he took the woman, Tamar, who later prostituted herself in order to continue the family line. Jacob's involvement with female Canaanites and their religious practices occurred just after his separation from his brother, Esau. Judah's involvement with a Canaanite wife and then with Tamar took place just after he separated from his brothers (Gen 38:1). In paying for her services as a cult prostitute (his description of her), he was in effect paying for the increase in Israel's family numbers, an outcome that would ordinarily warrant tangible thanks to Yahweh.

The Deuteronomist is typically interested in recurring patterns of behavior and experience from one generation to the next. He finds, for example, the taint that affected the first generation of the Ammonites and Moabites also affected their later ones. Generations of Israelites, after Jacob's and Judah's time, were themselves subjected to the contamination of Canaanite cultic prostitution, specifically the male variety (1 Kings 14:24, 15:12, 22:46; 2 Kings 23:7). For example, Judah's later ancestors, under their leader Rehoboam, again separated themselves from their brother Israelites. He, like Judah's sons, Perez and Zerah, was the product of a Judean, Solomon, and a foreign mother, Naamah the Ammonitess. The criticism leveled against his reign is that there were male cult prostitutes in the land (1 Kings 14:21–24). By ranging over Israelite history and contemplating the specific threat that Israelite daughters and sons may themselves become involved in a Canaanite religious practice (Tamar had become a mother of future Israelites), the lawgiver produces his law. When he specifically proscribes an Israelite from paying into the house of God the gains from such cultic practice, he is thinking of Jacob's promise on behalf of himself, but the promise would have been taken as also on behalf of later generations that a tenth of an Israelite's God-given wealth was to be paid into this house.[8]

Law: Loans on interest

[19] Thou shalt not lend upon interest to thy brother; interest of money, interest of victuals, interest of any thing that is lent upon interest: [20] unto a sojourner thou mayest lend upon interest; but unto thy brother thou shalt not lend upon interest: that Yahweh thy God may bless thee in all that thou settest thine hand to in the land whither thou goest to possess it. (Deut 23:19, 20)

Background: Esau's offer of assistance to Jacob, the later Edom's refusal and Jacob's trade negotiations with the Hivites

[14] Let my lord [Esau], I [Jacob] pray thee, pass over before his servant: and I will lead on softly, according as the cattle that goeth before me and the children be able to endure, until I come unto my lord unto Seir. [15] And Esau said, Let me now leave with thee some of the people that are with me. (Gen 33:14, 15)

[8]This point is well made by G. von Rad in *Das erste Buch Mose* ATD 4, 2d ed. (Göttingen: Vandenhoeck and Ruprecht, 1958), 249.

> [19] And the children of Israel said unto him [Edom], We will go by the high way: and if I and my cattle drink of thy water, then I will pay for it: I will only, without doing anything else, go through on my feet. [20] And he said, Thou shalt not go through. And Edom came out against him with much people, and with a strong hand. [21] Thus Edom refused to give Israel passage through his border: wherefore Israel turned away from him. (Num 20:19–21)

> [19] And he [Jacob] bought a parcel of a field, where he had spread his tent, at the hand of the children of Hamor, Shechem's father, for a hundred pieces of money. . . . [10] And ye [Jacob's group] shall dwell with us [Hamor's]: and the land shall be before you; dwell and trade ye therein, and get you possessions therein. (Gen 33:19, 34:10)

The law concerns the use of an Israelite's wealth. When giving loans to his fellow Israelite he should not exact interest, but in lending to a foreigner he should. The outcome will be that his wealth will increase, because God will bless him in all that he undertakes in the land. The motivation for this law comes from the lawgiver's reflection both upon the original Israel's situation at the time he acquired his wealth, when the deity was acting for him, and upon a parallel incident from later Israelite history. Jacob vowed at Bethel that if God caused him to prosper he would give some of his gains, a tenth, back to this sanctuary. Against all odds, Jacob did indeed prosper. He acquired much despite his servitude under Laban, and he was helped in maintaining it by his brother Esau's kindness. He was able to purchase a portion of land in Canaan and to enter into trading negotiations with the Canaanite group, the sons of Hamor.

The Deuteronomist would have observed that Esau wanted to give Jacob some of his men to help him look after his possessions. This offer was given freely and carried no obligation on Jacob's part to pay for their service. It was a fine brotherly example of lending without interest. In contrast, Esau's descendants, the Edomites, behaved in a contrary fashion. On the occasion of Israel's journey from Egypt to Canaan, when Israel, like the first ancestor Jacob, in going from Laban to Esau, was in the position of a fleeing slave, the Edomites showed a hostile, unaccommodating attitude. First they refused Israel's request to pass through Edomite territory, despite the assurance that the Israelites would keep out of field and vineyard and would not drink from their wells. Next they refused Israel's offer to pay for any water they might drink. Finally they threatened force should Israel approach. In weighing up the contrast between these two brotherly attitudes from different historical periods the Deuteronomist asks himself how brother Israelites should help each other out. He opts to recommend the example of Esau's helpful disposition to Jacob: the offer of a loan without benefit of material gain to the lender. The spirit of his law is in accord with that which resulted in the ruling—Esau's example was also the model—to receive a runaway slave with an open, welcoming attitude. There is a further connection between the two. A returning slave in most instances, if not in Jacob's, would need loans without interest to enable him to live a free life back in his homeland.

In formulating the second part of his law, the permission to lend with interest to foreigners, the Deuteronomist is responding to the issue that is raised but not followed through in the account of Jacob's dealings with the Hivites. If this foreign group had been acceptable to Israel, how should trading arrangements have proceeded? It happened that in the narrative Israel ended up much aggrandized at the expense of the Hivites. This development took place because of extraordinary circumstances. The lawgiver concentrates on normal Israelite relations with approved foreign groups and decides that gain accruing to Israel from straightforward business transactions is acceptable, perhaps even to be encouraged. A theological feature of these Genesis traditions is the recurring theme of the divinity's blessing upon Jacob and his family. Despite all adversities and potential disasters, their god protects them and they prosper and make progress. Yet someone observing these traditions, as the Deuteronomist does and as he imagines Moses must have done, would note the dubious nature of some of the advances. By putting the issues raised in these traditions into a proper legal and ethical perspective, the Deuteronomist believes that the Israel he is acquainted with will prosper under the same providential guidance available to the original Israel, should they follow the laws as constructed. Hence the statement added to the lending law: "That Yahweh thy God may bless thee in all that thou undertakest in the land which thou art entering to take possession of it." The geographical situation of the Israel addressed in the law is identical to that of Jacob at the time he negotiated with the sons of Hamor. Each was attempting to gain a foothold in Canaan.

Law: Prompt payment of a vow

[21] When thou shalt vow a vow unto Yahweh thy God, thou shalt not slack to pay it: for Yahweh thy God will surely require it of thee; and it would be sin in thee. [22] But if thou shalt forbear to vow, it shall be no sin in thee. [23] That which is gone out of thy lips thou shalt keep and perform; even a free-will offering, according as thou hast vowed unto Yahweh thy God, which thou hast promised with thy mouth. (Deut 23:21–23)

Background: Vows made in response to God's assistance to Israel in overcoming its enemies

[16] And Jacob awaked out of his sleep, and he said, Surely Yahweh is in this place. . . . [19] And he called the name of that place Bethel. . . . [20] And Jacob vowed a vow, saying, If God will be with me in this way that I go, and will give me bread to eat, and raiment to put on, [21] so that I come again to my father's house in peace; then shall Yahweh be my God: [22] and this stone, which I have set for a pillar, shall be God's house: and of all that thou shalt give me I will surely give the tenth unto thee. (Gen 28:16, 19–22)

[6] So Jacob came to Luz, which is in the land of Canaan, that is, Beth-el, he and all the people that were with him. [7] And he built there an altar, and called the place El-beth-el: because there God appeared unto him, when he fled from the face of his brother. . . . [9] And God appeared unto Jacob again, when he came out of Padan-aram, and blessed him. [10] And God said unto him, Thy name is Jacob: thy name shall not be called any more Jacob, but Israel shall be thy name: and he called his name Israel. [11] And God said unto him, I am God Almighty: be fruitful and multiply; a nation and a company of nations shall be of thee, and kings shall come out of thy loins. . . . [14] And Jacob set up a pillar in the place where he talked with him, even a pillar of stone: and he poured a drink offering thereon, and he poured oil thereon. [15] And Jacob called the name of the place where God spake with him, Beth-el. (Gen 35:6, 7, 9–11, 14, 15)

> [30] And Jephthah vowed a vow unto Yahweh, and said, If thou shalt without fail deliver the children of Ammon into mine hands, [31] then it shall be, that whatsoever cometh forth of the doors of my house to meet me, when I return in peace from the children of Ammon, shall surely be Yahweh's, and I will offer it up for a burnt offering. [32] So Jephthah passed over unto the children of Ammon to fight against them; and Yahweh delivered them into his hands. . . . [34] And Jephthah came to Mizpeh unto his house, and, behold, his daughter came out to meet him with timbrels and with dances: and she was his only child; besides her he had neither son nor daughter. [35] And it came to pass, when he saw her, that he rent his clothes, and said, Alas, my daughter! thou hast brought me very low, and thou art one of them that trouble me: for I have opened my mouth unto Yahweh, and I cannot go back. [36] And she said unto him, my father, if thou hast opened thy mouth unto Yahweh, do to me according to that which hath proceeded out of thy mouth; forasmuch as Yahweh hath taken vengeance for thee of thine enemies, even of the children of Ammon. [37] And she said unto her father, Let this thing be done for me: let me alone two months, that I may go up and down upon the mountains, and bewail my virginity, I and my companions. [38] And he said, Go. And he sent her away for two months: and she went with her companions, and bewailed her virginity upon the mountains. [39] And it came to pass at the end of two months, that she returned unto her father, who did with her according to his vow which he had vowed: and she knew no man. (Judg 11:30–32, 34–39)

This law has a similar subject matter to the preceding law on lending. In a vow there is a response from the human recipient to the deity's gift. He feels obliged, though unnecessarily, to give something in return. The law requires that should he feel so bound he must pay up immediately, without delay. This aspect of the law contrasts with lending on interest where a delayed payment is of the essence of the transaction. The law about cultic prostitution, which comes just before the lending law, is related in that it specifically concerns the kind of payment that might be made to the deity by way of fulfilling a vow.

By tracing the background traditions to these laws we can determine why they arise at certain points in the code and what motivates their construction. The laws in Deut 23:9–20 all emerge from the scrutiny of stories about Israel and its enemies, and the way in which the deity fights on behalf of the Israelite assembly. Thus, the law about the army camp corresponded directly the deity's protection of Israel and what they were required to do in order to maintain this support. God's protection of Jacob from a potentially destructive Esau was relevant to an understanding of the law about the reception of the fleeing slave. Simeon and Levi's slaughter of the males belonging to a Canaanite group, which would have been approved of by the Deuteronomist and therefore regarded by him as in accord with God's will, led to a conflict between Israel's religious duty and the influence of the religious orientation of the acquired Canaanite women. The law on cultic prostitution was alert to this influence and to later Canaanite influence upon the Israelites. Esau's change of heart, doubtless occasioned by the deity, was behind his offer of help to Jacob, but it was also contrasted with the later Edom's antagonism toward Israel when the Israelites were in need of provisions. The example of Esau's generous disposition was incorporated into the law on lending to a brother. The issue of trading with foreigners arose but was not developed in the context of Simeon and Levi's preparations for putting down the Hivites. The law took up the matter.

The reason why so much attention has been given to Jacob between his vow at Bethel in Gen 28:20–22 and its fulfillment in Gen 35:14, 15, after the episode in Shechem, is that this period of time marked the beginning of the Israelite nation. In that the period was defined by Jacob's vow and its fulfillment, the Deuteronomist scrutinizes the topic of vowing—not just Jacob's vow but two more: the vow made by Israel when some of its numbers were captured by the Canaanites of Arad, and, most influential of all, Jephthah's famous vow. All three were made in response to the deity's helping Israel to overcome opposition and enmity. The incident with the king of Arad occurred just after Edom refused the Israelites passage through their territory and would not even allow them to purchase water for payment. This negative attitude of the brother Edom highlighted the original Esau's generosity to Jacob and led to the formulation of the law on lending without interest to a brother. In face of the ensuing Canaanite menace, Israel vowed to God: "If thou wilt indeed deliver this people into my hand, then I will utterly destroy their cities" (Num 21:2). The deity kept his side of the arrangement and Israel duly destroyed, doubtless without delay, the Canaanite cities. Jephthah's vow was also made because of an imminent confrontation with an enemy.

Just before Jephthah uttered his vow he had addressed the king of the Ammonites and had referred to Israel's relations with them in the past. In recounting this history he mentioned Edom's refusal to let Israel pass through Edomite territory. Both the preceding law on lending and, as we shall see, the following law on eating from a neighbor's crops use this particular incident. The negotiations between Jephthah and the Ammonite king broke down, and God took the side of the Israelites and caused them to rout the opposition. Jephthah returned to his home and, "Behold, his daughter came out to meet him with timbrels and with dances; and she was his only child" (Judg 11:34). The vow required that she be sacrificed. The realization of what he has done and how he is obligated to carry out his vow are fully recognized. "I have opened my mouth unto Yahweh, and I cannot go back" (v. 35). Even his daughter sees its binding nature, "My father, if thou hast opened thy mouth unto Yahweh, do to me according to that which hath proceeded out of thy mouth" (v. 36). The law likewise underlines the strict necessity of keeping a vow. It would be a sin not to do so.

The law, however, is primarily interested in a narrower concern: once a vow has been made, its execution should not be delayed. This narrower focus is explained by the lawgiver's negative reaction to what occurred in Jephthah's case. He agreed to his daughter's request that the fulfillment of the vow be delayed until she spent two months lamenting her lot in life, that is, that she would die a virgin. The Deuteronomist, like the story, concentrates on the sacred, binding nature of the promise and judges that any delay in keeping it is simply inappropriate. It is, moreover, the shocking nature of what Jephthah's vow required that accounts for the seemingly unnecessary statement: if a person refrains from vowing no sin has been committed. Had Jephthah known that his daughter would be the sacrificial offering he would never have said what he did. If, in addition, he had asked himself whether any utterance was required in the first place, the answer would have been that no such necessity existed.

An underlying theme in so many of the laws and their traditions is the deity's preservation of Israel's numbers in the face of external threats. This aim was achieved in the defeat of the Ammonites, but the victory was accompanied by the subsequent loss of descendants to an Israelite. In lamenting that she would die a virgin, Jephthah's daughter was also declaring that no children would be born to her or to his line, because she was his only child. This loss in numbers would further justify the lawgiver's criticism of Jephthah's vow.

Law: Eating from a neighbor's crops

> [24] When thou comest into thy neighbour's vineyard, then thou mayest eat grapes thy fill at thine own pleasure; but thou shalt not put any in thy vessel. [25] When thou comest into the standing corn of thy neighbour, then thou mayest pluck the ears with thine hand; but thou shalt not move a sickle unto thy neighbour's standing corn. (Deut 23:24, 25)

Background: Israel's request to traverse Edom's land (Num 20:14–21)

The contrast between war and peace is an important feature in the formulation of so many of the laws. In the ones we have been looking at the lawgiver typically considers problems that arose in time of war and then legislates for comparable issues in that time of peacefulness that will characterize the land Israel is about to inherit. The law about permission to eat from a neighbor's vineyard and from his grain illustrates well the process in question.

When the Israelites, in an incident significant for the immediately preceding laws, were on their way to the new land they confronted a hostile Edom. The latter refused them permission to pass through their land (Num 20:17; Judg 11:17). At the time Israel gave assurances to Edom that they would not enter their fields or vineyards and that they would not drink from their wells. Such guarantees had no effect. Even the assurance that should they need water they would pay for it met with a hostile response. The Deuteronomist ponders this situation of enmity between two nations which traced their origin back to the two brothers, Jacob and Esau "(And Moses sent messengers from Kadesh unto the king of Edom. Thus saith thy brother Israel" [Num 20:14]). He notes the obvious need of the Israelites for food but notes further that the Edomites' negative response was motivated, in part at least, by their fear that this armed assembly of Israelites might take excessive amounts of grain and grapes should they turn aside into their fields and vineyards. In switching his attention to a peacetime Israelite setting, the lawgiver derives a solution to this kind of problem. When an Israelite feels the need to go into his neighbor's vineyard or standing grain he is free to eat as much as he wishes. He must not, however, fill a vessel with grapes and he must not apply a sickle to the grain. The lawgiver presumably thinks that Edom's response should have been similar. The Israelites should have been free to satisfy their hunger but should not have used any of their equipment to do so.

SUMMARY Genital mutilation in the form of circumcision is the sign of covenanting into Yahweh's assembly. Simeon and Levi's deceptive use of it to exclude the Canaanite group, the Hivites, raises the topic of whether there might in fact be a form of genital mutilation that would exclude anyone from being considered a member of the assembly. The lawgiver thinks of the person without testes or penis as unworthy because he cannot contribute to Israel's expansion. The Ammonites and Moabites came into existence by Lot's daughters' decision to preserve descendants for their father by getting him drunk and seducing him. Products of this kind of union are not to be included in the numbers that make up Yahweh's assembly. Those generations of Ammonites and Moabites who in Moses' lifetime tried to reduce Israel's numbers by not providing bread and water when they were in need of such, and who sought to curse them because of their great numbers, are themselves not to be counted among the members of Yahweh's assembly. The Edomites' and Egyptians' treatment of the Israelites had been inconsistent up to the time Moses issued his laws. The ancestor of the Edomites, Esau, treated them well in line with the blessing of expansion conferred upon Jacob and his family. But after the exodus from Egypt a generation of Edomites attacked the sojourning Israelites. Relations with Egypt were similar. First there was a period when the Egyptians encouraged their expansion, but it was followed by their attempt to kill off the Israelites. The law counsels that Edomite and Egyptian offspring of the third generation be reckoned as members of the Israelite assembly.

Jacob's was the first Israelite life saved—he survived an encounter with a divine warrior in God's army camp. The uncleanness caused at his thigh joint has sparked the issue of later Israelite armies and their need to keep themselves from bodily uncleanness when in their camps. God, we are informed, walks in the midst of them. Not only did Jacob survive as a slave in flight from a hostile master, Laban, but his new master, Esau, to whom he came as a slave, treated him as the brother he was. This kindly action was in keeping with God's promise that Jacob and his line would prosper. The law requires an Israelite not to return a runaway slave but to treat him well. After Jacob's kindly reception by Esau his group came into contact with a Canaanite group for the first time in Israel's history. Although the Hivite men were killed, because Shechem had treated Dinah as a harlot, their women and children joined Israel's ranks. In order to keep his earlier vow to go to Bethel and build an altar there, Jacob required that his household, including its recent additions, first purify itself. The lawgiver, thinking of later Canaanite cultic influence upon Israel, prohibits the payment of the gains from cultic prostitution to the house of God by way of keeping a vow. Esau offered his brother assistance without asking for anything in return. This was in contrast to the later Edom who refused to give the later Israel water even in return for payment. The first business transactions ever entered into by Israel were Jacob's dealings with the Hivites following Esau's generous treatment of Jacob and his family. Attempts to work out a trading agreement with this foreign group came to nothing because of Simeon and Levi's action against them. The lawgiver, thinking of relations between brother Israelites, supports Esau's example of offering Jacob assistance without requiring anything in return. The undeveloped example of trading with foreigners in the incident involving the Hivites is similarly taken up by the lawgiver.

Jephthah's vow was made in the context of fighting the Ammonites when he informed them about Israel's previous relationship with them and with, among others, Edom. In regard to the latter he cites their failure to let Israel traverse Edomite territory. In seeking divine assistance to counter Ammon's hostile response Jepthah uttered his vow. It proved to be a careless one, forcing him to sacrifice his daughter, and he was additionally at fault because he delayed its fulfillment. The lawgiver warns about such delays in paying a vow and notes that vows need not be made at all. The Edomites refused the brother Israel passage through their land because, it is implied, they feared that this armed assembly would help themselves to the produce of field and vineyard. The lawgiver takes up a parallel situation among brother Israelites when dwelling in their own land. Vines and grain may be taken freely but no instrument is to be used in doing so.

CHAPTER 10

PROBLEMS OF KIN

The preceding laws and corresponding incidents were dominated by Israel's interaction with foreign groups. There follows a succession of laws in which the focus switches to problems involving families belonging to the line of descent that began with Abraham. In the series of laws after those on sexual relations, the first, the exclusion of the bastard from Yahweh's assembly, referred to Abraham's kinship with Lot's descendants, the Ammonites and Moabites. Now we find three laws in which Abraham again figures. Concern with childlessness or loss of offspring is, as in the preceding laws, a common theme. Recall, for example, how there was an interest in Jephthah's vow. We should also remember that in the nonlegal parts of Deuteronomy this notion of Israel's fertility is also a dominant theme. That it shows up in the laws, or in the incidents inspiring them, is not surprising.

Law: Renovating a marriage

[1] If a man takes a wife, and marries her, and it come to pass that she find no favour in his eyes, because he hath found the nakedness of a thing in her: and he writes her a bill of divorcement, and gives it in her hand, and sends her out of his house, [2] and she departs out of his house, and she goes and becomes another man's

> wife. [3] And the latter husband hates her, and writes her a bill of divorcement, and gives it in her hand, and sends her out of his house; or the latter husband dies, which took her to be his wife; [4] her former husband, which sent her away, cannot take her again to be his wife, after that she is defiled; for that is abomination before Yahweh: and thou shalt not cause the land to sin, which Yahweh thy God giveth thee for an inheritance. (Deut 24:1–4)

Background: Abraham's use of his wife (Genesis 20; see p. 215)

The law prohibiting the renovation of a marriage, though so different in content from the preceding law about entering a neighbor's fields and vineyards, appears after it because the background incidents prompting each law are similar. Moses had sent messengers from Kadesh to the king of Edom with the request that the Israelites might pass through his land. They were aware that they might be faced with a hostile Edom rather than a helpful one. At an earlier period in time, Israel's renowned ancestor, Abraham, was likewise traveling near Kadesh and sojourned in Gerar (Genesis 20). He too anticipated enmity from the ruler of that region, Abimelech, king of Gerar. In order to meet this threat, not true as it turned out, Abraham let the local inhabitants think that his lovely wife, Sarah, was his sister. He reckoned that this piece of misinformation would save his own life because Sarah's great beauty would attract a protector for her and for himself also. The result was that the king did indeed desire her as his wife. Before he could consummate the union, however, a dream revealed to him that she was another man's wife. It turned out, moreover, that a plague of sterility had afflicted the other women of his household because of what had taken place. There is then a theological perspective in the narrative that is opposed to a man's wife being in effect transferred by one husband to another in order to help him cope with an oppressive situation. The intention of the divine intervention was to restore Sarah unsullied to Abraham. In a similar incident, recorded in Genesis 12, when Abram had had to go to Egypt because of famine, the pharaoh had actually taken Sarai as his spouse before the deity had pressured him into releasing her so that she became Abram's wife again.

An important, additional reason why the lawgiver turns back to the first ancestor, Abraham, is that his family life furnishes the earliest examples of problems involving offspring. This will become clear in the following two laws about exemption from military service and taking a millstone in pledge. Recall that at this period of time Sarah is childless. The laws we have been looking at share an interest in Israel as a nation destined to increase its numbers.

In making a typical switch from a problem that arose in a situation of enmity between an external power and Israel (or one of its ancestors), to a comparable problem that might arise in peacetime within Israel itself, the lawgiver produces the case laid out in the prohibition against renovating a marriage. Unlike the Genesis narrator, he concentrates on the man's role in permitting his partner to become another's wife and legislates accordingly. The man divorces the woman, not because he hates her, which is the usual reason for a divorce action, but because she finds no favor in his eyes, because there exists in her "the nakedness of a thing." The reference is to something about her which causes him to divorce her so that she becomes, immediately it appears,[1] the wife of another man. In other words, the parallel with the triangular case of Abraham, Sarah, and Abimelech is in mind. Sarah's great beauty, which in the nature of things could not be concealed from searching male eyes, constitutes an example of the "nakedness of a thing" in her.[2] The result was that as a wife she found no favor in his eyes.

Abraham did not actually divorce Sarah—the story has its peculiar, unconventional features—but she became free to be taken into Abimelech's house as his spouse. It was, moreover, the power that Abraham felt someone in Gerar would have over him that motivated him to declare that Sarah was his sister rather than his wife. Almost all interpreters, unaware of this background influence upon the law, have suggested a negative connotation for the expression, "the nakedness of a thing," and have assumed some undesirable feature in the woman that morally and legally justifies the husband's divorce action. There are serious problems with this view that I have discussed elsewhere,[3] not least of which is finding an explanation for

[1]Contrary to the RSV translation, for example, which adds a nonexistent "if" before "she becomes," the text states: "And she departs from his house and goes and becomes another man's wife."

[2]Cp. the disguised Joseph's allegation to his brothers that they came as spies to Egypt to see "the nakedness of the land" (Gen 42:9).

[3]See my *Women, Law, and the Genesis Traditions* (Edinburgh: Edinburgh University Press, 1979), 13, 14.

why the lawgiver would bother to prohibit a man from renovating his marriage after his wife has been married to another man. Once, however, we imagine a situation comparable to what took place in Genesis—for example, a man divorces his wife only because he stands to gain by her becoming another man's spouse—is it understandable why a lawgiver should formulate a prohibition whose primary aim is to discourage a man from releasing a woman for his personal advantage. No wonder he states that he cannot have her back after she has been defiled. He is referring to the apparently neutral fact that she has been legitimately married to a second husband and that he has divorced her or died. What is in the lawgiver's mind, however, are the circumstances in which the second husband acquired her. In reality a man was favoring another by permitting him to enjoy his wife. Carried out under cover of the law, at least from the first husband's side of things, in a way, this strategy used the law to encourage a wife's adultery. The appropriate term to characterize the woman is to say that she has been defiled (*ṭāmēʾ*). In the Genesis narrative the deity declared to Abimelech that his offense was one of adultery.[4] He had rightly protested his innocence. From our perspective the more accurate accusation would be against Sarah herself, with Abraham bearing the responsibility for encouraging her. In the Genesis 12 incident she was defiled; in Genesis 20 the deity intervened just in time.

Law: Giving pleasure to a new wife

> [5] When a man hath taken a new wife, he shall not go out to war, neither shall he be charged with any business: but he shall be free at home one year, and shall give joy to his wife which he hath taken. (Deut 24:5)

Background: Sarah receives pleasure

> [9] And they [angels] said unto him [Abraham], Where is Sarah thy wife? And he said, Behold, in the tent. [10] And he said, I will certainly return unto thee according to the time of life; and, lo, Sarah thy wife shall have a son. And Sarah heard it in the tent door,

[4]The law characterizes the woman's return to her first husband as "an abomination to Yahweh." This aptly describes Yahweh's reaction to Sarah's position.

> which was behind him. [11] Now Abraham and Sarah were old and well stricken in age; and it ceased to be with Sarah after the manner of women. [12] Therefore Sarah laughed within herself, saying, After I am waxed old shall I have pleasure, my lord being old also? (Gen 18:9–12)

Apart from his fear that a foreign potentate might take his wife and kill him, Abraham was also faced with the prospect that should he die he would have no heir by his chief wife, Sarah. Her barrenness had been a problem and to counter it she had given her maidservant, Hagar, to Abraham for the purpose of raising children by her and, no doubt, ensuring an heir for Abraham's line (Gen 16:1, 2). A child was born, Ishmael, but bad feeling between the two women complicated the ensuing relationships. Eventually, the deity promised Abraham a son by Sarah. She conceived a child, Isaac, who turned out to be Abraham's heir. This turn of events did not take place until after the danger of his sojourn in Gerar was past.

The law that comes after the one prohibiting the renovation of a marriage grants to a newly married man a year's exemption from military duty and from any other imposition. The reason—that he should give joy to his wife. It is a remarkable statement. The meaning is almost certain that a child is to be born—the period of a year is one indication—but the notion of giving pleasure to the woman, as spoken of by Sarah, seems to be the prominent factor. Again what has occurred is that the lawgiver has looked beyond the idiosyncratic features of Abraham and Sarah's situation and noted one salient feature: a man faced with the prospect of death at the hands of an enemy who has not yet given joy to his wife in the form of her conceiving a child. He asks himself in what more typical circumstances might this same problem arise for one of Abraham's descendants. The answer is when an Israelite has taken a new wife but is faced with the duty of military service and therefore the prospect of death at the hands of the enemy (see the comparable law in Deut 20:7, behind which was a focus upon the betrothed David).[5] The

[5]The differences between these two similar laws are explained by the traditions that underlie their construction. Abraham was married, David was betrothed. The attention to the woman in Deut 24:5 reflects the prominence given to Sarah. Michal's role, on the other hand, is not important in the struggle between Saul and David. The interest in procreation in Deut 24:5 reflects the similar interest in the story about Sarah.

specific motivation for the law is the fact that in the tradition Abraham had to suffer the danger before he gave conception to Sarah. Providential control could permit things to proceed that way. For a lawgiver, however, more earthly considerations apply, and practical wisdom requires that a man not face the danger of death before he has given his wife conception.

Law: A millstone as pledge

> [6] No man shall take the nether or the upper millstone to pledge: for he taketh a life to pledge. (Deut 24:6)

Background: Sarah's means of ensuring her son's superiority over Hagar's son

> [9] And Sarah saw the son of Hagar the Egyptian, which she had born unto Abraham, mocking. [10] Wherefore she said unto Abraham, Cast out this bondwoman and her son: for the son of this bondwoman shall not be heir with my son, even with Isaac. [11] And the thing was very grievous in Abraham's sight because of his son. [12] And God said unto Abraham, Let it not be grievous in thy sight because of the lad, and because of thy bondwoman; in all that Sarah hath said unto thee, hearken unto her voice; for in Isaac shall thy seed be called. (Gen 21:9–12)

Further inquiry into Abraham's family life also leads to an explanation for the law prohibiting the taking of a mill or a millstone in pledge. To take such an essential household item as collateral in order to pressure the recipient of a benefit, for example, a loan, into repaying is regarded as so oppressive that it is said to be the equivalent of taking a life in pledge. One can see the point, even if it is overstated. The hyperbole, however, is rooted in the lawgiver's response to what happened to Hagar, Sarah's maidservant. Not that the subject of a material loan on pledge arises in the Genesis narrative. We have come to see, however, that scrutiny of a narrative produces equivalent, not necessarily corresponding, concerns.

After Abraham had, to use the Deuteronomic language, given joy to his wife and she produced a son, Isaac (Gen 21:1–8), a problem arose in regard to this son's claim to be Abraham's heir. Sarah feared that the son, Ishmael, whom Hagar had borne, would inherit with him.[6] Her request, which was carried through, was harsh, even drastic. God is said by the narrator to be behind Abraham's decision to do Sarah's bidding. Abraham took some bread and water and sent Hagar and her son away. They wandered in the wilderness of Beersheba and the child's life was soon threatened with starvation. Providence, however, came to the rescue of child and mother. Isaac, not Ishmael, did in fact become Abraham's chief heir. Sarah achieved what she desired.

The lawgiver is interested in how she accomplished this. If the deity had not interfered on Ishmael's side, Isaac would have become chief heir at the cost of another's life. Sarah, in effect, pressured Abraham into ensuring that her son would receive the top inheritance by forcing him to cast out Hagar and her child. We are not dealing with the lending of an object, although at stake are considerable material advantages. It is nonetheless still accurate to paraphrase Abraham's agreement to Sarah's request by stating that it constituted his promise to give Isaac the prime inheritance because she had granted him the benefit of this son. By so agreeing, a life (Ishmael's and perhaps Hagar's too) was literally at stake.[7]

The lawgiver notes how the harshness of the situation might be glossed over because of the deity's role in rescuing Ishmael. Wondering what might constitute a comparably harsh situation in everyday life, he decides on a situation in which someone seeks to guarantee what is due to him by requesting a pledge that threatens the very existence of the members of a family which has received some important benefit from the creditor. An upper or lower millstone would be an example of a pledge that could lead to starvation within a family. Interestingly, a slave girl—Hagar was such—typically worked a millstone on behalf of a family. Also noteworthy is the fact that the issue of starvation comes up in both law and narrative. When Abraham gave Hagar some bread for her needs and her child's, it may well have

[6]See Z. W. Falk, *Hebrew Law in Biblical Times* (Jerusalem: Wahrmann, 1964), 168, on the sons of bondwomen as coheirs with the sons of the chief wife.

[7]This link to the Hagar story explains the personification of the pledge in the law. Commentators are puzzled by the expression "a life in pledge" and feel obliged to explain that this means "taking in pledge a means of livelihood" (see P. C. Craigie, *The Book of Deuteronomy* NICOT [Grand Rapids: Eerdmans, 1976], 307). Such a paraphrase, while correct, does not do justice to the lawgiver's expression.

been bread that she herself had prepared after working the millstone in Abraham and Sarah's household.

There is, however, no need to force the parallels between the law and the narrative. The relevant point is that Sarah had granted her husband a son and asked him in return to expel Hagar and her son by way of a pledge that Isaac would be recognized as the chief heir. The commercial aspect of such interfamily arrangements is well illustrated in another patriarchal story. Leah hired (*śākar*) her husband, Jacob, by means of the mandrakes her son had found for her (Gen 30:14–18). The purpose of the hire was to enable Leah to receive some love and joy from Jacob. Rachel, like Sarah, the barren wife, acquired the mandrakes so that she could conceive a child, Joseph, who, as it turned out, was to achieve the top inheritance in his time.

Law: Theft of a fellow Israelite

> [7] If a man be found stealing any of his brethren of the children of Israel, and treateth him oppressively, and selleth him; then that thief shall die; and thou shalt put evil away from thy midst. (Deut 24:7)

Background: The sale of Joseph

> [26] And Judah said unto his brethren, What profit is it if we slay our brother, and conceal his blood? [27] Come, and let us sell him to the Ishmaelites, and let not our hand be upon him; for he is our brother and our flesh. And his brethren hearkened. [28] Then there passed by Midianite merchantmen; and they drew and lifted up Joseph out of the pit, and sold Joseph to the Ishmaelites for twenty pieces of silver, and they brought Joseph into Egypt. (Gen 37:26–28)

By equating an oppressive demand for payment of an obligation with taking a life in pledge, the lawgiver moves close to the idea of forcibly acquiring a person. Not surprisingly the next law is about the theft of a man, in particular, of an Israelite who is stolen by a fellow Israelite, treated as a slave and sold. Moses in Exod 21:16, it was understood, had already dealt with the offense. In the later Deuteronomic law the focus narrows to the theft of one Israelite by another. It seems clear that the influential case is the sale of Joseph by his brothers, all sons of Israel, to the Egyptians through the hands of the Ishmaelites. Especially revealing are the links between the Hagar story and the one concerning Joseph. Hagar was the mother of Ishmael, the eponymous ancestor of the Ishmaelites. Oppression characterizes each story. Hagar and Ishmael were cast out from their home and family; so too was Joseph. Each time the cruelty arose within the family; each time material gain was involved. Sarah acquired the prime inheritance for Isaac, and Joseph's brothers received money from the Ishmaelites. There is an even closer parallel. Just as Isaac acquired the top position over his brother Ishmael, so too Judah tried to oust Joseph from his position as father's favorite (Gen 37:26; 38, 49:8–12). To be sure, Joseph in the end retained his advantage.

The Joseph story concentrates on what happened to Joseph, although at one point it recounts how the brothers received some recompence (in their dealings with the disguised Joseph in Egypt) for their misdeed. The law lays down the supreme penalty for the culprit. The fact that Joseph's brothers were not punished would have prompted the Deuteronomist to restate the law on kidnapping and to make clear that any comparable case among the sons of Israel (in the wider sense) should lead to a death sentence for the guilty party. An even stronger motivation may well stem from the Deuteronomist's need to respond at the legal level to the theological notion expressed in Gen 45:4–8, especially verse 5, "Now therefore be not grieved, nor angry with yourselves, that ye sold me hither: For God did send me before you to preserve life," and verse 8, "So now it was not you that sent me hither, but God" (cp., Gen 50:20). The restatement of a law about kidnapping, which addresses itself to the Israelite scene, would counter any confusion that might arise from this surprisingly favorable view of the brothers' action against Joseph.

The uncommon term *hitʿammer,* "to treat oppressively," is found in this law and in the one legislating against the bad treatment of a captive woman: an Israelite must not sell her after he has taken her as a wife (Deut 21:10–14). The narrative that contributed to the construction of the latter is the one about Laban's rebuke of Jacob for running off with his two daughters. From Laban's perspective Jacob had wrongfully removed them ("like captives of the sword") from their homeland, Aram (Gen 31:25–50). Joseph too was removed from his homeland.

Law: The cure of leprosy

[8] Take heed in the plague of leprosy, that thou observe diligently, and do according to all that the priests the Levites shall teach you: as I commanded them, so ye shall observe to do. [9] Remember what Yahweh thy God did unto Miriam by the way, after that ye were come forth out of Egypt. (Deut 24:8, 9)

Background: Miriam's leprosy

[1] And Miriam and Aaron spake against Moses. . . . [2] And they said, Hath Yahweh indeed spoken only by Moses? hath he not spoken also by us? And Yahweh heard it. . . . [6] And he said, Hear now my words: If there be a prophet among you, I Yahweh will make myself known unto him in a vision, and will speak unto him in a dream. [7] My servant Moses is not so, who is faithful in all mine house. [8] With him will I speak mouth to mouth, even apparently, and not in dark speeches; and the similitude of Yahweh shall he behold: wherefore then were ye not afraid to speak against my servant Moses? [9] And the anger of Yahweh was kindled against them; and he departed. [10] And the cloud departed from off the tabernacle; and, behold, Miriam became leprous, white as snow: and Aaron looked upon Miriam, and, behold, she was leprous. [11] And Aaron said unto Moses, Alas, my lord, I beseech thee, lay not the sin upon us, wherein we have done foolishly, and wherein we have sinned. [12] Let her not be as one dead, of whom the flesh is half consumed when he cometh out of his mother's womb. [13] And Moses cried unto Yahweh, saying, Heal her now, O God, I beseech thee. [14] And Yahweh said unto Moses, If her father had but spit in her face, should she not be ashamed seven days? let her be shut out from the camp seven days, and after that let her be received in again. (Num 12:1, 2, 6–14)

We have pointed out, without suggesting that the lawgiver himself placed much emphasis upon the fact, that he switches from a scrutiny of external threats to an Israelite (or an ancestor of Israel) to threats that arise within Israel itself or, even more specifically, within Israelite families. This law enjoins obedience to the Levitical priests in an outbreak of leprosy. Moses is, contrary to the other laws, made to declare himself in it: "As I commanded them [the priests], so ye shall observe to do."[8] Then follows a reference to what God did to his

[8]The use of the "You" form is again consistent with its use during Moses' own time. The form is found in Numbers 12.

sister Miriam. There is, in fact, as the law might lead us to conclude, no connection made in Numbers 12 between Miriam's cure and her obedience to the instructions of Moses concerning what to do in an outbreak of leprosy. Yet the lawgiver, clearly interested in this practical aspect of things, is led to ask what is to be done when someone has leprosy and divine intervention in human affairs is not to be anticipated. In that Moses emerges as the key authority in the incident, and in that Aaron as the head of the Levitical priests is made to recognize this,[9] the lawgiver infers that their instructions were the ones to be followed in curing leprosy. In the narrative Aaron was the one who first acknowledged that Moses was superior to him and that he and Miriam had been foolish in voicing their complaint. Aaron was, moreover, the one who first requested that she should be healed. The explicit affirmation of Moses' authority over the Levitical priests becomes readily intelligible in light of what took place in the narrative. The lawgiver would understand that Moses had proceeded to lay down instructions to Aaron about any future incident of leprosy, and these would have been passed on to the Levites who were under Aaron's charge.

In explaining why a law on leprosy is set down after the law against kidnapping, we can point to the common interest in conflicts over who possessed supreme authority. Joseph's brothers had rebelled against the top position that he had been granted in his dream. Just before they laid hands on him they had said to themselves, "Here comes this dreamer" (Gen 37:19), a negative reaction to his assumed superiority. Their sale of him constituted an illegitimate exclusion of a man from his family. Eventually they were saved from famine by acknowledging his authority. Interestingly, it is just after an incident concerning famine among the Israelites, when they lamented the fact that they no longer had the kind of food that was available to them in Egypt (Num 11:5), that Aaron and Miriam's rebelliousness against Moses surfaced. In the deity's resolution of this conflict, Moses' special position is marked by the fact that God speaks to him plainly and not, as with prophets (or with Joseph for that matter), in the dark speech of vision or dream. A further contrasting feature with the Joseph saga is that Miriam's exclusion from her family was a legitimate one as opposed to Joseph's exclusion.

[9]On Aaron's relationship to the Levites, see Numbers 8.

Law: Entering a house to fetch a neighbor's pledge

[10] When thou dost lend thy brother any thing, thou shalt not go into his house to fetch his pledge. [11] Thou shalt stand outside and the man to whom thou dost lend shall bring out the pledge outside unto thee. [12] And if the man be poor, thou shalt not sleep with his pledge: [13] in any case thou shalt deliver him the pledge again when the sun goeth down, that he may sleep in his own raiment, and bless thee: and it shall be righteousness unto thee before Yahweh thy God. (Deut 24:10–13)

Background: Benhadad's attempt to enter Ahab's house to collect his pledge

[1] And Ben-hadad the king of Aram gathered all his host together: and there were thirty and two kings with him, and horses, and chariots: and he went up and besieged Samaria, and warred against it. [2] And he sent messengers to Ahab king of Israel into the city, and said unto him, Thus saith Ben-hadad, [3] Thy silver and thy gold is mine; thy wives also and thy children, even the goodliest, are mine. [4] And the king of Israel answered and said, My lord, O king, according to thy saying, I am thine, and all that I have. [5] And the messengers came again, and said, Thus speaketh Ben-hadad, saying, Although I have sent unto thee, saying, Thou shalt deliver me thy silver and thy gold, and thy wives, and thy children; [6] yet I will send my servants unto thee to morrow about this time, and they shall search thine house, and the houses of thy servants; and it shall be, that whatsoever is pleasant in thine eyes, they shall put it in their hand, and take it away. [7] Then the king of Israel called all the elders of the land, and said, Mark, I pray you, and see how this man seeketh mischief; for he sent unto me for my wives, and for my children, and for my silver, and for my gold, and I denied him not. [8] And all the elders and all the people said unto him, Hearken not unto him, nor consent. [9] Wherefore he said unto the messengers of Ben-hadad, Tell my lord the king, All that thou didst send for to thy servant at the first I will do: but this thing I can not do. (1 Kings 20:1–9)

This law, remarkable in that it is solely concerned with a debtor's dignity, prohibits a lender from entering the borrower's house to fetch his pledge. The latter will already have been agreed to, or rather (for we are dealing with a pledge made under pressure),[10] the creditor

[10] As distinct from a pledge that is solely concerned with recouping the lender's loss should the borrower fail to repay his loan.

will have specified the collateral.[11] The requirement that he wait outside for the debtor to bring it to him is, as D. Daube in his analysis of shame in the Deuteronomic legal material has made clear, for the sake of preserving appearances. This way the debtor's dignity is salvaged. "To have the creditor inside the home, for the purpose of collecting his security, would be the most down-putting, dishonouring experience for the debtor and his family."[12] That we are dealing, not with a commercial transaction in which both sides stand to gain, but with a distressingly difficult situation for the borrower, emerges in the second part of the law. If the borrower is a poor man, and the only thing of value that he possesses is the garment with which he covers himself, the creditor must not put additional pressure upon him by failing to permit him to sleep in it at night. What situation of duress might have prompted the construction of this law?

Again a narrative incident, with all its unique, idiosyncratic features, stimulates the lawgiver to lay out the more usual circumstances in which a debtor is hard pressed both in a material sense but also in terms of his human dignity. In the two preceding laws there has been an underlying interest in legitimate assertion of authority, Joseph over his brothers, Moses over his brother and sister. This same topic comes to the fore in 1 Kings 20: Benhadad, king of Aram, exercised his authority over Ahab, king of Israel, and demanded that the latter submit to him. Moreover (not that the parallel needs to be pressed), we are eventually to learn that an important development takes place because they regard each other as brothers (1 Kings 20:32, 33).

The situation is a military one: Ahab has to bow to the threat of Benhadad's superior force. Initially he acknowledges Benhadad's demand: "Thy silver and thy gold is mine; thy wives also and thy children, even the goodliest, are mine" (1 Kings 20:3). These possessions of Ahab constitute a bond inherent in which is the recognition that his own person has come under the complete control of Benhadad. "My lord, O king, according to thy saying, I am thine, and all

[11]Commentators go badly astray when they suggest that the borrower is free to choose the article he wishes to give as collateral for the loan—see, for example, S. R. Driver, *Deuteronomy* ICC (Edinburgh: T. and T. Clark, 1902), 275, and Craigie, *Book of Deuteronomy,* 308. As Daube points out ("The Culture of Deuteronomy," *Orita* 3 [1969]: 34), there would be no lending at all (except where no security is required) if this were the law's requirement.

[12]Daube, "Culture," 34.

that I have" (v. 4). We recall, in the two laws preceding the one on leprosy, how a life could be taken in pledge and an Israelite be treated as an object for sale by a brother Israelite.

It is Benhadad's additional demand that causes Ahab to resist. Rather than have Ahab deliver over to him the possessions in question, Benhadad now demands that his servants enter Ahab's house (and the houses of his servants) and acquire what is owed. The reason for Ahab's resistance, which is supported by the elders and the people, is not stated. Commentators and translators wrongly think that Benhadad has escalated his demand to the point where it will amount to unlimited looting. They alter the Hebrew text to read "them" instead of "you" in his instruction that his servants should, having entered Ahab's house, "lay hands on whatever pleases you" (v. 6).[13] The Hebrew should not be altered. What Ahab is objecting to is the unnecessary, additional humiliation that is being placed upon him by those servants actually entering his house and taking the tribute that has more or less been specifically agreed to (silver and gold and the fairest among his wives and children).

We have yet another example in which the lawgiver first reflects upon a situation that arose in a time of military strife and then switches his attention to comparable circumstances in ordinary life. A man in dire need of material or monetary assistance comes under the power of his creditor.[14] The latter, the law commands, should not add to the humiliation of the debtor's oppressed state by insisting that he enter his house to fetch the already designated pledge.

Benhadad demanded in the form of wives and children a pledge from Ahab that would indicate that he was submitting to the Aramean's authority and, no doubt, that he would in the future be indebted to him for protection. These wives and children were to be removed from their homes and handed over to a foreign country. Hagar and Ishmael, we saw, also provided an example of a mother and child who were removed from their home as Abraham's pledge

[13]Already the Septuagint, the Peshitta, and the Vulgate read "them." For commentators see J. Gray, *I and II Kings* (Philadelphia: Westminster, 1964), 375; J. A. Montgomery, *The Books of Kings* ICC (New York: Scribner's, 1951), 320–21. David Daube noted the parallel with the law (*Wine in the Bible* [London: Diocesan Council for Christian-Jewish Understanding, 1974], 11).

[14]Cp. the perspective in Prov 22:7: "The rich ruleth over the poor, and the borrower is servant to the lender."

that Sarah's son, Isaac, would be the chief son. Judah, in particular, had Joseph removed from his home so that he would not be the chief son. Miriam was removed from her place because she refused to recognize Moses as head of her family. She and Aaron were wrong to question his authority. Ahab, in turn, was not in a position to question Benhadad's authority over him. Benhadad, however, exceeded his authority when he declared that he would send his servants into Ahab's house to fetch his bond. In contrast to Miriam (and Aaron), in standing up to Moses, Ahab was right to resist Benhadad at this point.

These common features indicate that there is in fact nothing haphazard about the way in which the lawgiver presents his laws. And this despite appearances; for example, the sequence is: taking a life in pledge (in the form of a millstone), kidnapping, leprosy, and the creditor-debtor relation. In going from the Miriam incident in Numbers 12 to Ahab's problem in 1 Kings 20, the Deuteronomist observes links between one period of Israelite history and another. This is no surprise in light of the well-recognized editorial activity attributed to this writer (or school of writers). What is especially interesting in the link between the Miriam story and the material in Kings is the further link between the Miriam story and the material that precedes the Ahab incident. In Numbers 12 God speaks to Moses in plain speech and not indirectly through dreams and visions. In 1 Kings 19 God speaks to Elijah plainly and not through wind or earthquake or fire. Elijah, moreover, is granted supreme authority such that his word will be paramount in matters domestic and foreign, for example, in deposing and setting up kings (1 Kings 19:15–17). If the Deuteronomist had a hand in the compiling of the material in Kings and if he was aware of Elijah as a successor to Moses (a prophet like him, according to his law in Deut 18:15), then his move from the one tradition to the other is far from arbitrary.

Law: The hired servant

[14] Thou shalt not oppress an hired servant that is poor and needy, whether he be of thy brethren, or of thy sojourners that are in thy land within thy gates: [15] at his day thou shalt give him his hire; neither shall the sun go down upon it; for he is poor, and

setteth his heart upon it: lest he cry against thee unto Yahweh, and it be sin unto thee. (Deut 24:14, 15)

Background: Jacob's experience as a hired servant

[4] And Jacob sent and called Rachel and Leah to the field unto his flock, [5] and said unto them, I see your father's countenance, that it is not toward me as before; but the God of my father hath been with me. [6] And ye know that with all my power I have served your father. [7] And your father hath deceived me, and changed my wages ten times; but God suffered him not to hurt me. . . . [40] Thus I was; in the day the drought consumed me, and the frost by night; and my sleep departed from mine eyes. [41] Thus have I been twenty years in thy [Laban's] house; I served thee fourteen years for thy two daughters, and six years for thy cattle: and thou hast changed my wages ten times. [42] Except the God of my father, the God of Abraham, and the fear of Isaac, had been with me, surely thou hadst sent me away now empty. God hath seen mine affliction and the labour of my hands, and rebuked thee yesternight. (Gen 31:4–7, 40–42)

If the oppression of an Israelite by an Aramean underlies the construction of the law about the debtor's dignity, the Aramean Laban's oppression of Jacob is behind the law on the mistreatment of the hired servant. This ancestor of the Arameans oppressed the ancestor of the Israelites in the matter of his wages. In fact, all the concerns that are mentioned in the law about mistreating a hired servant—he is poor and needy, he may be a brother Israelite or a sojourner, his hire should be given him on the day he earns it—show up in Laban's treatment of Jacob.

Initially their family relationship is stressed. Laban is the brother of Jacob's mother: "Surely thou art my bone and my flesh" (Gen 29:10, 14). Like Benhadad in relation to Ahab, a brotherly tie can be claimed to exist. Jacob, however, is also a sojourner in a land not his own. The shrewd Laban, moreover, ostensibly paying him wages as a mark of filial kindness (Gen 29:15), is in effect treating him as a hired servant. Like Joseph and Moses over their kin, Laban exercised power over his kinsman, but in capricious fashion. In his position as an employer he cheated him in the paying of his hire. The hand of the lovely Rachel was to be his wages, but he received instead the less desirable Leah. In other words, Laban oppressed his new servant by manipulating his wives, just as Benhadad oppressed his new vassal in the matter of his wives. Even more revealing of the lawgiver's concerns, for example, the requirement that the employer pay the servant's wages before the sun goes down, is Jacob's angry complaint in Gen 31:36–42. Jacob had served in exemplary fashion for twenty years; by day the heat consumed him and the cold by night, and sleep "had departed from his eyes." Worst of all, Jacob never knew when he was going to receive his wages. No less than ten times did he find that his wages had been changed. Fortunately for him the "God of his father" had responded to his oppression and had vindicated him against Laban. As a consequence of this divine intervention he had ended up well off.

In the law there is reference to the hired servant who in his downtrodden state cries out to God; and God finds fault, as he did with Laban, with the employer. Moreover, the apparently unnecessary reminder in the law that the hired servant is poor and needy has to be viewed against the background of the tradition. Jacob, because of divine assistance, which the lawgiver knows cannot be expected to repeat itself in ordinary, everyday affairs, acquired riches even though he was so badly treated. There is a sense in which the deity's interference is not helpful. Despite its merit in recognizing that there is injustice in the affairs of men, especially where one man has power over another, it can also obscure the need for human solutions to oppression. The hired servant's poverty and neediness is stressed in order to counter any confusion that might arise from observing the largesse which, despite everything, came Jacob's way. In the story the emphasis is upon God's aid to Jacob; the law, as we would expect, emphasizes God's condemnation of the oppressor.[15]

Law: Fathers and sons

> [16] The fathers shall not be put to death for the children, neither shall the children be put to death for the fathers: every man shall be put to death for his own sin. (Deut 24:16)

[15]For the deity's protection of Jacob against Laban, cp., Prov 22:22, 23: "Rob not the poor, because he is poor; neither oppress the afflicted in the gate; for Yahweh will plead their cause, and spoil the soul of those that spoiled them."

Background: Hamor and his son (Genesis 34; see pp. 193, 194)

This law is also about a grievous form of oppression: fathers being put to death because of their children's offenses and children being put to death because of their fathers' offenses. That this law fits into the context of those already presented may be seen by recalling such concerns as the life taken in pledge and the stealing of the "life" of a brother Israelite. In such background material as the Ahab story, his children (and his wives) were to be made to suffer because of him. In the Laban story his daughters suffered the consequences of their father's misdeed. Rachel received no children; Leah did, but she was hated by her husband, Jacob. How exactly Rachel's barrenness is tied to her father's cheating Jacob is, to be sure, complicated.[16] Leah's position is much less so: Jacob's hatred was directed at her as a substitute for her father. Such episodes illustrate the common injustice of children suffering for their fathers' offenses. Biblical literature is replete with examples. Even the Israelite god can visit death upon the Egyptian first-born as a means of striking at their fathers (Exod 11:4–9, 12:12, 29–32).[17] In 2 Kings 14:1–6 Amaziah kept this particular Deuteronomic law, but his fine example was again in regard to safeguarding the children. The proverbial statement on the subject, "The fathers have eaten sour grapes and the children's teeth are set on edge," is also confined to the typical situation (Jer 31:29, 30; Ezek 18:2). The much less usual injustice is where the father is put to death because of the son's misdeed. Yet the law formulates this instance first of all.[18] Its priority has to be accounted for.

In the preceding law Laban's mistreatment of Jacob determined the direction of the lawgiver's thinking. The most dramatic example of his cheating behavior occurred when he led Jacob to believe that Rachel would be the reward for his services. After Jacob had broken away from his Aramean oppressor, he went on to survive his encounter with his brother Esau. He then came into contact with the Shechemites. It is this story, which has already played a prominent role in the construction of other laws, that provides an instance (the only one in

[16]For one thing, her infertility is tied to Jacob's cheating Esau out of his birthright.

[17]Cp. the prophet's call to slaughter the sons for the iniquity of the fathers (Isa 14:21).

[18]Ezekiel has the reverse formulation: "The son shall not bear the iniquity of the father, neither shall the father bear the iniquity of the son" (Ezek 18:20).

biblical literature) of a father's being put to death because of his son's misdeed, namely, Shechem's seduction of Dinah. Moreover, a direct parallel to Laban's deception of Jacob is a crucial element in the story's outcome. Jacob's sons, Simeon and Levi, led Shechem's father to believe that Dinah would be given to his son as part of a larger pact involving marriage and trade between the two ethnic groups (Gen 34:8–17). It was a deception, however, that, because it involved the circumcision of all the male Shechemites, brought about the death of the offender Shechem as well as the death of his innocent father, and that of all the other fathers and sons of the clan. It is relevant to point out that Simeon and Levi were opposed to the whole notion of connubium, the prospect of other Hivite fathers wishing their sons to marry Israelite daughters. That the law refers to fathers and sons is intelligible in light of this element in the story. Like Laban's exploiting his position of power over Jacob, so Simeon and Levi took advantage of the power they temporarily had over the Hivites.

An important rationale for the lawgiver's concentration upon the inherent injustice of this aspect of the tradition would be the fact that Jacob condemns Simeon and Levi's action. What he is condemning, however, is not the death of an innocent father, or other innocents, but the difficulties his group faced because of what had been done. The other Canaanite groups would be incensed when they heard about the incident and likely to seek vengeance. The Deuteronomist, however, looks at the story with the detachment of hindsight and separates out the various issues it brings up. Some he has already taken up in other laws; in this law that insists on individual responsibility he focuses on the evil of a father's death, such as Hamor's, when only the son had offended. The law speaks of fathers being put to death together with (*ʿal*) the sons. Both Hamor and Shechem died. It is also worth noting that Jacob's complaint involved the recognition that his own life was jeopardized because of his sons' offense.

In 2 Kings 14:5, 6, it is said that King Amaziah obeyed the law of Moses on individual responsibility by not putting to death the sons of those servants who had murdered his father. His example, as noted, illustrates a resistance to the more common evil expressed in the second part of the law: children being put to death because of the fathers. What is most interesting is that the fable that follows upon the notice about Amaziah's example also serves as an illustration. In addition, it is about the same kind of issue that arose in the story in Genesis 34 about Shechem. Amaziah foolishly sought a military confrontation with Jehoash the king of Israel but was warned by the message embodied in the fable: "A thistle on Lebanon sent to a cedar on Lebanon, saying, 'Give thy daughter to my son for a wife'; and a wild beast of Lebanon passed by and trampled down the thistle" (2 Kings 14:9). The wild beast kills the thistle, the father, for its presumption, but not the son.

It is difficult to see how the fable fits its context. A rash proposal by an inferior to have his son marry above his station in life does not serve very well as a warning to a reckless aggressor. Amaziah was to recall what happened to the thistle. It is not a reference to himself and we have to ask: what was he to recall? The fable itself also raises some interesting questions. Why should the wild beast act on behalf of the cedar? Why should a third party be involved at all? The cedar could have dropped a branch on the thistle and dealt with the upstart that way. Still, the thistle is a menacing plant, indicating that some thought seems to have gone into the use of the fable in the context in question. Apart from the marital element there appears to be a military one as well. A context in which these two elements come together has to be sought.

The fable, like the law on individual responsibility, is a clever product of reflection upon an aspect of the story in Genesis 34. The thistle approached the cedar to ask for a marriage between his son and the cedar's daughter.[19] It was Hamor, the inferior being, who approached Jacob to ask if his son Shechem might marry Dinah, Jacob's daughter. In the world of animals, trees, and plants it is quite extraordinary (in a way that would not be true, say, for an ass to approach a horse) that a thistle should even begin to think of approaching a cedar with a view to discussing marital arrangements. It was only in the most extraordinary of ways that Hamor's proposal came to be put forth in the first place. It would never have come about if Dinah had not chosen to have a look at the women of the

[19]Apart from the special features in this piece, there is a universal element enshrined in it. Cp. the Arabic saying, "The mule says the horse was his father," quoted by Gray, *I and II Kings,* 550; and Freud's remark, "Every time two families become connected by a marriage, each of them thinks itself superior to or of better birth than the other" (*Group Psychology and the Analysis of the Ego,* 3d ed., [London: International Psycho-Analytical Press, 1945], 55).

area and had not been seduced by Shechem. An ass, moreover, should not be sexually involved with an ox. The incongruous element in the fable is inspired by observation upon this initial development in the story.

A further striking element in the fable is the death of the father at the hands of a third party in the form of a wild beast, or beasts, of the field.[20] The cedar was not involved in the attack. This particular feature is paralleled in the story. Jacob was a bystander as his two sons, who had been in the field when the initial incident took place and had come in from there when they heard about it, took the matter into their own hands. These sons of the ox resorted to violence and slew Hamor and all his men. Note that not just the father died but the son too and all their clansmen. In the fable only the father died, not the son. I shall return to this matter. In Assyrian sources we are informed that Tiglath-Pileser hunted and killed the *rîmu,* the wild ox (Hebrew *re'em*), at the foot of Lebanon. Shalmaneser II states, "His land I trod down like a *rîmu*."[21] Jacob's sons are of the ox family, but in their attack upon the Hivites they can be accurately identified as wild oxen.

The concern in the story with the superior standing of the house of Jacob should be further commented upon. The author is manifestly interested in matters of honor and disgrace. Shechem was the most honorable member of the princely house of his father (vv. 2, 19), yet he fell far short of Israelite community standards when he humiliated Dinah (v. 2, where *ʿinnāh* means to humble a woman by failing to observe the proper formalities). By lying with Jacob's daughter he had wrought folly in Israel, for such a thing ought not to be done (v. 7). Later when spurious negotiations were entered into by Jacob's sons, they expressed concern that if they chose to give their sister to one who was uncircumcised, their special standing in relation to the Hivites might be disgraced. Her marriage to the uncircumcised Shechem would be a reproach to them (v. 14). "We cannot do [*lō' nûkal*] this thing," they say. They could, of course, but their superior state and standards ("Should he deal with our sister as with an harlot" [v. 31]) forbid it.

[20]*rāmas* "to trample" is commonly used in the sense of destruction.

[21]See Driver, ICC *Deuteronomy,* 407; W. Von Soden *Akkadisches Handwörterbuch* (Wiesbaden: Harrassowitz, 1972), s.v. *rîmu.*

In a society in which shame plays a prominent role, sensitivity to one's name is important. Israelite superiority comes through clearly in the names given to Hamor and Shechem: ass and shoulder (of one). Recalling the proverbial beast of burden, their names are seen as suitable for those whose relationship to Israel should be that of servants. This relationship had supposedly originated when Noah had occasion to curse the sons of Ham (Gen 9:25).

It seems likely that the Deuteronomist is responsible not just for the expression of the law on individual responsibility and the shaping of the material about Amaziah's life but also for the composition of the fable itself. A suggestive detail that supports this view is the observation that in the fable, in contrast to what is found in Genesis 34, the principle of individual responsibility is recognized. The father thistle offended by his presumption, and even though he was acting on behalf of his son, only the offender suffered the consequences.

The links between the material in the book of Kings and the material in Genesis can be extended. The incident involving Shechem followed immediately after Jacob had overcome Esau's (Edom's) longstanding hostility. Amaziah's invitation to battle came in the wake of his having just defeated Edom (2 Kings 14:7, 10). King Jehoash, who pointed out to Amaziah that he was thinking too grandly of himself because of this victory, had newly defeated the Arameans and captured certain cities which they had previously taken from his father (2 Kings 13:25). Jacob in Genesis 31 had overcome the opposition of Laban the Aramean and acquired wealth that he felt rightly belonged to him rather than to the Arameans. After Jehoash defeated Amaziah, he took treasures from the house of God (2 Kings 14:14). Just after the Shechem incident Jacob had established Bethel, the first house of God ever.

It should not surprise us that in the writing of history an author looks back to an earlier period when similar issues arose among persons of the same ancestry. The account of the earlier events is liable to influence the writing up of the later ones; for example, only episodes seen to be in some way comparable are selected for presentation. Or the process may go further, and the wisdom and folly that are perceived in the reading of the earlier time may emerge among the participants of the later events. In this regard history writing has a tendency to create events. The attribution of the fable to King Jehoash may provide an example where the interpretation of an earlier event actually creates a later one.

Yet matters can be even more complicated. Historical writing that looks back on earlier events may influence the way in which they are interpreted and written up. The author of 2 Kings 13:22, 23 reports that the Arameans oppressed Israel but that God would not let Israel be destroyed because of his covenant with Abraham, Isaac, and Jacob. In Gen 35:11, at that point in time when Jacob, newly called Israel, feared the destruction of his group because of his sons' slaughter of the male Hivites, he was informed that kings would issue from his loins. Plainly, the two kings Jehoash and Amaziah were included in that prediction. To be sure, one was opposed to the other, but then Jacob's dispute with his two sons, Simeon and Levi, remained unresolved.

Despite the manifest awkwardness of the fable in its present context[22]—as an attempt to curb Amaziah's sabre rattling, its application does not seem especially appropriate—it is not inconceivable that it does fit after all, on the basis of the following consideration. The Deuteronomic laws and the fable itself belong to a setting in which it is likely that young men examined their national records and received instruction in the various topics that were extracted from them. If the two kings, no doubt unhistorically, are to be thought of as recipients of this instruction—it is said of Amaziah that he observed the law of Moses on individual responsibility[23]—then he should have understood the reference behind the fable. In their education each of them had scrutinized the story of Hamor and Shechem and had learnt how to encapsulate wisdom's lessons in the allusive language of proverb and fable.

[22]David Daube has also argued that there was a link between the fable and the story of Shechem. He noted that its context did not fit with the context in 2 Kings 14, namely, Amaziah's challenge to battle. Rather than originating in this historical setting, the fable more likely resulted from reflection upon the circumstances described in Genesis 34, and was then, somewhat awkwardly, applied to a reckless aggressor (*Ancient Hebrew Fables* [Oxford: Oxford Centre for Postgraduate Hebrew Studies, 1973], 19, 20).

[23]The fictional character of this statement should not be lost sight of. It is an interpretation after the event. Recall that it refers to the second part of the law in Deut 24:16. That a similar rule, probably of a proverbial nature, would have been recognized long before its distinctive Deuteronomic formulation, is certain.

SUMMARY Abraham sought to overcome an assumed threat to his life by passing his wife off as his sister. She was taken into Abimelech's harem but given back to Abraham before adultery took place. The law legislates against a situation in which a man, divorcing his wife so that another man can have her, might want to have her back again. Sarah was childless at this time. After the threat had passed she received sexual pleasure from Abraham that resulted in the birth of an heir. The law deals with an Israelite who has not yet given such pleasure to his wife and who is faced with death on the battlefield. In giving Abraham an heir, Sarah wanted an assurance, in the form of the expulsion of a bondwoman whose son had a claim to be Abraham's heir also, that he would receive the prime inheritance. In the law the taking of a part of a millstone as a pledge—the millstone is typically worked by a bondwoman—is an unacceptably harsh form of exercising power over someone to make him repay a benefit.

Joseph's brothers resisted his claim of superior authority and offended by selling him. The law is concerned with the offense of stealing a man and selling him. Miriam and Aaron resisted Moses' claim of superiority over them. This resistance was an offense in itself and resulted in Miriam's leprosy. The law is about obeying Levitical authority, which has been derived from Moses, in seeking a cure for leprosy. The Aramean Ahab resisted Benhadad's demand to enter his home to fetch his pledge, but, in contrast to the two preceding narratives, the offense resides in the wrongful nature of his demand. The concern of the law is that by nature of the relationship between them, a creditor is not thereby empowered to enter a debtor's house to collect the collateral to a loan. The Aramean Laban deceived Jacob in order to prolong and abuse his power over him. The deity resisted on behalf of Jacob. The law is concerned with an abuse of an employer's power. Simeon and Levi deceived Hamor and his son Shechem in order to exercise their will against them. In doing so they acted excessively. Jacob, after the event, opposed their excess. The law is concerned with a wrong application of justice in which an innocent father dies along with his guilty son.

CHAPTER II

PROTECTION OF THE VULNERABLE

In the remaining laws of the Deuteronomic code there is a pronounced interest in problems within the original Israel's family, with the focus on two sons in particular, Joseph and Judah. Such domestic conflicts simply continue the major trend found in the preceding laws. Also noted in these laws was the concern with the humiliation experienced by, for example, Hagar under Sarah's tyranny, Joseph at the hands of his brothers, Ahab under Benhadad's control, and Jacob in Laban's employ. As might be expected in situations where one party humiliates the other, there is typically an unequal balance of power in which one party is already strong and the other is weak. In the subsequent laws this aspect clearly plays a significant role, with the lawgiver showing sensitivity to the needs of the weak.

Laws: Perversion of justice, the forgotten sheaf, and brother Israelites in dispute

[17] Thou shalt not pervert the judgment of the sojourner, nor of the fatherless; nor take a widow's raiment to pledge: [18] but thou shalt remember that thou wast a bondman in Egypt, and Yahweh thy God redeemed thee thence: therefore I command thee to do this thing.

[19] When thou cuttest down thine harvest in thy field, and hast forgot a sheaf in the field, thou shalt not go again to fetch it: it shall be for the sojourner, for the fatherless, and for the widow: that Yahweh thy God may bless thee in all the work of thine hands. [20] When thou beatest thine olive tree, thou shalt not go over the boughs again: it shall be for the sojourner, for the fatherless, and for the widow. [21] When thou gatherest the grapes of thy vineyard, thou shalt not glean it afterward: it shall be for the sojourner, for the fatherless, and for the widow. [22] And thou shalt remember that thou wast a bondman in the land of Egypt: therefore I command thee to do this thing.

[1] If there be a controversy between men, then they shall come unto judgment, and the judges shall judge them; and they shall justify the righteous, and condemn the wicked. [2] And it shall be, if the wicked man be worthy to be beaten, that the judge shall cause him to lie down, and to be beaten before his face, according to his fault, by a certain number. [3] Forty stripes he may give him, and not exceed: lest if he should exceed, and beat him above these with many stripes, then thy brother should seem vile unto thee. (Deut 24:17–25:3)

Background: The Joseph story (Genesis 37–47)

Perversion of justice

[17] And she [Potiphar's wife] spake unto him, according to these words, saying, The Hebrew servant which thou hast brought unto us, came in unto me to mock me: [18] and it came to pass, as I lifted up my voice and cried, that he left his garment with me, and fled out. [19] And it came to pass, when his master heard the words of his wife, which she spake unto him, saying, After this manner did thy servant to me; that his wrath was kindled. [20] And Joseph's master took him, and put him into the prison, a place where the king's prisoners were bound: and he was there in the prison. (Gen 39:17–20)

[14] And she [Tamar] put her widow's garments off from her, and covered her with a vail, and wrapped herself, and sat at the entrance to Enaim, which is by the way to Timnath; for she saw that Shelah was grown, and she was not given unto him to wife. [15] When Judah saw her, he thought her to be an harlot; because she had covered her face. [16] And he turned unto her by the way, and said, Go to, I pray thee, let me come in unto thee; (for he knew

> not that she was his daughter in law.) And she said, What wilt thou give me, that thou mayest come in unto me? [17] And he said, I will send thee a kid from the flock. And she said, Wilt thou give me a pledge, till thou send it? [18] And he said, What pledge shall I give thee? And she said, Thy signet, and thy bracelets, and thy staff that is in thine hand. And he gave it her and came in unto her and she conceived by him. . . . [24] And it came to pass, about three months after, that it was told Judah, saying, Tamar thy daughter in law hath played the harlot; and also, behold, she is with child by whoredom. And Judah said, Bring her forth, and let her be burnt. [25] When she was brought forth, she sent to her father in law, saying, By the man, whose these are, am I with child: and she said, Discern, I pray thee, whose are these, the signet, and bracelets, and staff. [26] And Judah acknowledged them, and said, She hath been more righteous than I; because that I gave her not Shelah my son. (Gen 38:14–18, 24–26)

Three laws follow in which three incidents from Joseph's life have determined their subject matter. First is the law warning against perverting the justice due to the sojourner and the fatherless. There is also a prohibition against taking a widow's garment in pledge. The law's addressee is further urged to remember that he had been a slave in Egypt and that God had redeemed him from there. A blatant example of a perversion of justice was Joseph's imprisonment for an offense he never committed, namely, lying with Potiphar's wife. Joseph, moreover, was at this time a slave in Egypt (Potiphar's wife refers to him as the "Hebrew servant" [Gen 39:17]).

It is plain that the idea of wresting justice from the law carries over the same idea from the preceding law about fathers suffering for their sons' misdeeds and vice versa. There is, however, an even more specific link between the two laws, and we should note again how the lawgiver is alert to similar problems in the traditions he works with. In Genesis 34 Shechem's seduction of Dinah had wrongfully involved the punishment of his innocent father, as if he too had been guilty of the sexual offense. In Genesis 39 a false accusation that Joseph had seduced Potiphar's wife provides another example where a man is innocent of an offense but receives punishment for it.

The lawgiver addresses himself to the Israelite and is concerned about treating the sojourner and the fatherless justly. Like the sojourner Joseph in Egypt, himself in a sense also fatherless because of his brothers' misdeed, these two categories of persons constitute a vulnerable target for the unscrupulous. The other category included in the lawgiver's concern is the widow whose garment might be taken in pledge. That she is linked to the sojourner and the fatherless is understandable. The specific topic of her garment, however, requires an explanation because it is not clear why her having to pledge it provides a parallel to the *perversion* of justice.

Joseph's garment caused an injustice. So too, in the preceding story that has been inserted into the Joseph story, did Tamar's. Judah in effect forced her to put away her widow's garment in order to obtain what should have already been given to her, namely, seed that she would then return to him in the form of a child to continue the family line. The parallel to a material transaction exists.[1] She was to be lent the seed and her repayment would be the child that she produced. No pledge should have been taken from her for this loan, other than that she should remain a widow in her father's house until Shelah was grown enough to give it to her. What happened in fact was that she had to change out of her widow's garment and into prostitute's clothing in order to obtain the seed. In doing so, she was risking her life, and the initial removal of her widow's raiment symbolized this risk. As part of her strategy to right the wrong she herself took from Judah certain personal articles as a pledge that he would pay her for her sexual favors to him. What was really at stake, however, as the story reveals and the lawgiver picks up, was that she was pledging her life in order to obtain her rightful payment of a son from Judah's line. Had she died it would have been a perversion of justice, because there should have been no pressure upon her to put off her garment for the purpose in question.

As a parallel to this unusual development the lawgiver thinks of the widow who, under some unjust constraint, has to pledge her garment in order to receive a favor. In Prov 20:16 and 27:13, and in Job 22:6 a similar close association between taking a person's garment in pledge and taking him in pledge exists. Just as Joseph's alleged seduction of Potiphar's wife proved to be a perversion of justice, so Tamar's seduction of Judah pointed to an injustice done to her, because

[1]Recall the commercial element in Sarah's dealings with Abraham on behalf of her son, and Leah's hiring of Jacob from Rachel, which resulted in the birth of a fifth son to Leah and a first son to Rachel.

of his failure to send his surviving son, Shelah, into her. Judah was later to acknowledge the injustice (Gen 38:26). A highly idiosyncratic feature in a story again prompts the lawgiver to pinpoint the essential wrongdoing involved and to formulate the matter to express a more general evil.

By calling on the addressee to heed the cause of the sojourner, the fatherless, and the widow, the lawgiver appeals to his memory of the slavery in Egypt and God's redemptive activity on behalf of the Hebrew slaves. Once it is seen how the lawgiver thinks about Joseph, the first Hebrew slave, and God's aid on his behalf, it becomes much clearer why this appeal is embodied in this particular law.

The forgotten sheaf

> [6] And he [Joseph] said unto them [his brothers], Hear, I pray you, this dream which I have dreamed: [7] for, behold, we were binding sheaves in the field, and, lo, my sheaf arose, and also stood upright; and, behold, your sheaves stood round about, and made obeisance to my sheaf. [8] And his brethren said to him, Shalt thou indeed reign over us? or shalt thou indeed have dominion over us? (Gen 37:6–8)

> [12] And Joseph said unto them, This is the interpretation of it [the butler's dream]: The three branches are three days: [13] yet within three days shall Pharaoh lift up thine head, and restore thee unto thy place: and thou shalt deliver Pharaoh's cup into his hand, after the former manner when thou wast his butler. [14] But remember me with thee when it shall be well with thee, and shew kindness, I pray thee, unto me, and make remembrance of me unto Pharaoh. . . . [21] And he restored the chief butler unto his butlership again; and he gave the cup into Pharaoh's hand: [22] but he hanged the chief baker: as Joseph had interpreted to them. [23] Yet did not the chief butler remember Joseph, but forgat him. (Gen 40:12–14, 21–23)

> [25] And Joseph said unto Pharaoh, The dream of Pharaoh is one: God hath shewed Pharaoh what he is about to do. [26] The seven good kine are seven years; and the seven good ears are seven years; the dream is one. [27] And the seven thin and ill-favoured kine that came up after them are seven years; and the seven empty ears blasted with the east wind shall be seven years of famine. . . . [34] Let Pharaoh do this, and let him appoint officers over the land, and take up the fifth part of the land of Egypt in the seven

plenteous years. [35] And let them gather all the food of those good years that come, and lay up corn under the hand of Pharaoh, and let them keep food in the cities. [36] And that food shall be for store to the land against the seven years of famine, which shall be in the land of Egypt; that the land perish not through the famine. . . . [41] And Pharaoh said unto Joseph, See, I have set thee over all the land of Egypt. (Gen 41:25–27, 34–36, 41)

[7] And Joseph saw his brethren, and he knew them, but made himself strange unto them, and spake roughly unto them; and he said unto them, Whence come ye? [8] And they said, From the land of Canaan to buy food. And Joseph knew his brethren, but they knew not him. [9] And Joseph remembered the dreams which he dreamed of them, and said unto them, Ye are spies; to see the nakedness of the land ye are come. [10] And they said unto him, Nay, my lord, but to buy food are thy servants come. (Gen 42:7–10)

[26] And when Joseph came home, they [his brothers] brought him the present which was in their hand into the house, and bowed themselves to him to the earth. (Gen 43:26)

The same three categories of persons are the recipients of the next law's charitable intent: they should be allowed to take a harvest sheaf that the Israelite owner has forgotten and the olives and grapes that remain after the main harvesting. The call to remember Israel's slavery in Egypt is again given as the reason for observing the commandment. The best clue as to what has sparked the law lies in its puzzling initial statement. The injunction about the harvesting of a field of grain is different from the two about the harvesting of olives and grapes. Whereas in gathering them a regular practice of leaving some olives and grapes for the needy is enjoined, this practice does not apply to the grain. Only if a sheaf has been left forgotten in the field and the harvester then becomes aware that it is still there, is he counseled to leave it for the poor. The likelihood of this occurring on a regular basis is not very high. The Talmud informs us that the poor depended on such charity.[2] If this were the position during the Deuteronomist's time, they might well have gone without benefit many a year, at least so far as grain was concerned. It is noteworthy that the

[2]R. Johanan ben Nuri, at the beginning of the second century A.D., actually lived on the gleanings. See *Palestinian Peah* 20d.

corresponding requirement in Lev 19:9 and 23:22 lacks the peculiarity of the Deuteronomic rule: "And when ye reap the harvest of your land, thou shalt not wholly reap the corners of thy field, neither shalt thou gather the gleanings of thy harvest." There is nothing haphazard about requiring the harvester to leave the corners of his field unreaped.

Some commentators seem to be aware of the oddity in the Deuteronomic formulation. They imagine that in some remote, early period of Israelite history a sheaf might have been left in the field as a propitiatory offering to a god.[3] This view, for which no evidence is presented, appears to underlie their further point that the rule in question is ancient and that the lawgiver has incorporated it into his material without awareness of its original, and in his time almost certainly unacceptable, religious significance. This entire position is untenable, not in the least because these critics attribute an unthinking intelligence to the lawgiver, a failure on his part to see the peculiarity of his counsel.

The law is readily explained in the light of two perspectives. First is the well-recognized link between certain laws relating to food and agriculture, and the Israelite's historical experience in Egypt. The Passover lamb, the unleavened bread, the first fruits of the year's harvest are all given didactic, historical significance. The same is true for the forgotten sheaf. An indication of this connection is that the final exhortation in the law is for the Israelite to remember that he was a slave in Egypt. In all four instances, moreover—the lamb, the bread, the first fruits, and the sheaf—sensitivity to an oppressed state is expressed.

The second perspective highlights the link between law and wisdom. This particular injunction provides an excellent illustration of how certain biblical laws are like many a proverb in that they are condensed stories. They encapsulate the essential significance of the story in question, or at least some aspect of it. Proverbs often embody a clever, superficially concealing element that engages the hearer's attention and enables him or her to switch his or her focus from one

[3]See G. von Rad, *Deuteronomium*, ATD 8 (Göttingen: Vandenhoeck and Ruprecht, 1964), 109; A. Phillips, *Deuteronomy* CBC (Cambridge: Cambridge University Press, 1973), 166.

setting to another. The lawgiver's concentration on the sheaf that has been forgotten constitutes the proverbial element in the law.

The statement about the sheaf is not the most obvious kind of directive, and it is sensible to ask what prompted the statement. The answer lies in the Joseph story, a central element in which is Joseph's rise to a dominant position both among his brothers and the world at large. This rise was anticipated in his famous dream in which he was represented as a sheaf before whom his brothers, the other sheaves, bowed down.[4] Before he achieved superiority, however, he experienced the opposite, humiliation and oppression. In the preceding law we noted how this aspect, his imprisonment, was influential and provided the lawgiver with an example of a grievous injustice to an innocent man. The lawgiver continues his interest in Joseph's history because it is also the history of divine providence acting on behalf of the oppressed—Joseph in particular but also the nation Israel. During his incarceration the deity helped Joseph to solve the meaning of the dreams of the butler and the baker. Their dreams, about the three vine branches and the three bread baskets, recall Joseph's own dream. Moreover, just as they were going to find their dreams translated into action, so too was Joseph. He pleaded with the butler, whose dream betokened his successful restoration to the pharaoh's favor, that he remember him (*zākar* ["to remember"] occurs twice) when that came about. Joseph also informed him about how he had been stolen out of the land of the Hebrews and how he was wrongly imprisoned (Gen 40:14, 15).

Joseph was to be remembered but not on the occasion of the butler's restoration ("Yet did not the chief butler remember Joseph, but forgat him" [Gen 40:23]). Not until the pharaoh himself had his dreams, in each of which agricultural growth is again a central feature, and which the Egyptian sages could not interpret, did the butler remember Joseph and cause him to be brought before the pharaoh. When the Hebrew furnished the correct interpretation and predicted the seven years' famine, it was the beginning of his climb to the top as presaged in his own first dream about himself as a sheaf. The pharaoh

[4]Cp. the dream in which King Nebuchadnezzar is represented by a tree (Dan 4:10–22).

appointed him to oversee all arrangements necessary to cope with the coming famine. In effect, the plan, which was of Joseph's own devising, called for the putting aside of grain during the seven plenteous years so that when the famine struck the hungry would be fed. His plan was a piece of practical wisdom in which the idea was that an owner would not take all of his harvest so that the hungry and the deprived might be cared for. The same idea underlies the Deuteronomic concern. The one difference is that in the story the exceptional circumstances of the seven years' famine determine when the owner should leave aside some of the grain (a fifth, to be precise, during the seven years of plenty), whereas in the law the more typical situation contemplated is the annual harvest and the fact that, in the words of the law in Deut 15:11, "the poor shall never cease out of the land." The directives in both law and story are similar, however, in that they both deal with the future, the forthcoming seven years of famine, the new life in the new land.

Why then in the law do we have the emphasis upon the forgotten sheaf (a single one at that, and not a number of them)? The point is that the Deuteronomist, who has typically been open to the figurative nuances in the Genesis material, has accurately observed that so much in the Joseph saga, especially the scheme to save the Egyptians and the Israelites from starvation, has to do with Joseph in his role as the forgotten sheaf. His rise to dominance was first symbolized by his depiction as the separate sheaf at harvest time. That rise would not have taken place if he had not correctly interpreted the symbolism about vines and grain (the cakes in the baskets) in the dreams of the butler and baker. Yet at that point in time his own significance as the important sheaf of grain was neglected because the butler forgot about him. Only when the pharaoh's dream, again involving plants, needed interpretation was this forgotten sheaf remembered. The significance of the sheaf symbolism then came into its own. As overseer of the harvest Joseph saved everyone from starvation. His high position—in figurative terms he is the dominant sheaf—and the supply to needy people of sheaves of grain (in the literal sense) are intimately linked.[5]

[5]On the link, involving symmetrical plots, between the scene in Genesis 45 and Genesis 37, see Donald B. Redford, *A Study of the Biblical Story of Joseph (Genesis 37–50)* (Leiden: Brill, 1970), 71–74. His remark (249–50) that the rest of Scripture is

The law itself incorporates the same theme of remembering and forgetting. There is the reference to the forgotten sheaf (which, we might note, is in fact remembered by the harvester). When he so remembers it he is to leave it in the field so that the needy may take it. But there is also another, quite explicit, call to remembering, namely, "that thou wast a bondman in the land of Egypt."

For anyone reflecting upon the story, as the lawgiver did, and probably for the storyteller himself, Joseph can be characterized as the sheaf of grain whose significance was forgotten until he was called upon to predict the problem about the future harvests. He then became the deity's agent, saving the hungry from starvation. In particular, Joseph as the sheaf in the dream, who was eventually remembered in the context of the pharaoh's dream, provided the first example in Israelite tradition of someone who had set aside grain for the relief of the needy. Among those were his fellow Israelites who became sojourners in Egypt. In a sense they also became slaves there. They addressed the disguised Joseph as their lord, and this disposition was appropriate because they were being requited for having previously treated him as a slave. Like all the Egyptians, moreover, these Israelites would have thought of themselves as servants of the pharaoh. When the lawgiver appeals to the Israelite harvester to remember that he was once a slave in Egypt, he is recalling this period of time in Israelite experience. Providence had looked after the Israelites then in the person and position of Joseph. Moses, so we are to understand, reflects upon this providential activity and imitates its intent insofar as it is humanly possible. He focuses on the agricultural conditions that will prevail in Israel's new land. There the Israelite harvester is reminded to remember the role of Joseph and realize how, in the words of the law, God will bless all the work of his hands, just as he did for Joseph when the latter had provided food for the needy.[6]

The unsatisfactory aspect of the injunction about leaving a forgot-

---

completely silent on the subject of the Joseph story is simply wrong. His view becomes an important prop for his late dating of the story: "One can only conclude that the reason why the historical books and the Prophets say nothing of the Joseph Romance is because the narrative was not yet in existence when they were written."

[6]A.D.H. Mayes, *Deuteronomy* NCBC (Grand Rapids: Eerdmans, 1981), 327, is puzzled by the appearance of a concluding formula about God's blessing the work of the hands in the middle of the law. Again, however, the link with the blessing upon Joseph in the story clarifies.

ten sheaf in the field should not be viewed as a failure in practical wisdom. The directions about not going over the olive boughs a final time or gleaning the vines again indicate that the lawgiver knows what constitutes sensible procedure. He surely would have changed, as presumably the Levitical lawgiver did, the nature of his counsel if the practicable were the foremost of his concerns. It is the link rather to a historical precedent for his law that is the important consideration. This the lawgiver finds in his reflection upon the Joseph story.

The term for a sheaf as applied figuratively to Joseph is *'alūmmāh;* in the law it is *'ōmer*. Whatever other linguistic considerations might apply, it was sensible of the lawgiver to use a different term from the figurative one in the story. The metaphor of Joseph as the sheaf forgotten and then remembered primarily conveys his position of supremacy over his brothers and his overlordship of Egypt. His sphere of power was determined by his role in distributing grain. It is the connection between his position in the dream and the way in which it manifested itself that has caught the lawgiver's attention. For him to have used *'alūmmāh* in his law would have been overly clever and artificial, even misleading.

Brother Israelites in dispute

> [2] Joseph, being seventeen years old, was feeding the flock with his brethren; and the lad was with the sons of Bilhah, and with the sons of Zilpah, his father's wives: and Joseph brought an ill report of them to their father. . . . [8] And his brethren said to him, shall thou indeed reign over us? or shall thou indeed have dominion over us? And they hated him yet the more for his dreams, and for his words. . . . [19] And they said one to another, Behold, this dreamer cometh. [20] Come now therefore, and let us slay him, and cast him into some pit, and we will say, Some evil beast hath devoured him: and we shall see what will become of his dreams. [21] And Reuben heard it, and he delivered him out of their hands; and said, Let us not beat him to the life. (Gen 37:2, 8, 19–21)

The lawgiver's aim is first to have the disputants come into court to resolve their quarrel and then, once the judges have decided who is guilty and who is innocent, to insist that if the guilty party is to be beaten by way of punishment, no more than forty stripes should be administered lest, "if he should exceed, and beat him above these with many stripes, then thy brother should seem vile unto thee." The dispute between Joseph and his brothers inspires the construction of this law. The "settlement," obviously unsatisfactory, of that quarrel ended in a degrading punishment for Joseph: he was cast into a pit. The law is similarly narrow: its concern is with the degrading nature of punishment. In particular, it focuses upon physical punishment, as against, for example, monetary fines or imprisonment. Doubtless this makes it easier for the lawgiver to concentrate upon the subject of the possible degradation of the Israelite brother. Joseph was not beaten by his brothers, but he was truly humiliated by them. He was stripped, for example, before being cast into the pit. What is most interesting, however, is Reuben's attempt to moderate the other brothers' treatment of him. At one point he pleaded with them "not to beat [*hiphil nākāh*] him to the life" (Gen 37:21). He presumably felt that Joseph deserved to be punished with a beating but that it should not be excessive.

It is easy to see how the dispute between Joseph and his brothers would invite reflection upon how such matters should be handled. By resorting to their own remedy for resolving their antagonism to him, the brothers have committed a grievous form of injustice. The lawgiver's response to what he finds in this tradition shows that he sees the need to avoid arbitrary procedure in resolving disputes and to expect the matter to go through the courts.[7] In Genesis 37 we do not learn the full nature of the problem between Joseph and his brothers. Initially we hear about Joseph's bringing an ill report to his father about the doings of some of them, but nothing is elaborated. All of his brothers found fault with him because he was the father's favorite. The result was that they could not speak peaceably to him, and their jealousy was further aroused by his dreams. Only an impartial inquiry, such as would be found in a court, could get to the heart of the

[7]By stopping the protasis of the law after the reference to the dispute, we are able to note the lawgiver's concern with encouraging disputing parties to seek adjudication rather than to rely on themselves. It is possible that the protasis should proceed as far as the judges' decision, with the apodasis reading, "Then if the guilty man deserves to be beaten." If this is the correct point of division (the difficulty lies in the fact that the Hebrew particle *w*, "and," is used frequently as the conjunction), then the Deuteronomist is simply thinking of what might constitute a more conventional parallel to the Joseph narrative. The former alternative, because of the details of the story, is more likely.

dispute and decide where to fix the blame. Even when that step is reached, however, what follows by way of punishment has to be carefully scrutinized. A court, the lawgiver warns, has to beware of handing out excessive punishments. If the role of the court is simply to decide between the disputants but to leave the punishment in the hands of the vindicated party, there is all the more reason to limit the number of stripes that may be given and to have the punishment carried out in the presence of the judge. In the law it is not clear who administers the beating.

In linking the law to the narrative it might be noted that just as the reference to the guilty man as a brother of the innocent party recalls the family situation in the story, so too the law seems to indicate that the dispute is between one man, an Israelite, and a number of other Israelites. At least this numerical lineup is not excluded in the law's formulation. Again the model of one man, Joseph, being judged worthy of physical punishment by his many brothers seems to be in the lawgiver's mind.

It is also easy to see why this law comes at this point in the code. Incidents from Joseph's life led to the formulation of the two preceding laws. Moreover, in each of them court decisions—first about perverting justice and then about leaving food at harvest time to the poor—are part of the background narratives. Potiphar's wife's evidence for Joseph's seduction of her was, it is implied, decisive in determining his guilt. Likewise, the cases of the butler and baker came before the pharaoh's authority for arbitration. Joseph predicted that this resolution would happen eventually, and, consequently, his own dream as the dominant sheaf at harvest time was fulfilled. It is perhaps overstating what took place in these incidents to say that actual court proceedings were held. The idea of authoritative hearings for the settlement of cases is nonetheless compelling. It is therefore not surprising to find the lawgiver turning to this subject of a court at work. Another noteworthy feature is that an element of arbitrariness is found both in the judicial resolution of Potiphar's wife's complaint, where there was a definite miscarriage of justice, and in the butler's restoration to favor but not the baker's. The lawgiver shows sensitivity to the possibility that an Israelite court may handle an offender's punishment incorrectly. He had good reason to: Joseph's brothers constituted the greater part of the original Israel.

The move from the law of the forgotten sheaf to that of the dispute before the court can also be observed by noting a feature of the narrative in Genesis 45. Once Joseph was elevated to vizier, as originally his dream about the harvest sheaves had anticipated, he organized the distribution of grain so that both the Egyptians and his family were cared for. After giving provisions to the latter, who were (like those determined to be in need under the law) sojourners, he instructed them, "See that ye fall not out by the way" (v. 24). For both narrator and lawgiver, these words recall the quarrel between Joseph and his brothers and one major cause of it, namely, his dream about himself as the upright sheaf standing before the other prostrate ones. At this point in the narrative Joseph—the forgotten sheaf—has come into his own and can command his brothers.

Laws: The unmuzzled ox, an Israelite's refusal to give conception to his brother's widow, and a woman's immodest interference in a fight

[4] Thou shalt not muzzle an ox when he treadeth.

[5] If brethren dwell together, and one of them die, and have no
child, the wife of the dead shall not marry without unto a stranger:
her husband's brother shall go in unto her, and take her to him to
wife, and perform the duty of an husband's brother unto her. [6]
And it shall be, that the firstborn which she beareth shall succeed in
the name of his brother which is dead, that his name be not put out
of Israel. [7] And if the man like not to take his brother's wife, then
let his brother's wife go up to the gate unto the elders, and say, My
husband's brother refuseth to raise up unto his brother a name in
Israel, he will not perform the duty of my husband's brother. [8]
Then the elders of his city shall call him, and speak unto him: and if
he stand to it, and say, I like not to take her; [9] then shall his
brother's wife come unto him in the presence of the elders, and
loose his shoe from off his foot, and spit in his face, and shall
answer and say, So shall it be done unto that man that will not
build up his brother's house. [10] And his name shall be called in
Israel, The house of him that hath his shoe loosed.

[11] When men strive together one with another, and the wife of the one draweth near for to deliver her husband out of the hand of him that smiteth him, and putteth forth her hand, and taketh him

> by the shameful parts: [12] then thou shalt cut off her hand, thine eye shall not pity her. (Deut 25:4–12)

Background: The Tamar story (Genesis 38)

From three laws dependent upon the Joseph story, we have three laws dependent upon the story of Judah and Tamar. The topic of conflicts that arise within families dominates the laws beginning in Deut 24:6, which concerns the millstone. As an insertion into the story of Joseph, the account of Judah's family problems was designed to demonstrate the retribution visited upon him because of his attempt to eliminate Joseph from the favored place he enjoyed with their father.[8] The overlapping fortunes of Joseph, his experience with Potiphar's wife, and of Judah, his experience with Tamar, were already combined in the rule about perverting justice.

The unmuzzled ox

> [8] And Judah said unto Onan, Go in unto thy brother's wife, and marry her, and raise up seed to thy brother. [9] And Onan knew that the seed would not be his; and it came to pass, when he went in unto his brother's wife that he spilled it on the ground, lest that he should give seed to his brother. [10] And the thing which he did displeased Yahweh: wherefore he slew him also. (Gen 38:8–10)

The brief statement—only four words in the Hebrew text—"Thou shalt not muzzle an ox when he treadeth," invites an original figurative sense and not the literal one that is usually given to it. A number of reasons suggests this. First and foremost is the requirement to keep the animal unmuzzled, for as such it will simply not proceed with its task. The common belief that the animal deserves to enjoy the fruits of its labor fails to recognize that from a practical point of view the animal should be muzzled and, having done its work, then be fed.[9] In typical proverbial fashion the impracticality of the injunction catches the hearer's attention in order to direct it to another meaning. If a literal sense were read we would have to supply the reference to the

[8]See my *Women, Law, and the Genesis Traditions* (Edinburgh: Edinburgh University Press, 1979), 57–65.

[9]I went astray in my previous analysis (*ibid.*, 71–73) of the rule by failing to concentrate on its oddness.

grain. The fact that it is understood suggests a special significance for the kind of treading in mind. The parallel would be with the law against plowing with an ox and an ass together, in which attention is focused upon the plowing of these animals together, rather than upon plowing a field. In many languages, Hebrew, for example, both "to plow" and "to tread" are figurative of sexual intercourse.[10]

The last law to carry a figurative nuance was the one concerning the forgotten sheaf. The rule itself has a literal significance, but in the background was the notion of Joseph as the sheaf of grain forgotten for a while and then remembered. If this "sheaf" had remained forgotten there would have been no provision of grain either for the Egyptians or for his own family. In the law about the ox the figurative meaning resides in the rule and reminds us of the sense of the forgotten sheaf. If the ox is unmuzzled in its treading the final product, the provision of new seed, could be problematic. We are directed to a background in which the figurative sense of the law arises from some human situation.

In that the idea of the unmuzzled ox appears in part to have been stimulated by the idea of the forgotten sheaf we should consider a parallel phenomenon to Joseph's situation found in Genesis 38. From interest in the "dead" brother Joseph, we move to interest in a truly dead brother, Er. Judah experienced retribution for causing Jacob to lose his son. First Er died and then Onan, the latter in trying to make up for the loss of the former. In going into Tamar, in "treading" her for the purpose of producing seed on behalf of his dead brother,[11] Onan deliberately spilled it on the ground. This was an offense because it was an action against the family of Er, a refusal to continue his line for selfish reasons to do with enlarging Onan's own estate. The preceding law about the dispute was also concerned with brothers acting against a brother.

Onan, whose name means the "virile one" because of the misuse of his seed, is, according to Jacob in Gen 49:11, the "son of a she-ass," a reference to the fact that a Canaanite woman produced him. The same is true for Er (*'ēr*), whose name like Hamor's probably means ass (*'ayir*), and who is referred to in Gen 49:11 as Judah's ass (*'îrōh*) that was, along with the "son of the she-ass," tied to the vine. For the

[10]See my "'Treading' in the Book of Ruth," *ZAW* 92 (1980): 248–49.
[11]In *Genesis Rabba* 85, Onan "trod within but ejaculated without."

Deuteronomist such asses should not be part of the line of Jacob-Israel, the house of the ox, and should not be involved in enlarging the Israelite vine. True Israelites, however, should strive to enlarge it. He therefore focuses upon an Israelite brother's need to act for his dead one to ensure seed for his line. We have found before that whenever the lawgiver wishes to scrutinize a specific occurrence he resorts to allusive, cryptic language. This happens here in reference to Er's problem, but the lawgiver refers to a pure-bred son of Jacob's line and not to a son of mixed breed. Judah's family life was also the focus of the rule against plowing with an ox and an ass together.

The link between the literal sense of the rule and the transferred one has to be credible. The ox treads in order to produce seed. To require it to do so without a muzzle, as already noted, invites problems because it is just as likely to destroy the very seed it is supposed to be producing by consuming the ears of corn that lie scattered before it. The unmuzzled ox will tread but it will not produce the desired result for the family who need it. The oddness of a literal reading of the requirement is the clue that the meaning is to be displaced. In switching from one reading to the other, it is crucial to observe that a third party will have to be involved in getting the unmuzzled ox to produce seed.[12] The intent of the rule is to have its recipient narrowly concentrate on the problem between the ox and the grain and then to have him realize his role in solving it. "Thou shalt not muzzle an ox when he treadeth" first draws attention to the animal's negative contribution to a family. That way the precarious situation in the Israelite family is captured exactly. A man, left to himself like the ox with the grain, dies without producing offspring. As with the unmuzzled ox, a third party has to be involved. A relative, like the person responsible for attending to the ox, is under an obligation to ensure that seed is forthcoming. In sum, an Israelite hearing the law would be puzzled by the nature of the requirement as it applies to a treading ox but would then realize the human parallel. The message is that he possesses the solution to the problem of producing seed.

[12]S. R. Driver, *Deuteronomy* ICC (Edinburgh: T. and T. Clark, 1902), 280, draws attention to accounts of oxen with muzzles and without them. Presumably force in the form of a whip would have been used when working with an unmuzzled ox. This feature alone subverts the common view that a humane motive underlies the rule.

We have noted that the other figurative laws—uncovering a father's skirt, sowing a vineyard with two kinds of seed, plowing with an ox and an ass together, the *šaʿaṭnēz*—were each inspired by parallel comments and similarly figurative language in Jacob's sayings in Genesis 49.[13] The real inspiration for the superficial concentration upon the strange notion of unmuzzling an ox in its treading of the grain is Jacob's odd description of Judah's binding his ass (*ʿîrōh*) to the vine (Gen 49:11). As we noted in the analysis of the law about mixed seed in a vineyard, the reference is to Er's (*ʿēr*) union with Tamar for the purpose of adding to the family vine of Jacob. A real ass destroys a real vine (Er as Judah's son is part of this vine), suggesting the death of Er before he was able to produce offspring by Tamar (and thus cause the Israelite vine to grow). In switching from the Canaanite ass to the Israelite ox, the Deuteronomist comes up with a parallel clash between an animal and a plant, namely, the problem involving the ox and the grain.

Punishment for a brother who refuses to do his levirate duty

Precise links can be drawn between this law and the situation depicted in Genesis 38. We can make connections between a law and a narrative when some problem in the latter demands attention. Onan refused to do his duty by his dead brother. His punishment was death at the hands of God. By any reckoning this was an excessive punishment and reflects the complex interests of the narrator, in this instance, a desire to see Canaanite influence on Jacob's line removed. The lawgiver sets himself the task of devising a penalty appropriate to an Israelite who proves disloyal to his dead brother.

A second problem that stands out in the narrative is Judah's failure to have his remaining son, Shelah, go into Tamar for the purpose of fulfilling the levirate duty. Onan went through the motions of intercourse with Tamar to make his father think that he was fulfilling his duty. As head of the family, as the one who should ensure that his line is perpetuated, a father ordinarily will insist that a son be dutiful. It would be impossible for the lawgiver to address himself to Judah's reluctance to send Shelah into Tamar.[14] The problem will always

[13]The notion of Joseph as the forgotten sheaf should probably also be compared with Jacob's comments in Gen 49:22 about Joseph being a fruitful bough.

[14]For one thing, the law would not want to interfere with the father's *potestas*.

tend to be with the son. We have seen that typically the lawgiver presents an equivalent, less idiosyncratic parallel to what is found in a tradition. Here he does this by presenting a case in which brothers are living together; their father is not mentioned, presumably because he is dead.[15] That this is not stated but has to be inferred again suggests the influence of the story. In the context of Shelah's doing his duty, for all practical purposes Judah did not exist.

The law opens with a statement that an Israelite take his brother's widow and impregnate her in order to produce a child who will establish the dead brother's name in Israel. No such statement of this levirate custom would be necessary if a father, without Judah's complication, were around to tell his son what was required of him. In other words, the absence of the father explains why the initial part of the law is given. The law's main interest is in the question of a brother's refusal to impregnate the widow. Presumably his motivation is greed, his desire to retain his dead brother's portion of the estate.

After the widow takes her complaint against her brother-in-law to the local elders, they attempt to persuade him to fulfill his duty. If he continues to refuse, he is subjected to public humiliation at the hands of the widow. She takes off his shoe from his foot, spits in his face, and declares, "So shall it be done unto that man that will not build up his brother's house." Everafter his name in Israel is to be called, "The house of him that hath his shoe loosed." This ceremony of opprobium is entirely the product of the lawgiver's reflection upon the details of the story in Genesis 38.[16]

The Israelite whose passive response is his offense is compared to Onan. This comparison is the meaning of the woman's actions. The removal of the sandal from his foot signifies Onan's withdrawal from intercourse, and her spitting in his face, Onan's spilling of his seed to the ground. The shoe represents the female genitals, the foot the male organ, and the spitting semen.[17] Even the verb *ḥālaṣ*, "to loose, with-

[15]For other arguments that he is dead, see D. Daube, "Consortium in Roman and Hebrew Law," *Juridical Review* 62 (1950): 72–74. Many analyses of the law have gone badly wrong in failing to evaluate the omission of the father.

[16]In other words, I am claiming that no such sanction existed in the Deuteronomist's time or at any previous time. In that the matter belonged to the sphere of the family the law as a public instrument would have looked away.

[17]For the biblical, postbiblical, and extrabiblical evidence, see my *Women*, 65–70, and "A Ceremonial Crux: Removing a Man's Sandal as a Female Gesture of Contempt," *JBL* 96 (1977): 321–36.

draw," well conveys the notion of withdrawal from intercourse. In Hos 5:6, Israel's husband, God, finds that his wife has gone astray sexually and produced illicit children; hence he decides to withdraw (sexually) from her. In its nominal form the term means a man's loins, often in the specific sense of his virility. By her action the widow is mocking her brother-in-law's: she compares his attitude to that of the "virile one," Onan, who expressed his refusal to build up his brother's house by disengaging from intercourse with Tamar. The opprobrious name that everafter attaches to the man's house becomes intelligible in light of this background: "The house of the drawn off sandal." The link with the preceding figurative law about not muzzling an "ox" in its (sexual) treading can be seen from the fact that without a shoe the man cannot tread in order to produce seed for his brother.

At least three factors account for the Deuteronomist's motivation to devise a penalty that picks up from the details of the story in Genesis 38. First, as already noted, the punishment that befell Onan was extreme. Second, the Deuteronomist would have reacted negatively because the widow Tamar had proceeded beyond Onan's refusal, and Shelah's nonappearance, and taken active steps (namely, prostituting herself) to obtain a child. His view is plainly that if a man persists in being uncooperative he should be punished in some way, but that should be the end of the matter. Third, in that it is not easy to devise a punishment for someone whose offense is that he does nothing, Onan's action (which in effect amounted to the same thing) receives the lawgiver's primary attention. Onan's deed could be used to give expression to the Israelite brother's disgraceful and disloyal failure to act.[18]

A woman's interference in a dispute on behalf of her husband

> [25] When she [Tamar] was brought forth, she sent to her father in law, saying, By the man, whose these are, am I with child: and she said, Discern, I pray thee, whose are these, the signet, and bracelets, and staff. [26] And Judah acknowledged them, and said,

[18]Making him an Onan might be compared to our use of the expression "a peeping Tom" (derived from the story of Lady Godiva). Cp. too, but with different associations, the verb and adjective from the name Tupper; also Scrooge. Note how the offending brother is to be humiliated under proper supervision, and contrast the concern in the law about resolving a dispute where there is supervision to ensure that the offending brother is not humiliated.

> She hath been more righteous than I; because that I gave her not to Shelah my son. (Gen 38:25, 26)

This rule, in which a woman interferes in a fight between her husband and another man by grabbing the latter's genitals, shows the characteristic traits of the law code. First, little or no connection seems initially to exist between it and the preceding rule. Second, the substance of the law occasions surprise: it confines itself to a development that must have been out of the ordinary. As usual, the arresting feature reflects an idiosyncratic one in a tradition.[19]

In the preceding rule a woman was required, by means of a symbolic action, to uncover a man's genitals, thereby shaming him. She did so because the man, her brother-in-law, was being disloyal to her dead husband. A reason is suggested, even if only a desire to contrast a shameful female with a shameful male, why there follows a rule about the action of a woman in grabbing a man's genitals when he is engaged in a fight with her husband. Interestingly, the language of the rule speaks of the two men as brothers ("When men strive together, a man and his brother"), plainly in the broad sense of that term. The two preceding laws have been concerned with disputes involving blood brothers.

It is, however, not just the link to the preceding rule that illumines its content but the shared link with the story of Tamar in Genesis 38. A question that can be put to that narrative is why Tamar resorted to seducing her father-in-law. The answer is that she was in contention with him: "For she saw that Shelah was grown, and she was not given unto him to wife" (Gen 38:14). The dispute has to do with the levirate duty. In Judah's eyes, Tamar has been too closely associated

[19]Driver, (*Deuteronomy* ICC, 285) cites Dillmann with approval: "The case, significant for the manners of the age, was, nevertheless, assuredly not of such frequent occurrence as to call for prohibition by a special enactment: it is, however, selected typically out of a number of others, in order to serve as a standard for the judgment to be pronounced in similar cases." Apart from the pressing question why the law should be presented at just this point in the code, we need to know what principle of selection was at work and in what way this particular case served as a standard for others. There is no evidence for either view and we would be at a loss to uncover some. Why interpreters persist in trying to understand the law in terms of damage to the man's reproductive capacity when it simply does not raise the topic in any way is puzzling. The interpreters' reasons for bringing in the Middle Assyrian laws, in which this topic is raised, are equally obscure.

with the death of two of his sons, and he presumably does not want his third and last one to die too. In her eyes, Judah is acting against her dead husband, and she decides to intervene in the situation in order to salvage his name. Her mode of action requires that she pursue him sexually; in crude terms, she goes after his genitals. By dwelling upon the details and nature of this dispute, the Deuteronomist turns to what might constitute the closest parallel to it in real life, namely, a situation in which two men are involved in a physical fight, and the wife of one of them interferes on his behalf by going after his genitals.[20] In that the Deuteronomist often looks to existing laws in the Book of the Covenant in formulating his, the concern with the physical fight that causes a miscarriage in a woman (Exod 21:22) may also have directed him toward the example he works with.

Law: Weights and measures

> [13] Thou shalt not have in thy bag divers weights, a stone and a stone. [14] Thou shalt not have in thine house divers measures, an ephah and an ephah. [15] But thou shalt have a full and just weight, a full and just measure shalt thou have: that thy days may be lengthened in the land which Yahweh thy God giveth thee. [16] For all that do such things, and all that do unrighteously, are an abomination unto Yahweh thy God. (Deut 25:13–16)

Background: Joseph acts against his brothers, and God provides manna to the Israelites

> [25] Then Joseph commanded to fill their sacks with corn, and to restore every man's money into his sack, and to give them provision for the way: and thus did he unto them. [26] And they laded their asses with the corn, and departed thence. [27] And as one of them opened his sack to give his ass provender in the inn, he espied his money; for, behold, it was in his sack's mouth. [28] And he said unto his brethren, My money is restored; and, lo, it is even in my sack: and their heart failed them, and they were afraid, saying one to another, What is this that God hath done unto us? . . . . [35]

[20]For further comments on this law, regarding, for example, the nature of the woman's penalty, see my *Women*, 70–71. The severity of the law might owe something to the fact that Judah intended to penalize Tamar severely for her offense.

And it came to pass as they emptied their sacks, that, behold, every man's bundle of money was in his sack: and when both they and their father saw the bundles of money, they were afraid. (Gen 42:25–28, 35)

[34] And they [Joseph's brothers] drank, and were merry with him. [1] And he commanded the steward of his house, saying, Fill the men's sacks with food, as much as they can carry, and put every man's money in his sack's mouth. [2] And put my cup, the silver cup, in the sack's mouth of the youngest, and his corn money. And he did according to the word that Joseph had spoken. [3] As soon as the morning was light, the men were sent away, they and their asses. [4] And when they were gone out of the city, and not yet far off, Joseph said unto his steward, Up, follow after the men; and when thou dost overtake them, say unto them, Wherefore have ye rewarded evil for good? (Gen 43:34–44:4)

[3] And the children of Israel said unto them [Moses and Aaron], Would to God we had died by the hand of Yahweh in the land of Egypt, when we sat by the flesh pots, and when we did eat bread to the full; for ye have brought us forth into this wilderness, to kill this whole assembly with hunger. [4] Then said Yahweh unto Moses, Behold, I will rain bread from heaven for you; and the people shall go out and gather a certain rate every day, that I may prove them, whether they will walk in my law, or no. [5] And it shall come to pass, that on the sixth day they shall prepare that which they bring in; and it shall be twice as much as they gather daily. . . . [16] This is the thing which Yahweh hath commanded, Gather of it every man according to his eating, an omer for every man, according to the number of your persons; take ye every man for them which are in his tents. [17] And the children of Israel did so, and gathered, some more, some less. [18] And when they did mete it with an omer, he that gathered much had nothing over, and he that gathered little had no lack; they gathered every man according to his eating. . . . [32] And Moses said, This is the thing which Yahweh commandeth, Fill an omer of it to be kept for your generations; that they may see the bread wherewith I have fed you in the wilderness, when I brought you forth from the land of Egypt. . . . [36] Now an omer is the tenth part of an ephah. (Exod 16:3–5, 16–18, 32, 36)

Despite the abrupt change in subject matter from the immodest woman to correct weights and measures, the latter topic fits very well into the Deuteronomist's scheme. We are concerned with the Joseph story, with brothers in dispute, and with grain, precisely the subject matter of the preceding laws. In order to avenge his brothers for their ill-treatment of him, the "dead" Joseph took advantage of their lack of grain. Recall how Tamar on behalf of her dead husband proceeded against Judah because he owed her "seed." These brothers had sold the "sheaf," Joseph, for money. Their recompence was to receive sheaves of grain plus money. As Tamar disguised herself as a prostitute to seek compensation from Judah, so Joseph disguised himself as an Egyptian to trick his brothers in order to pay them back for their offense.

On returning to their father, the brothers recounted to him the problem of the money in their sacks of grain. Jacob suggested that there may have been an oversight (Gen 43:12). The issue in fact is about deception in a transaction, precisely the law's topic. Only the idiosyncratic, inverted feature in the tradition—they are being cheated not through loss but gain—is translated into the more conventional form of cheating by means of false weights. We are provided with an excellent illustration of how a rule, already known to its recipients,[21] has been brought into association with a narrative and presented again to the recipients because the aim has been to uncover the issues involved in the narrative.

Joseph deceived his brothers again when he had their money slipped into their sacks a second time. They should have been on guard because of the previous incident, but he took advantage of their inebriated state. When they had returned for more grain and reported to Joseph how they had found the money in their sacks the first time, he replied that God must have put such treasure there for he had received their money (Gen 43:23). According to the Deuteronomist, however, the deity should not be implicated in this kind of cheating. To prove his point, he recalls a tradition in Exodus 16 about the manna, in which God is viewed as equitable in his distribution of food to those in need. Before turning to it, we might note how the contrast between Joseph's partiality and the deity's impartiality in

[21]Probably from wisdom counsel, even if the formulations known to us (Prov 11:1, 16:11, 20:23) might be later than Deuteronomy. The fondness for antithetical cases—supervision to ensure that an Israelite is not humiliated when publicly punished, followed by a rule that requires that an Israelite be publicly shamed—and the fondness for figurative meaning, for example, in regard to seed (grain), are characteristic of the Book of Proverbs.

fact shows up in the Genesis material. When Joseph acts in person he is partial: "To all of them he gave each man changes of raiment; but to Benjamin he gave three hundred pieces of silver, and five changes of raiment" (Gen 45:22). When he acts for God, however, he is fair to all and provides the whole country with food during the famine. His claim that God had sent him to preserve life for his family has an echo in the law when it promises that God will prolong an Israelite's days on earth should he keep correct weights and measures.

In recalling a later, comparable episode in Israelite history, the Deuteronomist would primarily have been interested in the example it provided of how God himself used correct weights and measures in giving food to the Israelites. He would also have noted, however, that when the Israelites accused Moses and Aaron of bringing them to the wilderness so as to have them die of hunger, they recalled their previous experience in Egypt when they had plenty of food to eat (Exod 16:3). Not only is previous Egyptian history recalled, but the same context—in which the lives of starving people are threatened—raised.

The narrative is remarkable in that it represents God as adhering to some such rule about observing "a full and just weight thou shalt have, a full and just measure thou shalt have." Each day the people were to gather one day's portion of the manna, except on the sixth day when they were to gather twice the amount. Even technical standards are introduced into the account. Each man was to receive an omer, and the number of omers to be gathered was to be determined by the number of persons living in each man's tent. This exactness of measure is stressed throughout the entire episode.[22] An omer of the manna, for example, was kept to remind future generations about God's just treatment of the Israelites at that period of history. The narrative concludes with the technical notice that an omer is the tenth part of an ephah. The term in the law is the "ephah."

Resorting to false practices is described in the law as an "abomination to Yahweh." This phrase, with its religious overtones, is probably employed because of Yahweh's activity in Exodus 16.

A common feature of the laws is that they often range over different traditions in which the lawgiver notes some related topic. The law

[22]See my *The Laws of Deuteronomy* (Ithaca: Cornell University Press, 1974), 241–43.

on weights and measures is an excellent example of his method. Additional evidence that he has switched from the Joseph narrative to the one in Exodus 16 is that the narrative in Exodus 17 about Amalek's bad treatment of the Israelites inspires the law about Amalek that follows the law about weights and measures.

Mayes draws attention to what appears to be an awkward final form of the law in which the positive injunction about possessing "a full and just weight, a full and just measure," along with its statement promising long life, interrupts the connection between the prohibition in verse 14 and its condemnation in verse 16.[23] Rather than postulating some phantom, unskilled final redactor of the material, we might note that two traditions have been under scrutiny in the law. In that the second tradition serves to illustrate the example of God, it is subservient to the Genesis tradition that poses the primary human problem. The law therefore begins and concludes by addressing itself to the human problem.

Law: The extermination of the Amalekites

> [17] Remember what Amalek did unto thee by the way, when ye were come forth out of Egypt; [18] how he met thee by the way, and smote the hindmost of thee, even all that were feeble behind thee, when thou wast faint and weary; and he feared not God. [19] Therefore it shall be, when Yahweh thy God hath given thee rest from all thine enemies round about, in the land which Yahweh thy God giveth thee for an inheritance to possess it, that thou shalt blot out the remembrance of Amalek from under heaven; thou shalt not forget. (Deut 25:17–19)

Background: Amalek's attack on the Israelites

> [1] And all the congregation of the children of Israel journeyed from the wilderness of Sin, after their journeys, according to the commandment of Yahweh, and pitched in Rephidim: and there was no water for the people to drink. . . . [3] And the people thirsted there for water; and the people murmured against Moses, and said, Wherefore is this that thou hast brought us up out of Egypt, to kill

[23]Mayes, *Deuteronomy* NCBC, 331.

> us and our children and our cattle with thirst? . . . [5] And Yahweh said unto Moses, Go on before the people, and take with thee of the elders of Israel; and thy rod, wherewith thou smotest the river, take in thine hand, and go. [6] Behold, I will stand before thee there upon the rock in Horeb; and thou shalt smite the rock, and there shall come water out of it, that the people may drink. And Moses did so in the sight of the elders of Israel. . . . [8] Then came Amalek, and fought with Israel in Rephidim. [9] And Moses said unto Joshua, Choose us out men, and go out, fight with Amalek: to morrow I will stand on the top of the hill with the rod of God in mine hand. [10] So Joshua did as Moses had said to him, and fought with Amalek: and Moses, Aaron, and Hur went up to the top of the hill. [11] And it came to pass, when Moses held up his hand, that Israel prevailed: and when he let down his hand, Amalek prevailed. [12] But Moses' hands were heavy; and they took a stone, and put it under him, and he sat thereon; and Aaron and Hur stayed up his hands, the one on the one side, and the other on the other side; and his hands were steady until the going down of the sun. [13] And Joshua discomfited Amalek and his people with the edge of the sword. [14] And Yahweh said unto Moses, Write this for a memorial in a book, and rehearse it in the ears of Joshua: for I will utterly put out the remembrance of Amalek from under heaven. (Exod 17:1, 3, 5, 6, 8–14)

The reason for the presentation of the law on Amalek at this point is not just that the Deuteronomist moves from the tradition in Exodus 16 to the one in Exodus 17. In fact a substantive link exists between the two traditions, which in turn ties in with the lawgiver's dominant interest in the preceding laws. Israel had complained that Moses and Aaron had brought them to the wilderness to exploit their hungry state and have them die (Exod 16:3).[24] The deity intervened and strengthened them by feeding them. Amalek's offense is interpreted by the Deuteronomist to be that he took advantage of the Israelites' weakened condition to attack and destroy them. Initially this complaint, like the one in Exod 16:3 against Moses and Aaron, was directed against Moses (Exod 17:3). While providence had again come to their rescue by supplying them with water at a place some distance ahead of Rephidim, Amalek came and attacked those Isra-

[24]Consistent with preceding laws involving Moses' own experience, the lawgiver has him speak in the second-person plural, "Remember . . . when ye were come forth out of Egypt." The "You" form is found in the narrative in Exodus 17.

elites who had not yet left there (Exod 17:8).[25] Thus the law refers to Amalek's attacking "the hindmost of thee, even all that were feeble behind thee, when thou wast faint and weary." His attack upon the weak is also the reason why his action is judged so severely. In the biblical wisdom tradition the sages condemn such unsympathetic regard for the weak, even if there is enmity.[26]

In his preceding laws the Deuteronomist was concerned with Joseph's ill-treatment at his brothers' hands when he appealed to them in his distress (Gen 42:21). Joseph, in turn, took advantage of their starved state in order to make them realize their guilt. A true Israelite is not to be like Onan and derive benefit from his seedless, dead brother. Unlike Amalek, who in the law "feared not God" in attacking the physically weak Israelites, Joseph stated that he feared God and gave provision to his enemies, his brothers, because he wanted them to live (Gen 42:18). Amalek was a descendant of Esau (Gen 36:12). The conflict between the Amalekites and the Israelites can therefore be viewed as one between brothers. What the Amalekites did was what Esau almost did to Jacob and his struggling band (Gen 32:3–8, 33:1–4). Conflicts between brothers have dominated many of the preceding laws and the stories behind them. The judgment on the Amalekites, who are to be exterminated for their action against Israel, compares with the lawgiver's sentence of death upon an Israelite who steals his brother (Deut 24:7). Underlying this death sentence was Joseph's treatment at the hands of his brothers. In addition to the common factor of fraternal relationships in these laws, we might also note that the lawgiver's interest in the increase or decrease of numbers ties in with a focus established in so many of the preceding laws.

Law: Deliverance of the first fruits of the land to the sanctuary and the disposal of the triennial tithe (Deut 26:1–15; see following pages)

Background: The attacks by the Amalekites and the Edomites at Kadesh (Numbers 13, 14, 20; see following pages)

Just as Amalek's attack on Israel at Rephidim was behind the preceding law about Amalek, so one background to the law on the

[25]This observation has gone unnoticed by commentators.
[26]On this aspect, see my *Laws*, 245.

first fruits (grain yet again comes into focus) is the attack by the Amalekites on the occasion of Israel's attempt to conquer the land after receiving a sample of its fruits (Num 14:25, 43–45). The people had failed initially to proceed against the inhabitants of the land after the spies brought back not only the fruit but also a report of the daunting nature of these inhabitants. As in Exod 16:3 (related to the law on weights and measures) and Exod 17:3 (related to the law on Amalek), so the Israelites had complained that God's aim was to destroy them (Num 14:3). Their failure to proceed did indeed invoke God's wrath: the complainers were to be denied entry to the land in the future. Paying no attention to this pronouncement, they decided to invade but were defeated by the Amalekites and the Canaanites.

The larger context in which this attack occurred prompts the presentation of the law on the first fruits. The tradition records how at Kadesh twelve Israelite leaders from the tribes of their fathers were sent to spy out the new land and bring back some of its fruit. Their mission coincided with the appearance of the first ripe grapes (Num 13:20), and they duly brought back grapes, pomegranates, and figs. The event foreshadows the one the Deuteronomist lays down directions for, namely, the first complete entry to the land and the full enjoyment of its fruits: "And it shall be, when thou art come in unto the land which Yahweh thy God giveth thee for an inheritance, and possessest it, and dwellest therein; that thou shalt take of the first of all the fruit of the earth" (Deut 26:1). On this occasion the Israelite will place the first fruits in a basket and go to the priest and acknowledge that "I am come unto the country which Yahweh sware unto our fathers for to give us" (v. 3). The priest will then set it down before the altar. At Kadesh the twelve leaders of the individual tribes brought back a single cluster of grapes carried on a pole between two of them and presented them, along with the pomegranates and figs, to Moses and to Aaron, the first Israelite priest, and to all the congregation of Israel. There was no altar there but, perhaps significantly in light of the Deuteronomist's imaginative use of traditions,[27] the incident happened at a place whose name means "sanctuary," Kadesh.

The law then directs the Israelite to make another declaration about God's activity on behalf of Israel from the time of the ancestor

[27]Often these traditions themselves place significance on the names of persons and places, and the Deuteronomist would simply be following suit.

Jacob to its present situation. Impressive evidence exists in support of the idea that a subsequent attack at Kadesh by the Edomites (Numbers 20) underlies the need for the second speech of acknowledgment. The two incidents at Kadesh have features in common.[28] The Edomites and Amalekites are related (Gen 36:12). Their attacks upon the Israelites are similar to those conflicts between brothers that have been a dominant element in the immediately preceding laws. The context regarding Edom's attack in Numbers 20 again concerns the Israelites' need for sustenance, as in Num 14:3. Indeed they refer to the previous occasion at Kadesh when God brought a plague upon the spies because of the negative reaction they had caused in the people (Num 14:36, 37). In Num 20:3 the people express the wish that they had died then too. In the wilderness there is no water available, and "it is no place of seed, or of figs, or of vines, or of pomegranates" (Num 20:5). As in the incident involving the Amalekites in Exodus 17, water was provided to them from a rock.

The Israelites then sought to traverse Edomite territory but were refused permission and attacked in return. The Israelites' appeal to the Edomites when requesting freedom of passage is the model for the time when, no longer at the mercy of other groups and enjoying for the first time the fruit of the land as an actual resident of it, the Israelite recalls his previous history:

> [5] "An Aramean ready to perish was my father, and he went down into Egypt, and sojourned there with a few, and became there a nation, great, mighty, and populous; [6] And the Egyptians evil entreated us, and afflicted us, and laid upon us hard bondage; [7] And when we cried unto Yahweh God of our fathers, Yahweh heard our voice, and looked on our affliction, and our labour, and our oppression; [8] And Yahweh brought us forth out of Egypt with a mighty hand, and with an outstretched arm, and with great terribleness, and with signs, and with wonders; [9] And he hath brought us into this place, and hath given us this land, even a land that floweth with milk and honey. [10] And now, behold, I have brought the first fruits of the land, which thou, O Yahweh, has given me." (Deut 26:5–10)

Freedom from threats by other groups coupled with freedom from hunger and thirst constitute an important link with the preceding two

[28]See Driver, *Deuteronomy* ICC 31–33.

laws (regarding weights and measures, and Amalek) and traditions that influence them.

The structure and content of the Israelite's speech, even some of the language, are inspired by Israel's words to Edom in Num 20:14–17. Note, for example, how Israel is conceived of as an individual speaking for the group:

> [14] "Thus saith thy brother Israel, Thou knewest all the travail that befell us. [15] Then our fathers went down into Egypt, and we dwelt in Egypt a long time. Then the Egyptians vexed us, and our fathers; [16] And when we cried unto Yahweh, he heard our voice, and sent an angel, and hath brought us forth out of Egypt: and, behold, we are in Kadesh, a city in the uttermost of thy border. [17] Let us pass, I pray thee, through thy country: we will not pass through thy fields, or through the vineyards, neither will we drink of the water of the wells: we will go by the king's high way, we will not turn to the right hand nor to the left, until we have passed thy borders." (Num 20:14–17)

Both speeches have a triadic structure: pre-Egyptian history about Jacob's meeting with Esau after leaving Aram, the Egyptian experience, initially expansive but finally oppressive, and present reality concerning the fertility of each land. The form of the earlier speech in Numbers fits its social setting exactly: a retelling of past experience on the occasion of two related groups meeting after a long time. Contrariwise, only a desire to give didactic, historical content to an agricultural event can explain the artificial link that is forged between handing over first fruits to a sanctuary and recalling the nation's past on the same occasion. The incongruous relationship between form and setting for the Deuteronomic speech is itself an indication that the speech is borrowed from another context.

The Deuteronomic speech opens with an allusion to Jacob as "an Aramean ready to perish." The promise of the land was given to the patriarchs, and it is therefore to be expected that a recounting of the past will begin with a reference to one of them. As the father of the nation, Jacob found himself in double jeopardy when he decided to quit his life as an Aramean with his oppressive father-in-law, Laban, and return to the land of his birth (Gen 31:13). He had to steal away unawares from Laban who, however, caught up with him and would have harmed him had not Jacob's god saved him. As the first example in the nation's history of providence acting against an adversary on its behalf, the incident provides a suitable starting point for a recounting of how Israel's experiences led to its permanent settlement in the land. Threats to Jacob's well-being continued after Laban's departure. He had to face an Esau who sought vengeance for the loss of his birthright. To appeal to him Jacob sent messengers ahead. They returned and warned that Esau was approaching with four hundred men (Gen 32:6). Providence again, it is to be inferred, rescued Jacob.

It was at this time too that Jacob's name was changed to Israel, that his national identity, in anticipation of his future line, was established. To designate him an "Aramean ready to perish" accurately describes the situation he found himself in just before he acquired his true identity. Moreover, the Deuteronomist would have been encouraged to describe the ancestor in this way in light of God's first-time-ever deliverance of Jacob-Israel from his enemies, and because he was focusing upon Israel's next encounter with Edom in Num 20:14, when messengers were again sent ahead to see if Edom would receive Israel. In fact, as I have argued elsewhere,[29] the Israelite messengers began with an allusion to the last time Jacob had appealed to Esau: "Thou knewest all the travail that befell us," namely, the precarious journey Jacob took from Aram to the land of his fathers and his confrontation with Esau. The term *t^elā'āh,* "travail," is used in the Pentateuch only here and in Exod 18:8, in reference to God's delivery of the Israelites from the troubles they encountered after escaping their Egyptian oppressor, the pharaoh. With Laban and then with the pharaoh there had been a pursuit and each time providence had stepped in.

The triennial tithe

The Edomites refused the Israelites provision from the produce of their land, even when an offer was made to pay for it (Num 20:19). Their meanness was, by implication, condemned in the law that permits grapes and grain to be eaten by someone entering another's vineyard and field (Deut 23:24, 25). In that the event at Kadesh anticipated Israel's freedom from hunger when it came into its own land, Edom's negative attitude may have been a warning that an Israelite should not similarly treat the landless in his midst. From the

[29]See my *Laws,* 249–51.

significance of the first fruits, the Deuteronomist turns to the significance of the triennial tithe. He reminds the Israelite of his duty to give it to the Levite, the sojourner, the fatherless, and the widow.

The triennial tithe might also have been singled out at this point because of the Deuteronomist's continuing reflection upon the people's offense at Kadesh forty years before they met Edom at Kadesh. No Israelite over twenty years of age, except Joshua and Caleb, were allowed to enter the land and enjoy its fruits because they lacked trust in the deity's ability to take them into the land and they disobeyed his commandments. Over a period of forty years they would all die off, after which time their offspring would be in a position to enter. The law stipulates that after a period of three years in the land an Israelite of the surviving generation is required to state that he has duly given the triennial tithe to those in need. He declares that he has observed this particular obligation and that he has not transgressed any commandment or forgotten them. He then affirms that he has not eaten the tithe while mourning, or removed any of it while unclean, or offered any of it to the dead. He repeats yet again that he has obeyed the voice of God and that he has done all that he had been commanded to do. Finally, he requests that God "look down from thy holy habitation, from heaven, and bless thy people Israel, and the land which thou hast given us, as thou swarest unto our fathers, a land that floweth with milk and honey."

The emphasis in this law upon keeping the commandments may be linked to the exclusion from the land of that generation that failed to obey them at Kadesh.[30] Observation of the commandments is rewarded with life, in field, in animal, and in man (Deut 28:1–14, 30:15–20). The tithes are produce of the field and represent tangible evidence of this gift of life. Many of the laws, for example, those leading up to the presentation of the one on the tithes in Deut 14:22–29, are concerned with keeping life and death apart.[31] This same concern may underlie the instructions about not eating the tithe while

[30]If the meaning of Kadesh carried over into the Deuteronomist's reflection, it perhaps illuminates the language used in Deut 26:13, 15: "sacred portion" (*qōdeš*) and "thy holy habitation" (*māʿôn qodšᵉkā*).

[31]The prohibition against seething a kid in its mother's milk is a prime example. In Exod 23:19 this prohibition is paired with the requirement to bring the first fruits to the sanctuary. See my "On Separating Life and Death: An Explanation of Some Biblical Laws," *HTR* 69 (1976): 3.

mourning, not removing it while one is unclean (possibly because one has been in contact with a corpse), or not offering any of it to the dead. The lawgiver may be recalling that Yahweh prohibited Israel from entering the land until the last of the dead bodies of the preceding generation lay in the wilderness (Num 14:33). Their corpses, it is implied, must not come into contact with the life-giving, new land. The lawgiver's separation between life and death may be inspired by the separation found in the tradition.

SUMMARY The perversion of justice Joseph experienced at the hands of Potiphar's wife, and the injustice done to Tamar by Judah, prompt the rule about perverting the justice that is due to the sojourner and fatherless, and about taking the widow's garment in pledge. The role of Joseph as the forgotten sheaf in the dream, which is fulfilled when he brings relief from hunger for his kin, prompts the rule about the forgotten sheaf at harvest time. The dispute between Joseph and his brothers was unsatisfactorily resolved. A similar dispute among brother Israelites is to be resolved by a court, and the guilty brother is not to be humiliated when punishment is administered to him.

Judah had a problem when his son died childless and he sought to remedy it by having Onan give of his seed. Although this remedy is proper for an Israelite family, a complication existed within Judah's because he had married a Canaanite woman and consequently produced three "asses" by her. The figurative rule about not muzzling an "ox" in its (sexual) treading is inspired by Judah's problem. Onan sought to evade his duty to his dead brother by spilling his seed rather than having intercourse with his brother's widow. An Israelite brother who refuses to do his duty is to be likened to Onan by means of a symbolic ceremony in which the widow removes his sandal and spits in his face. Tamar, acting for her dead husband, resolved her contention with Judah by sexual conquest. The law condemns a woman who sexually assaults her husband's antagonist.

As Tamar disguised herself and took advantage of Judah, the disguised Joseph tricked his disadvantaged brothers when they bought grain from him. God was guiding Joseph, but the action contrasts sharply with God's fairness in distributing food to a later generation of hungry Israelites. The law declares that false weights and measures are an abomination to Yahweh. Amalek took advantage of Israel's thirsty state to attack them. The law imposes an obligation on the Israelites to destroy the Amalekites. Amalek had also attacked Israel after they had brought back a sample of the fruit of the new land to Kadesh. Because of a subsequent attack at Kadesh by the relatives of the Amalekites, the Edomites, Israel's account of the history of their hardship—going back to Jacob's escape from Laban—met with a negative response from the Edomites. According to the law, upon entering the new land, the Israelites are to present their first fruits to Yahweh. Beginning with Jacob's departure from Laban, Yahweh's deeds are to be recounted when presenting them. The Edomites' failure at Kadesh to provide for those in need serves as a reminder to the Israelites that they must set aside the triennial tithe for the needy.

CHAPTER 12

THE DECALOGUE

A host of questions about the decalogue remains either unsolved or without satisfactory solution. What accounts for the differences between both versions? Why does it include ten items, and why does the last one concentrate on a mental state, covetousness, and not upon an action? Why, given the limited scope of the decalogue and the fact that ordinarily tablets in the ancient Near East contained a great deal more material, are there two tablets? One would have been more than enough. Moses is apparently not on Sinai when God pronounces his words (Exod 19:25). Are we to accept the seemingly strange implication that both Moses and the people were too far off to hear what was actually said, that in effect there was no audience for the decalogue? Why, unlike other biblical laws that Moses receives from God and then communicates to the people, does God speak the decalogue on the occasion at Sinai? Why is the pronouncement of these laws accompanied by such a dramatic manifestation of divine power? Why are the individual items referred to as "words" (Exod 20:1, 34:28; Deut 4:13, 10:4) rather than "commandments"? New answers can be given to all of these questions.

It is widely acknowledged that Deuteronomic language is a feature of both versions. So pervasive is this language in fact that, as R. H. Pfeiffer pointed out, all attempts to remove it and recreate some original form of the decalogue has proved impossible.[1] Yet critics endlessly attempt to construct some such form, apparently motivated by the conviction that the decalogue is very old. They commonly reduce the length of the rules to as short and as metrical a form as possible, and suggest that the original rules had a similar form. Lurking behind the construction of such "a fantastic, homogenized *Urform* is probably the strange notion that as we go further back in time we find a greater preference for short, staccatolike, even rhythmic, utterances.[2]

The impossibility of disentangling the Deuteronomic language from some independent set of rules is one indication that the construction of the decalogue may in fact be Deuteronomic. This view encourages us to see if the individual rules are the outcome of the Deuteronomist's mediation between the laws and the narrative traditions. Immediately noteworthy is the link that is drawn between the event of the exodus, "I am Yahweh thy God, which brought thee out of the land of Egypt, from the house of bondage," and the presentation of the subsequent rules. There is too the specific link between the

[1]R. H. Pfeiffer, *Introduction to the Old Testament* (New York: Harper, 1941), 229–32. In his "The Structure of Deuteronomic Law," *Maarav* 1 (1979): 105–58, S. A. Kaufman revives in a detailed and systematic way the view that the order of the Deuteronomic laws follows that of the items in the decalogue. In doing so he is attempting to show that both sets of rules are more closely linked than has been hitherto realized. Alas, it takes little critical acumen to see that he forces the scheme to an extent beyond even a measure of plausibility. In order to make it work he interprets items in the decalogue either narrowly (e.g., taking Yahweh's name in vain) or broadly (e.g., murder), and interprets the topical unit of rules in Deuteronomy always as broadly as possible. The initial statement of the decalogue about Yahweh's deliverance from Egypt has to be merged with the prohibitions that follow so as to conceal the fact that the corresponding series of rules in Deuteronomy lacks any statement about the deliverance. But these grounds for scepticism are the least of the problem. Rules that have no link with the corresponding item in the decalogue are nonetheless somehow made to fit: removing boundary marks, a wife captured in war, the first-born son of the unloved wife, straying or broken down animals, and transvestism all come under murder; exampting a man from conscription to spend time with his wife comes under theft; leprosy comes under false witness, which by being interpreted to mean, "Be fair to one's fellow as regards both his substance and his dignity," permits a further range of rules to come under its sway. Rules about supposed state institutions come under the command to honor parents on the dubious basis that state authority has replaced that of the family. The obvious connection between the son who disobeys his parents and the item to honor parents comes under murder. I wonder what type of critic Kaufman was anticipating when he says that critics will view his scheme as "all too neat, too clean" (144)?

[2]David Daube's description in *Ancient Jewish Law* (Leiden: Brill, 1981), 98, 99.

sabbath command and the exodus in one version, and the same command and the creation story in the other. In fact, the presentation of the decalogue is in some ways—its opening statement, the clauses attached to some of the laws—in the form of a narrative itself.

Another factor that suggests that the basis for the decalogue's form can be found by scrutinizing certain narratives is that the decalogue cannot be viewed as a distinctive development in the history of law. Many of the rules in question are ageless. Those against murder, adultery, false accusation, stealing, and coveting apply to every time and place. Of his some two hundred publications, David Daube's "The Self-Understood in Legal History," first delivered on the occasion of the five hundred years' jubilee of the University of Munich, is widely regarded as among his most insightful. In it he discusses why it is that in early law codes, for example, the Roman Twelve Tables and the Bible's Book of the Covenant, some of the most basic rules of law are not found and concludes that "The author is not motivated to lay down what no one questions."[3] Everyone knows the laws. Only matters that require reform or about which there is doubt appear in these early compilations. From this perspective we cannot examine the decalogue as we would other early legal documents. We have to wonder why a lawgiver committed rules, such as those against murder, adultery, and stealing, to writing in the brief, unembellished, even banal, form in which we find them in the decalogue.

First tablet

Pronouncements: Yahweh as deliverer from Egypt; No other gods before him and no images; Not to use Yahweh's name for a vain thing; Recognition of the Sabbath

[2] I am Yahweh thy God, which have brought thee out of the land of Egypt, out of the house of bondage. [3] Thou shalt have no other gods before me. [4] Thou shalt not make unto thee any graven image, or any likeness of any thing that is in heaven above, or that is in the earth beneath, or that is in the water under the earth: [5] thou shalt not bow down thyself to them, nor serve them: for I Yahweh thy God am a jealous God, visiting the iniquity of the

[3]Daube, "The Self-Understood in Legal History," *Juridical Review* 18 (1973): 127.

fathers upon the children unto the third and fourth generation of them that hate me; [6] and shewing mercy unto thousands of them that love me and keep my commandments. [7] Thou shalt not take the name of Yahweh thy God in vain; for Yahweh will not hold him guiltless that taketh his name in vain. [8] Remember the sabbath day, to keep it holy. [9] Six days shalt thou labour, and do all thy work: [10] but the seventh day is the sabbath of Yahweh thy God: in it thou shalt not do any work, thou, nor thy son, nor thy daughter, thy manservant, nor thy maidservant, nor thy cattle, nor thy sojourner that is within thy gates: [11] for in six days Yahweh made heaven and earth, the sea, and all that in them is, and rested the seventh day: wherefore Yahweh blessed the sabbath day, and hallowed it. (Exod 20:2–11; cp., Deut 5:6–15)

Background: The making of the golden calf

[1] And when the people saw that Moses delayed to come down out of the mount, the people gathered themselves together unto Aaron, and said unto him, Up, make us gods, which shall go before us; for as for this Moses, the man that brought us up out of the land of Egypt, we wot not what is become of him. [2] And Aaron said unto them, Break off the golden earrings, which are in the ears of your wives, of your sons, and of your daughters, and bring them unto me. . . . [4] And he received them at their hand, and fashioned it with a graving tool, after he had made it a molten calf: and they said, These be thy gods, O Israel, which brought thee up out of the land of Egypt. [5] And when Aaron saw it, he built an altar before it; and Aaron made proclamation, and said, Tomorrow is a feast to Yahweh. [6] And they rose up early on the morrow, and offered burnt offerings, and brought peace offerings; and the people sat down to eat and to drink, and rose up to play. [7] And Yahweh said unto Moses, Go, get thee down; for thy people, which thou broughtest out of the land of Egypt, have corrupted themselves: [8] they have turned aside quickly out of the way which I commanded them: they have made them a molten calf, and have worshipped it, and have sacrificed thereunto, and said, These be thy gods, O Israel, which have brought thee up out of the land of Egypt. . . .[26] Then Moses stood in the gate of the camp, and said, Who is on Yahweh's side? let him come unto me. And all the sons of Levi gathered themselves together unto him. [27] And he said unto them, Thus saith Yahweh God of Israel, Put every man his sword by his side, and go in and out from gate to gate throughout the camp, and slay

every man his brother, and every man his companion, and every man his neighbour. [28] And the children of Levi did according to the word of Moses: and there fell of the people that day about three thousand men. . . . [33] And Yahweh said unto Moses, Whosoever hath sinned against me, him will I blot out of my book. [34] Therefore now go, lead the people unto the place of which I have spoken unto thee: behold, mine Angel shall go before thee: nevertheless in the day when I visit I will visit their sin upon them. . . . (Exod 32:1, 2, 4–8, 26–28, 33, 34)

[2] And on the seventh day God ended his work which he had made; and he rested on the seventh day from all his work which he had made. [3] And God blessed the seventh day, and sanctified it; because that in it he had rested from all his work which God created and made. (Gen 2:2, 3)

A primary feature of the Deuteronomic laws is Moses' capacity to anticipate problems that arose after his time, for example, during the reigns of the kings. This supernatural insight characterizes the pronouncements in the decalogue. God, not Moses, does the anticipating; consider, for example, the problem that arose when Moses was on the mountain awaiting—according to a later, Deuteronomic insertion into the story—delivery of the decalogue's written form. The people, impatient with his delay, requested of Aaron, "Up, make us gods, which shall go before us" (Exod 32:1). Neither in Egypt, nor in the aftermath of their escape until this development, did the Israelites manifest an inclination to acknowledge any god other than Yahweh.[4] The people's request to Aaron constituted the first example, or first open demonstration, in their history of idolatrous tendencies. This is the reason why judgments on what happened are incorporated in the first part of the decalogue. Realistically (if fictionally), they anticipate what will happen in the future.

We have noted over and again how the Deuteronomist focuses on such unique developments. In doing so, he shows he is alert not just to the incident in question but to the later history of the problem, and

[4]This statement is accurate if we follow the accounts in the Pentateuch about the experience in Egypt. In Josh 24:14 and Ezek 20:7, 8, however, the Israelites are said to have acknowledged the idols of Egypt. Whatever the basis for this view—for example, historical, or inferred on the ground that the Israelites were always inclined to idolatry—the perspective of the decalogue is that of the Pentateuch.

thus his formulations sometimes appear to combine different layers of material from various periods in Israelite history. In effect the fictional device of prophetic anticipation—really a looking back on events—accounts for this appearance of layering.

Once we view the first four pronouncements as the Deuteronomist's response to the making of the golden calf, much is clarified. Together the four might be viewed as constituting one tablet because they are dependent upon elements in the one narrative. Their order, as we shall see, also becomes intelligible. The opening statement about Yahweh's bringing the Israelites out of Egypt is the first item in the decalogue because we are dealing with ten utterances, not ten commandments. E. Nielsen makes an elementary error in excluding the statement from the enumeration on the ground that neither in form nor content was it a commandment.[5] Influenced by popular tradition in making this point, he ignores the plain textual description that "God spake all these words" (Exod 20:1).

Yahweh as deliverer from Egypt

The statement, "I am Yahweh thy God, which have brought thee out of the land of Egypt, out of the house of bondage," is significant in the context of the people's claim after Aaron had made the golden calf:[6] "These be thy gods, O Israel," they asserted, "which brought thee up out of the land of Egypt" (Exod 32:4).[7] Proper identification of Yahweh is a crucial consideration in light of the value the people placed upon a man-made object. The opening statement of the decalogue is a necessary response to this fundamental confusion about God's identity. He can only be identified in the context of the pattern of deliverance laid out in the story of the exodus. The larger background out of which the opening item of the decalogue has been

[5]E. Nielsen, *The Ten Commandments in New Perspective* (Naperville, Ill.: Allenson, 1968), 11.

[6]The statement is in fact a puzzling one in that it seems unnecessarily obvious. Consequently, we have to ask why the lawgiver felt it necessary to make. The situation that arose in Exodus 32 presents one such necessity. Although I do not exclude the general cultural influence of the language of international politics, for example, of vassal treaties, upon Deuteronomy, I fail to see its direct influence on the expression of Israelite religious perceptions.

[7]The Deuteronomist uses his own distinctive language, *yāṣāʾ*, and not *ʿālāh* as in Exod 32:4, and "the house of bondage." See S. R. Driver *Deuteronomy* ICC (Edinburgh: T. and T. Clark, 1902), lxxix.

fashioned is the Deuteronomist's constant emphasis upon Yahweh's power as manifested in his bringing the Israelites out of Egypt (Deut 4:34, 6:21–23, 7:18, 19). This emphasis is itself a reaction to the incident of the golden calf. The statement in Deut 6:4, "Hear, O Israel, Yahweh our God is one Yahweh," is probably one such reaction to the people's claim that the gods in the form of the calf brought the Israelites out of Egypt.

Other gods and the making of images

Not surprisingly, the item that follows addresses itself precisely to the remarks of the people about the gods they proclaimed as the ones responsible for bringing them out of Egypt: "Thou shalt have no other gods before me." Even the use of the preposition "before," which has caused exegetes so much trouble, can be explained as dependent upon the people's initial request to Aaron: "Up, make us gods, which shall go before us" (Exod 32:1). The underlying issue in the narrative is that Yahweh is "before" these other gods. The use of the first person in the divine utterance parallels its use by the deity in the narrative (Exod 32:8).

A prohibition follows against the making of images. This prohibition is also a response to Aaron's work with the gold earrings. After he fashioned them into a molten calf, the people identified it as their gods (plural). The Deuteronomist's condemnation of such developments on the basis of this particular example is all-encompassing. A tendency to be more inclusive also underlies the narrative in Exodus 32. Commentators generally agree that the narrative has been composed with Jeroboam's setting up the golden calves at Bethel and Dan in mind (1 Kings 12:25–33). This is why the story in Exodus 32 speaks of the calf in the plural and not in the singular. Some of its language is Deuteronomic, and it would not be surprising to find that the Deuteronomist altered the story at the same time that he included his negative judgment upon Jeroboam in his account of the history of the kings.

In any event, in the decalogue, he begins by proscribing a *pesel,* a term general in scope that would include Aaron's molten calf. That an image comparable to Aaron's earthly one is in the Deuteronomist's mind is indicated by the subsequent, similarly generalizing reference to "any likeness of any thing that is in heaven above, or that is in the earth beneath, or that is in the water under the earth." A problem for interpreters is that the language of the prohibition speaks of the image in the singular and then switches to the plural with the words, "Thou shalt not bow down thyself to them, nor serve them." This difficulty disappears when we recall that a singular image was fashioned by Aaron, yet it was given a plural designation: "These be thy gods, O Israel." In the context of the decalogue the antecedent of "them" is the "other gods," as in "Thou shalt have no other gods before me." Despite a common view that requires tortuous reasoning for support, this prohibition is not a separate item in the decalogue; instead, because of the identification between the gods and the golden calf in Exodus 32, the prohibition belongs together with the condemnation of image making.[8] Common sense alone suggests a close connection between them. What has probably misled interpreters into separating them is their inability to put aside the popular notion that they are dealing with ten commandments and not ten different pronouncements that may include, as here, two interrelated prohibitions.

The ground of these joint prohibitions is: "For I Yahweh thy God am a jealous God, visiting the iniquity of the fathers upon the children unto the third and fourth generation of them that hate me; and shewing mercy unto thousands of them that love me, and keep my commandments." If it is correct to relate them to the narrative in Exodus 32, as well as to the Deuteronomist's awareness of later developments, for example, Jeroboam's offense, then this statement about Yahweh's jealousy might also be illuminated by these contexts regarding calves. That very similar language about God's mercy to thousands and his visiting the iniquity of the fathers upon the children is used when God addresses Moses about the incident of the golden calf in Exod 34:7 helps verify my theory.

Although the language about the third and fourth generation can hardly reflect the narrative about the calf in Exodus 32, it is pertinent to note that a reference is made to Yahweh's decision to visit the people's sin upon them when they take up residence in the land (v. 34). In other words, both law and narrative are looking ahead and

[8]On W. Zimmerli's misunderstanding in "Das Zweite Gebot," *Gottes Offenbarung, Gesammelte Aufsätze zum Alten Testament* (Munich: Kaiser, 1963), 234–48, followed by B. S. Childs's in *The Book of Exodus* (Philadelphia: Westminster, 1974), 405, see my *The Ten Commandments,* Ninth Sacks Lecture (Oxford: Oxford Centre for Postgraduate Hebrew Studies, 1983), 14.

they are thinking of future instances of idolatry. In Exod 34:11–16, which is attributed to a Deuteronomic redactor, idolatry is also anticipated. As already noted, indications are that Exodus 32 was written up with Jeroboam's golden calves in mind. It therefore makes sense to see whether this period of history has possibly prompted the comment about idolatry in succeeding generations.

God's visiting the iniquity of the fathers upon the sons is not, contrary to the beliefs of almost all commentators, primarily about punishment. Nor, again contrary to common understanding, does the statement clash with the principle in Deut 24:16 that the sons should not be put to death for the offenses of the fathers. The latter directive concerns how human beings sometimes dispense justice, whereas the former attempts to embody a profound comment on the nature of providence. No problem of understanding is more intractable than accounting for repeated wrongdoing by those who fully know what they are about. Israel's history of apostasy would inevitably have occasioned reflection about why people continued to engage in it when they have been persistently warned against doing so. Nothing in human nature could explain this defiance. The Deuteronomist accordingly attributes its cause to the deity. Similar attempts to "explain" problems in such ultimate terms lie behind the descriptions of God "causing" Joseph's brothers to sell him into slavery (Gen 45:4–8), and God "hardening" the pharaoh's heart and preventing Israel's release from Egypt (Exod 4:21, 7:3, 9:12); note, too, Isa 63:17: "O Yahweh, why hast thou made us to err from thy ways, and hardened our hearts from thy fear."

The statement in the decalogue may have been prompted by observing a pattern of apostasy among Jeroboam's successors. The Deuteronomist judged the continued use of the golden calves in their reigns to have brought about the downfall of the northern kingdom (2 Kings 17:21–23). Jehu was one of Jeroboam's successors, and his sons to the fourth generation were permitted by the deity to sit on the throne (2 Kings 10:30). But they did not continue beyond the fourth generation. Of each father it is recorded that he imitated Jeroboam's offense (2 Kings 10:29, 13:2, 11, 14:24, 15:9). In regard to them it could have been said that just as God instituted their succession to the throne, so also he visited the iniquity of their apostasy upon the fourth generation.

The mention of Yahweh's mercy to thousands who love him and

keep his commandments is likewise less puzzling when related to the incident of the golden calf. Yahweh expressed an intention to destroy all the people on the occasion. It emerged, however, that some of them, namely, the Levites, were loyal and did his bidding in putting down some three thousand offenders. The number destroyed suggests that those loyal to Yahweh themselves numbered in the thousands, for the instruction was to slay "every man his brother, and every man his companion, and every man his neighbor" (Exod 32:27).

The vain use of Yahweh's name

Aaron built an altar for the golden calf and proclaimed, "Tomorrow is a feast to Yahweh" (Exod 32:5). Plainly, he identified the calf with Yahweh, or, at the very least, his words could be so interpreted. Insofar as the deity in the story, and hence the standard (usually) subscribed to by its teller, reacts to the development involving the calf, implicit rules exist prohibiting what took place. This observation should not be lost sight of. Anyone coming upon this narrative might want to know exactly what the nature of the offenses was and how the latent rules about them should be formulated. There is a sense in which the compiler of the decalogue is simply making these rules explicit. One such rule can be understood as a negative reaction to Aaron's use of the name Yahweh in his proclamation about the special day in honor of the calf. By setting the prohibition about the vain use of Yahweh's name against Aaron's statement, much is clarified.

The rule prohibits "taking up" (*nāśā'*) the name, upon one's lips in making a statement. The language is apt in regard to Aaron's proclamation. Moreover, his use of Yahweh's name in reference to the calf is accurately characterized as "vain" (*laššāw'*). This term, which denotes a lack of reality, more appropriately describes the misplaced application of the name Yahweh to the calf than the falsity of an oath (the usual interpretation given to the rule).[9] In Jer 18:15 the deity condemned Israel for forgetting him and burning (in the words of the AV) "incense to vanity" (*laššāw'*), presumably worshipping, like Aaron and company with the calf, some misperceived religious object. The Psalmist contrasts trust in Yahweh with adherence to vain idols (*hablē-šāw'*) (Ps. 31:6).

[9]B. S. Childs criticizes the inappropriateness of narrowly confining the term *laššāw'* to the notion of false swearing (*The Book of Exodus*, 410–11).

That Yahweh's name should be accompanied by appropriate statements about him is a condition both of earlier directives in the decalogue and of remarks by Moses in regard to the incident of the calf. Preceding the prohibition about the name we find: "I am Yahweh thy God which have brought thee out of the land of Egypt," and, "For I Yahweh thy God am a jealous God" (Exod 20:2, 5). When Moses again received the decalogue after the incident of the calf had taken place, God descended in the cloud, stood with him, and "proclaimed the name of Yahweh" (Exod 34:5–7). The content of the proclamation concerning his mercy as well as his visiting the iniquity of the fathers upon the children is directed at the people's apostasy in the matter of the calf. This proclamation is also Yahweh's personal statement that is incorporated into the prohibition that immediately precedes the rule about his name. In both contexts, the decalogue and the narratives about the calf, information about Yahweh's identity is a matter of some moment. An explicit rule that embodies a warning about the use of his name is all the more understandable in light of these two contexts.

In the decalogue we find statements about Yahweh, followed by statements about other gods, and then we return to Yahweh in the rule about the vain use of his name. A scrutiny of Exodus 32 accounts for this seemingly haphazard arrangement of material. First there was the need to assert Yahweh's role in Israel's experience in order to counter the value placed upon the god or gods of the people. Explicit opposition to these gods followed. Then came the need to attack Aaron's identification of Yahweh with the calf. It might be noted that each of the items is set against a background in which the concern is with gods other than Yahweh.

Attached to the prohibition about the name is the warning that Yahweh will not hold an offender guiltless. Unlike the preceding statements in which Yahweh speaks in the first person, his name is mentioned in the third person both in this warning and in the prohibition itself. What accounts in part for this change may be the fact that we do not actually learn that on the occasion of the celebration the name Yahweh was uttered in affirmation of the calf. The offense emerges as a potential one, not involving (unlike the others) Yahweh's direct response. Hence the lawgiver refrained from formulating the prohibition in language that indicated a response to a personal insult to Yahweh; hence, too, the use of language that warns about the future: "For Yahweh will not hold him guiltless." These same words occur in Exod 34:7, in Yahweh's proclamation of his identity when Moses prepared to receive the tablets a second time. This text provides important, additional support for linking the rule in the decalogue to the episode of the golden calf, in particular, to Aaron's claim that the feast was for Yahweh when in effect it was for the golden calf.

The Sabbath

Aaron's declaration that the day following the construction of the calf was to be set apart in celebration of Yahweh, which in the event caused the people "to rise up to play" ([Exod 32:6] and not to work), prompts the commandment about the sabbath. There is thus an easy transition from the rule about Yahweh's name to this one about his special day.

The statement about the special day is not, "Thou shalt not desecrate the sabbath," because this is not the issue in Exodus 32, contrary to, for example, the situation in Exodus 16 where the people gathered food on the seventh day. Rather, an opposing response, with an explanation, to Aaron's call for a special day to honor Yahweh in the shape of the calf is required. The form of the statement ("Remember the sabbath day") is consequently different from the preceding rules that required direct negative responses to developments in the narrative. The recipient of the instruction is directed to the link between the sabbath day and the creation of the world.[10] This is so because Aaron's religious object was man-made, and hence on the day in question he and the people were celebrating unawares the human capacity to create gods.[11] A basic confusion about the order

[10]This connection must have existed before its expression in the decalogue, otherwise the clause about the creation could not have been given in support of observing the sabbath. To communicate new teaching and simultaneously attempt to motivate people to observe a rule are not compatible tasks.

[11]M. Noth argues that it is not until Ezekiel (e.g., Ezek 20:11–21) that the sabbath became of central importance, so much so that the institution was later connected with the creation of the world. This explanation for the forging of the link between the latter and the rule in Exod 20:8 is tenuous, to say the least. Aside from whatever historical reality may lie behind the texts in Ezekiel, their main thrust is to link the sabbath with Israel's relationship to God by way of attacking Israel's idolatrous tendencies. The same position was taken by the compiler of the decalogue in response to the making of the golden calf (*Gesammelte Studien zum Alten Testament,* 2d ed. [Munich: Kaiser, 1966], 89).

of creation emerges. We are reminded of Hosea's comment about the calf of Samaria: "The workman made it: therefore it is not God" (8:6); or the Psalmist's judgment: "They made a calf in Horeb, and worshipped the molten image. Thus they changed their glory into the similitude of an ox that eateth grass" (Ps 106:20). The explanation attached to the rule is needed in this context to assert the correct relationship between the universe and its originator, who is referred to as Yahweh (rather than God). A satisfactory answer can thus be given to the important question why the sabbath rule carries an explanatory clause. It is plain, after all, that an injunction to observe the sabbath could have stood by itself, the more so in that the rule will already have been known to those addressed.

Aaron and the people thought that they were celebrating Yahweh as their deliverer from Egypt (Exod 32:4), but in fact they were wrongly identifying him with the calf. Their aim had been to have this object lead them in their future journeyings (Exod 32:1). Aaron's proclamation of a day in the calf's honor called for a response that affirmed Yahweh's role as it had been before the people's request to Aaron, namely, the role of their rescuer. The expression of Yahweh's day, the sabbath, in Deut 5:12–15, concentrates on the development involving the calf. Different facets of what transpired permit different responses and account for the variations in the sabbath rule as expressed in Exodus and Deuteronomy. The latter formulation with its reference to the seventh day as the "sabbath of Yahweh thy God" acknowledges Yahweh as the creator who rested on this day. In this respect both facets are incorporated in the version in Deuteronomy.

It must not be forgotten that the sabbath commandment existed before its particular formulations in the two versions of the decalogue. The incident in the narrative stimulates initial thinking on the subject, but the rule has to make sense in its own terms. In that its substance concerns rest from work, the reasons for its observance must be related to rest, which they are. The link between God's example at creation and the sabbath is satisfactory, but the link between God's rescue of the Israelites from Egypt and not working every seventh day is less easy to see. Why should the sabbath be viewed as commemorating at short, periodic intervals the deliverance from slavery?[12] The answer may well be that this rescue reestablished

[12]Driver (*Deuteronomy* ICC, 85, 86) expresses his puzzlement in the matter.

for the Israelites the institution of the sabbath as ordained at the beginning of time. During their bondage in Egypt they apparently experienced no respite from work every seventh day. An indication that this perspective may be accurate is the Deuteronomist's singling out (unlike in the Exodus version) of the manservant and maidservant as in need of rest on the seventh day. The implication is that they must not be subjected to work on that day because all Israelites had been freed by Yahweh's rescue of them from Egypt. A motivation for the deity's action would be not just opposition to oppression but a desire for assurance that the sabbath was again observed.

Second tablet

Pronouncements: Honor to parents; Murder; Adultery; Stealing; False witness; Coveting

[12] Honour thy father and thy mother: that thy days may be
long upon the land which Yahweh thy God giveth thee. [13] Thou
shalt not kill. [14] Thou shalt not commit adultery. [15] Thou shalt
not steal. [16] Thou shalt not bear false witness against thy neighbour. [17] Thou shalt not covet thy neighbor's house, thou shalt
not covet thy neighbour's wife, nor his manservant, nor his maidservant, nor his ox, nor his ass, nor any thing that is thy neighbour's. (Exod 20:12–17; cp., Deut 5:16–21)

Background: Adam and Eve, Cain and Abel

[23] And Adam said, This is now bone of my bones, and flesh of
my flesh: she shall be called Woman, because she was taken out of
Man. [24] Therefore shall a man leave his father and his mother,
and shall cleave unto his wife: and they shall be one flesh. . . . [6]
And when the woman saw that the tree was good for food, and that
it was pleasant to the eyes, and a tree to be desired to make one
wise, she took of the fruit thereof, and did eat; and gave also unto
her husband with her, and he did eat. . . . [11] And he [Yahweh]
said, Who told thee that thou wast naked? Hast thou eaten of the
tree, whereof I commanded thee that thou shouldest not eat? [12]
And the man said, The woman whom thou gavest to be with me,
she gave me of the tree, and I did eat. [13] And Yahweh God said
unto the woman, What is this that thou hast done? And the woman
said, The serpent beguiled me, and I did eat. . . . [17] And unto

Adam he said, Because thou hast hearkened unto the voice of thy wife, and hast eaten of the tree of which I commanded thee, saying, Thou shalt not eat of it: cursed is the ground for thy sake; in sorrow shalt thou eat of it all the days of thy life. . . . [21] Unto Adam also and to his wife did Yahweh God make coats of skins, and clothed them. [22] And Yahweh God said, Behold, the man is become as one of us, to know good and evil: and now, lest he put forth his hand, and take also of the tree of life, and eat, and live for ever: [23] therefore Yahweh God sent him forth from the garden of Eden, to till the ground from whence he was taken. . . .

[1] And Adam knew Eve his wife; and she conceived, and bare Cain, and said, I have gotten a man from Yahweh. [2] And she again bare his brother Abel. And Abel was a keeper of sheep, but Cain was a tiller of the ground. . . . [4] And Yahweh had regard for Abel and his offering: [5] but for Cain and his offering he had not regard. And Cain was very wroth, and his countenance fell. [6] And Yahweh said unto Cain, Why art thou wroth? and why is thy countenance fallen? [7] If thou doest well, shalt thou not be accepted? and if thou doest not well, sin lieth at the door. And unto thee shall be his desire, and thou shalt rule over him. [8] And Cain talked with Abel his brother: and it came to pass, when they were in the field, that Cain rose up against Abel his brother, and slew him. . . . [11] And now art thou [Cain] cursed from the earth, which hath opened her mouth to receive thy brother's blood from thy hand; [12] when thou tillest the ground, it shall not henceforth yield unto thee her strength; a fugitive and a wanderer shalt thou be in the earth. [13] And Cain said unto Yahweh, My punishment is greater than I can bear. [14] Behold, thou hast driven me out this day from the face of the earth; and from thy face shall I be hid; and I shall be a fugitive and a wanderer in the earth; and it shall come to pass, that every one that findeth me shall slay me. [15] And Yahweh said unto him, Therefore whosoever slayeth Cain, vengeance shall be taken on him sevenfold. And Yahweh set a mark upon Cain, lest any finding him should kill him. [16] And Cain went out from the presence of Yahweh, and dwelt in the land of Nod, on the east of Eden. [17] And Cain knew his wife; and she conceived, and bare Enoch. (Gen 2:23, 24, 3:6, 11–13, 17, 21–23, 4:1, 2, 4–8, 11–17).

Honoring parents

After the events surrounding the golden calf, Yahweh intended to destroy the Israelites and to start over again with seed through Moses

(Exod 32:10). Moses opposed his intentions on the ground that Yahweh would acquire a bad name among the Egyptians. They would note that he had brought them out from Egypt "to slay them in the mountains, and to consume them from the face of the earth" (Exod 32:12). Moses appealed to Yahweh's promise to the fathers of the nation, Abraham, Isaac, and Israel, that their seed would be greatly multiplied and would be given the land. By destroying the Israelites this promise would presumably be broken and not reconstituted, even should new seed be provided through Moses. The ancestors of the nation would thus be dishonored by the destruction of their seed and this dishonor would consist in denying them a perpetual inheritance in the land (*'ereṣ*). This line of reasoning brings us close to the substance of the rule about honoring parents and living long upon the land (*'ᵃdāmāh*).

Punishments for biblical offenses typically reflect the nature of the offense. There may then be a link between the people's honoring of a man-made god and Yahweh as the god of creation who disapproves by threatening to annihilate what he ultimately created. However that may be, the concern with the created order and its violation at human hands underlies the presentation of the commandment about honoring a father and a mother.

In formulating this commandment, the Deuteronomist in characteristic fashion returns to the first example of the problem, to the first children, Cain and Abel, of the first parents, Adam and Eve. It is noteworthy that the passage in Exod 32:7–14 is assigned to a Deuteronomic writer who recalls the generations as far back as Abraham's.[13] The tendency, in other words, to return to original developments, depending upon the perspective in question, shows up in this Deuteronomic passage.

What happened at the beginning of time has already shown up in the decalogue, in the commandment about the sabbath and in the prohibition against worshipping an image of something that might be found in the created order. The concern with creation is carried over into the injunction about parents. Even if we were unaware of the background that informs the rules, we might still speculate that a rule about honoring parents follows one about honoring the creator Yah-

[13]See Childs, *The Book of Exodus,* 559.

weh on the sabbath because parents create children.[14] This focus upon parents' reproductive role would be all the more intelligible in light of the issue raised by the story of the calf. The Israelites may have been confused about the significance of human capacity to create and whether reproduction was linked in any way to the deity's level of creative activity.

One indication that something as fundamental as procreation is the focus of this commandment is that both a father and a mother are mentioned as deserving honor (in Mal 1:6, only a father is singled out). Another indication might be that, if, as is universally assumed, the parental responsibility of inculcating moral values were in the lawgiver's mind, we would expect reference to this aspect in that only those parents who exercised the duty would deserve honor. We might then have expected, "Honor thy father and thy mother who direct thee in the way that thou shouldst walk." In that all parents without exception are included in the injunction, procreation seems to be the bottom line.

If the juxtaposition of the rules about Yahweh's sabbath and about parents reveals a shared interest in creation, this interest also characterizes Adam and Eve's relationship to Yahweh when producing Cain. As Eve put it, "I have produced (*qānāh*) a man with Yahweh" (Gen 4:2). The name of the child, Cain, is intended (even if from our irrelevant point of view the derivation is wrong) to represent this link. The description of Adam's procreative activity in Gen 5:1–3 shares the same language used to describe God's creating Adam.

A puzzling feature about the rule is the reason given why it should be observed, namely, "That thy days may be long upon the land which Yahweh thy God giveth thee" (Exod 20:12). It is far from apparent why this result should follow from the other. If, however, the example of Cain's relationship to his parents is looked at, the connection becomes clear. Cain destroyed what his parents had created, their other son, Abel. The consequence of his act was that he was not able to live upon the land of which he was a tiller. He became

[14]The admonition in Lev 19:3 to fear one's mother and father and keep God's sabbath, may be based upon the same consideration; cp., Isa 45:9, 10. Rabbinic exegetes noted the link, *Mekilta de-R. Simeon bar Yohai* to Exod 20:12. Cp. Philo, "Parents, in my opinion, are to their children what God is to the world, since just as he achieved existence for the non-existent, so they in imitation of his power, as far as they are capable, immortalize the race" (*De Specialibus Legibus* 2. 38.225).

a fugitive and a wanderer upon the earth (Gen 4:12). In both law and narrative the term *'ᵃdāmāh* is used in reference to a son's prospect of living upon the land. Cain's act of dishonoring his parents—in the fundamental sense of destroying what they had created—prompts the particular formulation of the rule in the decalogue. The rule's positive statement contrasts with Cain's negative deed.

If it is correct to argue that the Deuteronomist has compiled the decalogue, it is noteworthy that a frequent theme of his is that obedience to the commandments will lead to fertility in man and ground (*'ᵃdāmāh*, for example, Deut 7:13, 28:4).[15] The same concern with obedience and the same association with fertility underlie the composition of the injunction to honor parents. In the formulation that appears in Deuteronomy, the son who honors his parents is promised not just the prospect of doing well upon the land but also a long life. The consequence of Cain's killing Abel would also account for this expansion. As well as being denied access to the ground, Cain lived in fear of his life being cut short (Gen 4:14).

The transition from the story of the construction of the golden calf to that of creation arises naturally out of the Deuteronomist's judgments upon the issues raised. If, as is widely agreed, Exod 32:7–14, which contains the deity's pronouncement upon the people's offense, is a Deuteronomic insertion, then the narrative itself provides evidence for such a claim. The rules in the decalogue incorporate similar judgments, only the judgments are expressed outside of the narrative structure.

Murder

The logic of why a rule against murder follows one about honoring parents is apparent if Cain's act is understood. If a son honors his parents he will live long upon the land—unlike Cain who destroyed what his parents had created and was punished by his being unable to work the land. A further result of his misdeed was that he lived under the threat of being murdered himself. In that Yahweh acted to protect him from this fate, by putting a mark upon him, it is plain that he opposes such arbitrary killing. The incorporation of the prohibition about murder in the decalogue can be attributed to the implicit rule

[15]See M. Weinfeld, *Deuteronomy and the Deuteronomic School* (Oxford: Clarendon, 1972), 310–11.

that Yahweh is seen to be recognizing. The verb *hārag* is used for Cain's act of killing Abel and *nākāh* for someone's potential act of coming upon the fugitive Cain and killing him. The term *rāṣaḥ*, conveying the wrongfulness of the act, is used in the rule.[16]

Adultery

Cain had intercourse with his wife ("And Cain knew his wife") and produced a son himself (Gen 4:17). This information is related immediately after the account (which is introduced with, "And Adam knew Eve his wife") of Cain's killing of Abel and its consequences. The development represents the next stage in history after Adam's. The Deuteronomist himself typically dwells upon succeeding generations. Cain, not Adam, nonetheless represents the first son to leave his father and mother in order to marry, in line with the institution created by Yahweh in Gen 2:20–25. The Genesis narrator's reference to marriage, as part of his description of the origin of the male-female relationship, reveals the same kind of probing of social relationships as the Deuteronomist's.

Cain's killing of Abel violated his parent's participation in the process of creation. He destroyed what they produced. He in turn participated by producing a son himself. In that his violation consisted of destroying the result of the procreative act, the Deuteronomist naturally steps back and considers what constitutes a violation of sexual union itself.

According to the Genesis description the nature of marriage is such that "a man leaves his father and his mother and cleaves to his wife, and they become one flesh."[17] This union is presumably seen as part of the created order, and the Deuteronomist in his pursuit of Yahweh's rules considers the topic of its violation. He infers that Yahweh would oppose a man's having intercourse with a woman already married because it would interfere with the established bond between the couple. He therefore presents as one of Yahweh's fundamental

[16]Even in contexts where *rāṣaḥ* refers to unintentional killing (e.g., Deut 4:42; Josh 20:3), it basically denotes "to murder," as David Daube reminded me in commenting on the linguistic phenomenon that surfaces here. In English we might say of an overworked employee who dies, "Murder, sheer murder."

[17]Rabbinic exegesis (*Babylonian Sanhedrin* 58a) inferred prohibition of adultery in the statement about cleaving to a wife.

rules: "Thou shalt not commit adultery." Put differently, it is at this point in the Genesis narrative (to which the Deuteronomist was naturally drawn because of his interest in Cain) that the Deuteronomist sees room for the rule against adultery as having a basis in Yahweh's ordering of creation.[18]

Without any knowledge of how the items in the decalogue were given their order, we might have expected the rule about adultery to follow the one about honoring parents, because the male-female relationship is common to each. In various textual traditions of the Septuagint, Philo, the Nash Papyrus, and the New Testament there can be found a reversal of the rules about murder and adultery. But this is all the more reason why we must account for the apparently strange order in the original Hebrew texts. The sequence of events about Cain provides an explanation.

Stealing

Immediately after the statement about the male-female relationship in Gen 2:18–25, which enables the lawgiver to set down in Yahweh's name a rule about adultery, is the description of how Adam and Eve came to acquire a sense of shame. The crucial act is their eating from the tree of the knowledge of good and evil after they had been instructed not to do so. They had in fact stolen something that was Yahweh's. It was the first example of a wrongful taking, acquiring possession of what was known to belong to another.[19] The lawgiver is therefore able to present as the next of Yahweh's rules: "Thou shalt not steal." This prohibition was implicitly acknowledged by Yahweh when he instructed Adam not to eat from the tree.

False Witness

After Yahweh had found Adam and Eve experiencing the shame of their nakedness, he questioned Adam first of all about the fruit of the

[18]The reference to the institution of marriage in Gen 2:24 interrupts the flow of the narrative. The Deuteronomist may have inserted the reference at the same time as he compiled the decalogue.

[19]In this regard the rule that emerges reveals a concept of theft, namely, "a taking from possession against the will of the owner," so deeply rooted in all later conceptions of theft in western legal systems that it tended to exclude other forms of misappropriation. For a most useful, comparative perspective, see David Cohen, *Theft in Athenian Law, Münchener Beiträge zur Papyrusforschung und Antiken Rechtsgeschichte* 74 (Munich: Beck, 1983), 10–13.

tree. Adam's response was to say that the woman whom Yahweh had given to him had given him the fruit and he had eaten it. It was not a straight answer to the question in that Adam avoided acknowledging that he had violated the prohibition by placing the responsibility for what happened upon Eve. She in turn directed attention away from herself to the serpent's influence upon her. In evading blame for their own wrongdoing and placing it upon someone else when being questioned about an offense, Adam and Eve present a situation in which another kind of wrongdoing might easily arise, namely, falsely preferring a charge against someone. The narrative does not raise this issue, just as it had not raised the issue of adultery, but the lawgiver does, albeit indirectly.

In response to Adam and Eve's assertions, the deity actually accepts the partial truth in them, that Eve and the serpent had been instigators to Adam's offense. This is why the serpent is first punished, then the woman, and finally the man. The fact, however, that all three are punished means that Adam and Eve's attempts to absolve themselves from blame by transferring it to another were unacceptable. In noting Yahweh's rejection of this aspect of their testimony, the lawgiver recognizes the comparable problem in real life: the questioning by a person in authority of someone about an offense and his attempt to implicate, rightly or wrongly, someone else. A norm opposing false witness is readily derived.

The quasi-legal setting in the narrative explains why the prohibition in the decalogue uses language of a decidedly legal flavor about testifying as a false witness. Unaware of the story's influence we might have expected a condemnation of lying in general, which would include lying on one's own behalf. The narrower focus, the false charge against another, is a response to the narrative: Adam did not deny his action but concentrated on shifting attention to Eve, as did she to the serpent. Strictly speaking, they did not lie when testifying but, in the accurate description of the Deuteronomic formulation, they were "witnesses of emptiness" (*ʿēd šāw*ʾ) and, consequently, maliciously misleading.[20]

[20]Those who cite Hos 4:2 ("swearing and lying") and Jer 7:9 ("swear falsely") as evidence of the existence of some items of the decalogue prior to their appearance in Exodus and Deuteronomy fail to appreciate the specific focus upon witnessing falsely against another in the actual decalogue. These texts do not mention "witness" at all.

Coveting

The relationship between Yahweh and the first human beings again determines the presentation of the prohibition against coveting. Not only does the paradise narrative provide an explanation why this rule shows up at this point in the decalogue, it also explains why the subject of the rule is confined to coveting and not extended to any actions that might result from it.[21]

Both the last item of the decalogue and the climax of the paradise narrative are about coveting, and on the basis of the thesis under consideration this is no coincidence. After Adam and Eve had been punished for giving in to their desire to eat from the tree of knowledge, Yahweh expressed the fear that they would similarly proceed to eat of the fruit of the tree of life. To forestall this happening they were expelled from the garden. Having satisfied their desire to acquire the knowledge of good and evil that the gods possessed, they would be frustrated in any further attempt to be like them and possess unending life. The result, although it is not spelled out, is that human coveting aimed at acquiring "life" would remain, but its focus would be transferred to the existence that awaited human beings outside Eden. In that the life of the gods would not be a realistic focus for humans, the better life lived by a man's fellow would present itself as the potential, "natural" source of envy. The scene that follows the expulsion from Eden depicts Cain's envy of Yahweh's regard for Abel's sacrifice. In addressing Cain about his emotional state, Yahweh warned him about the influence of desire and the need to control it (Gen 4:7).

There is but a general affinity between them and the prohibition in the decalogue; a fact that occasions no surprise because the basic concern is an ageless one. For a recent, uncritical acceptance of a specific affinity, see A. Phillips, "The Decalogue—Ancient Israel's Criminal Law," *JJS* 34 (1983): 3. The subject of lying actually turns up in Gen 3:4, 5, in the serpent's point (which is justified) that Yahweh lied to Adam in telling him that on the day he ate of the fruit he would die (Gen 2:17). However, it seems unlikely that the serpent's assertion would have proved helpful as a basis for condemning human lying. On *šāw'*, in the more active sense of "damaging, malicious, bös willig," see J.F.A. Sawyer, *Theologisches Handwörterbuch zum Alten Testament,* 2, ed. E. Jenni, C. Westermann (Munich: Chr. Kaiser, 1976) cols. 882–83.

[21]For the unjustified attempt to understand the rule as involving an action too, see W. L. Moran, "The Conclusion of the Decalogue," *CBQ* 29 (1967): 543–48, and "Liability for Mere Intention in Early Jewish Law," in B. S. Jackson, *Essays in Jewish Comparative Legal History* (Leiden: Brill, 1975), 203–13.

In the final item of the decalogue the lawgiver has Yahweh address himself to the problem of desire in a post-Edenic setting. We might expect that a rule about coveting would consider the problem in relation to objects in life that are beyond most people's reach. The verb *ḥāmad,* "to covet," along with forms of the noun, is commonly used in reference to precious things, for example, silver and gold (Deut 7:25; Josh 7:21; Ps 19:10; Ezra 8:27; Nah 2:9). Yet the rule in the decalogue is much broader in scope and aimed at more ordinary possessions: a wife, a house, servants, and work animals. This orientation reflects the thrust of the paradise narrative. Already Yahweh's response to Adam and Eve's sense of shame, which was inextricably linked to their desire for something that was not theirs, namely, putting clothes on them, can be seen to anticipate future social life. The Genesis narrator concentrates on the male's future (Gen 3:22–24), and the act of covering male and female nakedness can be seen to imply Yahweh's attempt to control the sexual desire that had made Adam and Eve aware of their nakedness. Such desire should be kept within the bounds of a husband-wife relationship and not extended to another's wife, to a wish to view her nakedness, to "know" her.

Instead of living in the garden of Eden with its ready availability of food, Adam had to take up residence elsewhere "to till the ground from whence he was taken" (Gen 3:22). That ground, moreover, would prove intractable: "thorns also and thistles shall it bring forth to thee; and thou shalt eat the herb of the field; in the sweat of thy face shalt thou eat bread" (Gen 3:18, 19). In the post-Edenic state a desire for a better life could not have as its focus a return to Eden. Instead, living in houses, such desire had to take the form of another's house and another's easier life on the land. The explicit reference to servants and work animals, also to the neighbor's field in the version of Deuteronomy, makes sense in light of the unyielding earth in the Genesis story. The narrator anticipates the future. So too does the lawgiver, who has Yahweh address himself to the competition, based upon envy, between one man and another that replaced the unequal competition, similarly motivated by envy, between the first man and Yahweh. From Yahweh's perspective the motivation in each instance has to be condemned.

If the Deuteronomist has compiled the decalogue it is noteworthy that "life" in the book of Deuteronomy equals the secure possession of the land, which in turn means fertile fields and vines (Deut 8:7–9) and fine houses (Deut 6:11, 8:12). It also means the possession of a fruitful wife (Deut 24:5, 28:11). The indication is that in both the decalogue and Deuteronomy an amalgam of these desirable possessions defines "life."[22]

The two terms *ḥāmad,* "to covet," and *'āwāh,* "to desire," in Deut 5: 21 are also found in Gen 3:6. The tree of the knowledge of good and evil was something to be desired (*ta'awāh*) and to be coveted (*neḥmād*). The tree of life, it was feared, would inspire similar longings, and these had be restrained.

Unlike the version in Exod 20:13–17, the four rules in Deut 5:17–21, adultery, stealing, false witness, coveting another's wife, have the conjunction "neither" (*welō'*) appended to each. This feature, rather than suggesting the separation of one series of rules from another for the purposes of literary balance (not overly impressive as it turns out and also difficult to appreciate the rationale for),[23] may reflect an important element in the paradise narrative. Central to it, and playing a role in the presentation of each of the four rules, is the male-female relationship. This is obviously so in the prohibition against adultery. Its presentation was determined by a switch from Cain's destroying what his father and mother had created to his own involvement in procreation and the subsequent focus upon marriage. The conjunction "neither" links the two rules that come under consideration, murder and adultery. The topic of stealing likewise arises in a context in which Eve influences Adam to take the fruit, as does the topic of false witness. Adam's testimony when questioned about the tree brings out the role of the male-female relationship for the two rules in question: "The woman whom thou gavest to be with me, she gave me of the tree, and I did eat" (Gen 3:12). The topic of coveting a neighbor's wife was in turn derived from the significance of God's clothing the two sexes. In Deuteronomy the rule about coveting the neighbor's

[22]On the theme of "life" in Deuteronomy, see Weinfeld, *Deuteronomic School,* 307–13. Note how in the wisdom tradition one finds statements such as, "What man is he that desireth life and loveth many days, that he may see good?" (Ps 34:12). In light of the link with the paradise narrative, the Deuteronomic covenant could be understood as an agreement to overcome the negative consequences of Eden: man will work the land and be productive in it. As in Eden obedience to Yahweh's commands is required.

[23]See N. Lohfink, "Zur Dekalogfassung von Dt 5," *BZ* 9 (1965): 17–32.

possessions has the neighbor's wife listed first and not the house, as is the case in Exodus. Rather than this reversal representing, as is commonly claimed, an attempt to value a woman as something more than just a member of a house(hold),[24] it may reflect the linking together of those rules that are bound up with the relationship between the sexes in the Adam and Eve story. In other words, although both versions are related to the creation story, the one in Deuteronomy probes deeper.[25]

The narrative of creation in Gen 1:1–2:3, and the setting of the decalogue

Other aspects of the decalogue become clearer when we widen the scope of the links that have already been drawn between individual items and the Genesis narratives about the beginnings of things. If we focus upon the story of creation in Gen 1:1–2:3, as we are encouraged to do by the well-recognized reference to it in the Exodus version of the sabbath command,[26] we can provide explanations for some longstanding problems.

The voice that speaks at Sinai in giving the words of the decalogue also spoke the words that created the world. That Yahweh speaks the decalogue directly, and not through Moses, is explained by this parallel. The parallel also explains why the term "words," not "commandments," is found in reference to the contents of the decalogue. Equally revealing of a link is that just as there are ten pronouncements at creation, for example, "And God said, "Let there be light," so there are ten words at Sinai.[27]

[24]For example, Mayes, *Deuteronomy* NCBC, 171. It is far from clear, however, why house really means household (apparently in some version now lost), and why the lawgiver would bother to state this abstraction, especially in that one covets specific, concrete objects.

[25]The rule to honor parents obviously involves the male and the female, but it cannot be joined by the use of "neither" to the next rule about murder, for the simple reason that the former is a positive injunction.

[26]I take the position that if this story is to be assigned to P (the language might be an indication but not its substance), and a date later than Deuteronomy, a similar tradition lies behind the P version of it. Jer 4:23–26, understood to be earlier than Deuteronomy, appears to presuppose an account of creation similar to, or identical with, Genesis 1.

[27]"By ten sayings was the world created," *Pirqe Aboth* 5:1. The sayings are Gen

The comparison between the event at Sinai and the creation of the world can probably be taken further. The decalogue was presented amid a manifestation of the forces of nature, thunders, lightnings, a thick canopy of cloud upon the mountain, great noise, smoke, and fire (Exod 19:16–18). This exhibition of elemental power focuses attention upon the created world and its creator. There may even be a link between the fact that Yahweh, claiming all the earth to be his, made his appearance upon Mount Sinai on the third day after the people had prepared for it (Exod 19:11, 15, 16), and the fact that God created the dry land (which would include the mountains) on the third day (Gen 1:9–13).

A further puzzle may be clarified by comparing the two narratives. If we read the text of Exodus 19 as it stands, it is bewildering to find (v. 25) that Moses has descended the mountain to speak to the people at that point when God (Elohim as in Gen 1:1) "spoke all these words" (Exod 20:1). It is not said to whom he addressed them, and if we take the preceding verse seriously it seems, oddly, that there was no comprehending audience for them. Little wonder that scholars have spoken of displaced texts and of additions badly inserted into some previously existing narrative.[28] They may be right, although the evidence is nothing more than their perception of awkwardness.

The matter is otherwise, however, if we account for the influence of the creation narrative. There was no audience when God spoke his words at creation. The Deuteronomist may be attempting to explain

---

1:3, 6, 9, 11, 14, 20, 24, 26, 28, 29. The words are like those of the decalogue in that they command: "For he spake, and it was done; he commanded, and it stood fast" (Ps 33:9). Of all the sayings only the one in Gen 1:28 (about man's being fruitful and multiplying, replenishing the earth, subduing it, having dominion over the fish and fowl and every living thing), lacks a statement that the result took place. The statement, "And it was so," in verse 30, however, may also apply to verse 28. The one in verse 22, "And God blessed them [creatures of the sea and air], saying, 'Be fruitful and multiply,'" does not count as one of the ten utterances; unlike the others, it lacks the form, "And God said." J. Skinner likewise omits it in his listing of the ten, *Genesis* ICC, 2d ed. (Edinburgh: T. and T. Clark, 1930), 7, 8, 33, 34. If the link with the ten pronouncements in the creation story is the explanation for the number in the decalogue, we can appreciate better why this numerical designation does not appear to arise from any internal feature of the decalogue. The designation is found only in Exod 34:28 and Deut 4:13, 10:4.

[28]See, for a typical example of the supposed complications involved, F.-L. Hossfeld, *Der Dekalog. Seine späten Fassungen, die originale Komposition und seine Vorstufen* (Göttingen: Vandenhoeck and Ruprecht, 1982), 164–71.

the presentation of the decalogue on the basis of the view that what is incorporated in it goes back to the beginning of time. We noted how rules were presented because Yahweh acted upon them in his dealings with Adam, Eve, Cain, and Abel.

A curious element, more prominent in the description of events in Exodus than in Deuteronomy, is the depiction of God's voice whereby it is implied that the people heard the voice but not necessarily the actual words spoken (so notes Driver in his comment on Deut 5:5).[29] When Moses, preparing for the event, was on the mountain, God answered him "by a voice" (Exod 19:19). B. S. Childs rightly rejects the views that the reference is to thunder (see, for example, the RSV), or to audible language.[30] Although it is difficult to evaluate this odd feature, it at least ties in with the observations that even Moses himself was away from the mountain when the words of the decalogue were spoken, that no audience is cited for their reception, and that after they were uttered the people requested Moses not to let God speak to them but to hear through him (Exod 20:18, 19). The feature may have to do with the notion that the voice is an echo of God's voice at the time of creation.

The incident of the golden calf also suggests that the people, including Aaron, had not yet received the contents of the decalogue, that they only existed in written form in the deity's possession, and were brought down from the mountain by Moses. It is otherwise difficult to comprehend why, if they had just heard the decalogue, they proceeded to ignore its contents, and that no reference is made to this.[31] The fact rather that the written decalogue condemned what they had done was to be viewed as making its contents all the more significant.

There is, in fact, explicit textual evidence that the giving of the decalogue has been linked to the creation of the world: "For ask now of the days that are past, which were before thee, since the day that God created [*bārā'*, as in Gen 1:1, 27] man upon the earth, and ask from the one side of heaven unto the other, whether there hath been

[29]Driver, *Deuteronomy* ICC, 83, 84.

[30]Childs, *The Book of Exodus*, 343.

[31]To be sure, in Exod 32:8 (attributed to a Deuteronomic redactor) God complains that the people have turned aside from the path that he commanded by making a molten calf. This reference is just as likely to be to the prohibition in Exod 20:23, "Ye shall not make with me gods of silver, neither shall ye make unto you gods of gold." This rule had been transmitted to them through Moses (v. 22).

any such thing as this great thing, or hath been heard like it? Did ever people hear the voice of God speaking out of the midst of the fire, as thou has heard, and live?" (Deut 4:32, 33). This explicit link between the decalogue and creation is far more significant than has been realized. The author of the myth of the origin of the decalogue has patterned it after the myth of the creation of the universe. The decalogue serves the same purpose. Everyone would have known the basic structure of the universe, but it was nonetheless felt necessary to elaborate on it in the Genesis story. So too, everyone would have known the basic rules of the decalogue, but they are set down because an explanation of how they had come into existence was deemed important.

Concluding observations

If full recognition is given to the inventiveness that has gone into the decalogue and its "historical" setting, we are obliged to ponder its real-life setting. The indication is that Deuteronomic teaching circles, strongly influenced by the wisdom tradition, are responsible for its construction. We should imagine a teacher and his (male) pupils examining written records in order to glean legal and ethical rules from their contents. Most or probably all of the rules would be known in some form or another, and the purpose of the examination would be to recognize them on the basis of what was occurring in the narrative. The recipients of the Deuteronomic instruction could read and write (Deut 6:9, 11:20). The ten "words" were written, we are to believe, upon two tablets so that Moses might use them for instructional purposes (Exod 24:12; Deut 4:10). We have argued that two different experiences went into their construction. The model may well have been two different exercises whereby a teacher examined one body of material about the incident of the golden calf and another about the beginnings of human life. The resulting decalogue was then inserted into an existing narrative, Exodus 19 and 20, which originally told (and still does) of God's giving certain other laws to Moses.[32]

[32]Literary critics see the hand of a Deuteronomic editor in Exodus 19 (for example, Childs, *The Book of Exodus,* 360–61).

The narratives about the creation and the golden calf have certain features in common. Each is about first-time developments, the first human conduct and Israel's first documented demonstration of idolatrous tendencies. Each is concerned with distancing the deity from man: man cannot become like the gods (Gen 3:22), nor can he create a god (Exodus 32). An important need of the Deuteronomist's in response to what occurred in Exodus 32 is to assert that God created the world, including man and animals. Significantly, perhaps, the Genesis narrative about God's work of creation and his day of rest from it has been added (if the literary critics are right) to a narrative in which humans usurp divine attributes. The inspiration for this development may have come from the need to respond to Aaron's making the golden calf and proclaiming a special day for it. In other words, the putting together of the decalogue also prompted the juxtaposition of the two narratives about creation.

SUMMARY In the incident of the golden calf the people's claim, "These be thy gods, O Israel, which brought thee up out of the land of Egypt," is countered by Yahweh's declaration that it was his doing. The people's recognition of these gods, including any image of one such as Aaron made, is condemned. Aaron's identification of Yahweh with the golden calf is a misuse of Yahweh's name. Aaron's proclamation of a special day in honor of the calf Yahweh is countered by affirming the weekly sabbath of Yahweh, the creator of the universe and the deliverer of the Israelites from Egypt. Cain violated his parents' participation in creation by slaying Abel. He had to stop tilling of the land and live in fear of his life being cut short. A son has to honor his parents that he may live long upon the land. Cain murdered Abel, and Yahweh protected him from being murdered himself. Murder is prohibited. Cain married and produced a child himself. In doing so he furnishes the first example of a son who leaves his parents and forms a bond with a wife. In that he undermined his parents' act of procreation, consideration is now given to the violation of marital union itself, adultery. After Yahweh established the original male-female relationship, he was faced with the problem of their desire to eat from the fruit of the tree of the knowledge of good and evil. This development prompts the rule against stealing. In response to Yahweh's questioning about the offense, Adam blamed Eve and Eve blamed the serpent. This evasion anticipates the offense of bearing false witness against another. In order to forestall Adam and Eve from eating of the tree of life Yahweh expelled them from the garden. This frustration of their desire to attain unending life prompts a prohibition against coveting a neighbor's possessions.

INDEX OF BIBLICAL SOURCES

References are to the numbering in the English versions

Apocrypha

Rabbinic sources

SUBJECT INDEX

Y

Library of Congress Cataloging in Publication Data

Carmichael, Calum M.
Law and narrative in the Bible.

Includes index.
1. D document (Biblical criticism) 2. Ten commandments. 3. Law (Theology)—Biblical teaching. 4. Bible. O.T.—Criticism, Redaction. I. Title.
BS1181.17.C37 1985 222'.106 85-4214
ISBN 0-8014-1792-9 (alk. paper)